ALEXANDER POPE

Collected Poems

Introduction by Clive T. Probyn
Professor of English, Monash University

Edited by Bonamy Dobrée

J.M. Dent & Sons Ltd
London
Charles E. Tuttle Co. Inc.,
Rutland, Vermont
EVERYMANS' LIBRARY

Made in Great Britain by
The Guernsey Press Co. Ltd.,
Guernsey, C.I., for
J.M. Dent & Sons Ltd
91 Clapham High Street, London
SW4 7TA
and Charles E. Tuttle Co., Inc.
28 South Main Street
Rutland, Vermont 05701
U.S.A.

This edition was first published in
Everyman's Library in 1924
Last reprinted 1989
Reissued 1991

ISBN 0 460 87062 9

Everyman's Library
Reg. U.S. Patent Office

INTRODUCTION

FOR Alexander Pope, poetry was made from the interaction of past and present and of the private and public. No poet's career can be entirely self-determined, and even though Pope's career set a precedent in the eighteenth century for independent professionalism it was nevertheless directed by inherited modes of expression and contemporary circumstances. Man in society was both his subject and his audience. As for the making of the poet himself, there is no doubt that Pope was peculiarly disadvantaged from the start. He was born on 21 May 1688, the year which Leslie Stephen described as the 'annus mirabilis', the year which introduced a new era into English political life after the Glorious Revolution. A cause and an effect of the Revolution was the desire to end the civil and political aspirations of Catholics, and Pope was born into a Catholic family. This by itself excluded him from educational opportunities: the university was denied him, as was the chance of living in London – the centre of intellectual and artistic life. At about the age of twelve he contracted a tubercular disease of the spine which led to permanent physical deformity. In the words of Joshua Reynolds, 'He was about four feet six inches high, very humpbacked and deformed.' Pope himself referred to 'this long Disease, my Life'.

Pope's father had been a successful London linen merchant until forced to retire by anti-Catholic legislation passed after the accession of William III in 1689, thus the young Pope's life was very largely circumscribed by the statute book's attempt to secure the Protestant line of succession against the restoration of the Stuart monarchy. Even so, the Jacobites rebelled in 1715 and again in 1745, the year after Pope's death. In 1689 Catholics had been legally expelled from residence within a ten-mile radius of London, by an Act which was reinforced by royal proclamations in 1696, 1715 and 1744. Pope's family moved from Hammersmith to Binfield in Windsor Forest about 1700, and to Chiswick in 1716. Apart from one year of formal schooling at Twyford, near Winchester, Pope was taught by a succession of private Catholic tutors. In essence, he was self-taught.

Contemporary hostility towards Pope for the whole of his professional career (1711 to 1744) was comprehensively and uncomprehendingly violent, the natural antipathy of bad to good. Both poetry and poet were attacked. John Dennis opened the battle and set its tone with his remarks on Pope's *Essay on Criticism* (1711): 'There is nothing more wrong, more low, or more incorrect than this Rhap-

sody upon Criticism . . . As there is no Creature in Nature so
venomous, there is nothing so stupid and so impotent as a hunch-
back'd Toad.' Not surprisingly, then, Pope wrote in the 1717 Preface
to his *Works*: 'The life of a Wit is a warfare upon earth; and the present
spirit of the learned world is such, that to attempt to serve it (any way)
one must have the constancy of a martyr, and a resolution to suffer for
its sake.' These are significant words, for Pope was not only to
withstand the virulent criticism of his opponents but to make of their
attack and his self-defence a symbolic confrontation between anarchy
and order, with intellectual, moral and spiritual culture at stake. Even
today there is residual controversy about Pope's claims for artistic
integrity. No one seriously maintains, as Matthew Arnold did in
1880, that Pope (and Dryden) are 'classics of our prose', but some
recent criticism has reinforced Pope's reputation for poetry of a *merely*
technical excellence. In 1971 F. W. Bateson claimed that what we
admire and remember in Pope 'is not a vertebrate poetic structure,
such as Milton, for example, always provides, so much as an almost
haphazard shimmer of epigrams, characters, aphorisms and innuen-
does. If the parts hold together—as, miraculously, they almost
always do—it is the tone of voice and the metrical virtuosity that are
the principal agents.' Apart from the fact that such 'faults' are
specifically attacked by Pope in the *Essay on Criticism*, this kind of
criticism (partly subjective in any case) denies a crucial and remark-
able strength in Pope's poetry, i.e. its tensile energy, its wholeness of
vision, and its organic social commitment.

Pope's poetic career has a distinct shape, which in itself provides an
emblem of his literary loyalties, a source of inspiration and a measure
against which to judge the world around him. He inherited his poetic
idiom, the heroic couplet, from Dryden, but inherited a curriculum
vitae and a modus vivendi from Virgil and Horace. Pope's *Pastorals*
appeared in 1709, his Georgic *Windsor Forest* in 1713, his didactic *Essay
on Criticism* in 1711, his elegiac *Epistle to the Memory of an Unfortunate
Lady* in 1717, his 'heroic' *Eloisa to Abelard* in 1717, his mock-epic *The
Rape of the Lock* (five-canto version) in 1714, the first of his *Imitations of
Horace* in 1733 (printed as a parallel text, with the original on the facing
page). His *Moral Essays* and *An Essay on Man* (1733–4) were, he wrote
to Swift, 'a System of Ethics in the Horatian way'. His translations of
Homer (*Iliad* and *Odyssey*) were Pope's attempt to centre himself in the
classical tradition, and the same could be said for *The Dunciad* (1729 for
the *Variorum*, 1742 for the four-book version). From this it is clear that
classical literature provided Pope with the prototypes for his own
work. He completed the classical poet's *cursus honorum* by capping it
with a Virgilian *mock*-epic, so much more appropriate for what Pope
came to see as a mock-Augustan age, and a signal both of his cultural
allegiance to the past and of his close involvement with the
eighteenth-century present. Indeed, there is no greater or more

poignant contrast in Pope's career than that between the confident and visionary poetry of *Windsor Forest*'s 'Order in Variety' (soon to be destroyed by the death of Queen Anne and the collapse of the Tory ministry), and the apocalyptic visionary poetry of *The Dunciad*, where 'Universal Darkness buries all'. The classical confidence which Pope had learned from his reading of Theocritus, Horace, Longinus, Virgil and Ovid was to be increasingly strained, but it never fossilized into dogma. Wordsworth's remark to a minor poet, 'I do not think that great poems can be cast in a mould', is too arbitrary a prescription for Pope's poetry. Although his poetry *is* tied closely, and deliberately so, to the 'Kinds' of classical poetry, since it was Pope's intention from 1711 onwards to set English poetry in the context of classical and European Renaissance craftsmanship, it is the norm, not the exception, for Pope to transform his inherited resources.

Among Pope's personal resources there was none stronger than personal friendship. Writing to John Gay in 1730, Pope said: 'Nature, temper, and habit from my youth made me have but one strong desire. All other ambitions, my person, education, constitution, religion, etc. conspired to remove far from me. That desire was to fix and preserve a few lasting dependable friendships.' To a remarkable extent this ambition was fulfilled both in his life and in his art. The period from 1709 to 1717 witnessed the making of lifelong friendships: with John Gay (best known for *The Beggar's Opera*, 1728, and with whom Pope collaborated on that strangely surrealistic comedy *Three Hours after Marriage*, 1717); with Jonathan Swift (to whom Pope addresses *The Dunciad* as a gesture of cultural alliance); with Dr John Arbuthnot, one of Queen Anne's physicians and co-author, with Pope and others, of *The Memoirs of Martinus Scriblerus*, and to whom Pope addresses his satiric apologia, *An Epistle from Mr. Pope to Dr. Arbuthnot*; with Henry St John, Viscount Bolingbroke, 'My guide, philosopher, and friend', the addressee of *An Essay on Man*; and with Robert Harley, Earl of Oxford, who with Bolingbroke co-managed the Tory ministry under Queen Anne in what was the golden period for the Tories, from 1702 to 1714, celebrated in *Windsor Forest*. Equally important friendships developed with Lord Burlington, Maecenas of the arts, patron of Handel (and of his rival composer Buononcini), the painter Jervas (Pope's own tutor), the sculptor Guelfi, and the architect William Kent. The fourth Moral Essay is addressed to Burlington and celebrates (as Gay had done in the second book of *Trivia*) his aesthetic leadership in reviving Palladian architecture:

> You show us Rome was glorious, not profuse,
> And pompous buildings once were things of use,
> Yet shall (my lord) your just, your noble rules

Fill half the land with imitating fools;
Who random drawings from your sheets shall take,
And of one beauty many blunders make.   (lines 23–8)

(In these lines, it is clear, the positive and creative values emanate from the man himself: it is the spirit which gives life, the letter which kills, and there could be no clearer example of Pope's idea that the past is a living resource for the present to utilize. Even so, athwart the enlightenment of a Burlington lies the dark shadow of those who interpret tradition as a fashion, a living mode as modishness, and a model as an invitation to slavish copying.)

Many of Pope's poems arise from the contemplation of an individual friend: they begin in compliment and end in the public, emblematic celebration of ideas. A small example of this can be seen even in Pope's highly stylized *Pastorals*, where the importance of including invocations to his patrons is allowed precedence over the formal nicety that this sequence of seasonal poems totals (without them) 366 lines. In his *Life of Pope* Samuel Johnson discerned an emblematic quality in Pope's own life (his filial piety, and his artistic independence), and it is this exemplary quality which Pope carefully nurtures in his poetry, a continuity from private to public, a commemoration of friendships formed in private whose value is social, even institutional.

Pope's financial independence of patron was a liberation of his art. His translation of Homer's *Iliad* and *Odyssey* made him a free agent, 'Un-plac'd, un-pension'd, no Man's Heir, or Slave'. His early disadvantages had been turned into a combative self-reliance and a passionate desire to consolidate his values through friendship. We might have expected embittered alienation, but what emerges is a subtle double response. One critic, Pat Rogers, has remarked that Pope 'made himself a highly respected position in the world through poetry accommodated to the social forms of the day . . . He wrote of the social scene from within: but he was a fifth-columnist.' This, I think, catches the precise tone of Pope's loyalties. There is always the possibility that his poetic voice conveys a double-edged significance, combining celebration with execration, validating the status quo but often from a radical and dissenting angle. Irony and satire are, after all, generated at the flash-point of defence and attack, attraction and repulsion. In the *Second Satire of Dr. John Donne. . . . Versified* (1735), he opens with these lines: 'Yes, thank my stars! as early as I knew / This town, I had the sense to hate it too.' In *The Rape of the Lock* a shallow-minded society expending its energy on maintaining social rituals at the cost of sensible moral perspectives is both exposed for its inanity and celebrated for its dazzling elegance. Here is a world in which wretches hang that jurymen may dine, and blame is insinuated through passages of the most delicate complimentary appearance:

'Bright as the sun, her eyes the gazers strike, / And, like the sun, they shine on all alike' (II, 13–14).

In *The Dunciad* we see Pope assailed by an alien culture of entrepreneurial art, derivative, populist, modish, freakish and dull. Pope's defence against this is to mobilize a vast mythopoeic structure of classical literary norms tied, wherever possible, to examples of the Great Tradition threatened with extinction: Shakespeare, Molière, Milton, Swift, and of course Pope himself. Again, what one notices is Pope's unashamed commitment to the idea of the writer as central to the public life. Certainly, personal scores are settled against Pope's old antagonists (Cibber, Theobald, and a host of others), but what was at stake for Pope went far beyond professional revenge. If the Grub Street writers concerned themselves only with the satisfaction of the lowest common denominator of contemporary taste, then a vital continuity was broken. It is no accident that *The Dunciad* swarms with crowds and riotous noise, for the artist's duty to lead has been replaced by the tyranny of a ludicrous democracy of taste which drags everything down to one dead level. Just as Pope has made emblems of Burlington and others in the *Moral Essays*, so in *The Dunciad* he makes emblems of their negative equivalents: the man becomes a symbol of a reduced moral state, at times not even an individual but a collectivity:

> Now thousand tongues are heard in one loud din;
> The monkey-mimics rush discordant in;
> 'Twas chatt'ring, grinning, mouthing, jabb'ring all,
> And noise and Norton, brangling and Breval,
> Dennis and dissonance, and captious art,
> And snip-snap short, and interruption smart,
> And demonstration thin, and theses thick,
> And major, minor, and conclusion quick. (II, 235–42)

Tactically, Pope puts himself on the losing side in *The Dunciad*. By the end of the poem the duces have taken over, and Pope's final benediction is addressed to a world already lost. Yet Pope has also paraded the alternatives before us, and their collective significance is enormous. As Marshall McLuhan pointedly remarked, Pope in *The Dunciad* 'has not yet received his due as a serious analyst of the intellectual malaise of Europe'. It is as though Pope, as leader of the intellectual Resistance, has taken to the streets in an artistic equivalent of guerilla war.

The Dunciad is not, of course, the only poem by Pope which takes as its subject the minutiae of contemporary literary life, but it is certainly a climactic example of occasional satire which transcends its immediate causes. It was meant to do so, and perhaps the subtlest irony of all is that the duces' desperate anxiety for fame has been actually achieved. For most readers Orator Henley, John Dennis,

Colley Cibber and Lewis Theobald (deservedly or not) are *only* remembered for their dubious prominence in this poem. The early, and perhaps élitist preserve of classical values described in the *Essay on Criticism*, 'Still green with bays each ancient altar stands, / Above the reach of sacrilegious hands' (lines 181–2), has been vandalized, and if we respond to the language Pope uses to describe their crime, the full horror becomes apparent. In Colley Cibber's 'monster-breeding breast' the hierarchy of literary forms and the challenge of originality have degenerated to a chaos of plagiarism and freakish hybridization:

> Round him much embryo, much abortion lay,
> Much future ode, and abdicated play;
> Nonsense precipitate, like running lead,
> That slipp'd through cracks and zig-zags of the head;
> All that on folly frenzy could beget,
> Fruits of dull heat, and sooterkins of wit.
> Next, o'er his books his eyes began to roll,
> In pleasing memory of all he stole,
> How here he sipped, how there he plundered snug,
> And sucked all o'er, like an industrious bug.
> Here lay poor Fletcher's half-eat scenes, and here
> The frippery of crucified Molière;
> There hapless Shakespeare, yet of Tibbald sore,
> Wished he had blotted for himself before. (I, 121–34)

This is not primarily argumentative poetry, but fantastically inventive caricature built on intellectual contempt, just as the astonishing assassination of Sporus in the *Epistle to Arbuthnot* is built on contempt for ambivalence ('And he himself one vile antithesis', line 325). The language of the poetry is energized by associations, allusions, and even the syntax of such passages expresses the idea of a crazy and restless energy desperate to patch together something resembling a coat to cover its own poverty.

If Pope's career may be seen in terms of an increasing involvement with the agents of cultural decline, the progress of his own life indicates a kind of retrenchment. Significantly, Maynard Mack's brilliant study of the satires and epistles of the 1730s and of the final *Dunciad*, *The Garden and the City*, carries the apparently paradoxical subtitle *Retirement and Politics*. From 1719, and for a subsequent period of twenty-five years, Pope remodelled his Twickenham villa according to the architectural theories of Vitruvius, Palladio, and the indigenous neo-classical work of Inigo Jones and Burlington. Here he created a retreat from the City imbued with the values of Horace, the result of which was (in Mack's words) 'a confrontation of the actual world of Augustan England with a country of the mind'. As in his poetry, so in his house: an intellectual continuity was celebrated. Twickenham was adorned with portraits of his mother, Lord Peterborough, Martha Blount, Bolingbroke, Swift, Gay, Atterbury,

Arbuthnot, Prior, Burlington, Garth, the Earl of Oxford, and Walsh; the busts of Inigo Jones and Palladio were installed in the library. All functioned as indices to Pope's loyalties and roots, collectively imaging a world starkly opposed to the world of London (itself a symbolic place of the mind), where 'Nor public flame, nor private, dares to shine; / Nor human spark is left, nor glimpse divine!' Here Pope concentrated and nourished his resources, not, it should be said, from any desire to shut himself away. Though he wryly complained about uninvited guests besieging him at Twickenham, his house also became by design a kind of intellectual salon for Tory opposition writers. It objectified the moral error, as Pope saw it, of his times, the displacement of the poet from the centre of intellectual life. From the fastness of Twickenham he was able to organize his own profound opposition.

The cultural collapse of England prophesied at the end of *The Dunciad* has no basis in historical fact. Pope's is an idealized (or more appropriately a poet's) view, and his theatrical fourth book states a conviction that the bonds of the past have been untied, the cultural memory attenuated, and that under the influence of a materialistic society the traditional partnership of poet and patron has been replaced by literary prostitution, writing for a paymaster or to satisfy public taste. Though Pope is on the side of Order his poetry is remarkable *also* for depicting its opposite. This is not to say that he was secretly on the side of the Dunces, or gained more satisfaction from depicting anarchy than counteracting it. Like Swift, he gets under the skin of his antagonists and forces the disease to the surface in order to expose and condemn it. What he *was* drawn to was the conflict between opposing visions of civilized life, and this conflict is worked out with a dialectical clarity. In *Windsor Forest* he brilliantly distilled the idea of order in variety, for example in the couplet,

> Here in full light the russet plains extend:
> There, wrapt in clouds the bluish hills ascend   (lines 23–4)

where the closed antitheses embrace dimensions of space, light, colour and syntactic balance, the precise expressive form of the idea itself. In the following passage from Book I of *The Dunciad* Pope portrays a surrealistic, nightmarish burgeoning of literary dullness which confuses and corrodes the very language of artistic creation:

> How hints, like spawn, scarce quick in embryo lie,
> How new-born nonsense first is taught to cry,
> Maggots half-form'd in rhyme exactly meet,
> And learn to crawl upon poetic feet.
> Here one poor word an hundred clenches makes,
> And ductile Dulness new meanders takes;
> There motley images her fancy strike,
> Figures ill-pair'd, and similes unlike.   (lines 59–66)

The creating word of Genesis and the anarchy of contemporary literature are counterposed in a symbolic battle for the mind of man. Beneath the richly comic texture of *The Dunciad*'s negative image lies an insistent pattern of allusions to the world being lost: Colley Cibber is the Messiah, the new Anti-Christ of Wit; Bedlam and Grub Street have sprawled over what was once Parnassus; the Apocalypse blots out Genesis; the new watchword is a grotesque trinity of commandments: 'All my commands are easy, short, and full: / My sons! be proud, be selfish, and be dull' (IV, 581–2).

One of the major pleasures of *The Dunciad* is seeing how far Pope's linguistic shock-tactics can go. The unspeakable becomes the norm, the sanctified becomes a travesty, and the world runs down. In fact the challenge of reading Pope involves a constant invitation to discriminate between the elevating and the degrading, between the involvement of the mind and its denial, and between the affirmation of the artist's central social responsibilities and his abdication. These polarities are worked out in human and symbolic terms: the enlightened economic paternalism of the Man of Ross versus the arid self-aggrandisement of the social climber Sir Balaam (*Epistle to Bathurst*); Burlington's aesthetic co-operation with Nature versus the deadly mechanistic life-style of Timon (*Epistle to Burlington*); the gutless dilettantism of Atticus versus the moral decisiveness and literary seriousness of Pope's self-portrait in the *Epistle to Arbuthnot*; literature as a mere trick of words versus poetry as a faculty of the civilized mind (*Essay on Criticism*). In each case Pope moves out from the individual to the social, recognizing the essential fluidity of all things human and stressing man's paradoxical nature:

> Know then thyself, presume not God to scan,
> The proper study of mankind is man.
> Placed on this isthmus of a middle state,
> A being darkly wise, and rudely great:
> With too much knowledge for the sceptic side,
> With too much weakness for the stoic's pride,
> He hangs between; in doubt to act, or rest,
> In doubt to deem himself a god, or beast;
> In doubt his mind or body to prefer;
> Born but to die, and reasoning but to err;
> Alike in ignorance, his reason such,
> Whether he thinks too little, or too much:
> Chaos of Thought and Passion, all confused;
> Still by himself abused, or disabused;
> Created half to rise, and half to fall;
> Great lord of all things, yet a prey to all;
> Sole judge of truth, in endless error hurl'd:
> The glory, jest, and riddle of the world!
>
> (*An Essay on Man*, Epistle II, 1–18)

Hamlet, Rochester, and Swift had each wrestled with this ancient paradox, but it is typical of Pope that the paradox can be so neatly and decisively fixed. He revels in the glory of the antitheses. What should be emphasized is that neither here nor anywhere else does Pope argue that the response to man's instability should be passive acceptance. Like Spenser before him, Pope's sense of mutability was based on a positive and dynamic conception of the human personality. Antithesis is the single most prominent feature of his poetic grammar, the essence of his satirical technique, and (for Pope) the character of his times. In his life and poetry Pope's values were defined in conflict and through transformations.

For Pope, intellectual content is not something to be inferred from his poetry but a structural element. The idea carried is absorbed by rhythm, syntax and lexical choice. Not only in obvious examples of expressive form such as 'And ten low words oft creep in one dull line', or in the mellifluous couplet, 'Not so, when swift Camilla scours the plain, / Flies o'er the unbending corn, and skims along the main' (*Essay on Criticism*, 347; 372–3), which are showcase samples, but also in the total architectural conception of lines like these:

> Two principles in human nature reign;
> Self-love, to urge, and Reason, to restrain;
> Nor this a good, nor that a bad we call,
> Each works its end, to move or govern all:
> And to their proper operation still,
> Ascribe all good; to their improper, ill.
>
> (*An Essay on Man*, Epistle II, 53–8)

Such a passage might strike us as having no more than a *minimal* poetic quality, since it is denotative and prose-like in its apparent function. Yet the prose surface is built upon a poetic grammar of rhythmic and syntactic persuasiveness. The argument is insinuated through the force of an elegant stylistic movement, just as the Dunces and Sporus are locked into a syntactic perversion (maggots crawling on poetic feet, or an antithesis). Style is the man.

After Pope, no poet assumed the public domain as his rightful territory to the same extent. When Dr Johnson has Imlac say in *Rasselas* (1759) that the poet must write as 'the interpreter of nature, and the legislator of mankind . . . as a being superior to time and place', the daunting implications of fulfilling such a role again were becoming clear (the Prince reacts to Imlac's enthusiastic fit by declaring that 'no human being can ever be a poet'). Yet Pope had attempted it. In *The Dunciad* he had taken on the whole cultural scene around him and judged it as a mock-epic falling away from the norms of Humanism, a vast comic insult and a cultural betrayal. Changes in the relationship between the writer and his audience were a fundamental concern in this poem, and in some details we would perhaps challenge Pope's view (Defoe is chosen by Pope probably for his pamphleteering and political opportunism; there is no reference to the importance, for us, of his pioneer work in the now dominant form of the novel). Pope owed no favour or loyalty to a patron and his sense of the writer's public contract remained intense: he discerned and praised this commitment in Swift's Irish writings and, one feels, regarded his own ten-year stint of translating Homer as a public duty. It is perhaps significant that the next long poem in English of epic proportions was Wordsworth's *The Prelude*, eventually to be subtitled 'Growth of a Poet's Mind, An Autobiographical Poem'.

Pope's demotion of egocentricity does not make his poetry either impersonal or conventional. If, as has been said, Pope was a man talking to men and Wordsworth was a poet talking to the poet in each of us, the argument that Pope puts forward is the necessity for an integrity of relationships between the artist and the work, the work and the reader, and the reader and society at large. It was a conviction needing every ounce of Pope's courage to realize. In *An Essay on Man* the plentiful evidence of the disordered world of man takes its sometimes crazy toll in a nonetheless ordered cosmos. Whilst recognizing the intuitive, inspirational basis of the finest literature, through 'a grace beyond the reach of art', Pope maintained a general distrust of the individual's ability. Certainly, the man who arrogates to himself the task of self-definition runs the risk of self-delusion:

> All-seeing in thy mists, we want no guide,
> Mother of arrogance, and source of pride!
> We nobly take the high Priori Road,
> And reason downward, till we doubt of God;
> Make nature still incroach upon His plan;
> And shove Him off as fast as e'er we can:
> Thrust some mechanic cause into His place;
> Or bind in matter, or diffuse in space.
> Or, at one bound o'erleaping all His laws,
> Make God man's image, man the final cause,
> Find virtue local, all relation scorn,
> See all in self, and but for self be born.
> (*The Dunciad*, IV, 469–80.)

Like Swift before him and Johnson after, Pope's public message is a secular one, however much his moral programme was based on religious convictions. The Horatian image of *beatus ille*, the virtuous recluse, which Pope created for himself in his life and poetry, was constructed as an emblem for society: the two are inextricable. The converse relationship is seen in Cibber plagiarizing the plays of Molière in a Grub Street attic, in Bentley and Theobald submerging the text of Milton and Shakespeare under editorial pedantry, in Chloe (*Epistle to a Lady*), who while her lover 'pants upon her breast, / Can mark the figures on an Indian chest', in Timon (a 'puny insect' in a

Brobdingnagian villa), in all those whose image of the world is merely a reflection of the self.

Pope's victory over the Dunces was much more than a matter of a superior style, of course, but it is the style which comprehends the negative forces in a positive vision through irony. *The Dunciad*, for all its sombre evidence of the ruin of the nation, conveys its meaning through the rich liveliness of intellectual energy and imaginative irony. T. S. Eliot's *The Waste Land* also surveys the landscape of a twentieth-century *Dunciad*, but the comparison immediately highlights Pope's greater confidence. It is a disembodied voice which weakly asks at the end of Eliot's poem, 'Shall I at least set my lands in order?', whereas in *The Dunciad* the theatrical exhibition of cosmic collapse is stage-managed by Pope as a warning, not a surrender. Neither does Pope see himself alone in the audience: in this particular battle of the books and the man, Pope had both history and posterity on his side.

1983   Clive T. Probyn

SELECT BIBLIOGRAPHY

The standard edition of Pope's works is *The Twickenham Edition of the Poems of Alexander Pope*, general editor John Butt, 11 volumes (Methuen, 1939–69):

I   *Pastoral Poetry and An Essay on Criticism*, ed. A. Audra and A. Williams, 1961

II   *The Rape of the Lock and Other Poems*, ed. G. Tillotson, 1940; revised 1962

III i *An Essay on Man*, ed. Maynard Mack, 1950

III ii *Epistles to Several Persons*, ed. F. W. Bateson, 1951; revised 1961

IV   *Imitations of Horace*, ed. J. Butt, 1939; revised 1953

V   *The Dunciad*, ed. J. Sutherland, 1943; revised 1963

VI   *Minor Poems*, ed. N. Ault and J. Butt, 1954

VII–X *Iliad and Odyssey*, ed. Maynard Mack, N. Callan, R. Fagles, W. Frost and D. Knight, 1967

XI   *Index*, ed. Maynard Mack, 1969

A convenient one-volume edition (which excludes only the Homer translations and the 1712 version of *The Rape of the Lock*) is *The Poems of Alexander Pope*, ed. J. Butt (Methuen, 1963). For the prose, see *The Prose Works of Alexander Pope*, ed. N. Ault (Blackwell, 1936) – earlier works only. Edna L. Steeves has edited *The Art of Sinking in Poetry* (Russell and Russell, 1968), Charles Kerby Miller *The Memoirs of Martinus Scriblerus* (Yale, 1950), and the standard edition of the letters is *The Correspondence of Alexander Pope*, ed. George Sherburn, 5 volumes (Clarendon Press, Oxford, 1956).

The standard and complete biography of Pope is Maynard Mack, *Alexander Pope: A Life* (New Haven and London, 1985). George Sherburn's *Early Career of Alexander Pope* (Oxford, 1934) goes up to 1727, and there are useful supplements available in Johnson's life of Pope in *Lives of the Poets* (1779–81) and in the headnotes to Sherburn's *Correspondence* volumes. Apart from their intrinsic value, biographical information is also found in Howard Erskine-Hill's *The Social Milieu of Alexander Pope* (New Haven and London, 1975), and in Maynard Mack's *The Garden and the City* (Toronto and London, 1969). For background studies, the following are useful: A. R. Humphreys's *The Augustan World* (1954); Isaac Kramnick, *Bolingbroke and His Circle* (Harvard, 1968); Jean Hagstrum, *The Sister Arts* (Chicago, 1958); Pat Rogers, *Grub Street* (Methuen, 1972: a slimmer version focused on Swift and Pope, *Hacks and Dunces*, appeared in 1980); Paul Fussell, *The Rhetorical World of Augustan Humanism* (Oxford, 1965); Morris R. Brownell, *Alexander Pope and the Arts of Georgian England* (Oxford, 1973); Peter Dixon, ed., *Alexander Pope* (Writers and Their Background series, London, 1972); J. V. Guerinot, *Pamphlet Attacks on Alexander Pope 1711–1744: A Descriptive Bibliography* (Methuen, 1969).

General studies of Pope include: Geoffrey Tillotson, *On the Poetry of Pope* (Oxford, 1938; revised 1950), and *Pope and Human Nature* (Oxford, 1958); the third chapter of F. R. Leavis, *Revaluation: Tradition and Development in English Poetry* (Chatto and Windus, 1936); Reuben Brower, *Alexander Pope: The Poetry of Allusion* (Oxford, 1959)—the best single study of the poetry; and

Maynard Mack's classic essay, 'Wit and Poetry and Pope' (reprinted in *Eighteenth-Century English Literature: Modern Essays in Criticism*, ed. J. L. Clifford, Oxford, 1959). Important studies of individual poems are found in: Aubrey Williams, *Pope's Dunciad: A Study of Its Meaning* (Methuen, 1955); J. S. Cunningham, *Pope: The Rape of the Lock* (Edward Arnold, 1961); Howard Erskine-Hill, *Pope: The Dunciad* (Edward Arnold, 1972); Miriam Leranbaum, *Alexander Pope's 'Opus Magnum' 1729–1744* (Oxford, 1977: on *An Essay on Man*); Ian Jack, *Augustan Satire: Intention and Idiom in English Poetry 1660–1750* (Oxford, 1952: includes chapters on *The Dunciad*, *Moral Essays* and *The Rape of the Lock*); Earl Wasserman, *The Subtler Language* (Baltimore, 1959: 67 pages on *Windsor Forest*).

The following collections of critical essays are notable: F. W. Bateson and N. A. Joukovsky, eds., *Alexander Pope: A Critical Anthology* (Penguin, London, 1971); Maynard Mack, ed., *Essential Articles for the Study of Alexander Pope* (Archon, Connecticut, 1968); Howard Erskine-Hill and Anne Smith, eds., *The Art of Alexander Pope* (Vision, London, 1979).

The standard bibliography is R. H. Griffith's *Alexander Pope: A Bibliography* (Austin, 1922–7). Supplementary aids are: J. E. Tobin, *Pope: A List of Critical Studies, 1895–1944* (New York, 1945); Cecilia L. Lopez, *Alexander Pope: An Annotated Bibliography, 1945–1967* (Gainesville, Florida, 1970).

Two recently published introductory volumes are: Pat Rogers, *An Introduction to Pope* (Methuen, 1975); I. R. F. Gordon, *A Preface to Pope* (Longman, 1976).

NOTE

THE text of this edition is substantially that produced by Ernest Rhys in 1924. Since that date, however, much progress has been made in the knowledge of Pope's references and allusions, thus where necessary the notes have been corrected. Some poems now ascribed to others have been replaced by some almost certainly his, and a number have been added. The publishers gratefully acknowledge their debt to the Twickenham Edition (Messrs Methuen), from which most of the corrections have been made. The extra poems, moreover, are taken from vol. vi of that edition, *Minor Poems*, with permission of the late Norman Ault's executor and of Professor John Butt. The text of the replacements and additions has been modernized to conform with the remainder of the volume.

CONTENTS

CONTENTS

CONTENTS

EARLY POEMS

ODE ON SOLITUDE

HAPPY the man, whose wish and care
  A few paternal acres bound,
Content to breathe his native air
        In his own ground.

Whose herds with milk, whose fields with bread,   5
  Whose flocks supply him with attire,
Whose trees in summer yield him shade,
        In winter fire.

Blest, who can unconcern'dly find
  Hours, days, and years slide soft away,
In health of body, peace of mind,   10
        Quiet by day.

Sound sleep by night; study and ease,
  Together mixt; sweet recreation:
And innocence, which most does please   15
        With meditation.

Thus let me live, unseen, unknown,
  Thus unlamented let me die,
Steal from the world, and not a stone
        Tell where I lie   20

TO THE AUTHOR OF A POEM ENTITLED "SUCCESSIO"[1]

BEGONE, ye critics, and restrain your spite,
Codrus writes on, and will for ever write.
The heaviest Muse the swiftest course has gone,
As clocks run fastest when most lead is on;

[1] The author of *Successio* was Elkanah Settle, the London City Poet, the Doeg of Dryden's satire.

What though no bees around your cradle flew,   5
Nor on your lips distill'd the golden dew,
Yet have we oft discover'd in their stead
A swarm of drones that buzz'd about your head.
When you, like Orpheus, strike the warbling lyre,
Attentive blocks stand round you and admire.   10
Wit pass'd through thee no longer is the same,
As meat digested takes a different name,
But sense must sure thy safest plunder be,
Since no reprisals can be made on thee.
Thus thou may'st rise, and in thy daring flight   15
(Though ne'er so weighty) reach a wondrous height.
So, forced from engines, lead itself can fly,
And pond'rous slugs move nimbly through the sky.
Sure Bavius copied Mævius to the full,
And Chærilus taught Codrus to be dull;   20
Therefore, dear friend, at my advice give o'er
This needless labour; and contend no more
To prove a *dull succession* to be true,
Since 'tis enough we find it so in you.

IMITATIONS OF ENGLISH POETS

DONE BY THE AUTHOR IN HIS YOUTH

I

CHAUCER

Women ben full of ragerie,
Yet swinken nat sans secresie.
Thilke moral shall ye understond,
From schoole-boy's tale of fayre Irelond;
Which to the fennes hath him betake,   5
To filche the grey ducke fro the lake.
Right then there passen by the way
His aunt, and eke her daughters tway.
Ducke in his trowses hath he hent,
Not to be spied of ladies gent,   10
" But ho! our nephew," crieth one;
" Ho!" quoth another, " Cozen John ";

And stoppen, and lough, and callen out—
This sely clerke full low doth lout:
They asken that, and talken this. 15
" Lo, here is coz, and here is miss."
But, as he glozeth with speeches soote,
The ducke sore tickleth his erse roote:
Fore-piece and buttons all to-brest
Forth thrust a white neck and red crest. 20
" Te-hee! " cried ladies: clerk nought spake:
Miss star'd, and grey ducke crieth " quaake."
" O moder, moder! " quoth the daughter,
" Be thilke same thing maids longen a'ter?
Bette is to pine on coals and chalke, 25
Then trust on mon whose yerde can talke."

[The above, when first published in the Miscellanies, was entitled
" A Tale of Chaucer lately found in an old Manuscript."]

II

SPENSER

THE ALLEY

In every town where Thamis rolls his tyde,
A narrow pass there is, with houses low.
Where ever and anon the stream is ey'd,
And many a boat soft sliding to and fro:
There oft are heard the notes of infant woe, 5
The short thick sob, loud scream, and shriller squall:
How can ye, mothers, vex your children so?
Some play, some eat, some cack against the wall,
And as they crouchen low for bread and butter call.

And on the broken pavement, here and there, 10
Doth many a stinking sprat and herring lie;
A brandy and tobacco shop is near,
And hens, and dogs, and hogs, are feeding by;
And here a sailor's jacket hangs to dry.
At every door are sunburnt matrons seen 15
Mending old nets to catch the scaly fry;
Now singing shrill, and scolding eft between;
Scolds answer foul-mouth'd scolds; bad neighbourhood I ween.

The snappish cur (the passenger's annoy)
Close at my heel with yelping treble flies;   20
The whimpering girl, and hoarser screaming boy,
Join to the yelping treble shrilling cries;
The scolding quean to louder notes doth rise,
And her full pipes those shrilling cries confound:
To her full pipes the grunting hog replies: 25
The grunting hogs alarm the neighbours round,
And curs, girls, boys, and scolds, in the deep base are drown'd.[1]

Hard by a sty, beneath a roof of thatch,
Dwelt Obloquy, who in her early days
Baskets of fish at Billingsgate did watch,   30
Cod, whiting, oyster, mackrel, sprat, or plaice:
There learn'd she speech from tongues that never cease,
Slander beside her like a magpie chatters,
With Envy (spitting cat), dread foe to peace;
Like a curs'd cur, Malice before her clatters,   35
And, vexing every wight, tears clothes and all to tatters.

Her dugs were mark'd by every collier's hand;
Her mouth was black as bull-dogs at the stall:
She scratched, bit, and spar'd ne lace ne band,
And bitch and rogue her answer was to all;   40
Nay, ev'n the parts of shame by name would call:
Yea, when she passed by or lane or nook,
Would greet the man who turn'd him to the wall,
And by his hand obscene the porter took,
Nor ever did askance like modest virgin look.   45

Such place hath Deptford, navy-building town,
Woolwich and Wapping, smelling strong of pitch;
Such Lambeth, envy of each band and gown,
And Twickenham such, which fairer scenes enrich,

---

[1] Evidently a parody of the descriptive verse quoted in *The Faerie Queene*:
> " The joyous birds, shrouded in cheerful shade,
> Their notes unto the voice attemper'd sweet;
> Th' angelical soft trembling voices made
> To th' instruments divine respondence meet;
> The silver-sounding instruments did meet
> With the base murmur of the water's fall;
> The water's fall, with difference discreet,
> Now soft, now loud, unto the wind did call;
> The gently warbling wind low answered to all."

Grots, statues, urns, and Jo—n's [1] dog and bitch,   50
Ne village is without, on either side,
All up the silver Thames, or all adown;
Ne Richmond's self, from whose tall front are ey'd
Vales, spires, meandering streams, and Windsor's towery pride.

III

WALLER

ON A LADY SINGING TO HER LUTE

FAIR charmer! cease; nor make your voice's prize
A heart resign'd the conquest of your eyes:
Well might, alas! that threaten'd vessel fail,
Which winds and lightning both at once assail.
We were too bless'd with these enchanting lays,   5
Which must be heavenly when an angel plays:
But killing charms your lover's death contrive,
Lest heavenly music should be heard alive.
Orpheus could charm the trees; but thus a tree,
Taught by your hand, can charm no less than he,   10
A poet made the silent wood pursue;
This vocal wood had drawn the poet too.

ON A FAN OF THE AUTHOR'S DESIGN,

*In which was painted the story of Cephalus and Procris, with
the motto, " Aura veni."*

"COME, gentle air," th' Æolian shepherd said,
While Procris panted in the secret shade,
"Come, gentle air!" the fairer Delia cries,
While at her feet her swain expiring lies.
Lo! the glad gales o'er all her beauties stray,   5
Breathe on her lips, and in her bosom play!
In Delia's hand this toy is fatal found,
Nor could that fabled dart more surely wound:
Both gifts destructive to the givers prove;
Alike both lovers fall by those they love.   10

[1] Mr. James Johnston, the retired Scotch Secretary of State, who lived
at Twickenham. The dog and bitch were leaden figures.

Yet guiltless too this bright destroyer lives,
At random wounds, nor knows the wound she gives:
She views the story with attentive eyes,
And pities Procris while her lover dies.

IV

COWLEY

THE GARDEN

Fain would my Muse the flowery treasure sing,
And humble glories of the youthful Spring;
Where opening roses breathing sweets diffuse,
And soft carnations shower their balmy dews;
Where lilies smile in virgin robes of white,   5
The thin undress of superficial light,
And varied tulips show so dazzling gay,
Blushing in bright diversities of day.
Each painted floweret in the lake below
Surveys its beauties, whence its beauties grow;   10
And pale Narcissus on the bank, in vain
Transformed, gazes on himself again.
Here aged trees cathedral walks compose,
And mount the hill in venerable rows;
There the green infants in their beds are laid,   15
The garden's hope, and its expected shade.
Here orange trees with blooms and pendants shine,
And vernal honours to their autumn join;
Exceed their promise in the ripen'd store,
Yet in the rising blossom promise more.   20
There in bright drops the crystal fountains play,
By laurels shielded from the piercing day:
Where Daphne, now a tree, as once a maid,
Still from Apollo vindicates her shade;
Still turns her beauties from th' invading beam,   25
Nor seeks in vain for succour to the stream.
The stream at once preserves her virgin leaves,
At once a shelter from her boughs receives,
Where summer's beauty midst of winter stays,
And winter's coolness spite of summer's rays.   30

WEEPING

WHILE Celia's tears make sorrow bright,
  Proud grief sits swelling in her eyes;
The sun, next those the fairest light,
  Thus from the ocean first did rise:
And thus through mists we see the sun,   5
Which else we durst not gaze upon.

These silver drops, like morning dew,
  Foretell the fervour of the day:
So from one cloud soft showers we view,
  And blasting lightnings burst away.   10
The stars that fall from Celia's eye
Declare our doom in drawing nigh.

The baby in that sunny sphere
  So like a Phaëton appears,
That Heaven, the threaten'd world to spare,   15
  Thought fit to drown him in her tears;
Else might th' ambitious nymph aspire
To set, like him, heaven too on fire.

V

EARL OF ROCHESTER

ON SILENCE

SILENCE! coeval with eternity,
Thou wert ere Nature's self began to be;
'Twas one vast nothing all, and all slept fast in thee.

Thine was the sway ere heaven was form'd, or earth,
Ere fruitful thought conceived creation's birth,   5
Or midwife word gave aid, and spoke the infant forth.

Then various elements against thee join'd,
In one more various animal combined,
And framed the clamorous race of busy human-kind.

The tongue moved gently first, and speech was low,　　10
Till wrangling science taught it noise and show,
And wicked wit arose, thy most abusive foe.

But rebel wit deserts thee oft in vain:
Lost in the maze of words he turns again,
And seeks a surer state, and courts thy gentle reign.　　15

Afflicted sense thou kindly dost set free,
Oppress'd with argumental tyranny,
And routed reason finds a safe retreat in thee.

With thee in private modest dulness lies,
And in thy bosom lurks in thought's disguise;　　20
Thou varnisher of fools, and cheat of all the wise!

Yet thy indulgence is by both confess'd:
Folly by thee lies sleeping in the breast,
And 'tis in thee at last that wisdom seeks for rest.

Silence! the knave's repute, the whore's good name,　　25
The only honour of the wishing dame;
The very want of tongue makes thee a kind of fame.

But couldst thou seize some tongues that now are free,
How Church and State should be obliged to thee!
At Senate and at Bar how welcome wouldst thou be!　　30

Yet speech even there submissively withdraws
From rights of subjects, and the poor man's cause:
Then pompous Silence reigns, and stills the noisy laws.

Past services of friends, good deeds of foes,
What favourites gain, and what the nation owes,　　35
Fly the forgetful world, and in thy arms repose.

The country wit, religion of the town,
The courtier's learning, policy of the gown,
Are best by thee express'd, and shine in thee alone.

The parson's cant, the lawyer's sophistry,　　40
Lord's quibble, critic's jest, all end in thee;
All rest in peace at last, and sleep eternally.

VI

EARL OF DORSET

ARTEMISIA

THOUGH Artemisia talks by fits
Of councils, classics, fathers, wits;
   Reads Malbranche, Boyle, and Locke:
Yet in some things methinks she fails;
'Twere well if she would pare her nails,   5
   And wear a cleaner smock.

Haughty and huge as High-Dutch bride,
Such nastiness and so much pride
   Are oddly joined by fate:
On her large squab you find her spread,   10
Like a fat corpse upon a bed,
   That lies and stinks in state.

She wears no colours (sign of grace)
On any part except her face:
   All white and black beside:
Dauntless her look, her gesture proud,   15
Her voice theatrically loud,
   And masculine her stride.

So have I seen, in black and white,
A prating thing, a magpie hight,
   Majestically stalk;   20
A stately worthless animal,
That plies the tongue, and wags the tail,
   All flutter, pride, and talk.

PHRYNE

PHRYNE had talents for mankind,
Open she was and unconfined,
   Like some free port of trade:
Merchants unloaded here their freight,
And agents from each foreign state
   Here first their entry made.   5

Her learning and good breeding such,
Whether the Italian or the Dutch,
   Spaniards or French came to her;
To all obliging she'd appear;   10
'Twas "Si, Signior," 'twas "Yaw, Mynheer,"
   'Twas "S'il vous plaît, Monsieur."

Obscure by birth, renown'd by crimes,
Still changing names, religions, climes,
   At length she turns a bride: 15
In diamonds, pearls, and rich brocades,
She shines the first of batter'd jades,
   And flutters in her pride.

So have I known those insects fair
(Which curious Germans hold so rare)   20
   Still vary shapes and dyes;
Still gain new titles with new forms;
First grubs obscene, then wriggling worms,
   Then painted butterflies.

VII

DR. SWIFT

THE HAPPY LIFE OF A COUNTRY PARSON

PARSON, these things in thy possessing
Are better than the bishop's blessing:—
A wife that makes conserves; a steed
That carries double when there's need;
October store, and best Virginia,   5
Tithe pig, and mortuary guinea;
Gazettes sent gratis down and frank'd,
For which thy patron's weekly thank'd;
A large Concordance, bound long since;
Sermons to Charles the First when prince; 10
A Chronicle of ancient standing;
A Chrysostom to smooth thy band in:
The Polyglot—three parts—my text,
Howbeit—likewise—now to my next:
Lo, here the Septuagint—and Paul,   15
To sum the whole—the close of all.

He that has these may pass his life,
Drink with the 'squire, and kiss his wife;
On Sundays preach, and eat his fill,
And fast on Fridays—if he will;   20
Toast Church and Queen, explain the news,
Talk with churchwardens about pews,
Pray heartily for some new gift,
And shake his head at Doctor S—t.

PASTORALS

WRITTEN IN THE YEAR MDCCIV

Rura mihi, et rigui placeant in vallibus amnes;
Flumina amem, sylvasque, inglorius!—VIRG.

My next desire is, void of care and strife,
To lead a soft, secure, inglorious life—
A country cottage near a crystal flood,
A winding valley and a lofty wood.—DRYDEN.

SPRING: THE FIRST PASTORAL,
OR DAMON

FIRST in these fields I try the sylvan strains,
Nor blush to sport on Windsor's blissful plains:
Fair Thames, flow gently from thy sacred spring,
While on thy banks Sicilian Muses sing;
Let vernal airs through trembling osiers play,   5
And Albion's cliffs resound the rural lay.

You, that too wise for pride, too good for power,
Enjoy the glory to be great no more,
And carrying with you all the world can boast,
To all the world illustriously are lost!   10
O let my Muse her slender reed inspire,
Till in your native shades you tune the lyre:
So when the nightingale to rest removes,
The thrush may chant to the forsaken groves,
But, charm'd to silence, listens while she sings,   15
And all th' aërial audience clap their wings.
Soon as the flocks shook off the nightly dews,
Two swains, whom love kept wakeful and the Muse,

Pour'd o'er the whitening vale their fleecy care,
Fresh as the morn, and as the season fair: 20
The dawn now blushing on the mountain's side,
Thus Daphnis spoke, and Strephon thus replied.

DAPHNIS

Hear how the birds, on every bloomy spray,
With joyous music wake the dawning day!
Why sit we mute, when early linnets sing,   25
When warbling Philomel salutes the spring?
Why sit we sad, when Phosphor shines so clear,
And lavish Nature paints the purple year?

STREPHON

Sing then, and Damon shall attend the strain,
While yon' slow oxen turn the furrow'd plain.   30
Here the bright crocus and blue violet glow;
Here western winds on breathing roses blow.
I'll stake yon' lamb, that near the fountain plays,
And from the brink his dancing shade surveys.

DAPHNIS

And I this bowl, where wanton ivy twines,   35
And swelling clusters bend the curling vines:
Four figures rising from the work appear,
The various seasons of the rolling year;
And what is that, which binds the radiant sky,
Where twelve fair signs in beauteous order lie?   40

DAMON

Then sing by turns, by turns the Muses sing,
Now hawthorns blossom, now the daisies spring,
Now leaves the trees, and flowers adorn the ground;
Begin, the vales shall every note rebound.

STREPHON

Inspire me, Phœbus, in my Delia's praise,   45
With Waller's strains, or Granville's moving lays![1]

[1] George Granville, afterwards Lord Lansdowne.

A milk-white Bull shall at your altars stand,
That threats a fight, and spurns the rising sand.

DAPHNIS

O Love! for Sylvia let me gain the prize,
And make my tongue victorious as her eyes: 50
No lambs or sheep for victims I'll impart,
Thy victim, Love, shall be the shepherd's heart.

STREPHON

Me gentle Delia beckons from the plain,
Then hid in shades, eludes her eager swain;
But feigns a laugh, to see me search around, 55
And by that laugh the willing pair is found.

DAPHNIS

The sprightly Sylvia trips along the green,
She runs, but hopes she does not run unseen;
While a kind glance at her pursuer flies,
How much at variance are her feet and eyes! 60

STREPHON

O'er golden sands let rich Pactolus flow,
And trees weep amber on the banks of Po!
Blest Thames's shores the brightest beauties yield,
Feed here my lambs, I'll seek no distant field.

DAPHNIS

Celestial Venus haunts Idalia's groves; 65
Diana Cynthus, Ceres Hybla loves,
If Windsor-shades delight the matchless maid,
Cynthus and Hybla yield to Windsor-shade.

STREPHON

All Nature mourns, the skies relent in showers,
Hush'd are the birds, and closed the drooping flowers; 70
If Delia smile, the flowers begin to spring,
The skies to brighten, and the birds to sing.

DAPHNIS

All Nature laughs, the groves are fresh and fair,
The sun's mild lustre warms the vital air;
If Sylvia smiles, new glories gild the shore,   75
And vanquish'd nature seems to charm no more.

STREPHON

In spring the fields, in autumn hills I love,
At morn the plains, at noon the shady grove,
But Delia always; absent from her sight,
Nor plains at morn, nor groves at noon delight.   80

DAPHNIS

Sylvia's like autumn ripe, yet mild as May,
More bright than noon, yet fresh as early day;
E'en spring displeases, when she shines not here;
But bless'd with her, 'tis spring throughout the year.

STREPHON

Say, Daphnis, say, in what glad soil appears,   85
A wondrous tree that sacred monarchs bears:
Tell me but this, and I'll disclaim the prize,
And give the conquest to thy Sylvia's eyes.

DAPHNIS

Nay, tell me first, in what more happy fields
The thistle springs, to which the lily yields: 90
And then a nobler prize I will resign;
For Sylvia, charming Sylvia, shall be thine.

DAMON

Cease to contend, for, Daphnis, I decree,
The bowl to Strephon, and the lamb to thee:
Blest swains, whose nymphs in every grace excel;   95
Blest nymphs, whose swains those graces sing so well!
Now rise, and haste to yonder woodbine bowers,
A soft retreat from sudden vernal showers;
The turf with rural dainties shall be crown'd,
While opening blooms diffuse their sweets around.   100
For see! the gathering flocks to shelter tend,
And from the Pleiads fruitful showers descend.

SUMMER: THE SECOND PASTORAL,
OR ALEXIS [1]

A SHEPHERD's boy (he seeks no better name)
Led forth his flock along the silver Thame,
Where dancing sun-beams on the waters play'd,
And verdant alders form'd a quivering shade.
Soft as he mourn'd, the streams forgot to flow,   5
The flocks around a dumb compassion show,
The Naïads wept in every watery bower,
And Jove consented in a silent shower.

   Accept, O Garth, the Muse's early lays,[2]
That adds this wreath of ivy to thy bays;   10
Hear what from love unpractised hearts endure,
From love, the sole disease thou canst not cure.

   Ye shady beeches, and ye cooling streams,
Defence from Phœbus', not from Cupid's beams,
To you I mourn, nor to the deaf I sing,   15
"The woods shall answer, and their echo ring."
The hills and rocks attend my doleful lay:
Why art thou prouder and more hard than they?
The bleating sheep with my complaints agree,
They parch'd with heat, and I inflamed by thee.   20
The sultry Sirius burns the thirsty plains,
While in thy heart eternal winter reigns.

   Where stray ye, Muses, in what lawn or grove,
While your Alexis pines in hopeless love?
In those fair fields where sacred Isis glides,   25
Or else where Cam his winding vales divides?
As in the crystal spring I view my face,
Fresh rising blushes paint the watery glass;
But since those graces please thy eyes no more,
I shun the fountains which I sought before.   30
Once I was skill'd in every herb that grew,
And every plant that drinks the morning dew;
Ah, wretched shepherd, what avails thy art,
To cure thy lambs, but not to heal thy heart!

   Let other swains attend the rural care,   35

[1] The scene of this pastoral by the river's side, suitable to the heat of the season; the time, noon.

[2] Dr. Samuel Garth, author of *The Dispensary*, one of Pope's first friends.

Feed fairer flocks, or richer fleeces shear:
But nigh yon mountain let me tune my lays,
Embrace my love, and bind my brows with bays.
That flute is mine which Colin's tuneful breath
Inspired when living, and bequeath'd in death: 40
He said, "Alexis, take this pipe, the same
That taught the groves my Rosalinda's name:"
But now the reeds shall hang on yonder tree,
For ever silent, since despised by thee.
O, were I made by some transforming power,   45
The captive bird that sings within thy bower!
Then might my voice thy listening ears employ,
And I those kisses he receives enjoy.
  And yet my numbers please the rural throng,
Rough satyrs dance, and Pan applauds the song: 50
The nymphs, forsaking every cave and spring,
Their early fruit, and milk-white turtles bring!
Each amorous nymph prefers her gifts in vain,
On you their gifts are all bestow'd again,
For you the swains the fairest flowers design,   55
And in one garland all their beauties join;
Accept the wreath which you deserve alone,
In whom all beauties are comprised in one.
  See what delights in sylvan scenes appear!
Descending gods have found Elysium here.   60
In woods bright Venus with Adonis stray'd,
And chaste Diana haunts the forest shade.
Come, lovely nymph, and bless the silent hours,
When swains from shearing seek their nightly bowers;
When weary reapers quit the sultry field,   65
And crown'd with corn their thanks to Ceres yield.
This harmless grove no lurking vapour hides,
But in my breast the serpent love abides.
Here bees from blossoms sip the rosy dew,
But your Alexis knows no sweets but you.   70
O deign to visit our forsaken seats,
The mossy fountains, and the green retreats!
Where'er you walk, cool gales shall fan the glade,
Trees, where you sit, shall crowd into a shade:
Where'er you tread, the blushing flowers shall rise,   75
And all things flourish where you turn your eyes.
Oh, how I long with you to pass my days,
Invoke the Muses, and resound your praise!

Your praise the birds shall chant in every grove,
And winds shall waft it to the powers above. 80
But would you sing, and rival Orpheus' strain,
The wondering forests soon should dance again,
The moving mountains hear the powerful call,
And headlong streams hang listening in their fall!
　　But see, the shepherds shun the noonday heat, 85
The lowing herds to murmuring brooks retreat,
To closer shades the panting flocks remove;
Ye gods! and is there no relief for Love?
But soon the sun with milder rays descends
To the cool ocean, where his journey ends: 90
On me Love's fiercer flames for ever prey,
By night he scorches, as he burns by day.

AUTUMN: THE THIRD PASTORAL, OR HYLAS AND ÆGON [1]

Beneath the shade a spreading beech displays,
Hylas and Ægon sung their rural lays:
This mourn'd a faithless, that an absent, Love;
And Delia's name and Doris' fill'd the grove.
Ye Mantuan nymphs, your sacred succour bring; 5
Hylas and Ægon's rural lays I sing.
　　Thou, whom the Nine, with Plautus' wit inspire,
The art of Terence, and Menander's fire;
Whose sense instructs us, and whose humour charms,
Whose judgment sways us, and whose spirit warms! 10
Oh, skill'd in Nature! see the hearts of swains,
Their artless passions, and their tender pains.
　　New setting Phœbus shone serenely bright,
And fleecy clouds were streak'd with purple light.
When tuneful Hylas with melodious moan, 15
Taught rocks to weep, and made the mountains groan.
　　Go, gentle gales, and bear my sighs away!
To Delia's ear the tender notes convey.
As some sad turtle his lost love deplores,
And with deep murmurs fills the sounding shores; 20

[1] This pastoral consists of two parts, like the eighth of Virgil: the scene a hill; the time, at sunset.

Thus, far from Delia, to the winds I mourn,
Alike unheard, unpitied, and forlorn.
  Go, gentle gales, and bear my sighs along!
For her, the feather'd quires neglect their song:
For her, the limes their pleasing shades deny;   25
For her, the lilies hang their heads and die.
Ye flowers that droop, forsaken by the spring,
Ye birds that, left by summer, cease to sing,
Ye trees that fade when autumn-heats remove,
Say, is not absence death to those who love?   30
  Go, gentle gales, and bear my sighs away!
Cursed be the fields that cause my Delia's stay;
Fade every blossom, wither every tree,
Die every flower, and perish all, but she.
What have I said? where'er my Delia flies,   35
Let spring attend, and sudden flowers arise;
Let opening roses knotted oaks adorn,
And liquid amber drop from every thorn.
  Go, gentle gales, and bear my sighs along!
The birds shall cease to tune their evening song,   40
The winds to breathe, the waving woods to move,
And streams to murmur, ere I cease to love.
Not bubbling fountains to the thirsty swain,
Not balmy sleep to labourers faint with pain,
Not showers to larks, or sunshine to the bee,   45
Are half so charming as thy sight to me.
  Go, gentle gales, and bear my sighs away!
Come, Delia, come; ah, why this long delay?
Through rocks and cave the name of Delia sounds,
Delia, each cave and echoing rock rebounds.   50
Ye powers, what pleasing frenzy soothes my mind!
Do lovers dream, or is my Delia kind?
She comes, my Delia comes!—Now cease my lay,
And cease, ye gales, to bear my sighs away!
  Next Ægon sung, while Windsor groves admired;   55
Rehearse, ye Muses, what yourselves inspired.
  Resound, ye hills, resound my mournful strain!
Of perjured Doris, dying I complain:
Here where the mountains, lessening as they rise,
Lose the low vales, and steal into the skies;   60
While labouring oxen, spent with toil and heat,
In their loose traces from the field retreat;
While curling smokes from village-tops are seen,

And the fleet shades glide o'er the dusky green.
   Resound, ye hills, resound my mournful lay! 65
Beneath yon' poplar oft we pass'd the day:
Oft on the rind I carved her amorous vows,
While she with garlands hung the bending boughs:
The garlands fade, the vows are worn away;
So dies her love, and so my hopes decay. 70
   Resound, ye hills, resound my mournful strain!
Now bright Arcturus glads the teeming grain,
Now golden fruits on loaded branches shine,
And grateful clusters swell with floods of wine;
Now blushing berries paint the yellow grove; 75
Just Gods! shall all things yield returns but love?
   Resound, ye hills, resound my mournful lay!
The shepherds cry, " Thy flocks are left a prey."—
Ah! what avails it me, the flocks to keep,
Who lost my heart while I preserved my sheep? 80
Pan came, and ask'd, what magic caused my smart,
Or what ill eyes malignant glances dart?
What eyes but hers, alas, have power to move?
And is there magic but what dwells in love?
   Resound, ye hills, resound my mournful strains! 85
I'll fly from shepherds, flocks, and flowery plains.
From shepherds, flocks, and plains, I may remove,
Forsake mankind, and all the world—but Love!
I know thee, Love! on foreign mountains bred,
Wolves gave thee suck, and savage tigers fed. 90
Thou wert from Ætna's burning entrails torn,
Got by fierce whirlwinds, and in thunder born!
   Resound, ye hills, resound my mournful lay!
Farewell, ye woods, adieu the light of day!
One leap from yonder cliff shall end my pains; 95
No more, ye hills, no more resound my strains!
   Thus sung the shepherds till th' approach of night,
The skies yet blushing with departing light,
When falling dews with spangles deck'd the glade,
And the low sun had lengthen'd every shade. 100

WINTER: THE FOURTH PASTORAL,
OR DAPHNE

LYCIDAS

THYRSIS, the music of that murmuring spring
Is not so mournful as the strains you sing.
Nor rivers winding through the vales below,
So sweetly warble, or so smoothly flow.
Now sleeping flocks on their soft fleeces lie,   5
The moon, serene in glory, mounts the sky,
While silent birds forget their tuneful lays,
Oh sing of Daphne's fate, and Daphne's praise!

THYRSIS

Behold the groves that shine with silver frost,
Their beauty wither'd, and their verdure lost.   10
Here shall I try the sweet Alexis' strain,
That call'd the listening Dryads to the plain?
Thames heard the numbers, as he flow'd along,
And bade his willows learn the moving song.

LYCIDAS

So may kind rains their vital moisture yield,   15
And swell the future harvest of the field,
Begin; this charge the dying Daphne gave,
And said, " Ye shepherds, sing around my grave!"
Sing, while beside the shaded tomb I mourn,
And with fresh bays her rural shrine adorn.   20

THYRSIS

Ye gentle Muses, leave your crystal spring,
Let Nymphs and Sylvans cypress garlands bring;
Ye weeping loves, the stream with myrtles hide,
And break your bows as when Adonis died;
And with your golden darts, now useless grown,   25
Inscribe a verse on this relenting stone:
"Let nature change, let heaven and earth deplore,
Fair Daphne's dead, and love is now no more!"

'Tis done, and Nature's various charms decay,
See gloomy clouds obscure the cheerful day!   30

Now hung with pearls the dropping trees appear,
Their faded honours scatter'd on her bier.
See where, on earth, the flowery glories lie,
With her they flourish'd, and with her they die.
Ah, what avail the beauties Nature wore?   35
Fair Daphne's dead, and beauty is no more!
  For her the flocks refuse their verdant food,
The thirsty heifers shun the gliding flood,
The silver swans her hapless fate bemoan,
In notes more sad than when they sing their own; 40
In hollow caves sweet Echo silent lies,
Silent, or only to her name replies;
Her name with pleasure once she taught the shore,
Now Daphne's dead, and pleasure is no more!
  No grateful dews descend from evening skies, 45
Nor morning odours from the flowers arise;
No rich perfumes refresh the fruitful field,
Nor fragrant herbs their native incense yield.
The balmy Zephyrs, silent since her death,
Lament the ceasing of a sweeter breath;   50
The industrious bees neglect their golden store!
Fair Daphne's dead, and sweetness is no more!
  No more the mounting larks, while Daphne sings,
Shall, listening in mid-air, suspend their wings;
No more the birds shall imitate her lays,   55
Or, hush'd with wonder, hearken from the sprays:
No more the streams their murmurs shall forbear,
A sweeter music than their own to hear;
But tell the reeds, and tell the vocal shore,
Fair Daphne's dead, and music is no more!   60
  Her fate is whisper'd by the gentle breeze,
And told in sighs to all the trembling trees;
The trembling trees, in every plain and wood,
Her fate remurmur to the silver flood:
The silver flood, so lately calm, appears   65
Swell'd with new passion, and o'erflows with tears;
The winds and trees and floods her death deplore,
Daphne, our grief! our glory now no more!
  But see! where Daphne wondering mounts on high
Above the clouds, above the starry sky!
Eternal beauties grace the shining scene,   70
Fields ever fresh, and groves for ever green!
There while you rest in Amaranthine bowers,

Or from those meads select unfading flowers,
Behold us kindly, who your name implore, 75
Daphne, our goddess, and our grief no more!

LYCIDAS

How all things listen, while thy Muse complains!
Such silence waits on Philomela's strains,
In some still evening, when the whispering breeze
Pants on the leaves, and dies upon the trees. 80
To thee, bright goddess, oft a lamb shall bleed,
If teeming ewes increase my fleecy breed.
While plants their shade, or flowers their odours give,
Thy name, thy honour, and thy praise shall live!

THYRSIS

But see, Orion sheds unwholesome dews; 85
Arise, the pines a noxious shade diffuse;
Sharp Boreas blows, and Nature feels decay,
Time conquers all, and we must time obey.
Adieu, ye vales, ye mountains, streams, and groves;
Adieu, ye shepherds' rural lays and loves; 90
Adieu, my flocks; farewell, ye sylvan crew;
Daphne, farewell; and all the world adieu!

WINDSOR FOREST

TO THE RIGHT HONOURABLE GEORGE LORD LANSDOWNE

Non injussa cano: Te nostræ, Vare, myricæ,
Te Nemus omne canet; nec Phœbo gratior ulla est,
Quam sibi quæ Vari præscripsit pagina nomen.—VIRG.

[My pastoral Muse her humble tribute brings;
And yet not wholly uninspir'd she sings:
For all who read, and reading, not disdain
These rural poems, and their lowly strain,
The name of Varus oft inscribed shall see
In every grove and every vocal tree,
And all the sylvan reign shall sing of thee:
Thy name, to Phœbus and the Muses known,
Shall in the front of every page be shown;
For he who sings thy praise secures his own.—DRYDEN.]

THY forest, Windsor! and thy green retreats,
At once the Monarch's and the Muse's seats,
Invite my lays. Be present, sylvan maids!
Unlock your springs, and open all your shades.

GRANVILLE commands; your aid, O Muses, bring!   5
What Muse for GRANVILLE can refuse to sing?
    The groves of Eden, vanish'd now so long,
Live in description, and look green in song:
These, were my breast inspired with equal flame,
Like them in beauty, should be like in fame.   10
Here hills and vales, the woodland and the plain,
Here earth and water seem to strive again;
Not chaos-like together crush'd and bruised,
But, as the world harmoniously confused:
Where order in variety we see,   15
And where, though all things differ, all agree.
Here waving groves a chequer'd scene display,
And part admit, and part exclude the day;
As some coy nymph her lover's warm address
Not quite indulges, nor can quite repress.   20
There, interspersed in lawns and opening glades,
Thin trees arise that shun each other's shades.
Here in full light the russet plains extend:
There, wrapt in clouds the bluish hills ascend.
Even the wild heath displays her purple dyes,   25
And 'midst the desert, fruitful fields arise,
That crown'd with tufted trees and springing corn,
Like verdant isles the sable waste adorn.
Let India boast her plants, nor envy we
The weeping amber, or the balmy tree,   30
While by our oaks the precious loads are borne,
And realms commanded which those trees adorn.
Not proud Olympus yields a nobler sight,
Though gods assembled grace his towering height,
Than what more humble mountains offer here,   35
Where, in their blessings, all those gods appear.
See Pan with flocks, with fruits Pomona crown'd,
Here blushing Flora paints th' enamell'd ground,
Here Ceres' gifts in waving prospect stand,
And nodding tempt the joyful reaper's hand;   40
Rich Industry sits smiling on the plains,
And peace and plenty tell, a STUART reigns.
    Not thus the land appear'd in ages past,
A dreary desert, and a gloomy waste,
To savage beasts and savage laws a prey,   45
And kings more furious and severe than they;
Who claim'd the skies, dispeopled air and floods,

The lonely lords of empty wilds and woods:
Cities laid waste, they storm'd the dens and caves
(For wiser brutes were backward to be slaves).   50
What could be free, when lawless beasts obey'd,
And even the elements a tyrant sway'd?
In vain kind seasons swell'd the teeming grain,
Soft showers distill'd, and suns grew warm in vain;
The swain with tears his frustrate labour yields,   55
And famish'd dies amidst his ripen'd fields.
What wonder then, a beast or subject slain
Were equal crimes in a despotic reign?
Both doom'd alike for sportive tyrants bled,
But while the subject starv'd, the beast was fed.   60
Proud Nimrod first the bloody chase began,
A mighty hunter, and his prey was man;
Our haughty Norman boasts that barbarous name,
And makes his trembling slaves the royal game.
The fields are ravish'd from th' industrious swains,   65
From men their cities, and from gods their fanes:
The levell'd towns with weeds lie cover'd o'er;
The hollow winds through naked temples roar;
Round broken columns clasping ivy twined;
O'er heaps of ruin stalk'd the stately hind;   70
The fox obscene to gaping tombs retires,
And savage howlings fill the sacred quires.
Awed by his Nobles, by his Commons cursed,
Th' oppressor ruled tyrannic where he durst,
Stretch'd o'er the poor and Church his iron rod,   75
And served alike his vassals and his God.
Whom even the Saxon spared, and bloody Dane,
The wanton victims of his sport remain.
But see, the man who spacious regions gave
A waste for beasts, himself denied a grave!   80
Stretch'd on the lawn his second hope survey,
At once the chaser, and at once the prey:
Lo Rufus, tugging at the deadly dart,
Bleeds in the forest like a wounded hart.
Succeeding monarchs heard the subjects' cries,   85
Nor saw displeased the peaceful cottage rise,
Then gathering flocks on unknown mountains fed,
O'er sandy wilds were yellow harvests spread.
The forests wonder'd at th' unusual grain,
And sacred transport touch'd the conscious swain.   90

Fair Liberty, Britannia's goddess, rears
Her cheerful head, and leads the golden years.
    Ye vigorous swains! while youth ferments your blood,
And purer spirits swell the sprightly flood,
Now range the hills, the gameful woods beset,   95
Wind the shrill horn, or spread the waving net.
When milder autumn summer's heat succeeds,
And in the new-shorn field the partridge feeds,
Before his lord the ready spaniel bounds,
Panting with hope, he tries the furrow'd grounds;   100
But when the tainted gales the game betray,
Couch'd close he lies, and meditates the prey:
Secure they trust th' unfaithful field beset,
Till hovering o'er them sweeps the swelling net.
Thus (if small things we may with great compare)   105
When Albion sends her eager sons to war,
Some thoughtless town, with ease and plenty blest,
Near, and more near, the closing lines invest;
Sudden they seize th' amazed, defenceless prize,
And high in air Britannia's standard flies.   110
See! from the brake the whirring pheasant springs,
And mounts exulting on triumphant wings:
Short is his joy; he feels the fiery wound,
Flutters in blood, and panting beats the ground,
Ah! what avail his glossy, varying dyes,   115
His purple crest, and scarlet-circled eyes,
The vivid green his shining plumes unfold,
His painted wings and breast that flames with gold?
    Nor yet, when moist Arcturus clouds the sky
The woods and fields their pleasing toils deny.   120
To plains with well-breath'd beagles we repair,
And trace the mazes of the circling hare:
(Beasts, urged by us, their fellow beast pursue,
And learn of man each other to undo)
With slaughtering guns the unwearied fowler roves,   125
When frosts have whiten'd all the naked groves;
Where doves in flocks the leafless trees o'ershade,
And lonely woodcocks haunt the watery glade.
He lifts the tube, and levels with his eye;
Straight a short thunder breaks the frozen sky: 130
Oft, as in airy rings they skim the heath,
The clamorous lapwings feel the leaden death:
Oft, as the mounting larks their notes prepare,

They fall, and leave their little lives in air.
    In genial spring, beneath the quivering shade,   135
Where cooling vapours breathe along the mead,
The patient fisher takes his silent stand,
Intent, his angle trembling in his hand:
With looks unmoved, he hopes the scaly breed,
And eyes the dancing cork, and bending reed.   140
Our plenteous streams a various race supply,
The bright-eyed perch with fins of Tyrian dye,
The silver eel, in shining volumes roll'd,
The yellow carp, in scales bedropp'd with gold,
Swift trouts, diversified with crimson stains,   145
And pikes, the tyrants of the watery plains.
    Now Cancer glows with Phœbus' fiery car:
The youth rush eager to the sylvan war,
Swarm o'er the lawns, the forest walks surround,
Rouse the fleet hart, and cheer the opening hound.   150
The impatient courser pants in every vein,
And pawing, seems to beat the distant plain:
Hills, vales, and floods appear already cross'd,
And ere he starts, a thousand steps are lost.
See the bold youth strain up the threat'ning steep,   155
Rush through the thickets, down the valleys sweep,
Hang o'er their coursers' heads with eager speed,
And earth rolls back beneath the flying steed.
Let old Arcadia boast her ample plain,
The immortal huntress, and her virgin train;   160
Nor envy, Windsor! since thy shades have seen
As bright a goddess, and as chaste a QUEEN;
Whose care, like hers, protects the sylvan reign,
The earth's fair light, and empress of the main.
    Here too, 'tis sung, of old Diana stray'd,   165
And Cynthus' top forsook for Windsor shade!
Here was she seen o'er airy wastes to rove,
Seek the clear spring, or haunt the pathless grove;
Here arm'd with silver bows, in early dawn,
Her buskin'd virgins traced the dewy lawn.   170
    Above the rest a rural nymph was famed,
Thy offspring, Thames! the fair Lodona named:
(Lodona's fate, in long oblivion cast,
The Muse shall sing, and what she sings shall last.)
Scarce could the goddess from her nymph be known,   175
But by the crescent, and the golden zone.

She scorn'd the praise of beauty, and the care;
A belt her waist, a fillet binds her hair;
A painted quiver on her shoulder sounds,
And with her dart the flying deer she wounds.   180
It chanced, as eager of the chase, the maid
Beyond the forest's verdant limits stray'd,
Pan saw and loved, and, burning with desire,
Pursued her flight, her flight increased his fire.
Not half so swift the trembling doves can fly,   185
When the fierce eagle cleaves the liquid sky;
Not half so swiftly the fierce eagle moves,
When through the clouds he drives the trembling doves;
As from the god she flew with furious pace,
Or as the god, more furious, urged the chase.   190
Now fainting, sinking, pale, the nymph appears;
Now close behind, his sounding steps she hears;
And now his shadow reach'd her as she run,
His shadow lengthen'd by the setting sun;
And now his shorter breath, with sultry air,   195
Pants on her neck, and fans her parting hair.
In vain on Father Thames she calls for aid,
Nor could Diana help her injured maid.
Faint, breathless, thus she pray'd, nor pray'd in vain:
" Ah, Cynthia! ah—though banish'd from thy train,   200
Let me, O let me, to the shades repair,
My native shades—there weep, and murmur there."
She said, and melting as in tears she lay,
In a soft silver stream dissolved away.
The silver stream her virgin coldness keeps,   205
For ever murmurs, and for ever weeps;
Still bears the name the hapless virgin bore,[1]
And bathes the forest where she ranged before.
In her chaste current oft the goddess laves,
And with celestial tears augments the waves.   210
Oft in her glass the musing shepherd spies
The headlong mountains and the downward skies,
The watery landskip of the pendant woods,
And absent trees that tremble in the floods;
In the clear azure gleam the flocks are seen,   215
And floating forests paint the waves with green,
Through the fair scene roll slow the ling'ring streams,
Then foaming pour along, and rush into the Thames.

[1] The River Loddon.

Thou, too, great father of the British floods!
With joyful pride survey'st our lofty woods; 220
Where towering oaks their growing honours rear
And future navies on thy shores appear.
Not Neptune's self from all her streams receives
A wealthier tribute, than to thine he gives.
No seas so rich, so gay no banks appear. 225
No lake so gentle, and no spring so clear.
Nor Po so swells the fabling poet's lays,
While led along the skies his current strays,
As thine, which visits Windsor's famed abodes,
To grace the mansion of our earthly gods: 230
Nor all his stars above a lustre show,
Like the bright beauties on thy banks below;
Where Jove, subdued by mortal passion still,
Might change Olympus for a nobler hill.

Happy the man whom this bright court approves, 235
His sovereign favours, and his country loves;
Happy next him, who to these shades retires,
Whom Nature charms, and whom the Muse inspires;
Whom humbler joys of home-felt quiet please,
Successive study, exercise, and ease. 240
He gathers health from herbs the forest yields,
And of their fragrant physic spoils the fields:
With chemic art exalts the mineral powers,
And draws the aromatic souls of flowers:
Now marks the course of rolling orbs on high; 245
O'er figured worlds now travels with his eye;
Of ancient writ unlocks the learned store,
Consults the dead, and lives past ages o'er:
Or wandering thoughtful in the silent wood,
Attends the duties of the wise and good, 250
To observe a mean, be to himself a friend,
To follow Nature, and regard his end;
Or looks on heaven with more than mortal eyes,
Bids his free soul expatiate in the skies,
Amid her kindred stars familiar roam, 255
Survey the region, and confess her home!
Such was the life great Scipio once admired,
Thus Atticus, and TRUMBULL thus retired.

Ye sacred Nine! that all my soul possess,
Whose raptures fire me, and whose visions bless, 260
Bear me, oh bear me to sequester'd scenes,

The bowery mazes, and surrounding greens:
To Thames's banks which fragrant breezes fill,
Or where ye Muses sport on COOPER'S HILL.
(On COOPER'S HILL eternal wreaths shall grow, 265
While lasts the mountain, or while Thames shall flow.)
I seem through consecrated walks to rove,
I hear soft music die along the grove:
Led by the sound, I roam from shade to shade,
By godlike poets venerable made: 270
Here his first lays majestic DENHAM sung;
There the last numbers flow'd from COWLEY'S tongue.
O early lost! what tears the river shed,
When the sad pomp along his banks was led!
His drooping swans on every note expire, 275
And on his willows hung each Muse's lyre.

Since fate relentless stopp'd their heavenly voice,
No more the forests ring, or groves rejoice;
Who now shall charm the shades, where COWLEY strung
His living harp, and lofty DENHAM sung? 280
But hark! the groves rejoice, the forest rings!
Are these revived? or is it GRANVILLE sings?
'Tis yours, my lord, to bless our soft retreats,
And call the Muses to their ancient seats;
To paint anew the flowery sylvan scenes, 285
To crown the forests with immortal greens,
Make Windsor hills in lofty numbers rise,
And lift her turrets nearer to the skies;
To sing those honours you deserve to wear,
And add new lustre to her silver star. 290

Here noble SURREY felt the sacred rage,[1]
SURREY, the GRANVILLE of a former age:
Matchless his pen, victorious was his lance,
Bold in the lists, and graceful in the dance:
In the same shades the Cupids tuned his lyre, 295
To the same notes, of love and soft desire:
Fair Geraldine, bright object of his vow,
Then fill'd the groves, as heavenly Mira now.

Oh would'st thou sing what heroes Windsor bore,
What kings first breathed upon her winding shore, 300
Or raise old warriors, whose adored remains
In weeping vaults her hallow'd earth contains!
With Edward's acts adorn the shining page,[2]

[1] Henry Howard, Earl of Surrey, the poet.   [2] Edward III.

Stretch his long triumphs down through every age,
Draw monarchs chain'd, and Cressy's glorious field,   305
The lilies blazing on the regal shield;
Then, from her roofs when Verrio's colours fall,[1]
And leave inanimate the naked wall,
Still in thy song should vanquish'd France appear,
And bleed for ever under Britain's spear.   310
    Let softer strains ill-fated Henry mourn,[2]
And palms eternal flourish round his urn.
Here o'er the martyr-king the marble weeps,
And, fast beside him, once-fear'd Edward sleeps:[3]
Whom not th' extended Albion could contain,   315
From old Belerium to the northern main,
The grave unites; where e'en the great find rest,
And blended lie th' oppressor and th' oppress'd!
    Make sacred Charles's tomb for ever known,
(Obscure the place, and uninscribed the stone)   320
O fact accursed! what tears has Albion shed,
Heavens, what new wounds! and how her old have bled!
She saw her sons with purple deaths expire,
Her sacred domes involved in rolling fire,
A dreadful series of intestine wars,   325
Inglorious triumphs and dishonest scars.
At length great Anna said: "Let discord cease!"
She said, the world obey'd, and all was peace!
    In that blest moment from his oozy bed
Old Father Thames advanced his reverend head;   330
His tresses dropp'd with dews, and o'er the stream
His shining horns diffused a golden gleam:
Graved on his urn appear'd the moon, that guides
His swelling waters, and alternate tides;
The figured streams in waves of silver roll'd,   335
And on her banks Augusta rose in gold;
Around his throne the sea-born brothers stood,
Who swell with tributary urns his flood:
First the famed authors of his ancient name,
The winding Isis, and the fruitful Thame: 340
The Kennet swift, for silver eels renown'd;
The Loddon slow, with verdant alders crown'd;

[1] Verrio, whose paintings at Windsor and Hampton Court were on ceilings and staircases, "where one should be sorry to place the works of a better master " (Walpole).
[2] Henry VI.
[3] Edward IV.

Cole, whose dark streams his flowery islands lave;
And chalky Wey, that rolls a milky wave;
The blue, transparent Vandalis appears;   345
The gulphy Lee his sedgy tresses rears;
And sullen Mole, that hides his diving flood;
And silent Darent, stain'd with Danish blood.

High in the midst, upon his urn reclined,
(His sea-green mantle waving with the wind,)   350
The god appear'd: he turn'd his azure eyes
Where Windsor-domes and pompous turrets rise;
Then bow'd and spoke; the winds forgot to roar,
And the hush'd waves glide softly to the shore.

Hail, sacred peace! hail, long expected days,   355
That Thames's glory to the stars shall raise!
Though Tiber's streams immortal Rome behold,
Though foaming Hermus swells with tides of gold,
From Heaven itself though sevenfold Nilus flows,
And harvests on a hundred realms bestows;   360
These now no more shall be the Muse's themes,
Lost in my fame, as in the sea their streams.
Let Volga's banks with iron squadrons shine,
And groves of lances glitter on the Rhine,
Let barbarous Ganges arm a servile train;   365
Be mine the blessings of a peaceful reign.
No more my sons shall dye with British blood
Red Iber's sands, or Ister's foaming flood:
Safe on my shore each unmolested swain
Shall tend the flocks, or reap the bearded grain;   370
The shady empire shall retain no trace
Of war or blood, but in the sylvan chase;
The trumpet sleep, whilst cheerful horns are blown,
And arms employ'd on birds and beasts alone.
Behold! th' ascending villas on my side   375
Project long shadows o'er the crystal tide.
Behold! Augusta's glittering spires increase,
And temples rise, the beauteous works of Peace,
I see, I see, where two fair cities bend
Their ample bow, a new Whitehall ascend!   380
There mighty nations shall inquire their doom,
The world's great oracle in times to come;
There kings shall sue, and suppliant states be seen
Once more to bend before a British queen.

Thy trees, fair Windsor! now shall leave their woods,

And half thy forest rush into thy floods,   386
Bear Britain's thunder, and her cross display,
To the bright regions of the rising day:
Tempt icy seas, where scarce the waters roll,
Where clearer flames glow round the frozen pole;   390
Or under southern skies exalt their sails,
Led by new stars, and borne by spicy gales!
For me the balm shall bleed, and amber flow,
The coral redden, and the ruby glow,
The pearly shell its lucid globe infold,   395
And Phœbus warm the ripening ore to gold.
The time shall come, when free as seas or wind
Unbounded Thames shall flow for all mankind,
Whole nations enter with each swelling tide,
And seas but join the regions they divide;   400
Earth's distant ends our glory shall behold,
And the new world launch forth to seek the old.
Then ships of uncouth form shall stem the tide,
And feather'd people crowd my wealthy side,
And naked youths and painted chiefs admire   405
Our speech, our colour, and our strange attire!
O stretch thy reign, fair Peace! from shore to shore,
Till conquest cease, and slavery be no more;
Till the freed Indians in their native groves
Reap their own fruits, and woo their sable loves,   410
Peru once more a race of kings behold,
And other Mexicos be roof'd with gold.
Exiled by thee from earth to deepest hell,
In brazen bonds, shall barbarous Discord dwell:
Gigantic Pride, pale Terror, gloomy Care,   415
And mad Ambition shall attend her there:
There purple Vengeance bathed in gore retires,
Her weapons blunted, and extinct her fires:
There hateful Envy her own snakes shall feel,
And Persecution mourn her broken wheel: 420
There Faction roar, Rebellion bite her chain,
And gasping Furies thirst for blood in vain.
    Here cease thy flight, nor with unhallow'd lays
Touch the fair fame of Albion's golden days:
The thoughts of gods let Granville's verse recite,   425
And bring the scenes of opening fate to light:
My humble Muse, in unambitious strains,
Paints the green forests and the flowery plains.

Where Peace descending bids her olives spring,
And scatters blessings from her dove-like wing.   430
Even I more sweetly pass my careless days,
Pleased in the silent shade with empty praise;
Enough for me, that to the listening swains
First in these fields I sung the sylvan strains.

MESSIAH

A SACRED ECLOGUE

IN IMITATION OF VIRGIL'S POLLIO

Ye nymphs of Solyma! begin the song:
To heavenly themes sublimer strains belong.
The mossy fountains, and the sylvan shades,
The dreams of Pindus and Aonian maids,
Delight no more—O thou my voice inspire   5
Who touch'd Isaiah's hallowed lips with fire!
  Rapt into future times, the bard begun:
A Virgin shall conceive, a Virgin bear a Son!
From Jesse's root behold a Branch arise,
Whose sacred flower with fragrance fills the skies: 10
The ethereal spirit o'er its leaves shall move,
And on its top descends the mystic Dove.
Ye heavens! from high the dewy nectar pour,
And in oft silence shed the kindly shower!
The sick and weak the healing plant shall aid,   15
From storms a shelter, and from heat a shade.
All crimes shall cease, and ancient fraud shall fail;
Returning Justice lift aloft her scale;
Peace o'er the world her olive wand extend,
And white-robed Innocence from heaven descend.   20
Swift fly the years, and rise the expected morn!
Oh spring to light, auspicious Babe, be born!
See Nature hastes her earliest wreaths to bring,
With all the incense of the breathing spring:
See lofty Lebanon his head advance,   25
See nodding forests on the mountains dance:
See spicy clouds from lowly Saron rise,
And Carmel's flowery top perfumes the skies!

Hark! a glad voice the lonely desert cheers:—
"Prepare the way! a God, a God appears";   30
"A God, a God!" the vocal hills reply,
The rocks proclaim the approaching Deity.
Lo, earth receives him from the bending skies!
Sink down, ye mountains, and ye valleys, rise;
With heads declined, ye cedars, homage pay;   35
Be smooth, ye rocks; ye rapid floods, give way;
The Saviour comes! by ancient bards foretold!
Hear him, ye deaf, and all ye blind, behold!
He from thick films shall purge the visual ray,
And on the sightless eyeball pour the day: 40
'Tis he th' obstructed paths of sound shall clear,
And bid new music charm th' unfolding ear:
The dumb shall sing, the lame his crutch forego,
And leap exulting like the bounding roe.
No sigh, no murmur the wide world shall hear,   45
From every face he wipes off every tear.
In adamantine chains shall Death be bound,
And Hell's grim tyrant feel the eternal wound.
As the good shepherd tends his fleecy care,
Seeks freshest pasture and the purest air,   50
Explores the lost, the wandering sheep directs,
By day o'ersees them, and by night protects;
The tender lambs he raises in his arms,
Feeds from his hands, and in his bosom warms;
Thus shall mankind his guardian care engage,   55
The promised Father of the future age.
No more shall nation against nation rise,
Nor ardent warriors meet with hateful eyes,
Nor fields with gleaming steel be cover'd o'er,
The brazen trumpets kindle rage no more;   60
But useless lances into scythes shall bend,
And the broad falchion in a ploughshare end.
Then palaces shall rise; the joyful son
Shall finish what his short-lived sire begun;
Their vines a shadow to their race shall yield,   65
And the same hand that sow'd, shall reap the field.
The swain in barren deserts with surprise
See lilies spring, and sudden verdure rise;
And start, amidst the thirsty wilds to hear
New falls of water murmuring in his ear.   70
On rifted rocks, the dragon's late abodes,

The green reed trembles, and the bulrush nods.
Waste sandy valleys, once perplex'd with thorn,
The spiry fir and shapely box adorn;
To leafless shrubs the flowering palms succeed,   75
And odorous myrtle to the noisome weed.
The lambs with wolves shall graze the verdant mead,
And boys in flowery bands the tiger lead;
The steer and lion at one crib shall meet,
And harmless serpents lick the pilgrim's feet;   80
The smiling infant in his hand shall take
The crested basilisk and speckled snake,
Pleased the green lustre of the scales survey,
And with their forky tongue shall innocently play.
Rise, crown'd with light, imperial Salem, rise!   85
Exalt thy towery head, and lift thy eyes!
See, a long race thy spacious courts adorn;
See future sons, and daughters yet unborn,
In crowding ranks on every side arise,
Demanding life, impatient for the skies!   90
See barbarous nations at thy gates attend,
Walk in thy light, and in thy temple bend;
See thy bright altars throng'd with prostrate kings,
And heap'd with products of Sabean springs!
For thee Idume's spicy forests blow,   95
And seeds of gold in Ophir's mountains glow.
See heaven its sparkling portals wide display,
And break upon thee in a flood of day.
No more the rising sun shall gild the morn,
Nor evening Cynthia fill her silver horn;   100
But lost, dissolved in thy superior rays,
One tide of glory, one unclouded blaze
O'erflow thy courts: the Light himself shall shine
Reveal'd, and God's eternal day be thine!
The seas shall waste, the skies in smoke decay,   105
Rocks fall to dust, and mountains melt away;
But fix'd his word, his saving power remains:
Thy realms for ever lasts, thy own MESSIAH reigns!

THE TEMPLE OF FAME [1]

WRITTEN IN THE YEAR 1711

In that soft season, when descending showers
Call forth the greens, and wake the rising flowers;
When opening buds salute the welcome day,
And earth relenting feels the genial ray;
As balmy sleep had charm'd my cares to rest,   5
And love itself was banish'd from my breast,
(What time the morn mysterious visions brings,
While purer slumbers spread their golden wings,)
A train of phantoms in wild order rose,
And, join'd, this intellectual scene compose.   10
    I stood, methought, betwixt earth, seas, and skies:
The whole creation open to my eyes:
In air self-balanced hung the globe below,
Where mountains rise, and circling oceans flow;
Here naked rocks and empty wastes were seen,   15
There towery cities, and the forests green:
Here sailing ships delight the wandering eyes;
There trees, and intermingled temples rise:
Now a clear sun the shining scene displays,
The transient landscape now in clouds decays.   20
    O'er the wide prospect as I gazed around,
Sudden I heard a wild promiscuous sound,
Like broken thunders that at distance roar,
Or billows murmuring on the hollow shore:
Then gazing up, a glorious pile beheld,   25
Whose towering summit ambient clouds conceal'd,
High on a rock of ice the structure lay,
Steep its ascent, and slippery was the way:
The wondrous rock like Parian marble shone,
And seem'd, to distant sight, of solid stone.   30
Inscriptions here of various names I view'd,
The greater part by hostile time subdued;
Yet wide was spread their fame in ages past,
And poets once had promised they should last.
Some fresh engraved appear'd of wits renown'd;   35
I look'd again, nor could their trace be found.

[1] "The hint of the following piece was taken from Chaucer's *Hous of Fame*. The design is in a manner entirely altered, the descriptions and most of the particular thoughts my own: yet I could not suffer it to be printed without this acknowledgment."

Critics I saw that other names deface,
And fix their own, with labour, in their place:
Their own, like others, soon their place resign'd,
Or disappear'd, and left the first behind.   40
Nor was the work impair'd by storms alone,
But felt the approaches of too warm a sun;
For Fame, impatient of extremes, decays
Not more by envy than excess of praise.
Yet part no injuries of heaven could feel,   45
Like crystal faithful to the graving steel:
The rock's high summit, in the temple's shade,
Nor heat could melt, nor beating storm invade.
Their names inscribed unnumber'd ages past
From Time's first birth, with Time itself shall last;   50
These ever new, nor subject to decays,
Spread, and grow brighter with the length of days.
   So Zembla's rocks (the beauteous work of frost)
Rise white in air, and glitter o'er the coast;
Pale suns, unfelt, at distance roll away,   55
And on the impassive ice the lightnings play;
Eternal snows the growing mass supply,
Till the bright mountains prop the incumbent sky:
As Atlas fix'd, each hoary pile appears,
The gather'd winter of a thousand years.   60
On this foundation Fame's high temple stands;
Stupendous pile! not rear'd by mortal hands.
Whate'er proud Rome or artful Greece beheld,
Or elder Babylon, its frame excell'd.
Four faces had the dome, and every face   65
Of various structure, but of equal grace:
Four brazen gates, on columns lifted high,
Salute the different quarters of the sky,
Here fabled chiefs in darker ages born,
Or worthies old, whom arms or arts adorn,   70
Who cities raised, or tamed a monstrous race,
The walls in venerable order grace:
Heroes in animated marble frown,
And legislators seem to think in stone.
   Westward, a sumptuous frontispiece appear'd,   75
On Doric pillars of white marble rear'd,
Crown'd with an architrave of antique mould,
And sculpture rising on the roughen'd gold.
In shaggy spoils ere Theseus was beheld,

And Perseus dreadful with Minerva's shield: 80
There great Alcides stopping with his toil,
Rests on his club, and holds th' Hesperian spoil.
Here Orpheus sings; trees, moving to the sound,
Start from their roots, and form a shade around:
Amphion there the loud creating lyre   85
Strikes, and beholds a sudden Thebes aspire!
Cythæron's echoes answer to his call,
And half the mountain rolls into a wall:
There might you see the lengthening spires ascend,
The domes swell up, the widening arches bend,   90
The growing towers, like exhalations rise,
And the huge columns heave into the skies.

The Eastern front was glorious to behold,
With diamond flaming, and barbaric gold.
There Ninus shone, who spread the Assyrian fame,   95
And the great founder of the Persian name: [1]
There in long robes the royal Magi stand,
Grave Zoroaster waves the circling wand,
The sage Chaldeans robed in white appear'd,
And Brachmans, deep in desert woods revered,   100
These stopp'd the moon, and call'd th' unbodied shades
To midnight banquets in the glimm'ring glades;
Made visionary fabrics round them rise,
And airy spectres skim before their eyes;
Of talismans and sigils knew the power,   105
And careful watch'd the planetary hour.
Superior, and alone, Confucius stood,
Who taught that useful science—to be good.

But on the South, a long majestic race
Of Egypt's priests the gilded niches grace,   110
Who measured earth, described the starry spheres,
And traced the long records of lunar years.
High on his car Sesostris struck my view,
Whom sceptred slaves in golden harness drew:
His hands a bow and pointed javelin hold;   115
His giant-limbs are arm'd in scales of gold.
Between the statues obelisks were placed,
And the learn'd walls with hieroglyphics graced.

Of Gothic structure was the Northern side,
O'erwrought with ornaments of barbarous pride.   120
There huge Colosses rose, with trophies crown'd,

[1] Cyrus.

And Runic characters were graved around.
There sat Zamolxis with erected eyes,
And Odin here in mimic trances dies.
There on rude iron columns, smear'd with blood,   125
The horrid forms of Scythian heroes stood,
Druids and bards (their once loud harps unstrung),
And youths that died to be by poets sung.
These and a thousand more of doubtful fame,
To whom old fables gave a lasting name,   130
In ranks adorn'd the temple's outward face;
The wall in lustre and effect like glass,
Which o'er each object casting various dyes,
Enlarges some, and others multiplies:
Nor void of emblem was the mystic wall,   135
For thus romantic Fame increases all.
    The temple shakes, the sounding gates unfold,
Wide vaults appear, and roofs of fretted gold:
Rais'd on a thousand pillars, wreath'd around
With laurel foliage, and with eagles crown'd: 140
Of bright, transparent beryl were the walls,
The friezes gold, and gold the capitals:
As heaven with stars, the roof with jewels glows,
And ever-living lamps depend in rows.
Full in the passage of each spacious gate,   145
The sage historians in white garments wait;
Graved o'er their seats the form of Time was found,
His scythe reversed, and both his pinions bound.
Within stood heroes, who through loud alarms
In bloody fields pursued renown in arms.   150
High on a throne, with trophies charged, I view'd
The youth that all things but himself subdued;[1]
His feet on sceptres and tiaras trod,
And his horn'd head belied the Libyan god.
There Cæsar, graced with both Minervas shone;   155
Cæsar, the world's great master, and his own;
Unmoved, superior still in every state,
And scarce detested in his country's fate.
But chief were those, who not for empire sought,
But with their toils their people's safety brought: 160
High o'er the rest Epaminondas stood;
Timoleon, glorious in his brother's blood;
Bold Scipio, saviour of the Roman state,

[1] Alexander the Great.

Great in his triumphs, in retirement great;
And wise Aurelius, in whose well-taught mind 165
With boundless power unbounded virtue join'd,
His own strict judge, and patron of mankind.

Much-suffering heroes next their honours claim,
Those of less noisy, and less guilty fame,
Fair Virtue's silent train: supreme of these 170
Here ever shines the godlike Socrates:
He whom ungrateful Athens could expel,[1]
At all times just, but when he sign'd the shell:
Here his abode the martyr'd Phocion claims,
With Agis, not the last of Spartan names: 175
Unconquer'd Cato shows the wound he tore,
And Brutus his ill genius meets no more.

But in the centre of the hallow'd choir,
Six pompous columns o'er the rest aspire;
Around the shrine itself of Fame they stand, 180
Hold the chief honours, and the fane command.
High on the first, the mighty Homer shone;
Eternal adamant composed his throne;
Father of verse! in holy fillets dress'd,
His silver beard waved gently o'er his breast; 185
Though blind, a boldness in his looks appears;
In years he seem'd, but not impair'd by years.
The wars of Troy were round the pillar seen:
Here fierce Tydides wounds the Cyprian queen;
Here Hector, glorious from Patroclus' fall, 190
Here dragg'd in triumph round the Trojan wall:
Motion and life did every part inspire,
Bold was the work, and proved the master's fire;
A strong expression most he seem'd t' affect,
And here and there disclosed a brave neglect. 195

A golden column next in rank appear'd,
On which a shrine of purest gold was rear'd;
Finish'd the whole, and labour'd every part,
With patient touches of unwearied art:
The Mantuan there in sober triumph sat, 200
Composed his posture, and his look sedate;
On Homer still he fix'd a reverent eye,
Great without pride, in modest majesty.
In living sculpture on the sides were spread
The Latian wars, and haughty Turnus dead; 205

[1] Aristides, " the Just."

Eliza stretch'd upon the funeral pyre,
Æneas bending with his aged sire:
Troy flamed in burning gold, and o'er the throne
ARMS AND THE MAN in golden ciphers shone.

    Four swans sustain a car of silver bright,   210
With heads advanced, and pinions stretch'd for flight:
Here, like some furious prophet, Pindar rode,
And seem'd to labour with th' inspiring god.
Across the harp a careless hand he flings,
And boldly sinks into the sounding strings.   215
The figured games of Greece the column grace,
Neptune and Jove survey the rapid race.
The youths hang o'er their chariots as they run;
The fiery steeds seem starting from the stone;
The champions in distorted postures threat;   220
And all appear'd irregularly great.

    Here happy Horace tuned the Ausonian lyre
To sweeter sounds, and temper'd Pindar's fire;
Pleased with Alcæus' manly rage t' infuse
The softer spirit of the Sapphic muse.   225
The polish'd pillar different sculptures grace;
A work outlasting monumental brass.

    Here smiling Loves and Bacchanals appear,
The Julian star, and great Augustus here.
The doves that round the infant poet spread   230
Myrtles and bays, hung hovering o'er his head.

    Here in a shrine that cast a dazzling light,
Sat fix'd in thought the mighty Stagyrite;
His sacred head a radiant zodiac crown'd,
And various animals his side surround;   235
His piercing eyes, erect, appear to view
Superior worlds, and look all Nature through.
With equal rays immortal Tully shone,
The Roman rostra deck'd the Consul's throne:
Gathering his flowing robe, he seem'd to stand   240
In act to speak, and graceful stretch'd his hand.
Behind, Rome's genius waits with civic crowns,
And the great father of his country owns.

    These massy columns in a circle rise,
O'er which a pompous dome invades the skies   245
Scarce to the top I stretch'd my aching sight,
So large it spread, and swell'd to such a height.
Full in the midst proud Fame's imperial seat

With jewels blazed, magnificently great;
The vivid emeralds there revive the eye,   250
The flaming rubies show their sanguine dye,
Bright azure rays from lively sapphires stream,
And lucid amber casts a golden gleam.
With various-colour'd light the pavement shone,
And all on fire appear'd the glowing throne;   255
The dome's high arch reflects the mingled blaze,
And forms a rainbow of alternate rays.
When on the goddess first I cast my sight,
Scarce seem'd her stature of a cubit's height;
But swell'd to larger size, the more I gazed,   260
Till to the roof her towering front she raised.
With her, the temple every moment grew,
And ampler vistas open'd to my view:
Upward the columns shoot, the roofs ascend,
And arches widen, and long aisles extend,   265
Such was her form, as ancient bards have told,
Wings raise her arms, and wings her feet infold;
A thousand busy tongues the goddess hears,
And thousand open eyes, and thousand listening ears.
Beneath, in order ranged, the tuneful Nine   270
(Her virgin handmaids) still attend the shrine:
With eyes on Fame for ever fix'd, they sing:
For Fame they raise the voice, and tune the string:
With Time's first birth began the heavenly lays,
And last, eternal, through the length of days.   275
  Around these wonders as I cast a look,
The trumpet sounded, and the temple shook,
And all the nations, summon'd at the call,
From different quarters fill the crowded hall:
Of various tongues the mingled sounds were heard;   280
In various garbs promiscuous throngs appear'd;
Thick as the bees, that with the spring renew
Their flowery toils, and sip the fragrant dew,
When the wing'd colonies first tempt the sky,
O'er dusky fields and shaded waters fly,   285
Or settling, seize the sweets the blossoms yield,
And a low murmur runs along the field.
Millions of suppliant crowds the shrine attend,
And all degrees before the goddess bend;
The poor, the rich, the valiant, and the sage,   290
And boasting youth, and narrative old age.

Their pleas were different, their requests the same:
For good and bad alike are fond of Fame.
Some she disgraced, and some with honours crown'd;
Unlike successes equal merits found.   295
Thus her blind sister, fickle Fortune, reigns,
And, undiscerning, scatters crowns and chains.
  First at the shrine the learned world appear,
And to the goddess thus prefer their prayer,
" Long have we sought to instruct and please mankind,
With studies pale, with midnight-vigils blind;   301
But thank'd by few, rewarded yet by none,
We here appeal to thy superior throne:
On wit and learning the just prize bestow,
For Fame is all we must expect below."   305
  The goddess heard, and bade the muses raise
The golden trumpet of eternal praise.
From pole to pole the winds diffuse the sound,
That fills the circuit of the world around;
Not all at once, as thunder breaks the cloud;   310
The notes at first were rather sweet than loud:
By just degrees they every moment rise,
Fill the wide earth, and gain upon the skies.
At every breath were balmy odours shed,
Which still grew sweeter as they wider spread!   315
Less fragrant scents the unfolding rose exhales,
Or spices breathing in Arabian gales.
  Next these the good and just, an awful train,
Thus on their knees address the sacred fane,
"Since living virtue is with envy curst,   320
And the best men are treated like the worst,
Do thou, just goddess, call our merits forth,
And give each deed the exact intrinsic worth."
" Not with bare justice shall your act be crown'd,
(Said Fame) but high above desert renown'd: 325
Let fuller notes the applauding world amaze,
And the loud clarion labour in your praise."
  This band dismiss'd, behold another crowd
Preferr'd the same request, and lowly bow'd;
The constant tenor of whose well-spent days   330
No less deserved a just return of praise.
But straight the direful trump of slander sounds;
Through the big dome the doubling thunder bounds;
Loud as the burst of cannon rends the skies,

The dire report through every region flies,   335
In every ear incessant rumours rung,
And gathering scandals grew on every tongue.
From the black trumpet's rusty concave broke
Sulphureous flames, and clouds of rolling smoke:
The poisonous vapour blots the purple skies,   340
And withers all before it as it flies.

A troop came next, who crowns and armour wore,
And proud defiance in their looks they bore:
"For thee, (they cried) amidst alarms and strife,
We sail'd in tempests down the stream of life;   345
For thee whole nations fill'd with flames and blood,
And swam to empire through the purple flood.
Those ills we dared, thy inspiration own,
What virtue seemed, was done for thee alone."
"Ambitious fools! (the Queen replied, and frown'd,)   350
Be all your acts in dark oblivion drown'd;
There sleep forgot, with mighty tyrants gone,
Your statues moulder'd, and your names unknown!"
A sudden cloud straight snatch'd them from my sight,
And each majestic phantom sunk in night.   355

Then came the smallest tribe I yet had seen;
Plain was their dress, and modest was their mien.
"Great idol of mankind! we neither claim
The praise of merit, nor aspire to fame!
But safe in deserts from the applause of men,   360
Would die unheard of, as we lived unseen.
'Tis all we beg thee, to conceal from sight
Those acts of goodness, which themselves requite.
O let us still the secret joy partake,
To follow virtue ev'n for virtue's sake."   365
"And live there men, who slight immortal fame?
Who then with incense shall adore our name?
But, mortals! know, 'tis still our greatest pride
To blaze those virtues which the good would hide.
Rise! Muses, rise! add all your tuneful breath;   370
These must not sleep in darkness and in death."
She said: in air the trembling music floats,
And on the winds triumphant swell the notes;
So soft, though high, so loud, and yet so clear,
Even listening angels lean'd from Heaven to hear: 375
To farthest shores the ambrosial spirit flies
Sweet to the world, and grateful to the skies.

Next these a youthful train their vows express'd.
With feathers crown'd, with gay embroidery dress'd:
"Hither (they cried) direct your eyes, and see   380
The men of pleasure, dress, and gallantry;
Ours is the place at banquets, balls, and plays,
Sprightly our nights, polite are all our days;
Courts we frequent, where 'tis our pleasing care
To pay due visits, and address the fair: 385
In fact, 'tis true, no nymph we could persuade,
But still in fancy vanquish'd every maid;
Of unknown duchesses lewd tales we tell,
Yet, would the world believe us, all were well.
The joy let others have, and we the name: 390
And what we want in pleasure grant in fame."
   The Queen assents, the trumpet rends the skies,
And at each blast a lady's honour dies.
   Pleased with the strange success, vast numbers press'd
Around the shrine, and made the same request.   395
"What! you (she cried) unlearn'd in arts to please,
Slaves to yourselves, and even fatigued with ease,
Who lose a length of undeserving days,
Would you usurp the lover's dear-bought praise?
To just contempt, ye vain pretenders, fall,   400
The people's fable, and the scorn of all."
Straight the black clarion sends a horrid sound,
Loud laughs burst out, and bitter scoffs fly round,
Whispers are heard, with taunts reviling loud,
And scornful hisses run through all the crowd.   405
   Last, those who boast of mighty mischiefs done,
Enslave their country, or usurp a throne:
Or who their glory's dire foundation laid
On sovereigns ruin'd, or on friends betray'd;
Calm, thinking villains, whom no faith could fix,   410
Of crooked counsels and dark politics;
Of these a gloomy tribe surround the throne,
And beg to make the immortal treasons known.
The trumpet roars, long flaky flames expire,
With sparks, that seem'd to set the world on fire.   415
At the dread sound, pale mortals stood aghast,
And startled Nature trembled with the blast.
   This having heard and seen, some power unknown
Straight changed the scene, and snatch'd me from the throne.
Before my view appear'd a structure fair   420

Its site uncertain, if in earth or air:
With rapid motion turn'd the mansion round;
With ceaseless noise the ringing walls resound;
Not less in number were the spacious doors,
Than leaves on trees, or sands upon the shores;   425
Which still unfolded stand, by night, by day,
Pervious to winds, and open every way.
As flames by nature to the skies ascend,
As weighty bodies to the centre tend,
As to the sea returning rivers roll,   430
And the touch'd needle trembles to the pole;
Hither, as to their proper place, arise
All various sounds from earth, and seas, and skies,
Or spoke aloud, or whisper'd in the ear;
Nor ever silence, rest, or peace is here.   435
As on the smooth expanse of crystal lakes,
The sinking stone at first a circle makes;
The trembling surface by the motion stirr'd,
Spreads in a second circle, then a third;
Wide, and more wide, the floating rings advance,   440
Fill all the watery plain, and to the margin dance:
Thus every voice and sound, when first they break,
On neighb'ring air a soft impression make;
Another ambient circle then they move;
That, in its turn, impels the next above;   445
Through undulating air the sounds are sent,
And spread o'er all the fluid element.
    There various news I heard of love and strife,
Of peace and war, health, sickness, death, and life,
Of loss and gain, of famine and of store,   450
Of storms at sea, and travels on the shore,
Of prodigies, and portents seen in air,
Of fires and plagues, and stars with blazing hair,
Of turns of fortune, changes in the state,
The falls of fav'rites, projects of the great,   455
Of old mismanagements, taxations new:
All neither wholly false, nor wholly true.
    Above, below, without, within, around,
Confused, unnumber'd multitudes are found,
Who pass, repass, advance, and glide away;   460
Hosts raised by fear, and phantoms of a day:
Astrologers, that future fates foreshew,
Projectors, quacks, and lawyers not a few;

And priests, and party-zealots, numerous bands
With home-born lies, or tales from foreign lands;   465
Each talk'd aloud, or in some secret place,
And wild impatience stared in every face.
The flying rumours gather'd as they roll'd,
Scarce any tale was sooner heard than told;
And all who told it added something new,   470
And all who heard it made enlargements too,
In every ear it spread, on every tongue it grew.
Thus flying east and west, and north and south,
News travelled with increase from mouth to mouth.
So from a spark, that kindled first by chance,   475
With gathering force the quickening flames advance;
Till to the clouds their curling heads aspire,
And towers and temples sink in floods of fire.
    When thus ripe lies are to perfection sprung,
Full grown, and fit to grace a mortal tongue,   480
Through thousand vents, impatient, forth they flow,
And rush in millions on the world below.
Fame sits aloft, and points them out their course,
Their date determines, and prescribes their force:
Some to remain, and some to perish soon;   485
Or wane and wax alternate like the moon.
Around, a thousand winged wonders fly,
Borne by the trumpet's blast, and scatter'd through the sky.
    There, at one passage, oft you might survey
A lie and truth contending for the way;   490
And long 'twas doubtful, both so closely pent,
Which first should issue through the narrow vent:
At last agreed, together out they fly,
Inseparable now, the truth and lie;
The strict companions are for ever join'd,   495
And this or that unmix'd, no mortal e'er shall find.
    While thus I stood, intent to see and hear,
One came, methought, and whisper'd in my ear:
"What could thus high thy rash ambition raise?
Art thou, fond youth, a candidate for praise?"   500
    "'Tis true," said I, "not void of hopes I came,
For who so fond as youthful bards of fame?
But few, alas! the casual blessing boast,
So hard to gain, so easy to be lost.
How vain that second life in others' breath,   505
The estate which wits inherit after death!

Ease, health, and life, for this they must resign,
(Unsure the tenure, but how vast the fine!)
The great man's curse, without the gains, endure,
Be envied, wretched, and be flatter'd, poor;   510
All luckless wits their enemies profess'd,
And all successful, jealous friends at best.
Nor fame I slight, nor for her favours call;
She comes unlook'd for, if she comes at all.
But if the purchase cost so dear a price,   515
As soothing folly, or exalting vice:
Oh! if the Muse must flatter lawless sway,
And follow still where fortune leads the way;
Or if no basis bear my rising name,
But the fallen ruins of another's fame;   520
Then teach me, Heaven! to scorn the guilty bays,
Drive from my breast that wretched lust of praise;
Unblemish'd let me live, or die unknown;
Oh, grant an honest fame, or grant me none!"

ODE ON ST. CECILIA'S DAY

MDCCVIII

I

DESCEND, ye Nine! descend and sing;
  The breathing instruments inspire,
Wake into voice each silent string,
  And sweep the sounding lyre!
    In a sadly-pleasing strain   5
    Let the warbling lute complain;
      Let the loud trumpet sound,
      Till the roofs all around
      The shrill echoes rebound:
While in more lengthen'd notes and slow,   10
The deep, majestic, solemn organs blow.
      Hark! the numbers soft and clear
      Gently steal upon the ear;
      Now louder, and yet louder rise,
      And fill with spreading sounds the skies;   15
Exulting in triumph now swell the bold notes,
In broken air, trembling, the wild music floats;

Till, by degrees, remote and small,
    The strains decay,
    And melt away,
In a dying, dying fall.   20

II

By music, minds an equal temper know,
  Nor swell too high, nor sink too low.
If in the breast tumultuous joys arise,
Music her soft, assuasive voice applies;   25
  Or, when the soul is press'd with cares,
  Exalts her in enlivening airs.
Warriors she fires with animated sounds;
Pours balm into the bleeding lover's wounds:
    Melancholy lifts her head,   30
    Morpheus rouses from his bed,
    Sloth unfolds her arms and wakes,
    Listening Envy drops her snakes;
Intestine war no more our passions wage,
And giddy factions hear away their rage.   35

III

But when our country's cause provokes to arms,
How martial music every bosom warms!
So when the first bold vessel dared the seas,
High on the stern the Thracian raised his strain,
    While Argo saw her kindred trees   40
      Descend from Pelion to the main.
    Transported demi-gods stood round,
    And men grew heroes at the sound,
      Inflam'd with glory's charms:
Each chief his sevenfold shield display'd,   45
And half unsheath'd the shining blade,
And seas, and rocks, and skies rebound,
"To arms, to arms, to arms!"

IV

But when through all the infernal bounds,
Which flaming Phlegethon surrounds,   50
    Love, strong as Death, the Poet led [1]
    To the pale nations of the dead,

[1] "For death is not more strong than love."—SANDYS.

What sounds were heard,
What scenes appear'd,
   O'er all the dreary coasts!   55
    Dreadful gleams,
    Dismal screams,
    Fires that glow,
    Shrieks of woe,
    Sullen moans,   60
    Hollow groans,
  And cries of tortured ghosts!
But, hark! he strikes the golden lyre:
And see! the tortured ghosts respire.
      See shady forms advance!   65
   Thy stone, O Sisyphus, stands still,
   Ixion rests upon his wheel,
      And the pale spectres dance!
The Furies sink upon their iron beds,
And snakes uncurl'd hang listening round their heads. 70

V

"By the streams that ever flow,
  By the fragrant winds that blow
   O'er the Elysian flowers;
  By those happy souls who dwell
  In yellow meads of Asphodel,   75
   Or Amaranthine bowers;
  By the hero's armed shades,
  Glittering through the gloomy glades;
  By the youths that died for love,
  Wandering in the myrtle grove,   80
Restore, restore Eurydice to life:
O take the husband, or return the wife!"
   He sung, and hell consented
    To hear the Poet's prayer:
   Stern Proserpine relented,   85
    And gave him back the fair.
    Thus song could prevail
    O'er death, and o'er hell,
A conquest how hard and how glorious:
   Though fate had fast bound her   90
   With Styx nine times round her,
Yet music and love were victorious.

VI

But soon, too soon, the lover turns his eyes:
Again she falls, again she dies, she dies!
How wilt thou now the fatal sisters move?   95
No crime was thine, if 'tis no crime to love.
  Now under hanging mountains,
  Beside the falls of fountains,
  Or where Hebrus wanders,
  Rolling in meanders,   100
    All alone,
    Unheard, unknown,
    He makes his moan;
    And calls her ghost,
For ever, ever, ever lost!   105
Now with Furies surrounded,
Despairing, confounded,
He trembles, he glows,
  Amidst Rhodope's snows:
See, wild as the winds, o'er the desert he flies;   110
Hark! Hæmus resounds with the Bacchanals' cries—
               Ah see, he dies!
Yet ev'n in death Eurydice he sung,
Eurydice still trembled on his tongue,
    Eurydice the woods,
    Eurydice the floods,   115
Eurydice the rocks, and hollow mountains rung.

VII

Music the fiercest grief can charm,
  And fate's severest rage disarm:
  Music can soften pain to ease,
  And make despair and madness please: 120
  Our joys below it can improve,
  And antedate the bliss above.
This the divine Cecilia found,
And to her Maker's praise confined the sound.   125
When the full organ joins the tuneful quire,
  Th' immortal powers incline their ear;
Borne on the swelling notes our souls aspire,
While solemn airs improve the sacred fire;
  And Angels lean from heaven to hear.   130

Of Orpheus now no more let Poets tell,
　　To bright Cecilia greater power is given;
His numbers raised a shade from hell,
　　Hers lift the soul to heaven.

TWO CHORUSES TO THE TRAGEDY OF BRUTUS[1]

CHORUS OF ATHENIANS

STROPHE I

YE shades, where sacred truth is sought;
Groves, where immortal sages taught;
　　Where heavenly visions Plato fired,
　　And Epicurus lay inspired;
　　In vain your guiltless laurels stood　　　　　5
　　Unspotted long with human blood.
War, horrid war, your thoughtful walks invades,
And steel now glitters in the Muses' shades.

ANTISTROPHE I

　　Oh heaven-born sisters! source of art!
　　Who charm the sense or mend the heart;　　10
　　Who lead fair Virtue's train along,
　　Moral truth, and mystic song!
　　To what new clime, what distant sky,
　　Forsaken, friendless, shall ye fly?
Say, will ye bless the bleak Atlantic shore?　　15
Or bid the furious Gaul be rude no more?

STROPHE II

　　When Athens sinks by fates unjust,
　　When wild barbarians spurn her dust;
　　Perhaps even Britain's utmost shore
　　Shall cease to blush with strangers' gore;　　20
　　See arts her savage sons control,
　　And Athens rising near the pole!
Till some new tyrant lifts his purple hand,
And civil madness tears them from the land.

[1] Altered from Shakespeare by the Duke of Buckingham, at whose desire these two choruses were composed.

ANTISTROPHE II

Ye gods! what justice rules the ball?   25
Freedom and arts together fall;
Fools grant whate'er Ambition craves,
And men, once ignorant, are slaves.
Oh cursed effects of civil hate,
In every age, in every state!   30
Still, when the lust of tyrant power succeeds,
Some Athens perishes, some Tully bleeds.

CHORUS OF YOUTHS AND VIRGINS

SEMICHORUS

Oh, tyrant Love! hast thou possess'd
The prudent, learn'd, and virtuous breast?
Wisdom and wit in vain reclaim,
And arts but soften us to feel thy flame.
Love, soft intruder, enters here,   5
But entering learns to be sincere.
Marcus with blushes owns he loves,
And Brutus tenderly reproves.
Why, Virtue, dost thou blame desire,
Which Nature hath impress'd?   10
Why, Nature, dost thou soonest fire
The mild and generous breast?

CHORUS

Love's purer flames the gods approve;
The gods and Brutus bend to love:
Brutus for absent Portia sighs,   15
And sterner Cassius melts at Junia's eyes.
What is loose love? a transient gust,
Spent in a sudden storm of lust,
A vapour fed from wild desire,
A wandering, self-consuming fire.   20
But Hymen's kinder flames unite,
And burn for ever one;
Chaste as cold Cynthia's virgin light,
Productive as the Sun.

SEMICHORUS

Oh source of every social tie,   25
United wish, and mutual joy!
What various joys on one attend,
As son, as father, brother, husband, friend!
Whether his hoary sire he spies,
While thousand grateful thoughts arise;   30
Or meets his spouse's fonder eye;
Or views his smiling progeny;
    What tender passions take their turns,
    What home-felt raptures move!
His heart now melts, now leaps, now burns,   35
    With reverence, hope, and love.

CHORUS

Hence, guilty joys, distastes, surmises,
Hence, false tears, deceits, disguises,
Dangers, doubts, delays, surprises!
    Fires that scorch, yet dare not shine: 40
Purest love's unwasting treasure,
Constant faith, fair hope, long leisure;
Days of ease, and nights of pleasure;
    Sacred Hymen! these are thine.

THE DYING CHRISTIAN TO HIS SOUL [1]

ODE

I

Vital spark of heavenly flame!
Quit, oh quit this mortal frame!
Trembling, hoping, lingering, flying,
Oh the pain, the bliss of dying!
Cease, fond Nature, cease thy strife,   5
And let me languish into life!

[1] Steele in a letter to Pope, 4th December, 1712, requested the poet to "make an Ode as of a cheerful dying spirit, that is to say, the Emperor Adrian's *Animula vagula*, put into two or three stanzas for music." Pope sent the above: " You have it (as Cowley calls it, just warm from the brain. It came to me the first moment I waked this morning; yet you will see it was not so absolutely inspiration, but that I had in my head not only the verses of Adrian, but the fine fragment of Sappho."

II

Hark! they whisper; angels say,
"Sister Spirit, come away!"
What is this absorbs me quite?
Steals my senses, shuts my sight,
Drowns my spirits, draws my breath?   10
Tell me, my Soul, can this be death?

III

The world recedes; it disappears!
Heaven opens on my eyes! my ears
With sounds seraphic ring:
Lend, lend your wings! I mount! I fly!   15
O Grave! where is thy victory?
O Death! where is thy sting?

ELEGY

TO THE MEMORY OF AN UNFORTUNATE LADY

What beckoning ghost along the moonlight shade
Invites my steps, and points to yonder glade?
'Tis she!—but why that bleeding bosom gored,
Why dimly gleams the visionary sword?
Oh, ever beauteous, ever friendly! tell,   5
Is it, in heaven, a crime to love too well?
To bear too tender or too firm a heart,
To act a lover's or a Roman's part?
Is there no bright reversion in the sky
For those who greatly think, or bravely die? ·   10
  Why bade ye else, ye powers! her soul aspire
Above the vulgar flight of low desire?
Ambition first sprung from your blest abodes,
The glorious fault of angels and of gods:
Thence to their images on earth it flows,   15
And in the breast of kings and heroes glows.
Most souls, 'tis true, but peep out once an age,
Dull, sullen prisoners in the body's cage:
Dim lights of life, that burn a length of years,
Useless, unseen, as lamps in sepulchres;   20

Like Eastern kings a lazy state they keep,
And, close confined to their own palace, sleep.
    From these perhaps (ere Nature bade her die)
Fate snatched her early to the pitying sky.
As into air the purer spirits flow,   25
And separate from their kindred dregs below;
So flew the soul to its congenial place,
Nor left one virtue to redeem her race,
    But thou, false guardian of a charge too good,
Thou, mean deserter of thy brother's blood!   30
See on these ruby lips the trembling breath,
These cheeks now fading at the blast of death;
Cold is that breast which warm'd the world before,
And those love-darting eyes must roll no more.
Thus, if eternal justice rules the ball,   35
Thus shall your wives, and thus your children fall:
On all the line a sudden vengeance waits,
And frequent hearses shall besiege your gates;
There passengers shall stand, and pointing say,
(While the long funerals blacken all the way,)   40
"Lo! these were they, whose souls the Furies steel'd,
And cursed with hearts unknowing how to yield."
    Thus unlamented pass the proud away,
The gaze of fools, and pageant of a day!
So perish all, whose breast ne'er learn'd to glow   45
For others' good, or melt at others' woe.
    What can atone (oh ever-injured shade!)
Thy fate unpitied, and thy rites unpaid?
No friend's complaint, no kind domestic tear
Pleased thy pale ghost, or graced thy mournful bier.   50
By foreign hands thy dying eyes were closed,
By foreign hands thy decent limbs composed,
By foreign hands thy humble grave adorn'd,
By strangers honour'd, and by strangers mourn'd!
What, though no friends in sable weeds appear,   55
Grieve for an hour, perhaps then mourn a year,
And bear about the mockery of woe
To midnight dances, and the public show?
What, though no weeping loves thy ashes grace,
Nor polish'd marble emulate thy face?   60
What, though no sacred earth allow thee room,
Nor hallow'd dirge be mutter'd o'er thy tomb?
Yet shall thy grave with rising flowers be dress'd

And the green turf lie lightly on thy breast:
There shall the morn her earliest tears bestow,　　65
There the first roses of the year shall blow;
While angels with their silver wings o'ershade
The ground now sacred by thy reliques made.
　　So peaceful rests, without a stone, a name,
What once had beauty, titles, wealth, and fame.　　70
How loved, how honour'd once, avails thee not,
To whom related, or by whom begot;
A heap of dust alone remains of thee,
'Tis all thou art, and all the proud shall be!
　　Poets themselves must fall, like those they sung,　　75
Deaf the praised ear, and mute the tuneful tongue.
Even he, whose soul now melts in mournful lays,
Shall shortly want the generous tear he pays;
Then from his closing eyes thy form shall part,
And the last pang shall tear thee from his heart,　　80
Life's idle business at one gasp be o'er,
The Muse forgot, and thou beloved no more!

PROLOGUE TO MR. ADDISON'S TRAGEDY OF CATO[1]

To wake the soul by tender strokes of art,
To raise the genius, and to mend the heart,
To make mankind, in conscious virtue bold,
Live o'er each scene, and be what they behold:
For this the tragic Muse first trod the stage,　　5
Commanding tears to stream through every age;
Tyrants no more their savage nature kept,
And foes to virtue wonder'd how they wept.
Our author shuns by vulgar springs to move
The hero's glory, or the virgin's love;　　10
In pitying love, we but our weakness show,
And wild ambition well deserves its woe.
Here tears shall flow from a more generous cause,
Such tears as patriots shed for dying laws:
He bids your breasts with ancient ardour rise,　　15
And calls forth Roman drops from British eyes.
Virtue confess'd in human shape he draws,
What Plato thought, and godlike Cato was:

[1] Brought on the stage in April, 1713.

No common object to your sight displays,
But what with pleasure Heaven itself surveys, 20
A brave man struggling in the storms of fate,
And greatly falling with a falling state.
While Cato gives his little senate laws,
What bosom beats not in his country's cause?
Who sees him act, but envies every deed? 25
Who hears him groan, and does not wish to bleed?
Even when proud Cæsar midst triumphal cars,
The spoils of nations, and the pomp of wars,
Ignobly vain, and impotently great,
Show'd Rome her Cato's figure drawn in state; 30
As her dead father's reverend image pass'd,
The pomp was darken'd, and the day o'ercast;
The triumph ceased, tears gush'd from every eye;
The world's great victor pass'd unheeded by;
Her last good man dejected Rome adored, 35
And honour'd Cæsar's less than Cato's sword.
    Britons, attend: be worth like this approved,
And show, you have the virtue to be moved.
With honest scorn the first famed Cato view'd
Rome learning arts from Greece, whom she subdued. 40
Your scene precariously subsists too long
On French translation, and Italian song.
Dare to have sense yourselves; assert the stage,
Be justly warm'd with your own native rage:
Such plays alore should win a British ear, 45
As Cato's self had not disdain'd to hear.

AN ESSAY ON CRITICISM

I

'Tis hard to say, if greater want of skill
Appear in writing or in judging ill;
But, of the two, less dangerous is the offence
To tire our patience, than mislead our sense.
Some few in that, but numbers err in this, 5
Ten censure wrong for one who writes amiss;
A fool might once himself alone expose,
Now one in verse makes many more in prose.
    'Tis with our judgments as our watches, none
Go just alike, yet each believes his own. 10

In poets as true genius is but rare,
True taste as seldom is the critic's share,
Both must alike from Heaven derive their light,
These born to judge, as well as those to write.
Let such teach others who themselves excel, 15
And censure freely who have written well.
Authors are partial to their wit, 'tis true,
But are not critics to their judgment too?
Yet, if we look more closely, we shall find
Most have the seeds of judgment in their mind: 20
Nature affords at least a glimmering light;
The lines, though touch'd but faintly, are drawn right.
But as the slightest sketch, if justly traced,
Is by ill colouring but the more disgraced,
So by false learning is good sense defaced; 25
Some are bewilder'd in the maze of schools,
And some made coxcombs Nature meant but fools.
In search of wit these lose their common sense,
And then turn critics in their own defence:
Each burns alike, who can, or cannot write, 30
Or with a rival's, or an eunuch's spite.
All fools have still an itching to deride,
And fain would be upon the laughing side.
If Mævius scribble in Apollo's spite,
There are who judge still worse than he can write. 35
Some have at first for wits, then poets pass'd,
Turn'd critics next, and proved plain fools at last.
Some neither can for wits nor critics pass,
As heavy mules are neither horse nor ass.
Those half-learn'd witlings, numerous in our isle, 40
As half-form'd insects on the banks of Nile;
Unfinish'd things, one knows not what to call,
Their generation's so equivocal:
To tell them would a hundred tongues require,
Or one vain wit's, that might a hundred tire. 45
But you who seek to give and merit fame,
And justly bear a critic's noble name,
Be sure yourself and your own reach to know,
How far your genius, taste, and learning go;
Launch not beyond your depth, but be discreet, 50
And mark that point where sense and dulness meet.
Nature to all things fix'd the limits fit,
And wisely curb'd proud man's pretending wit.

As on the land while here the ocean gains,
In other parts it leaves wide sandy plains;   55
Thus in the soul while memory prevails,
The solid power of understanding fails;
Where beams of warm imagination play,
The memory's soft figures melt away.
One science only will one genius fit: 60
So vast is art, so narrow human wit:
Not only bounded to peculiar arts,
But oft in those confined to single parts.
Like kings we lose the conquests gain'd before,
By vain ambition still to make them more: 65
Each might his servile province well command,
Would all but stoop to what they understand.
   First follow Nature, and your judgment frame
By her just standard, which is still the same:
Unerring Nature, still divinely bright,   70
One clear, unchanged, and universal light,
Life, force, and beauty, must to all impart,
At once the source, and end, and test of Art.
Art from that fund each just supply provides;
Works without show, and without pomp presides: 75
In some fair body thus th' informing soul
With spirits feeds, with vigour fills the whole,
Each motion guides, and every nerve sustains;
Itself unseen, but in th' effects remains.
Some, to whom Heaven in wit has been profuse,   80
Want as much more to turn it to its use;
For wit and judgment often are at strife,
Though meant each other's aid, like man and wife.
'Tis more to guide, than spur the Muse's steed;
Restrain his fury, than provoke his speed: 85
The winged courser, like a generous horse,
Shows most true mettle when you check his course.
   Those rules of old discover'd, not devised,
Are Nature still, but Nature methodised:
Nature, like liberty, is but restrain'd   90
By the same laws which first herself ordain'd.
   Hear how learn'd Greece her useful rules indites,
When to repress, and when indulge our flights:
High on Parnassus' top her sons she show'd,
And pointed out those arduous paths they trod;   95
Held from afar, aloft, the immortal prize,

And urged the rest by equal steps to rise.
Just precepts thus from great examples given,
She drew from them what they derive from Heaven.
The generous critic fann'd the poet's fire,   100
And taught the world with reason to admire.
Then criticism the Muse's handmaid proved,
To dress her charms, and make her more beloved:
But following wits from that intention stray'd,
Who could not win the mistress, woo'd the maid;   105
Against the poets their own arms they turn'd,
Sure to hate most the men from whom they learn'd.
So modern 'pothecaries, taught the art
By doctor's bills to play the doctor's part,
Bold in the practice of mistaken rules,   110
Prescribe, apply, and call their masters fools.
Some on the leaves of ancient authors prey,
Nor time nor moths e'er spoil'd so much as they:
Some drily plain, without invention's aid,
Write dull receipts how poems may be made.   115
These leave the sense, their learning to display,
And those explain the meaning quite away.
   You then whose judgment the right course would steer,
Know well each Ancient's proper character:
His fable, subject, scope in every page;   120
Religion, country, genius of his age:
Without all these at once before your eyes,
Cavil you may, but never criticise.
Be Homer's works your study and delight,
Read them by day, and meditate by night;   125
Thence form your judgment, thence your maxims bring,
And trace the Muses upward to their spring.
Still with itself compared, his text peruse;
And let your comment be the Mantuan Muse.
   When first young Maro in his boundless mind   130
A work to outlast immortal Rome design'd,
Perhaps he seem'd above the critic's law,
And but from Nature's fountains scorn'd to draw:
But when to examine every part he came,
Nature and Homer were, he found, the same.   135
Convinced, amazed, he checks the bold design;
And rules as strict his labour'd work confine,
As if the Stagyrite o'erlook'd each line.
Learn hence for ancient rules a just esteem;

To copy Nature is to copy them.   140
   Some beauties yet no precepts can declare,
For there's a happiness as well as care.
Music resembles poetry, in each
Are nameless graces which no methods teach,
And which a master-hand alone can reach.   145
If, where the rules not far enough extend,
(Since rules were made but to promote their end)
Some lucky licence answer to the full
The intent proposed, that licence is a rule.
Thus Pegasus, a nearer way to take,   150
May boldly deviate from the common track.
Great wits sometimes may gloriously offend,
And rise to faults true critics dare not mend;
From vulgar bounds with brave disorder part,
And snatch a grace beyond the reach of art,   155
Which, without passing through the judgment, gains
The heart, and all its end at once attains.
In prospects thus, some objects please our eyes,
Which out of Nature's common order rise,
The shapeless rock, or hanging precipice.   160
But though the ancients thus their rules invade,
(As kings dispense with laws themselves have made)
Moderns, beware! or if you must offend
Against the precept, ne'er transgress its end;
Let it be seldom, and compell'd by need;   165
And have, at least, their precedent to plead.
The critic else proceeds without remorse,
Seizes your fame, and puts his laws in force.
   I know there are, to whose presumptuous thoughts
Those freer beauties, even in them, seem faults.   170
Some figures monstrous and misshaped appear,
Consider'd singly, or beheld too near,
Which, but proportion'd to their light, or place,
Due distance reconciles to form and grace.
A prudent chief not always must display   175
His powers, in equal ranks, and fair array,
But with the occasion and the place comply,
Conceal his force, nay seem sometimes to fly.
Those oft are stratagems which errors seem,
Nor is it Homer nods, but we that dream.   180
   Still green with bays each ancient altar stands,
Above the reach of sacrilegious hands;

Secure from flames, from envy's fiercer rage,
Destructive war, and all-involving age.
See from each clime the learn'd their incense bring! 185
Hear in all tongues consenting pæans ring!
In praise so just let every voice be join'd,
And fill the general chorus of mankind.
Hail, bards triumphant! born in happier days;
Immortal heirs of universal praise! 190
Whose honours with increase of ages grow,
As streams roll down, enlarging as they flow;
Nations unborn your mighty names shall sound,
And worlds applaud that must not yet be found!
O may some spark of your celestial fire, 195
The last, the meanest of your sons inspire,
(That on weak wings, from far, pursues your flights;
Glows while he reads, but trembles as he writes)
To teach vain wits a science little known,
To admire superior sense, and doubt their own! 200

II

Of all the causes which conspire to blind
Man's erring judgment, and misguide the mind,
What the weak head with strongest bias rules,
Is PRIDE, the never-failing vice of fools.
Whatever Nature has in worth denied, 205
She gives in large recruits of needless pride;
For as in bodies, thus in souls we find
What wants in blood and spirits, swell'd with wind:
Pride, where wit fails, steps in to our defence,
And fills up all the mighty void of sense. 210
If once right reason drives that cloud away,
Truth breaks upon us with resistless day.
Trust not yourself; but your defects to know,
Make use of every friend—and every foe.
A little learning is a dangerous thing; 215
Drink deep, or taste not the Pierian spring:
There shallow draughts intoxicate the brain,
And drinking largely sobers us again.
Fired at first sight with what the Muse imparts,
In fearless youth we tempt the height of arts, 220
While from the bounded level of our mind,
Short views we take, nor see the lengths behind;

But more advanced, behold with strange surprise
New distant scenes of endless science rise!
So pleased at first the towering Alps we try,   225
Mount o'er the vales, and seem to tread the sky,
The eternal snows appear already passed,
And the first clouds and mountains seem the last:
But, those attain'd, we tremble to survey
The growing labours of the lengthen'd way,   230
The increasing prospect tires our wandering eyes,
Hills peep o'er hills, and Alps on Alps arise!
    A perfect judge will read each work of wit
With the same spirit that its author writ:
Survey the WHOLE, nor seek slight faults to find   235
Where Nature moves, and rapture warms the mind,
Nor lose, for that malignant dull delight,
The generous pleasure to be charm'd with wit.
But in such lays as neither ebb nor flow,
Correctly cold, and regularly low,   240
That shunning faults, one quiet tenor keep;
We cannot blame indeed—but we may sleep.
In wit, as Nature, what affects our hearts
Is not th' exactness of peculiar parts;
'Tis not a lip, or eye, we beauty call,   245
But the joint force and full result of all.
Thus when we view some well-proportion'd dome,
(The world's just wonder, and ev'n thine, O Rome!)
No single parts unequally surprise,
All comes united to th' admiring eyes;   250
No monstrous height, or breadth or length appear;
The whole at once is bold and regular.
    Whoever thinks a faultless piece to see,
Thinks what ne'er was, nor is, nor e'er shall be,
In every work regard the writer's end,   255
Since none can compass more than they intend;
And if the means be just, the conduct true,
Applause, in spite of trivial faults, is due.
As men of breeding, sometimes men of wit,
To avoid great errors, must the less commit: 260
Neglect the rules each verbal critic lays,
For not to know some trifles, is a praise.
Most critics, fond of some subservient art,
Still make the whole depend upon a part:
They talk of principles, but notions prize,   265

And all to one loved folly sacrifice.
Once on a time, La Mancha's knight, they say
A certain bard encountering on the way,
Discoursed in terms as just, with looks as sage,
As e'er could Dennis, of the Grecian stage;   270
Concluding all were desperate sots and fools,
Who durst depart from Aristotle's rules.
Our author, happy in a judge so nice,
Produced his play, and begg'd the knight's advice;
Made him observe the subject and the plot,   275
The manners, passions, unities; what not?
All which, exact to rule, were brought about,
Were but a combat in the lists left out.
"What! leave the combat out?" exclaims the knight;
Yes, or we must renounce the Stagyrite.   280
"Not so, by heaven, (he answers in a rage)
"Knights, squires, and steeds, must enter on the stage."
So vast a throng the stage can ne'er contain.
"Then build a new, or act it in a plain."
Thus critics of less judgment than caprice,   285
Curious, not knowing, not exact but nice,
Form short ideas; and offend in arts
(As most in manners) by a love to parts.
Some to Conceit alone their taste confine,
And glittering thoughts struck out at every line;   290
Pleased with a work where nothing's just or fit;
One glaring chaos and wild heap of wit.
Poets, like painters, thus, unskill'd to trace
The naked Nature and the living grace,
With gold and jewels cover every part,   295
And hide with ornaments their want of art.
True wit is Nature to advantage dress'd;
What oft was thought, but ne'er so well express'd;
Something, whose truth convinced at sight we find,
That gives us back the image of our mind.   300
As shades more sweetly recommend the light,
So modest plainness sets off sprightly wit.
For works may have more wit than does 'em good,
As bodies perish through excess of blood.
Others for Language all their care express,   305
And value books, as women men, for dress:
Their praise is still,—The style is excellent;
The sense, they humbly take upon content.

Words are like leaves; and where they most abound,
Much fruit of sense beneath is rarely found.   310
False eloquence, like the prismatic glass,
Its gaudy colours spreads on every place;
The face of Nature we no more survey,
All glares alike, without distinction gay:
But true expression, like th' unchanging sun,   315
Clears and improves whate'er it shines upon,
It gilds all objects, but it alters none.
Expression is the dress of thought, and still
Appears more decent, as more suitable;
A vile conceit in pompous words express'd   320
Is like a clown in regal purple dress'd:
For different styles with different subjects sort,
As several garbs, with country, town, and court.
Some by old words to fame have made pretence,
Ancients in phrase, mere moderns in their sense;   325
Such labour'd nothings, in so strange a style,
Amaze the unlearn'd, and make the learned smile.
Unlucky as Fungoso in the play,
These sparks with awkward vanity display
What the fine gentleman wore yesterday;   330
And but so mimic ancient wits at best,
As apes our grandsires, in their doublets dress'd.
In words, as fashions, the same rule will hold;
Alike fantastic, if too new, or old:
Be not the first by whom the new are tried,   335
Nor yet the last to lay the old aside.
   But most by numbers judge a poet's song:
And smooth or rough, with them, is right or wrong:
In the bright muse, though thousand charms conspire,
Her voice is all these tuneful fools admire;   340
Who haunt Parnassus but to please their ear,
Not mend their minds; as some to church repair,
Not for the doctrine, but the music there.
These equal syllables alone require,
Though oft the ear the open vowels tire;   345
While expletives their feeble aid do join;
And ten low words oft creep in one dull line:
While they ring round the same unvaried chimes,
With sure returns of still expected rhymes;
Where'er you find " the cooling western breeze,"   350
In the next line, it "whispers through the trees":

If crystal streams "with pleasing murmurs creep":
The reader's threaten'd (not in vain) with "sleep."
Then, at the last and only couplet fraught
With some unmeaning thing they call a thought,   355
A needless Alexandrine ends the song,
That, like a wounded snake, drags its slow length along.
Leave such to tune their own dull rhymes, and know
What's roundly smooth, or languishingly slow;
And praise the easy vigour of a line,   360
Where Denham's strength, and Waller's sweetness join.
True ease in writing comes from art, not chance,
As those move easiest who have learn'd to dance.
'Tis not enough no harshness gives offence,
The sound must seem an echo to the sense: 365
Soft is the strain when Zephyr gently blows,
And the smooth stream in smoother numbers flows;
But when loud billows lash the sounding shore,
The hoarse, rough verse should like the torrent roar.
When Ajax strives some rock's vast weight to throw,   370
The line too labours, and the words move slow:
Not so, when swift Camilla scours the plain,
Flies o'er the unbending corn, and skims along the main.
Hear how Timotheus' varied lays surprise,
And bid alternate passions fall and rise!   375
While, at each change, the son of Libyan Jove
Now burns with glory, and then melts with love;
Now his fierce eyes with sparkling fury glow,
Now sighs steal out, and tears begin to flow:
Persians and Greeks like turns of Nature found,   380
And the world's victor stood subdued by sound!
The power of music all our hearts allow,
And what Timotheus was, is DRYDEN now.
    Avoid extremes; and shun the fault of such,
Who still are pleased too little or too much.   385
At every trifle scorn to take offence,
That always shows great pride, or little sense;
Those heads, as stomachs, are not sure the best,
Which nauseate all, and nothing can digest.
Yet let not each gay turn thy rapture move;   390
For fools admire, but men of sense approve:
As things seem large which we through mists descry,
Dulness is ever apt to magnify.
    Some foreign writers, some our own despise;

The ancients only, or the moderns prize. 395
Thus wit, like faith, by each man is applied
To one small sect, and all are damn'd beside.
Meanly they seek the blessing to confine,
And force that sun but on a part to shine,
Which not alone the southern wit sublimes, 400
But ripens spirits in cold northern climes;
Which from the first has shone on ages past,
Enlights the present, and shall warm the last;
Though each may feel increases and decays,
And see now clearer and now darker days. 405
Regard not then if wit be old or new,
But blame the false, and value still the true.

Some ne'er advance a judgment of their own,
But catch the spreading notion of the town;
They reason and conclude by precedent, 410
And own stale nonsense which they ne'er invent.
Some judge of authors' names, not works, and then
Nor praise nor blame the writings, but the men.
Of all this servile herd, the worst is he
That in proud dulness joins with quality, 415
A constant critic at the great man's board,
To fetch and carry nonsense for my lord.
What woful stuff this madrigal would be,
In some starved hackney sonnetteer, or me?
But let a lord once own the happy lines, 420
How the wit brightens! how the style refines!
Before his sacred name flies every fault,
And each exalted stanza teems with thought!

The vulgar thus through imitation err;
As oft the learn'd by being singular; 425
So much they scorn the crowd, that if the throng
By chance go right, they purposely go wrong:
So schismatics the plain believers quit,
And are but damn'd for having too much wit.
Some praise at morning what they blame at night; 430
But always think the last opinion right.
A Muse by these is like a mistress used,
This hour she's idolized, the next abused;
While their weak heads, like towns unfortified,
'Twixt sense and nonsense daily change their side. 435
Ask them the cause; they're wiser still, they say;
And still to-morrow's wiser than to-day.

We think our fathers fools, so wise we grow;
Our wiser sons, no doubt, will think us so.
Once school-divines this zealous isle o'erspread;   440
Who knew most sentences, was deepest read:
Faith, Gospel, all seem'd made to be disputed,
And none had sense enough to be confuted:
Scotists and Thomists, now in peace remain,[1]
Amidst their kindred cobwebs in Duck-lane.[2]   445
If Faith itself has different dresses worn,
What wonder modes in wit should take their turn?
Oft leaving what is natural and fit,
The current folly proves the ready wit;
And authors think their reputation safe,   450
Which lives as long as fools are pleased to laugh.
    Some valuing those of their own side or mind,
Still make themselves the measure of mankind:
Fondly we think we honour merit then,
When we but praise ourselves in other men.   455
Parties in wit attend on those of state,
And public faction doubles private hate.
Pride, malice, folly, against Dryden rose,
In various shapes of parsons, critics, beaus;
But sense survived when merry jests were past;   460
For rising merit will buoy up at last.
Might he return, and bless once more our eyes,
New Blackmores and new Milbourns must arise:
Nay, should great Homer lift his awful head,
Zoilus again would start up from the dead.   465
Envy will merit, as its shade, pursue;
But like a shadow, proves the substance true:
For envied wit, like Sol eclipsed, makes known
The opposing body's grossness, not its own.
When first that sun too powerful beams displays,   470
It draws up vapours which obscure its rays;
But even those clouds at last adorn its way,
Reflect new glories, and augment the day.
    Be thou the first true merit to befriend;
His praise is lost, who stays till all commend.   475
Short is the date, alas! of modern rhymes,
And 'tis but just to let them live betimes.

[1] John Duns Scotus, the " subtle doctor," who opposed Aquinas on the subject of grace; hence the Scotists as opposed to the Thomists.
[2] A place where old and secondhand books were sold formerly, near Smithfield.

No longer now that golden age appears,
When patriarch-wits survived a thousand years:
Now length of fame (our second life) is lost,   480
And bare threescore is all even that can boast;
Our sons their fathers' failing language see,
And such as Chaucer is, shall Dryden be.
So when the faithful pencil has design'd
Some bright idea of the master's mind,   485
Where a new world leaps out at his command,
And ready Nature waits upon his hand;
When the ripe colours soften and unite,
And sweetly melt into just shade and light;
When mellow years their full perfection give,   490
And each bold figure just begins to live,
The treacherous colours the fair art betray,
And all the bright creation fades away!

    Unhappy wit, like most mistaken things,
Atones not for that envy which it brings.   495
In youth alone its empty praise we boast,
But soon the short-lived vanity is lost:
Like some fair flower the early spring supplies,
That gaily blooms, but even in blooming dies.
What is this wit, which must our cares employ?   500
The owner's wife, that other men enjoy;
Then most our trouble still when most admired,
And still the more we give, the more required;
Whose fame with pains we guard, but lose with ease,
Sure some to vex, but never all to please;   505
'Tis what the vicious fear, the virtuous shun,
By fools 'tis hated, and by knaves undone!

    If wit so much from ignorance undergo,
Ah, let not learning too commence its foe!
Of old, those met rewards who could excel,   510
And such were praised who but endeavour'd well:
Though triumphs were to generals only due,
Crowns were reserved to grace the soldiers too.
Now, they who reach Parnassus' lofty crown,
Employ their pains to spurn some others down;   515
And while self-love each jealous writer rules,
Contending wits become the sport of fools:
But still the worst with most regret commend,
For each ill author is as bad a friend.
To what base ends, and by what abject ways,   520

Are mortals urged through sacred lust of praise!
Ah ne'er so dire a thirst of glory boast,
Nor in the critic let the man be lost.
Good nature and good sense must ever join;
To err is human, to forgive, divine.   525
  But if in noble minds some dregs remain,
Not yet purged off, of spleen and sour disdain;
Discharge that rage on more provoking crimes,
Nor fear a dearth in these flagitious times.
No pardon vile obscenity should find,
Though wit and art conspire to move your mind;   530
But dulness with obscenity must prove
As shameful sure as impotence in love.
In the fat age of pleasure, wealth, and ease,
Sprung the rank weed, and thrived with large increase: 535
When love was all an easy monarch's care;
Seldom at council, never in a war:
Jilts ruled the state, and statesmen farces writ;
Nay wits had pensions, and young lords had wit:
The fair sat panting at a courtier's play,   540
And not a mask went unimproved away:
The modest fan was lifted up no more,
And virgins smiled at what they blush'd before.
The following licence of a foreign reign
Did all the dregs of bold Socinus drain;
Then unbelieving priests reform'd the nation,   545
And taught more pleasant methods of salvation;
Where Heaven's free subjects might their rights dispute,
Lest God Himself should seem too absolute:
Pulpits their sacred satire learn'd to spare,
And vice admired to find a flatterer there!   550
Encouraged thus, Wit's Titans braved the skies,
And the press groan'd with licensed blasphemies.
These monsters, critics! with your darts engage,
Here point your thunder, and exhaust your rage!
Yet shun their fault, who, scandalously nice,   555
Will needs mistake an author into vice;
All seems infected that th' infected spy,
As all looks yellow to the jaundiced eye.

III

  Learn then what morals critics ought to show,
For 'tis but half a judge's task, to know.   560

'Tis not enough, taste, judgment, learning, join;
In all you speak, let truth and candour shine:
That not alone what to your sense is due
All may allow; but seek your friendship too.   565

  Be silent always, when you doubt your sense;
And speak, though sure, with seeming diffidence:
Some positive, persisting fops we know,
Who, if once wrong, will needs be always so;
But you, with pleasure own your errors past,   570
And make each day a critique on the last.

  'Tis not enough your counsel still be true;
Blunt truths more mischief than nice falsehoods do;
Men must be taught as if you taught them not,
And things unknown proposed as things forgot.   575
Without good-breeding, truth is disapproved;
That only makes superior sense beloved.

  Be niggards of advice on no pretence;
For the worst avarice is that of sense.
With mean complaisance ne'er betray your trust,   580
Nor be so civil as to prove unjust.
Fear not the anger of the wise to raise;
Those best can bear reproof who merit praise.

  'Twere well might critics still this freedom take,
But Appius reddens at each word you speak,   585
And stares, tremendous, with a threatening eye,
Like some fierce tyrant in old tapestry.[1]
Fear most to tax an Honourable fool,
Whose right it is, uncensured, to be dull;
Such, without wit, are poets when they please,   590
As without learning they can take degrees.
Leave dangerous truths to unsuccessful satires,
And flattery to fulsome dedicators,
Whom, when they praise, the world believes no more,
Than when they promise to give scribbling o'er.   595
'Tis best sometimes your censure to restrain,
And charitably let the dull be vain:
Your silence there is better than your spite,
For who can rail so long as they can write?
Still humming on, their drowsy course they keep,   600
And lash'd so long, like tops, are lash'd asleep.

[1] A reference to Dennis, the critic, whose *Appius and Virginia* was acted
in 1709.   He promptly retorted with *Reflections Historical and Critical upon
a Late Rhapsody call'd, An Essay upon Criticism*, where coarse personalities
were mixed with fair and acute criticism.

False steps but help them to renew the race,
As, after stumbling, jades will mend their pace.
What crowds of these, impenitently bold,
In sounds and jingling syllables grown old,   605
Still run on poets in a raging vein,
Even to the dregs and squeezings of the brain,
Strain out the last dull dropping of their sense,
And rhyme with all the rage of impotence!

    Such shameless bards we have; and yet 'tis true   610
There are as mad, abandon'd critics too.
The bookful blockhead, ignorantly read,
With loads of learned lumber in his head,
With his own tongue still edifies his ears,
And always listening to himself appears.   615
All books he reads, and all he reads assails,
From Dryden's Fables down to D'Urfey's Tales:
With him, most authors steal their works, or buy;
Garth did not write his own Dispensary.
Name a new play, and he's the poet's friend,   620
Nay show'd his faults—but when would poets mend?
No place so sacred from such fops is barr'd,
Nor is Paul's church more safe than Paul's church-yard:
Nay, fly to altars; there they'll talk you dead;
For fools rush in where angels fear to tread,   625
Distrustful sense with modest caution speaks,
It still looks home, and short excursions makes;
But rattling nonsense in full volleys breaks,
And never shock'd, and never turn'd aside,
Bursts out, resistless, with a thundering tide.   630

    But where's the man who counsel can bestow,
Still pleased to teach, and yet not proud to know?
Unbiass'd, or by favour, or by spite;
Not dully prepossess'd, nor blindly right;
Though learn'd, well-bred; and though well-bred, sincere;   635
Modestly bold, and humanly severe:
Who to a friend his faults can freely show,
And gladly praise the merit of a foe?
Bless'd with a taste exact, yet unconfined;
A knowledge both of books and human kind;   640
Generous converse; a soul exempt from pride;
And love to praise, with reason on his side?

    Such once were critics; such the happy few,
Athens and Rome in better ages knew.

The mighty Stagyrite first left the shore,   645
Spread all his sails, and durst the deeps explore;
He steer'd securely, and discover'd far,
Led by the light of the Mæonian star.
Poets, a race long unconfined, and free,
Still fond and proud of savage liberty,   650
Received his laws; and stood convinced 'twas fit,
Who conquer'd Nature, should preside o'er Wit.
   Horace still charms with graceful negligence,
And without method talks us into sense,
Will, like a friend, familiarly convey   655
The truest notions in the easiest way.
He, who supreme in judgment, as in wit,
Might boldly censure, as he boldly writ,
Yet judged with coolness, though he sung with fire;
His precepts teach but what his works inspire.   660
Our critics take a contrary extreme,
They judge with fury, but they write with phlegm:
Nor suffers Horace more in wrong translations
By wits, than critics in as wrong quotations.
   See Dionysius Homer's thoughts refine,   665
And call new beauties forth from every line!
   Fancy and art in gay Petronius please,
The scholar's learning with the courtier's ease.
   In grave Quintilian's copious work, we find
The justest rules and clearest method join'd: 670
Thus useful arms in magazines we place,
All ranged in order, and disposed with grace,
But less to please the eye, than arm the hand,
Still fit for use, and ready at command.
   Thee, bold Longinus! all the Nine inspire,   675
And bless their critic with a poet's fire.
An ardent judge, who, zealous in his trust,
With warmth gives sentence, yet is always just:
Whose own example strengthens all his laws:
And is himself that great sublime he draws.   680
   Thus long succeeding critics justly reign'd,
Licence repress'd, and useful laws ordain'd.
Learning and Rome alike in empire grew;
And arts still follow'd where her eagles flew;
From the same foes, at last, both felt their doom,   685
And the same age saw Learning fall, and Rome.
With Tyranny, then Superstition join'd,

As that the body, this enslaved the mind;
Much was believed, but little understood,
And to be dull was construed to be good;   690
A second deluge learning thus o'errun,
And the monks finish'd what the Goths begun.

At length Erasmus, that great injured name,
(The glory of the priesthood, and the shame!)
Stemm'd the wild torrent of a barbarous age,   695
And drove those holy Vandals off the stage.

But see! each Muse, in Leo's golden days,
Starts from her trance, and trims her wither'd bays;
Rome's ancient Genius, o'er its ruins spread,
Shakes off the dust, and rears his reverend head. 700
Then Sculpture and her sister-arts revive;
Stones leaped to form, and rocks began to live;
With sweeter notes each rising temple rung;
A Raphael painted, and a Vida sung.
Immortal Vida: on whose honour'd brow   705
The poet's bays and critic's ivy grow:
Cremona now shall ever boast thy name,
As next in place to Mantua, next in fame!

But soon by impious arms from Latium chased,
Their ancient bounds the banish'd Muses pass'd;   710
Thence Arts o'er all the northern world advance,
But critic-learning flourish'd most in France;
The rules a nation, born to serve, obeys;
And Boileau still in right of Horace sways.

But we, brave Britons, foreign laws despised,   715
And kept unconquer'd, and uncivilised;
Fierce for the liberties of wit and bold,
We still defied the Romans, as of old.
Yet some there were, among the sounder few
Of those who less presumed, and better knew,   720
Who durst assert the juster ancient cause,
And here restored Wit's fundamental laws.
Such was the Muse, whose rules and practice tell,[1]
"Nature's chief Masterpiece is writing well,"
Such was Roscommon, not more learn'd than good, 725
With manners generous as his noble blood;
To him the wit of Greece and Rome was known,
And every author's merit, but his own.
Such late was Walsh—the Muse's judge and friend,

[1] The *Essay on Poetry*, by the Earl of Mulgrave, later Duke of Buckingham.

Who justly knew to blame or to commend: 730
To failings mild, but zealous for desert;
The clearest head, and the sincerest heart.
This humble praise, lamented shade! receive,
This praise at least a grateful Muse may give:
The Muse, whose early voice you taught to sing,   735
Prescribed her heights, and pruned her tender wing,
(Her guide now lost) no more attempts to rise,
But in low numbers short excursions tries:
Content, if hence the unlearn'd their wants may view,
The learn'd reflect on what before they knew;   740
Careless of censure, nor too fond of fame;
Still pleased to praise, yet not afraid to blame;
Averse alike to flatter, or offend;
Not free from faults, nor yet too vain to mend.

THE RAPE OF THE LOCK

DEDICATION TO MRS. ARABELLA FERMOR

MADAM,—It will be in vain to deny that I have some regard for this piece, since I dedicate it to you. Yet you may bear me witness, it was intended only to divert a few young ladies, who have good sense and good humour enough to laugh not only at their sex's little unguarded follies, but at their own. But as it was communicated with the air of a secret, it soon found its way into the world. An imperfect copy having been offered to a bookseller, you had the good-nature for my sake to consent to the publication of one more correct: this I was forced to before I had executed half my design, for the machinery was entirely wanting to complete it.

The machinery, Madam, is a term invented by the critics to signify that part which the Deities, Angels, or Dæmons are made to act in a Poem: for the ancient Poets are in one respect like many modern ladies: let an action be never so trivial in itself, they always make it appear of the utmost importance. These machines I determined to raise on a very new and odd foundation, the Rosicrucian doctrine of Spirits.

I know how disagreeable it is to make use of hard words before a lady; but 'tis so much the concern of a Poet to have his works understood, and particularly by your sex, that you must give me leave to explain two or three difficult terms.

The Rosicrucians are a people I must bring you acquainted with. The best account I know of them is in a French book called *Le Comte de Gabalis*, which, both in its title and size, is so like a novel that many of the fair sex have read it for one by mistake. According to these gentlemen, the four elements are inhabited by Spirits which they call Sylphs, Gnomes, Nymphs and Salamanders. The Gnomes, or Dæmons of Earth, delight in mischief; but the Sylphs, whose habitation is in the air, are the best-conditioned creatures imaginable. For they say any mortals may enjoy the most intimate familiarities with these gentle Spirits, upon a condition very easy to all true adepts, an inviolate preservation of chastity.

As to the following Cantos, all the passages of them are as fabulous as the vision at the beginning, or the transformation at the end (except the loss of your hair, which I always mention with reverence). The human persons are as fictitious as the airy ones; and the character of Belinda, as it is now managed, resembles you in nothing but in beauty.

If this Poem had as many graces as there are in your person, or in your mind, yet I could never hope it should pass through the world half so uncensured as you have done. But let its fortune be what it will, mine is happy enough, to have given me this occasion of assuring you that I am, with the truest esteem, Madam, your most obedient, humble Servant,

A. POPE.

Nolueram, Belinda, tuos violare capillos;
Sed juvat, hoc precibus me tribuisse tuis.—Mart.

CANTO I

What dire offence from amorous causes springs,
What mighty contests rise from trivial things,
I sing—This verse to Caryll, Muse! is due:
This, even Belinda may vouchsafe to view;
Slight is the subject, but not so the praise,   5
If she inspire, and he approve my lays.
    Say what strange motive, goddess! could compel
A well-bred lord to assault a gentle belle?
O say what stranger cause, yet unexplored,
Could make a gentle belle reject a lord?   10
In tasks so bold, can little men engage,
And in soft bosoms dwells such mighty rage?
    Sol through white curtains shot a tim'rous ray,
And oped those eyes that must eclipse the day:
Now lap-dogs give themselves the rousing shake,   15
And sleepless lovers, just at twelve awake:
Thrice rung the bell, the slipper knock'd the ground,
And the press'd watch return'd a silver sound.
Belinda still her downy pillow press'd,
Her guardian sylph prolong'd the balmy rest: 20
'Twas he had summon'd to her silent bed

The morning-dream that hover'd o'er her head?
A youth more glittering than a birth-night beau,
(That ev'n in slumber caused her cheek to glow)
Seem'd to her ear his winning lips to lay,   25
And thus in whispers said, or seem'd to say:
  "Fairest of mortals, thou distinguish'd care
Of thousand bright inhabitants of air!
If e'er one vision touch'd thy infant thought,
Of all the nurse and all the priest have taught;   30
Of airy elves by moonlight shadows seen,
The silver token, and the circled green,
Or virgins visited by angel powers,
With golden crowns and wreaths of heavenly flowers;
Hear and believe! thy own importance know,   35
Nor bound thy narrow views to things below.
Some secret truths, from learned pride conceal'd,
To maids alone and children are reveal'd:
What though no credit doubting wits may give?
The fair and innocent shall still believe.   40
Know, then, unnumbered spirits round thee fly,
The light militia of the lower sky:
These, though unseen, are ever on the wing,
Hang o'er the box, and hover round the ring.
Think what an equipage thou hast in air,   45
And view with scorn two pages and a chair.
As now your own, our beings were of old,
And once inclosed in woman's beauteous mould;
Thence, by a soft transition, we repair
From earthly vehicles to these of air.   50
Think not, when woman's transient breath is fled,
That all her vanities at once are dead;
Succeeding vanities she still regards,
And though she plays no more, o'erlooks the cards.
Her joy in gilden chariots, when alive,   55
And love of ombre, after death survive.
For when the fair in all their pride expire,
To their first elements their souls retire:
The sprites of fiery termagants in flame
Mount up, and take a Salamander's name.   60
Soft yielding minds to water glide away,
And sip, with nymphs, their elemental tea.
The graver prude sinks downward to a gnome,
In search of mischief still on earth to roam.

The light coquettes in sylphs aloft repair, 65
And sport and flutter in the fields of air.
  "Know further yet; whoever fair and chaste
Rejects mankind, is by some sylph embraced:
For spirits, freed from mortal laws, with ease
Assume what sexes and what shapes they please. 70
What guards the purity of melting maids,
In courtly balls, and midnight masquerades,
Safe from the treach'rous friend, the daring spark,
The glance by day, the whisper in the dark,
When kind occasion prompts their warm desires, 75
When music softens, and when dancing fires?
'Tis but their sylph, the wise celestials know,
Though honour is the word with men below.
  "Some nymphs there are, too conscious of their face,
For life predestined to the gnomes' embrace. 80
These swell their prospects and exalt their pride,
When offers are disdain'd and love denied:
Then gay ideas crowd the vacant brain,
While peers, and dukes, and all their sweeping train,
And garters, stars, and coronets appear, 85
And in soft sounds, 'Your Grace' salutes their ear.
'Tis these that early taint the female soul,
Instruct the eyes of young coquettes to roll,
Teach infant cheeks a bidden blush to know,
And little hearts to flutter at a beau. 90
  "Oft when the world imagine women stray,
The sylphs through mystic mazes guide their way,
Through all the giddy circle they pursue,
And old impertinence expel by new.
What tender maid but must a victim fall 95
To one man's treat, but for another's ball?
When Florio speaks, what virgin could withstand,
If gentle Damon did not squeeze her hand?
With varying vanities, from ev'ry part,
They shift the moving toy-shop of their heart; 100
Where wigs with wigs, with sword-knots sword-knots strive,
Beaux banish beaux, and coaches coaches drive.
This erring mortals levity may call,
Oh, blind to truth! the sylphs contrive it all.
  "Of these am I, who thy protection claim, 105
A watchful sprite, and Ariel is my name.
Late, as I ranged the crystal wilds of air,

In the clear mirror of thy ruling star
I saw, alas! some dread event impend,
Ere to the main this morning sun descend;   110
But heaven reveals not what, or how, or where:
Warn'd by the sylph, oh, pious maid, beware!
This to disclose is all thy guardian can:
Beware of all, but most beware of man!"
    He said; when Shock, who thought she slept too long, 115
Leap'd up, and waked his mistress with his tongue.
'Twas then, Belinda, if report say true,
Thy eyes first open'd on a billet-doux;
Wounds, charms, and ardours, were no sooner read,
But all the vision vanish'd from thy head.   120
    And now, unveil'd, the toilet stands display'd,
Each silver vase in mystic order laid.
First, robed in white, the nymph intent adores,
With head uncover'd, the cosmetic powers.
A heav'nly image in the glass appears,   125
To that she bends, to that her eye she rears;
Th' inferior priestess. at her altar's side,
Trembling, begins the sacred rites of pride.
Unnumber'd treasures ope at once, and here
The various offerings of the world appear;   130
From each she nicely culls with curious toil,
And decks the goddess with the glitt'ring spoil.
This casket India's glowing gems unlocks,
And all Arabia breathes from yonder box.
The tortoise here and elephant unite,   135
Transform'd to combs, the speckled and the white.
Here files of pins extend their shining rows,
Puffs, powders, patches, Bibles, billet-doux.
Now awful beauty puts on all its arms;
The fair each moment rises in her charms,   140
Repairs her smiles, awakens every grace,
And calls forth all the wonders of her face:
Sees by degrees a purer blush arise,
And keener lightnings quicken in her eyes.
The busy sylphs surround their darling care,   145
These set the head, and those divide the hair,
Some fold the sleeve, while others plait the gown;
And Betty's praised for labours not her own.

CANTO II

Not with more glories, in th' ethereal plain,
The sun first rises o'er the purpled main,
Than, issuing forth, the rival of his beams
Launch'd on the bosom of the silver Thames.
Fair nymphs and well-dress'd youths around her shone, 5
But every eye was fix'd on her alone.
On her white breast a sparkling cross she wore,
Which Jews might kiss, and infidels adore.
Her lively looks a sprightly mind disclose,
Quick as her eyes, and as unfix'd as those: 10
Favours to none, to all she smiles extends;
Oft she rejects, but never once offends.
Bright as the sun, her eyes the gazers strike,
And, like the sun, they shine on all alike.
Yet graceful ease, and sweetness void of pride, 15
Might hide her faults, if belles had faults to hide:
If to her share some female errors fall,
Look on her face, and you'll forget them all.
   This nymph, to the destruction of mankind,
Nourish'd two locks, which graceful hung behind 20
In equal curls, and well conspired to deck
With shining ringlets the smooth ivory neck.
Love in these labyrinths his slaves detains,
And mighty hearts are held in slender chains.
With hairy springes we the birds betray,. 25
Slight lines of hair surprise the finny prey,
Fair tresses man's imperial race insnare,
And beauty draws us with a single hair.
   Th' adventurous baron the bright locks admired;
He saw, he wish'd, and to the prize aspired. 30
Resolved to win, he meditates the way,
By force to ravish, or by fraud betray;
For when success a lover's toils attends,
Few ask, if fraud or force attain'd his ends.
   For this, ere Phœbus rose, he had implored 35
Propitious Heaven, and every power adored:
But chiefly Love—to Love an altar built,
Of twelve vast French romances, neatly gilt.
There lay three garters, half a pair of gloves;
And all the trophies of his former loves: 40
With tender billet-doux he lights the pyre,

And breathes three amorous sighs to raise the fire.
Then prostrate falls, and begs with ardent eyes
Soon to obtain, and long possess the prize:
The powers gave ear, and granted half his prayer,　45
The rest, the winds dispersed in empty air.
　But now secure the painted vessel glides,
The sun-beams trembling on the floating tides;
While melting music steals upon the sky,
And soften'd sounds along the waters die;　50
Smooth flow the waves, the zephyrs gently play,
Belinda smiled, and all the world was gay.
All but the sylph—with careful thoughts oppress'd,
Th' impending woe sat heavy on his breast.
He summons straight his denizens of air;　55
The lucid squadrons round the sails repair:
Soft o'er the shrouds aërial whispers breathe,
That seem'd but zephyrs to the train beneath.
Some to the sun their insect-wings unfold,
Waft on the breeze, or sink in clouds of gold;　60
Transparent forms, too fine for mortal sight,
Their fluid bodies half dissolved in light.
Loose to the wind their airy garments flew,
Thin glittering textures of the filmy dew,
Dipp'd in the richest tincture of the skies,　65
Where light disports in ever-mingling dyes;
While ev'ry beam new transient colours flings,
Colours that change whene'er they wave their wings.
Amid the circle on the gilded mast,
Superior by the head, was Ariel placed;　70
His purple pinions op'ning to the sun,
He raised his azure wand, and thus begun:
　"Ye sylphs and sylphids, to your chief give ear;
Fays, fairies, genii, elves, and dæmons, hear:
Ye know the spheres, and various tasks assign'd　75
By laws eternal to the aërial kind.
Some in the fields of purest ether play,
And bask and whiten in the blaze of day.
Some guide the course of wand'ring orbs on high,
Or roll the planets through the boundless sky.　80
Some less refined beneath the moon's pale light
Pursue the stars that shoot athwart the night,
Or suck the mists in grosser air below,
Or dip their pinions in the painted bow,

Or brew fierce tempests on the wintry main,   85
Or o'er the glebe distil the kindly rain.
Others on earth o'er human race preside,
Watch all their ways, and all their actions guide:
Of these the chief the care of nations own,
And guard with arms divine the British throne.   90
  "Our humbler province is to tend the fair,
Not a less pleasing, though less glorious care;
To save the powder from too rude a gale,
Nor let the imprison'd essences exhale;
To draw fresh colours from the vernal flowers;   95
To steal from rainbows, ere they drop in showers,
A brighter wash; to curl their waving hairs,
Assist their blushes and inspire their airs;
Nay, oft, in dreams, invention we bestow,
To change a flounce, or add a furbelow.   100
  "This day, black omens threat the brightest fair
That e'er deserved a watchful spirit's care;
Some dire disaster, or by force, or slight;
But what, or where, the Fates have wrapp'd in night.
Whether the nymph shall break Diana's law,   105
Or some frail china-jar receive a flaw;
Or stain her honour or her new brocade;
Forget her prayers, or miss a masquerade;
Or lose her heart, or necklace, at a ball;
Or whether Heaven has doom'd that Shock must fall.   110
Haste, then, ye spirits! to your charge repair:
The flutt'ring fan be Zephyretta's care;
The drops to thee, Brillante, we consign;
And, Momentilla, let the watch be thine;
Do thou, Crispissa, tend her fav'rite lock;   115
Ariel himself shall be the guard of Shock.
  "To fifty chosen sylphs, of special note,
We trust th' important charge, the petticoat:
Oft have we known that seven-fold fence to fail,
Though stiff with hoops, and arm'd with ribs of whale; 120
Form a strong line about the silver bound,
And guard the wide circumference around.
  "Whatever spirit, careless of his charge,
His post neglects, or leaves the fair at large,
Shall feel sharp vengeance soon o'ertake his sins,   125
Be stopp'd in vials, or transfix'd with pins;
Or plunged in lakes of bitter washes lie,

Or wedged whole ages in a bodkin's eye:
Gums and pomatums shall his flight restrain,
While clogg'd he beats his silken wings in vain:　　130
Or alum styptics with contracting power
Shrink his thin essence like a rivell'd flower:
Or, as Ixion fix'd, the wretch shall feel
The giddy motion of the whirling wheel,
In fumes of burning chocolate shall glow,　　135
And tremble at the sea that froths below!"
　　He spoke; the spirits from the sails descend;
Some, orb in orb, around the nymph extend;
Some thrid the mazy ringlets of her hair;
Some hang upon the pendants of her ear:　　140
With beating hearts the dire event they wait,
Anxious and trembling for the birth of Fate.

CANTO III

CLOSE by those meads, for ever crown'd with flowers,
Where Thames with pride surveys his rising towers,
There stands a structure of majestic frame,
Which from the neighb'ring Hampton takes its name.
Here Britain's statesmen oft the fall foredoom　　5
Of foreign tyrants, and of nymphs at home;
Here thou, great ANNA! whom three realms obey,
Dost sometimes counsel take—and sometimes tea.
　　Hither the heroes and the nymphs resort,
To taste a while the pleasures of a court;　　10
In various talk th' instructive hours they pass'd,
Who gave the ball, or paid the visit last;
One speaks the glory of the British Queen,
And one describes a charming Indian screen;
A third interprets motions, looks, and eyes;　　15
At every word a reputation dies.
Snuff, or the fan, supply each pause of chat,
With singing, laughing, ogling, *and all that*.
　　Meanwhile, declining from the noon of day,
The sun obliquely shoots his burning ray;　　20
The hungry judges soon the sentence sign,
And wretches hang that jurymen may dine;
The merchant from th' exchange returns in peace,
And the long labours of the toilet cease.

Belinda now, whom thirst of fame invites, 25
Burns to encounter two adventurous knights,
At ombre singly to decide their doom;
And swells her breast with conquests yet to come.
Straight the three bands prepare in arms to join,
Each band the number of the sacred nine. 30
Soon as she spreads her hand, th' aërial guard
Descend, and sit on each important card:
First Ariel perch'd upon a Matadore,
Then each according to the rank he bore;
For sylphs, yet mindful of their ancient race, 35
Are, as when women, wondrous fond of place.

Behold, four Kings in majesty revered,
With hoary whiskers and a forky beard;
And four fair Queens, whose hands sustain a flower,
Th' expressive emblem of their softer power; 40
Four knaves in garbs succinct, a trusty band;
Caps on their heads, and halberts in their hand;
And party-colour'd troops, a shining train,
Drawn forth to combat on the velvet plain.

The skilful nymph reviews her force with care: 45
"Let Spades be trumps!" she said, and trumps they were.

Now move to war her sable Matadores,
In show like leaders of the swarthy Moors.
Spadillio first, unconquerable lord!
Led off two captive trumps, and swept the board. 50
As many more Manillio forced to yield,
And march'd a victor from the verdant field.
Him Basto follow'd; but his fate more hard
Gain'd but one trump, and one plebeian card.
With his broad sabre next, a chief in years, 55
The hoary Majesty of Spades appears,
Puts forth one manly leg, to sight reveal'd,
The rest, his many-colour'd robe conceal'd.
The rebel Knave, who dares his prince engage,
Proves the just victim of his royal rage. 60
Ev'n mighty Pam, that kings and queens o'erthrew,
And mow'd down armies in the fights of Lu,
Sad chance of war! now destitute of aid,
Falls undistinguish'd by the victor Spade!

Thus far both armies to Belinda yield; 65
Now to the baron fate inclines the field.
His warlike Amazon her host invades,

Th' imperial consort of the crown of Spades.
The Club's black tyrant first her victim dyed,
Spite of his haughty mien, and barb'rous pride: 70
What boots the regal circle on his head,
His giant limbs, in state unwieldy spread;
That long behind he trails his pompous robe,
And, of all monarchs, only grasps the globe?

The baron now his Diamonds pours apace;   75
Th' embroider'd King who shows but half his face,
And his refulgent Queen, with powers combined
Of broken troops an easy conquest find.
Clubs, Diamonds, Hearts, in wild disorder seen,
With throngs promiscuous strow the level green.   80
Thus when dispersed a routed army runs,
Of Asia's troops, and Afric's sable sons,
With like confusion different nations fly,
Of various habit, and of various dye,
The pierced battalions disunited fall,   85
In heaps on heaps; one fate o'erwhelms them all.

The Knave of Diamonds tries his wily arts,
And wins (oh shameful chance!) the Queen of Hearts.
At this, the blood the virgin's cheek forsook,
A livid paleness spreads o'er all her look;   90
She sees, and trembles at th' approaching ill,
Just in the jaws of ruin, and Codille.
And now (as oft in some distemper'd state)
On one nice trick depends the gen'ral fate,
An Ace of Hearts steps forth: the King unseen   95
Lurk'd in her hand, and mourn'd his captive Queen:
He springs to vengeance with an eager pace,
And falls like thunder on the prostrate Ace.
The nymph exulting fills with shouts the sky;
The walls, the woods, and long canals reply.   100

O thoughtless mortals! ever blind to fate,
Too soon dejected, and too soon elate.
Sudden, these honours shall be snatch'd away,
And cursed for ever this victorious day.

For lo! the board with cups and spoons is crown'd,   105
The berries crackle, and the mill turns round:
On shining altars of Japan they raise
The silver lamp; the fiery spirits blaze:
From silver spouts the grateful liquors glide,
While China's earth receives the smoking tide: 110

At once they gratify their scent and taste,
And frequent cups prolong the rich repast.
Straight hover round the fair her airy band;
Some, as she sipp'd, the fuming liquor fann'd,
Some o'er her lap their careful plumes display'd,   115
Trembling, and conscious of the rich brocade.
Coffee (which makes the politician wise,
And see through all things with his half-shut eyes)
Sent up in vapours to the baron's brain
New stratagems, the radiant lock to gain.   120
Ah cease, rash youth! desist ere 'tis too late,
Fear the just gods, and think of Scylla's fate!
Changed to a bird, and sent to flit in air,
She dearly pays for Nisus' injured hair!
    But when to mischief mortals bend their will,   125
How soon they find fit instruments of ill!
Just then, Clarissa drew with tempting grace
A two-edged weapon from her shining case:
So ladies, in romance, assist their knight,
Present the spear, and arm him for the fight.   130
He takes the gift with reverence and extends
The little engine on his fingers' ends;
This just behind Belinda's neck he spread,
As o'er the fragrant steams she bends her head.
Swift to the lock a thousand sprites repair,   135
A thousand wings, by turns, blow back the hair;
And thrice they twitch'd the diamond in her ear;
Thrice she look'd back, and thrice the foe drew near.
Just in that instant, anxious Ariel sought
The close recesses of the virgin's thought: 140
As on the nosegay in her breast reclin'd,
He watch'd th' ideas rising in her mind,
Sudden he view'd, in spite of all her art,
An earthly lover lurking at her heart.
Amazed, confused, he found his power expired,   145
Resign'd to fate, and with a sigh retired.
The peer now spreads the glitt'ring forfex wide,
T' inclose the lock; now joins it, to divide.
Ev'n then, before the fatal engine closed,
A wretched sylph too fondly interposed;   150
Fate urged the shears, and cut the sylph in twain,
(But airy substance soon unites again)
The meeting points the sacred hair dissever

From the fair head, for ever, and for ever!
   Then flash'd the living lightning from her eyes,   155
And screams of horror rend th' affrighted skies.
Not louder shrieks to pitying Heaven are cast,
When husbands or when lap-dogs breathe their last;
Or when rich China vessels, fall'n from high,
In glitt'ring dust and painted fragments lie!   160
   "Let wreaths of triumph now my temples twine,
(The victor cried) the glorious prize is mine!
While fish in streams, or birds delight in air,
Or in a coach and six the British fair,
As long as *Atalantis* shall be read,[1]   165
Or the small pillow grace a lady's bed,
While visits shall be paid on solemn days,
When numerous wax-lights in bright order blaze,
While nymphs take treats, or assignations give,
So long my honour, name, and praise shall live!"   170
What Time would spare, from steel receives its date,
And monuments, like men, submit to fate!
Steel could the labour of the gods destroy,
And strike to dust th' imperial towers of Troy;
Steel could the works of mortal pride confound,   175
And hew triumphal arches to the ground.
What wonder then, fair nymph! thy hairs should feel
The conquering force of unresisted steel?

CANTO IV

But anxious cares the pensive nymph oppress'd,
And secret passions labour'd in her breast.
Not youthful kings in battle seized alive,
Not scornful virgins who their charms survive,
Not ardent lovers robb'd of all their bliss,   5
Not ancient ladies when refused a kiss,
Not tyrants fierce that unrepenting die,
Not Cynthia when her manteau's pinn'd awry,
E'er felt such rage, resentment, and despair,
As thou, sad virgin! for thy ravish'd hair.   10
   For, that sad moment, when the sylphs withdrew,

[1] The *New Atalantis*, a famous book written about that time by Mrs. Manley, dramatist, political writer, and woman of intrigue; frequently mentioned in Swift's *Journal to Stella*.

And Ariel weeping from Belinda flew,
Umbriel, a dusky, melancholy sprite,
As ever sullied the fair face of light,
Down to the central earth, his proper scene,   15
Repair'd to search the gloomy Cave of Spleen.
    Swift on his sooty pinions flits the gnome,
And in a vapour reach'd the dismal dome.
No cheerful breeze this sullen region knows,
The dreaded east is all the wind that blows.   20
Here in a grotto, shelter'd close from air,
And screen'd in shades from day's detested glare,
She sighs for ever on her pensive bed,
Pain at her side, and Megrim at her head.
Two handmaids wait the throne: alike in place,   25
But diff'ring far in figure and in face.
Here stood Ill-nature like an ancient maid,
Her wrinkled form in black and white array'd;
With store of prayers, for mornings, nights, and noons,
Her hand is fill'd; her bosom with lampoons.   30
    There Affectation, with a sickly mien,
Shows in her cheek the roses of eighteen,
Practised to lisp, and hang the head aside,
Faints into airs, and languishes with pride,
On the rich quilt sinks with becoming woe,   35
Wrapp'd in a gown, for sickness, and for show.
The fair ones feel such maladies as these,
When each new night-dress gives a new disease.
    A constant vapour o'er the palace flies;
Strange phantoms rising as the mists arise;   40
Dreadful, as hermits' dreams in haunted shades,
Or bright, as visions of expiring maids.
Now glaring fiends, and snakes on rolling spires,
Pale spectres, gaping tombs, and purple fires:
Now lakes of liquid gold, Elysian scenes,   45
And crystal domes, and angels in machines.
    Unnumber'd throngs on every side are seen
Of bodies changed to various forms by Spleen.
Here living tea-pots stand, one arm held out,
One bent; the handle this, and that the spout: 50
A pipkin there, like Homer's tripod walks;
Here sighs a jar, and there a goose-pie talks:
Men prove with child, as powerful fancy works,
And maids turn'd bottles call aloud for corks.

Safe pass'd the gnome through this fantastic band,   55
A branch of healing spleen-wort in his hand.
Then thus address'd the power: "Hail, wayward Queen!
Who rule the sex to fifty from fifteen;
Parent of vapours, and of female wit,
Who give th' hysteric or poetic fit;   60
On various tempers act by various ways,
Make some take physic, others scribble plays;
Who cause the proud their visits to delay,
And send the godly in a pet to pray;
A nymph there is, that all thy power disdains,   65
And thousands more in equal mirth maintains.
But oh! if e'er thy gnome could spoil a grace,
Or raise a pimple on a beauteous face,
Like citron waters matrons' cheeks inflame,
Or change complexions at a losing game;   70
If e'er with airy horns I planted heads,
Or rumpled petticoats, or tumbled beds,
Or caused suspicion when no soul was rude,
Or discomposed the head-dress of a prude,
Or e'er to costive lap-dog gave disease,   75
Which not the tears of brightest eyes could ease;
Hear me, and touch Belinda with chagrin,
That single act gives half the world the spleen."
   The Goddess with a discontented air
Seems to reject him, though she grants his prayer.   80
A wondrous bag with both her hands she binds,
Like that where once Ulysses held the winds;
There she collects the force of female lungs,
Sighs, sobs, and passions, and the war of tongues.
A vial next she fills with fainting fears,   85
Soft sorrows, melting griefs, and flowing tears.
The gnome rejoicing bears her gifts away,
Spreads his black wings, and slowly mounts to day.
   Sunk in Thalestris' arms the nymph he found,
Her eyes dejected, and her hair unbound.   90
Full o'er their heads the swelling bag he rent,
And all the furies issued at the vent.
Belinda burns with more than mortal ire,
And fierce Thalestris fans the rising fire;
"O wretched maid!" she spread her hands, and cried,   95
(While Hampton's echoes, "Wretched maid!" replied)
"Was it for this you took such constant care

The bodkin, comb, and essence to prepare?
For this your locks in paper durance bound?
For this with torturing irons wreathed around?   100
For this with fillets strain'd your tender head,
And bravely bore the double loads of lead?
Gods! shall the ravisher display your hair,
While the fops envy and the ladies stare?
Honour forbid! at whose unrivall'd shrine   105
Ease, pleasure, virtue, all our sex resign.
Methinks already I your tears survey,
Already hear the horrid things they say,
Already see you a degraded toast,
And all your honour in a whisper lost!   110
How shall I then your helpless fame defend?
'Twill then be infamy to seem your friend!
And shall this prize, th' inestimable prize,
Exposed through crystal to the gazing eyes,
And heighten'd by the diamond's circling rays,   115
On that rapacious hand for ever blaze?
Sooner shall grass in Hyde Park Circus grow,
And wits take lodgings in the sound of Bow;
Sooner let earth, air, sea, to Chaos fall,
Men, monkeys, lap-dogs, parrots, perish all!"   120
    She said; then raging to Sir Plume repairs,
And bids her beau demand the precious hairs:
(Sir Plume of amber snuff-box justly vain,
And the nice conduct of a clouded cane)
With earnest eyes, and round, unthinking face,   125
He first the snuff-box open'd, then the case,
And then broke out—"My Lord, why, what the devil!
Z—ds! damn the lock! 'fore Gad, you must be civil!
Plague on't! 'tis past a jest—nay prithee, pox!
Give her the hair"—he spoke, and rapp'd his box.   130
"It grieves me much (replied the peer again)
Who speaks so well should ever speak in vain,
But by this lock, this sacred lock, I swear,
(Which never more shall join its parted hair;
Which never more its honours shall renew,   135
Clipp'd from the lovely head where late it grew)
That while my nostrils draw the vital air,
This hand, which won it, shall for ever wear."
He spoke, and speaking, in proud triumph spread
The long-contended honours of her head.   140

But Umbriel, hateful gnome! forbears not so;
He breaks the vial whence the sorrows flow.
Then see! the nymph in beauteous grief appears,
Her eyes half-languishing, half-drowned in tears;
On her heaved bosom hung her drooping head,   145
Which, with a sigh, she raised; and thus she said:
    "For ever cursed be this detested day,
Which snatch'd my best, my fav'rite curl away!
Happy! ay ten times happy had I been,
If Hampton Court these eyes had never seen!   150
Yet am I not the first mistaken maid,
By love of courts to numerous ills betray'd,
Oh had I rather unadmired remain'd
In some lone isle, or distant northern land;
Where the gilt chariot never marks the way,   155
Where none learn ombre, none e'er taste bohea!
There kept my charms conceal'd from mortal eye,
Like roses that in deserts bloom and die.
What moved my mind with youthful lords to roam?
Oh had I stayed, and said my prayers at home!   160
'Twas this the morning omens seem'd to tell:
Thrice from my trembling hand the patch-box fell;
The tott'ring china shook without a wind;
Nay, Poll sat mute, and Shock was most unkind!
A sylph too warn'd me of the threats of Fate,   165
In mystic visions, now believed too late!
See the poor remnants of these slighted hairs!
My hands shall rend what e'en thy rapine spares:
These in two sable ringlets taught to break,
Once gave new beauties to the snowy neck;   170
The sister-lock now sits uncouth, alone,
And in its fellow's fate foresees its own;
Uncurl'd it hangs, the fatal shears demands,
And tempts, once more, thy sacrilegious hands.
Oh hadst thou, cruel! been content to seize   175
Hairs less in sight, or any hairs but these!"

CANTO V

SHE said: the pitying audience melt in tears;
But Fate and Love had stopp'd the baron's ears.
In vain Thalestris with reproach assails,
For who can move when fair Belinda fails?

Not half so fix'd the Trojan could remain, 5
While Anna begg'd and Dido raged in vain.
Then grave Clarissa graceful waved her fan;
Silence ensued, and thus the nymph began:
    "Say, why are beauties praised and honoured most,
The wise man's passion, and the vain man's toast? 10
Why deck'd with all that land and sea afford?
Why angels call'd, and angel-like adored?
Why round our coaches crowd the white-gloved beaux?
Why bows the side-box from its inmost rows?
How vain are all these glories, all our pains, 15
Unless good sense preserve what beauty gains;
That men may say, when we the front-box grace,
'Behold the first in virtue as in face!'
Oh! if to dance all night, and dress all day,
Charm'd the small-pox, or chased old age away; 20
Who would not scorn what housewife's cares produce,
Or who would learn one earthly thing of use?
To patch, nay, ogle, might become a saint,
Nor could it sure be such a sin to paint.
But since, alas! frail beauty must decay, 25
Curl'd or uncurl'd, since locks will turn to grey;
Since painted, or not painted, all shall fade,
And she who scorns a man must die a maid;
What then remains, but well our power to use,
And keep good-humour still, whate'er we lose? 30
And trust me, dear, good-humour can prevail,
When airs, and flights, and screams, and scolding fail.
Beauties in vain their pretty eyes may roll;
Charms strike the sight, but merit wins the soul."
    So spoke the dame, but no applause ensued; 35
Belinda frown'd, Thalestris call'd her prude.
"To arms, to arms!" the fierce virago cries,
And swift as lightning to the combat flies.
All side in parties, and begin th' attack:
Fans clap, silks rustle, and tough whalebones crack; 40
Heroes' and heroines' shouts confusedly rise,
And bass and treble voices strike the skies.
No common weapons in their hands are found,
Like Gods they fight, nor dread a mortal wound.
    So when bold Homer makes the Gods engage, 45
And heavenly breasts with human passions rage;
'Gainst Pallas, Mars; Latona, Hermes arms;

And all Olympus rings with loud alarms;
Jove's thunder roars, Heaven trembles all around,
Blue Neptune storms, the bellowing deeps resound: 50
Earth shakes her nodding towers, the ground gives way,
And the pale ghosts start at the flash of day!

 Triumphant Umbriel on a sconce's height
Clapp'd his glad wings, and sate to view the fight:
Propp'd on their bodkin spears, the sprites survey   55
The growing combat, or assist the fray.

 While through the press enraged Thalestris flies,
And scatters death around from both her eyes,
A beau and witling perish'd in the throng,
One died in metaphor, and one in song.   60
"O cruel nymph! a living death I bear,"
Cried Dapperwit, and sunk beside his chair.
A mournful glance Sir Fopling upwards cast,
"Those eyes are made so killing,"—was his last.[1]
Thus on Mæander's flowery margin lies   65
Th' expiring swan, and as he sings he dies.

 When bold Sir Plume had drawn Clarissa down,
Chloe stepp'd in, and kill'd him with a frown;
She smiled to see the doughty hero slain,
But, at her smile, the beau revived again.   70

 Now Jove suspends his golden scales in air,
Weighs the men's wits against the lady's hair:
The doubtful beam long nods from side to side;
At length the wits mount up, the hairs subside.

 See fierce Belinda on the baron flies,   75
With more than usual lightning in her eyes:
Nor fear'd the chief th' unequal fight to try,
Who sought no more than on his foe to die.
But this bold lord with manly strength endued,
She with one finger and a thumb subdued: 80
Just where the breath of life his nostrils drew,
A charge of snuff the wily virgin threw;
The gnomes direct, to every atom just,
The pungent grains of titillating dust.
Sudden, with starting tears each eye o'erflows,   85
And the high dome re-echoes to his nose.

 "Now meet thy fate," incensed Belinda cried,
And drew a deadly bodkin from her side.
(The same, his ancient personage to deck,

---

[1] The words of a song in the opera of *Camilla*.

Her great-great-grandsire wore about his neck, 90
In three seal rings; which after, melted down,
Form'd a vast buckle for his widow's gown:
Her infant grandame's whistle next it grew,
The bells she jingled, and the whistle blew;
Then in a bodkin graced her mother's hairs, 95
Which long she wore, and now Belinda wears.)
  "Boast not my fall, (he cried) insulting foe!
Thou by some other shalt be laid as low.
Nor think, to die dejects my lofty mind:
All that I dread is leaving you behind! 100
Rather than so, ah let me still survive,
And burn in Cupid's flames—but burn alive."
  "Restore the lock!" she cries; and all around
"Restore the lock!" the vaulted roofs rebound.
Not fierce Othello in so loud a strain 105
Roar'd for the handkerchief that caused his pain.
But see how oft ambitious aims are cross'd,
And chiefs contend till all the prize is lost!
The lock, obtain'd with guilt, and kept with pain,
In every place is sought, but sought in vain: 110
With such a prize no mortal must be blest,
So Heaven decrees! with Heaven who can contest?
  Some thought it mounted to the lunar sphere,
Since all things lost on earth are treasured there.
There heroes' wits are kept in pond'rous vases, 115
And beaux' in snuff-boxes and tweezer-cases.
There broken vows, and death-bed alms are found,
And lovers' hearts with ends of riband bound,
The courtier's promises, and sick man's prayers,
The smiles of harlots, and the tears of heirs, 120
Cages for gnats, and chains to yoke a flea,
Dried butterflies, and tomes of casuistry.
  But trust the Muse—she saw it upward rise,
Though mark'd by none but quick, poetic eyes:
(So Rome's great founder to the heavens withdrew, 125
To Proculus alone confess'd in view)
A sudden star it shot through liquid air,
And drew behind a radiant trail of hair.
Not Berenice's lock first rose so bright,
The heavens bespangling with dishevell'd light. 130
The sylphs behold it kindling as it flies,
And pleased pursue its progress through the skies.

This the beau-monde shall from the Mall survey,
And hail with music its propitious ray.
This the blest lover shall for Venus take,   135
And send up vows from Rosamonda's lake.
This Partridge soon shall view in cloudless skies,[1]
When next he looks through Galileo's eyes;
And hence th' egregious wizard shall foredoom
The fate of Louis, and the fall of Rome.   140
    Then cease, bright nymph! to mourn thy ravish'd hair,
Which adds new glory to the shining sphere!
Not all the tresses that fair head can boast
Shall draw such envy as the lock you lost.
For, after all the murders of your eye,   145
When, after millions slain, yourself shall die;
When those fair suns shall set, as set they must,
And all those tresses shall be laid in dust;
This lock, the Muse shall consecrate to fame,
And 'midst the stars inscribe Belinda's name.   150

ELOISA TO ABELARD

In these deep solitudes and awful cells,
Where heavenly-pensive Contemplation dwells,
And ever-musing Melancholy reigns,
What means this tumult in a Vestal's veins?
Why rove my thoughts beyond this last retreat?   5
Why feels my heart its long-forgotten heat?
Yet, yet I love! From Abelard it came,
And Eloisa yet must kiss the name.
    Dear fatal name! rest ever unreveal'd,
Nor pass these lips in holy silence seal'd: 10
Hide it, my heart, within that close disguise,
Where, mix'd with God's, his loved idea lies:
Oh, write it not, my hand—the name appears
Already written—wash it out, my tears!
In vain lost Eloisa weeps and prays,   15
Her heart still dictates, and her hand obeys.
    Relentless walls! whose darksome round contains
Repentant sighs, and voluntary pains:

[1] John Partridge, who was the subject of Swift's satire, *Predictions for the Year* 1708, *by Isaac Bickerstaff, Esq.*

Ye rugged rocks! which holy knees have worn;
Ye grots and caverns shagg'd with horrid thorn!   20
Shrines! where their vigils pale-eyed virgins keep,
And pitying saints, whose statues learn to weep!
Though cold like you, unmoved and silent grown,
I have not yet forgot myself to stone.
All is not Heaven's while Abelard has part,   25
Still rebel nature holds out half my heart;·
Nor prayers nor fasts its stubborn pulse restrain,
Nor tears for ages taught to flow in vain.
  Soon as thy letters trembling I unclose,
That well-known name awakens all my woes.   30
Oh name for ever sad! for ever dear!
Still breathed in sighs, still usher'd with a tear.
I tremble too, where'er my own I find,
Some dire misfortune follows close behind.
Line after line my gushing eyes o'erflow,   35
Led through a sad variety of woe;
Now warm in love, now with'ring in my bloom,
Lost in a convent's solitary gloom!
There stern religion quench'd th' unwilling flame,
There died the best of passions, Love and Fame.   40
  Yet write, oh write me all, that I may join
Griefs to thy grief, and echo sighs to thine.
Nor foes nor fortune take this power away;
And is my Abelard less kind than they?
Tears still are mine, and those I need not spare,   45
Love but demands what else were shed in prayer;
No happier task these faded eyes pursue;
To read and weep is all they now can do.
  Then share thy pain, allow that sad relief;
Ah, more than share it, give me all thy grief.   50
Heaven first taught letters for some wretch's aid,
Some banish'd lover, or some captive maid:
They live, they speak, they breathe what love inspires,
Warm from the soul, and faithful to its fires;
The virgin's wish without her fears impart,   55
Excuse the blush, and pour out all the heart;
Speed the soft intercourse from soul to soul,
And waft a sigh from Indus to the pole.
  Thou know'st how guiltless first I met thy flame,
When love approach'd me under friendship's name;   60
My fancy form'd thee of angelic kind,

Some emanation of th' all-beauteous mind.
Those smiling eyes, attemp'ring every ray,
Shone sweetly lambent with celestial day.
Guiltless I gazed; Heaven listen'd while you sung; 65
And truths divine came mended from that tongue.
From lips like those what precepts fail to move?
Too soon they taught me 'twas no sin to love:
Back through the paths of pleasing sense I ran,
Nor wish'd an angel whom I loved a man. 70
Dim and remote the joys of saints I see;
Nor envy them that Heaven I lose for thee.
　　How oft, when press'd to marriage, have I said,
Curse on all laws but those which Love has made!
Love, free as air, at sight of human ties, 75
Spreads his light wings, and in a moment flies.
Let wealth, let honour, wait the wedded dame,
August her deed, and sacred be her fame;
Before true passion all those views remove;
Fame, wealth, and honour! what are you to love? 80
The jealous God, when we profane his fires,
Those restless passions in revenge inspires,
And bids them make mistaken mortals groan,
Who seek in love for aught but love alone.
Should at my feet the world's great master fall, 85
Himself, his throne, his world, I'd scorn them all:
Not Cæsar's empress would I deign to prove;
No, make me mistress to the man I love;
If there be yet another name more free,
More fond than mistress, make me that to thee! 90
Oh, happy state! when souls each other draw,
When love is liberty, and Nature law:
All then is full, possessing, and possessed,
No craving void left aching in the breast:
Even thought meets thought ere from the lips it part, 95
And each warm wish springs mutual from the heart.
This sure is bliss, if bliss on earth there be,
And once the lot of Abelard and me.
　　Alas, how changed! what sudden horrors rise!
A naked lover bound and bleeding lies! 100
Where, where was Eloïse? her voice, her hand,
Her poniard had opposed the dire command.
Barbarian, stay! that bloody stroke restrain;
The crime was common, common be the pain.

I can no more, by shame, by rage suppress'd,   105
Let tears, and burning blushes speak the rest.
   Canst thou forget that sad, that solemn day,
When victims at yon altar's foot we lay?
Canst thou forget what tears that moment fell,
When warm in youth I bade the world farewell?   110
As with cold lips I kiss'd the sacred veil,
The shrines all trembled, and the lamps grew pale:
Heaven scarce believed the conquest it survey'd,
And saints with wonder heard the vows I made.
Yet then, to those dread altars as I drew,   115
Not on the cross my eyes were fix'd, but you:
Not grace, or zeal, love only was my call;
And if I lose thy love, I lose my all.
Come! with thy looks, thy words, relieve my woe;
Those still at least are left thee to bestow.   120
Still on that breast enamour'd let me lie,
Still drink delicious poison from thy eye,
Pant on thy lip, and to thy heart be press'd;
Give all thou canst—and let me dream the rest.
Ah no! instruct me other joys to prize,   125
With other beauties charm my partial eyes:
Full in my view set all the bright abode,
And make my soul quit Abelard for God.
   Ah, think at least thy flock deserves thy care,
Plants of thy hand, and children of thy prayer.   130
From the false world in early youth they fled,
By thee to mountains, wilds, and deserts led.
You raised these hallow'd walls; the desert smiled,
And Paradise was open'd in the wild.
No weeping orphan saw his father's stores   135
Our shrines irradiate, or emblaze the floors;
No silver saints by dying misers given,
Here bribed the rage of ill-requited Heaven:
But such plain roofs as Piety could raise,
And only vocal with the Maker's praise.   140
In these lone walls, (their day's eternal bound)
These moss-grown domes with spiry turrets crown'd,
Where awful arches make a noon-day night,
And the dim windows shed a solemn light;
Thy eyes diffused a reconciling ray,   145
And gleams of glory brighten'd all the day.
But now no face divine contentment wears,

'Tis all blank sadness, or continual tears.
See how the force of others' pray'rs I try,
(O pious fraud of amorous charity!)   150
But why should I on others' prayers depend?
Come thou, my father, brother, husband, friend!
Ah, let thy handmaid, sister, daughter move,
And all those tender names in one, thy love!
The darksome pines that o'er yon rocks reclined   155
Wave high, and murmur to the hollow wind,
The wand'ring streams that shine between the hills,
The grots that echo to the tinkling rills,
The dying gales that pant upon the trees,
The lakes that quiver to the curling breeze;   160
No more these scenes my meditation aid,
Or lull to rest the visionary maid.
But o'er the twilight groves and dusky caves,
Long-sounding aisles, and intermingled graves,
Black Melancholy sits, and round her throws   165
A death-like silence, and a dread repose:
Her gloomy presence saddens all the scene,
Shades ev'ry flow'r, and darkens ev'ry green,
Deepens the murmur of the falling floods,
And breathes a browner horror on the woods.   170
    Yet here for ever, ever must I stay;
Sad proof how well a lover can obey!
Death, only death, can break the lasting chain;
And here, ev'n then, shall my cold dust remain,
Here all its frailties, all its flames resign,   175
And wait till 'tis no sin to mix with thine.
    Ah, wretch! believed the spouse of God in vain,
Confess'd within the slave of love and man.
Assist me, Heaven! but whence arose that prayer?
Sprung it from piety, or from despair?   180
Ev'n here, where frozen chastity retires,
Love finds an altar for forbidden fires.
I ought to grieve, but cannot what I ought;
I mourn the lover, not lament the fault;
I view my crime, but kindle at the view,   185
Repent old pleasures, and solicit new:
Now turn'd to Heaven, I weep my past offence,
Now think of thee, and curse my innocence.
Of all affliction taught a lover yet,
'Tis sure the hardest science to forget!   190

How shall I lose the sin, yet keep the sense,
And love the offender, yet detest th' offence?
How the dear object from the crime remove,
Or how distinguish penitence from love?
Unequal task! a passion to resign,   195
For hearts so touch'd, so pierced, so lost as mine.
Ere such a soul regains its peaceful state,
How often must it love, how often hate!
How often hope, despair, resent, regret,
Conceal, disdain,—do all things but forget!   200
But let Heaven seize it, all at once 'tis fired;
Not touch'd, but rapt; not weaken'd, but inspired!
Oh come! oh teach me nature to subdue,
Renounce my love, my life, myself—and you.
Fill my fond heart with God alone, for He   205
Alone can rival, can succeed to thee.
      How happy is the blameless Vestal's lot!
The world forgetting, by the world forgot:
Eternal sunshine of the spotless mind!
Each prayer accepted, and each wish resign'd;   210
Labour and rest that equal periods keep;
"Obedient slumbers that can wake and weep";
Desires composed, affections ever even;
Tears that delight, and sighs that waft to Heaven.
Grace shines around her with serenest beams,   215
And whisp'ring angels prompt her golden dreams.
For her th' unfading rose of Eden blooms,
And wings of seraphs shed divine perfumes;
For her the spouse prepares the bridal ring,
For her white virgins hymeneals sing;   220
To sounds of heavenly harps she dies away,
And melts in visions of eternal day.
      Far other dreams my erring soul employ,
Far other raptures, of unholy joy:
When at the close of each sad, sorrowing day,   225
Fancy restores what vengeance snatch'd away,
Then conscience sleeps, and leaving Nature free,
All my loose soul unbounded springs to thee.
O cursed, dear horrors of all-conscious night!
How glowing guilt exalts the keen delight!   230
Provoking demons all restraint remove,
And stir within me ev'ry source of love.
I hear thee, view thee, gaze o'er all thy charms,

And round thy phantom glue my clasping arms.
I wake:—no more I hear, no more I view, 235
The phantom flies me, as unkind as you.
I call aloud; it hears not what I say:
I stretch my empty arms; it glides away.
To dream once more I close my willing eyes;
Ye soft illusions, dear deceits, arise! 240
Alas, no more! methinks we wand'ring go
Through dreary wastes, and weep each other's woe,
Where round some mould'ring tower pale ivy creeps,
And low-brow'd rocks hang nodding o'er the deeps.
Sudden you mount, you beckon from the skies; 245
Clouds interpose, waves roar, and winds arise.
I shriek, start up, the same sad prospect find,
And wake to all the griefs I left behind.
     For thee the Fates, severely kind, ordain
A cool suspense from pleasure and from pain; 250
Thy life a long dead calm of fix'd repose;
No pulse that riots, and no blood that glows.
Still as the sea, ere winds were taught to blow,
Or moving spirit bade the waters flow;
Soft as the slumbers of a saint forgiven, 255
And mild as opening gleams of promised Heaven.
     Come, Abelard! for what hast thou to dread?
The torch of Venus burns not for the dead.
Nature stands check'd; religion disapproves:
Ev'n thou art cold—yet Eloïsa loves. 260
Ah hopeless, lasting flames! like those that burn
To light the dead, and warm th' unfruitful urn.
     What scenes appear where'er I turn my view?
The dear ideas, where I fly, pursue,
Rise in the grove, before the altar rise, 265
Stain all my soul, and wanton in my eyes.
I waste the matin lamp in sighs for thee,
Thy image steals between my God and me,
Thy voice I seem in ev'ry hymn to hear,
With ev'ry bead I drop too soft a tear. 270
When from the censer clouds of fragrance roll,
And swelling organs lift the rising soul,
One thought of thee puts all the pomp to flight,
Priests, tapers, temples, swim before my sight:
In seas of flame my plunging soul is drowned, 275
While altars blaze, and angels tremble round.

While prostrate here in humble grief I lie,
Kind, virtuous drops just gath'ring in my eye,
While praying, trembling, in the dust I roll,
And dawning grace is opening on my soul: 280
Come, if thou dar'st, all charming as thou art!
Oppose thyself to Heaven; dispute my heart;
Come, with one glance of those deluding eyes
Blot out each bright idea of the skies;
Take back that grace, those sorrows, and those tears;
Take back my fruitless penitence and prayers;   286
Snatch me, just mounting, from the bless'd abode;
Assist the fiends and tear me from my God!
  No, fly me, fly me, far as pole from pole;
Rise Alps between us! and whole oceans roll!   290
Ah, come not, write not, think not once of me,
Nor share one pang of all I felt for thee,
Thy oaths I quit, thy memory resign;
Forget, renounce me, hate whate'er was mine.
Fair eyes, and tempting looks, (which yet I view!)   295
Long loved, adored ideas, all adieu!
O Grace serene! O Virtue heavenly fair!
Divine oblivion of low-thoughted care!
Fresh blooming Hope, gay daughter of the sky!
And Faith, our early immortality!   300
Enter, each mild, each amicable guest:
Receive, and wrap me in eternal rest!
  See in her cell sad Eloïsa spread,
Propped on some tomb, a neighbour of the dead.
In each low wind methinks a spirit calls,   305
And more than echoes talk along the walls.
Here, as I watch'd the dying lamps around,
From yonder shrine I heard a hollow sound.
"Come, sister, come! (it said, or seem'd to say,)
Thy place is here, sad sister, come away!   310
Once, like thyself, I trembled, wept, and prayed,
Love's victim then, though now a sainted maid:
But all is calm in this eternal sleep;
Here Grief forgets to groan, and Love to weep,
Ev'n Superstition loses ev'ry fear: 315
For God, not man, absolves our frailties here."
I come, I come! prepare your roseate bowers,
Celestial palms, and ever-blooming flowers.
Thither, where sinners may have rest, I go,

Where flames refined in breasts seraphic glow: 320
Thou, Abelard! the last sad office pay,
And smooth my passage to the realms of day;
See my lips tremble, and my eye-balls roll,
Suck my last breath, and catch my flying soul!
Ah no—in sacred vestments may'st thou stand,   325
The hallow'd taper trembling in thy hand,
Present the cross before my lifted eye,
Teach me at once, and learn of me to die.
Ah then, thy once-loved Eloïsa see!
It will be then no crime to gaze on me.   330
See from my cheek the transient roses fly!
See the last sparkle languish in my eye!
Till ev'ry motion, pulse, and breath be o'er,
And ev'n my Abelard be lov'd no more.
O Death all-eloquent! you only prove   335
What dust we dote on, when 'tis man we love.
    Then too, when fate shall thy fair frame destroy,
(That cause of all my guilt, and all my joy,)
In trance ecstatic may thy pangs be drowned,
Bright clouds descend, and angels watch thee round; 340
From opening skies may streaming glories shine,
And saints embrace thee with a love like mine.
    May one kind grave unite each hapless name,
And graft my love immortal on thy fame!
Then, ages hence, when all my woes are o'er,   345
When this rebellious heart shall beat no more;
If ever chance two wand'ring lovers brings
To Paraclete's white walls and silver springs,
O'er the pale marble shall they join their heads,
And drink the falling tears each other sheds;   350
Then sadly say, with mutual pity moved,
"Oh may we never love as these have loved!"
From the full choir when loud Hosannas rise,
And swell the pomp of dreadful sacrifice,
Amid that scene, if some relenting eye   355
Glance on the stone where our cold relics lie,
Devotion's self shall steal a thought from Heaven,
One human tear shall drop, and be forgiven.
And sure, if Fate some future bard shall join,
In sad similitude of griefs to mine,   360
Condemn'd whole years in absence to deplore,
And image charms he must behold no more;

Such if there be, who love so long, so well,
Let him our sad, our tender story tell;
The well-sung woes will soothe my pensive ghost;   365
He best can paint them who shall feel them most.

EPISTLES

TO MR. ADDISON

OCCASIONED BY HIS DIALOGUES ON MEDALS

SEE the wild waste of all devouring years!
How Rome her own sad sepulchre appears,
With nodding arches, broken temples spread!
The very tombs now vanish'd like their dead!
Imperial wonders raised on nations spoil'd,   5
Where mix'd with slaves the groaning martyr toil'd:
Huge theatres, that now unpeopled woods,
Now drain'd a distant country of her floods:
Fanes, which admiring Gods with pride survey,
Statues of men, scarce less alive than they!   10
Some felt the silent stroke of mould'ring age,
Some hostile fury, some religious rage.
Barbarian blindness, Christian zeal conspire,
And Papal piety, and Gothic fire.
Perhaps, by its own ruins saved from flame,   15
Some buried marble half preserves a name;
That name the learn'd with fierce disputes pursue,
And give to Titus old Vespasian's due.
  Ambition sighed: she found it vain to trust
The faithless column and the crumbling bust: 20
Huge moles, whose shadow stretch'd from shore to shore,
Their ruins perish'd, and their place no more!
Convinced, she now contracts her vast design,
And all her triumphs shrink into a coin.
A narrow orb each crowded conquest keeps,   25
Beneath her palm here sad Judea weeps.
Now scantier limits the proud arch confine,
And scarce are seen the prostrate Nile or Rhine;
A small Euphrates through the piece is roll'd,
And little eagles wave their wings in gold.   30

The Medal, faithful to its charge of fame,
Through climes and ages bears each form and name:
In one short view subjected to our eye
Gods, Emperors, Heroes, Sages, Beauties, lie.
With sharpen'd sight pale antiquaries pore, 35
Th' inscription value, but the rust adore.
This the blue varnish, that the green endears,
The sacred rust of twice ten hundred years!
To gain Pescennius one employs his schemes;
One grasps a Cecrops in ecstatic dreams. 40
Poor Vadius, long with learned spleen devour'd,
Can taste no pleasure since his shield was scour'd:
And Curio, restless by the fair-one's side,
Sighs for an Otho, and neglects his bride.

Theirs is the vanity, the learning thine: 45
Touch'd by thy hand, again Rome's glories shine;
Her Gods, and godlike heroes rise to view,
And all her faded garlands bloom anew.
Nor blush, these studies thy regard engage;
These pleased the fathers of poetic rage: 50
The verse and sculpture bore an equal part,
And Art reflected images to Art.

Oh when shall Britain, conscious of her claim,
Stand emulous of Greek and Roman fame:
In living medals see her wars enroll'd, 55
And vanquish'd realms supply recording gold?
Here, rising bold, the patriot's honest face;
There, warriors frowning in historic brass:
Then, future ages with delight shall see
How Plato's, Bacon's, Newton's looks agree; 60
Or in fair series laurell'd bards be shown,
A Virgil there, and here an Addison.
Then shall thy CRAGGS (and let me call him mine)
On the cast ore, another Pollio, shine;
With aspect open shall erect his head, 65
And round the orb in lasting notes be read,
"Statesman, yet friend to Truth! of soul sincere,
In action faithful, and in honour clear;
Who broke no promise, served no private end,
Who gain'd no title, and who lost no friend; 70
Ennobled by himself, by all approved,
And praised, unenvied, by the Muse he loved."

TO ROBERT EARL OF OXFORD, AND EARL MORTIMER [1]

SUCH were the notes thy once-loved Poet sung,
Till Death untimely stopp'd his tuneful tongue.
Oh just beheld and lost! admired and mourn'd!
With softest manners, gentlest arts adorn'd!
Blest in each science, blest in ev'ry strain!   5
Dear to the Muse! to HARLEY dear—in vain!
  For him, thou oft hast bid the world attend,
Fond to forget the statesman in the friend;
For SWIFT and him, despised the farce of state,
The sober follies of the wise and great;   10
Dext'rous, the craving, fawning crowd to quit,
And pleased to 'scape from Flattery to Wit.
  Absent or dead, still let a friend be dear,
(A sigh the absent claims, the dead a tear,)
Recall those nights that closed thy toilsome days,   15
Still hear thy Parnell in his living lays,
Who, careless now of Int'rest, Fame, or Fate,
Perhaps forgets that OXFORD e'er was great;
Or deeming meanest what we greatest call,
Beholds thee glorious only in thy fall.   20
And sure, if aught below the seats divine
Can touch Immortals, 'tis a soul like thine:
A soul supreme, in each hard instance tried,
Above all pain, all passion, and all pride,
The rage of power, the blast of public breath,   25
The lust of lucre, and the dread of death.
  In vain to deserts thy retreat is made;
The Muse attends thee to thy silent shade:
'Tis hers, the brave man's latest steps to trace,
Rejudge his acts, and dignify disgrace.   30
When Interest calls off all her sneaking train,
And all th' obliged desert, and all the vain;
She waits, or to the scaffold, or the cell,
When the last lingering friend has bid farewell.
Ev'n now, she shades thy evening-walk with bays,   35
(No hireling she, no prostitute to praise,)

[1] This epistle was sent to the Earl of Oxford with Dr. Parnell's *Poems*, published by our author, after the said earl's imprisonment in the Tower, and retreat into the country, in the year 1721.

Ev'n now, observant of the parting ray,
Eyes the calm sunset of thy various day,
Through Fortune's cloud one truly great can see,
Nor fears to tell, that MORTIMER is he.   40

TO JAMES CRAGGS, ESQ.

SECRETARY OF STATE [1]

A SOUL as full of worth as void of pride,
Which nothing seeks to show, or needs to hide,
Which nor to guilt nor fear its caution owes,
And boasts a warmth that from no passion flows.
A face untaught to feign; a judging eye,   5
That darts severe upon a rising lie,
And strikes a blush through frontless flattery.
All this thou wert; and being this before,
Know, kings and fortune cannot make thee more.
Then scorn to gain a friend by servile ways,   10
Nor wish to lose a foe these virtues raise;
But candid, free, sincere, as you began,
Proceed—a minister, but still a man.
Be not (exalted to whate'er degree)
Ashamed of any friend, not ev'n of me: 15
The patriot's plain, but untrod, path pursue;
If not, 'tis I must be ashamed of you.

TO MR. JERVAS [2]

WITH MR. DRYDEN'S TRANSLATION OF FRESNOY'S ART OF PAINTING

THIS verse be thine, my friend, nor thou refuse
This, from no venal or ungrateful Muse.
Whether thy hand strike out some free design,
Where life awakes, and dawns at ev'ry line;

[1] He died at the age of thirty-five, on 15th February, 1720. He had been early engaged in missions at foreign courts, and in 1717 was made Secretary at War. In the following year he was appointed one of the Secretaries of State.

[2] Jervas studied under Sir Godfrey Kneller, and was a fashionable portrait painter in the reigns of George I. and George II. Walpole says he was defective in drawing, colouring and composition; " his pictures are a light flimsy kind of fan-painting, as large as life." He took several portraits of Pope; one of these is in the Bodleian Library, Oxford; another at Maplodurham, and a third at Elton Hall, Huntingdonshire.

Or blend in beauteous tints the colour'd mass, 5
And from the canvas call the mimic face:
Read these instructive leaves, in which conspire
Fresnoy's close art and Dryden's native fire:
And reading wish like theirs our fate and fame,
So mix'd our studies, and so join'd our name; 10
Like them to shine through long succeeding age,
So just thy skill, so regular my rage.

Smit with the love of sister-arts we came,
And met congenial, mingling flame with flame;
Like friendly colours found them both unite, 15
And each from each contract new strength and light.
How oft in pleasing tasks we wear the day,
While summer suns roll unperceived away?
How oft our slowly-growing works impart,
While images reflect from art to art; 20
How oft review; each finding like a friend
Something to blame, and something to commend?

What flatt'ring scenes our wand'ring fancy wrought,
Rome's pompous glories rising to our thought!
Together o'er the Alps methinks we fly, 25
Fired with ideas of fair Italy.
With thee on Raphael's monument I mourn,
Or wait inspiring dreams at Maro's urn:
With thee repose where Tully once was laid,
Or seek some ruin's formidable shade: 30
While Fancy brings the banish'd piles to view,
And builds imaginary Rome anew.
Here thy well-studied marbles fix our eye;
A fading fresco here demands a sigh;
Each heavenly piece unwearied we compare, 35
Match Raphael's grace with thy loved Guido's air,
Carracci's strength, Correggio's softer line,
Paulo's free stroke, and Titian's warmth divine.
How finish'd with illustrious toil appears
This small, well-polish'd Gem, the work of years! 40
Yet still how faint by precept is express'd
The living image in the painter's breast!
Thence endless streams of fair ideas flow,
Strike in the sketch, or in the picture glow;
Thence Beauty, waking all her forms, supplies 45
An angel's sweetness, or Bridgewater's eyes.

Muse! at that name thy sacred sorrows shed,

Those tears eternal, that embalm the dead:
Call round her tomb each object of desire,
Each purer frame inform'd with purer fire: 50
Bid her be all that cheers or softens life,
The tender sister, daughter, friend, and wife:
Bid her be all that makes mankind adore;
Then view this marble, and be vain no more!

Yet still her charms in breathing paint engage;   55
Her modest cheek shall warm a future age.
Beauty, frail flower that ev'ry season fears,
Blooms in thy colours for a thousand years.
Thus Churchill's race shall other hearts surprise,
And other beauties envy Worsley's eyes;   60
Each pleasing Blount shall endless smiles bestow,
And soft Belinda's blush for ever glow.[1]

Oh lasting as those colours may they shine,
Free as thy stroke, yet faultless as thy line;
New graces yearly like thy works display,   65
Soft without weakness, without glaring gay;
Led by some rule, that guides, but not constrains;
And finish'd more through happiness than pains.
The kindred arts shall in their praise conspire,
One dip the pencil, and one string the lyre.   70
Yet should the Graces all thy figures place,
And breathe an air divine on ev'ry face;
Yet should the Muses bid my numbers roll
Strong as their charms, and gentle as their soul;
With Zeuxis' Helen thy Bridgewater vie,   75
And these be sung till Granville's Myra die:
Alas! how little from the grave we claim!
Thou but preserv'st a face, and I a name.

---

[1] The ladies grouped together in this passage were all remarkable for
their beauty. The " Churchill race " were the four celebrated daughters of
the great duke, the Countess of Godolphin (afterwards Duchess of Marl-
borough, Congreve's friend), the Countess of Sunderland, the Countess of
Bridgewater, and Mary, Duchess of Montagu. Lady Worsley, the mother
of Lady Carteret, was the wife of Sir Robert Worsley, Bart., of Appulder-
combe, in the Isle of Wight; and " soft Belinda " was Arabella Fermor.

TO MISS BLOUNT[1]

WITH THE WORKS OF VOITURE

In these gay thoughts the Loves and Graces shine,
And all the writer lives in ev'ry line;
His easy art may happy nature seem,
Trifles themselves are elegant in him.
Sure to charm all was his peculiar fate,   5
Who without flattery pleased the fair and great;
Still with esteem no less conversed than read;
With wit well-natured, and with books well-bred;
His heart, his mistress and his friend did share,
His time, the Muse, the witty and the fair.   10
Thus wisely careless, innocently gay,
Cheerful he play'd the trifle, Life, away;
Till fate scarce felt his gentle breath suppressed,
As smiling infants sport themselves to rest.
Even rival wits did Voiture's death deplore,   15
And the gay mourn'd who never mourn'd before;
The truest hearts for Voiture heaved with sighs,
Voiture was wept by all the brightest eyes:
The Smiles and Loves had died in Voiture's death,
But that for ever in his lines they breathe.   20
  Let the strict life of graver mortals be
A long, exact, and serious comedy;
In ev'ry scene some moral let it teach,
And, if it can, at once both please and preach.
Let mine, an innocent gay farce appear,   25
And more diverting still than regular,
Have humour, wit, a native ease and grace,
Though not too strictly bound to time and place:
Critics in wit, or life, are hard to please,
Few write to those, and none can live to these.   30
  Too much your sex is by their forms confined,
Severe to all, but most to womankind;
Custom, grown blind with age, must be your guide;
Your pleasure is a vice, but not your pride;
By nature yielding, stubborn but for fame;   35
Made slaves by honour, and made fools by shame.
Marriage may all those petty tyrants chase,
But sets up one, a greater, in their place:

[1] Almost certainly Martha Blount.

Well might you wish for change by those accursed,
But the last tyrant ever proves the worst.   40
Still in constraint your suff'ring sex remains,
Or bound in formal or in real chains:
Whole years neglected, for some months adored,
The fawning servant turns a haughty lord.
Ah quit not the free innocence of life,   45
For the dull glory of a virtuous wife;
Nor let false shows nor empty titles please:
Aim not at joy, but rest content with ease.

The gods, to curse Pamela with her prayers,
Gave the gilt coach and dappled Flanders mares,   50
The shining robes, rich jewels, beds of state,
And, to complete her bliss, a fool for mate.
She glares in balls, front boxes, and the Ring,
A vain, unquiet, glitt'ring, wretched thing!
Pride, pomp, and state but reach her outward part;   55
She sighs, and is no duchess at her heart.

But Madam, if the Fates withstand, and you
Are destined Hymen's willing victim too;
Trust not too much your now resistless charms,
Those, age or sickness soon or late disarms: 60
Good humour only teaches charms to last,
Still makes new conquests, and maintains the past:
Love, raised on beauty, will like that decay,
Our hearts may bear its slender chain a day;
As flowery bands in wantonness are worn,   65
A morning's pleasure, and at evening torn;
This binds in ties more easy, yet more strong,
The willing heart, and only holds it long.

Thus Voiture's early care still shone the same,
And Monthausier was only changed in name;   70
By this, ev'n now they live, ev'n now they charm,
Their wit still sparkling, and their flames still warm.

Now crown'd with myrtle, on th' Elysian coast,
Amid those lovers, joys his gentle ghost:
Pleased, while with smiles his happy lines you view,   75
And finds a fairer Rambouillet in you.
The brightest eyes in France inspired his Muse;
The brightest eyes of Britain now peruse;
And dead, as living, 'tis our author's pride
Still to charm those who charm the world beside.   80

TO THE SAME

ON HER LEAVING THE TOWN AFTER THE CORONATION [1]

As some fond virgin, whom her mother's care
Drags from the town to wholesome country air,
Just when she learns to roll a melting eye,
And hear a spark, yet think no danger nigh;
From the dear man unwilling she must sever,   5
Yet takes one kiss before she parts for ever:
Thus from the world fair Zephalinda flew,
Saw others happy, and with sighs withdrew;
Not that their pleasures caused her discontent,
She sigh'd not that they stay'd, but that she went.   10

　　She went to plain-work, and to purling brooks,
Old-fashion'd halls, dull aunts, and croaking rooks:
She went from opera, park, assembly, play,
To morning walks, and prayers three hours a-day;
To part her time 'twixt reading and bohea,   15
To muse, and spill her solitary tea,
Or o'er cold coffee trifle with the spoon,
Count the slow clock, and dine exact at noon;
Divert her eyes with pictures in the fire,
Hum half a tune, tell stories to the 'squire;   20
Up to her godly garret after seven,
There starve and pray, for that's the way to Heaven.

　　Some 'squire, perhaps, you take delight to rack;
Whose game is whisk, whose treat a toast in sack;
Who visits with a gun, presents you birds,   25
Then gives a smacking buss and cries,—No words!
Or with his hound comes hallooing from the stable,
Makes love with nods, and knees beneath a table;
Whose laughs are hearty, though his jests are coarse,
And loves you best of all things—but his horse.   30

　　In some fair ev'ning, on your elbow laid,
You dream of triumphs in the rural shade;
In pensive thought recall the fancied scene,
See coronations rise on ev'ry green;
Before you pass th' imaginary sights   35
Of lords, and earls, and dukes, and garter'd knights,
While the spread fan o'ershades your closing eyes;
Then give one flirt, and all the vision flies.

[1] Of King George the First, 1715. [The poet was careless as to dates.
The coronation of George I. took place on 20th October, 1714.]
　　In spite of the title, this is certainly addressed to Teresa Blount.

Thus vanish sceptres, coronets, and balls,
And leave you in lone woods, or empty walls!　　40
　So when your slave, at some dear idle time,
(Not plagued with head-aches, or the want of rhyme)
Stands in the streets, abstracted from the crew,
And while he seems to study, thinks of you;
Just when his fancy points your sprightly eyes,　　45
Or sees the blush of soft Parthenia rise,[1]
Gay pats my shoulder, and you vanish quite,
Streets, chairs, and coxcombs rush upon my sight;
Vex'd to be still in town, I knit my brow,
Look sour, and hum a tune as you may now.　　50

TO MRS. M. B. ON HER BIRTHDAY [2]

OH be thou blest with all that Heaven can send,
Long health, long youth, long pleasure, and a friend:
Not with those toys the female world admire,
Riches that vex, and vanities that tire.
With added years, if life bring nothing new,　　5
But like a sieve let every blessing through,
Some joy still lost, as each vain year runs o'er,
And all we gain, some sad reflection more;
Is that a birthday? 'tis alas! too clear,
'Tis but the funeral of the former year.　　10
　Let joy or ease, let affluence or content,
And the gay conscience of a life well spent,
Calm ev'ry thought, inspirit ev'ry grace,
Glow in thy heart and smile upon thy face.
Let day improve on day, and year on year,　　15
Without a pain, a trouble, or a fear;
Till death unfelt that tender frame destroy,
In some soft dream, or ecstasy of joy,
Peaceful sleep out the Sabbath of the tomb,
And wake to raptures in a life to come.　　20

[1] In the original it is "the blush of Parthenissa," which was the fanciful designation of Martha Blount in the correspondence of the sisters with James Moore, as Zephalinda was of Teresa.
[2] Martha Blount was the lady addressed. The original copy of the verses is preserved at Mapledurham, addressed to Martha, and entitled "Written June 15, on your Birth-day, 1723." In a letter written in 1724, on the anniversary of Miss Blount's birthday, Pope says, "Were I to tell you what I wish for you in particular, it would be only to repeat in prose what I told you last year in rhyme, so sincere is my poetry."

TO MR. THOMAS SOUTHERN

ON HIS BIRTHDAY, 1742

RESIGN'D to live, prepared to die,
With not one sin but poetry,
This day Tom's fair account has run
(Without a blot) to eighty-one.
Kind Boyle, before his poet lays   5
A table, with a cloth of bays; [1]
And Ireland, mother of sweet singers,
Presents his harp still to his fingers. [2]
The feast, his tow'ring genius marks
In yonder wild-goose and the larks!   10
The mushrooms show his wit was sudden!
And for his judgment, lo a pudden!
Roast beef, though old, proclaims him stout,
And grace, although a bard, devout.
May Tom, whom Heaven sent down to raise   15
The price of prologues and of plays, [3]
Be ev'ry birthday more a winner,
Digest his thirty-thousandth dinner;
Walk to his grave without reproach,
And scorn a rascal and a coach.   20

TO MR. JOHN MOORE

AUTHOR OF THE CELEBRATED WORM-POWDER

How much, egregious Moore, are we
Deceived by shows and forms!
Whate'er we think, whate'er we see,
All human kind are worms.

[1] He was invited to dine on his birthday with this nobleman, who had prepared for him the entertainment of which the bill of fare is here set down.—WARBURTON.

[2] The harp is generally wove on the Irish linen, etc.—WARBURTON.

[3] Alludes to a story Mr. Southern told of Dryden. Dryden was so famous for his prologues that the players would act nothing without that decoration. His usual price had been four guineas: but when Southern came to him for the prologue he had bespoke, Dryden told him he must have six guineas for it; " which," said he, " young man, is out of no disrespect to you; but the players have had my goods too cheap."—WARBURTON.

Man is a very worm by birth,   5
    Vile reptile, weak and vain:
Awhile he crawls upon the earth,
    Then shrinks to earth again.

That woman is a worm, we find
    E'er since our grandame's evil;   10
She first conversed with her own kind,
    That ancient worm, the devil.

The learn'd themselves we book-worms name,
    The blockhead is a slow-worm;
The nymph whose tail is all on flame,   15
    Is aptly term'd a glow-worm.

The fops are painted butterflies,
    That flutter for a day;
First from a worm they take their rise,
    And in a worm decay.   20

The flatterer an earwig grows;
    Thus worms suit all conditions;
Misers are muck-worms, silk-worms beaus,
    And death-watches physicians.

That statesmen have the worm, is seen   25
    By all their winding play;
Their conscience is a worm within,
    That gnaws them night and day.

Ah, Moore! thy skill were well employ'd,
    And greater gain would rise,   30
If thou could'st make the courtier void
    The worm that never dies!

O learned Friend of Abchurch Lane,
    Who sett'st our entrails free;
Vain is thy art, thy powder vain,   35
    Since worms shall eat e'en thee.[1]

[1] The *Gentleman's Magazine* announces the death of this worthy as
having taken place 12th April, 1737. "He will now shortly," says the
grave Sylvanus Urban, "verify Mr. Pope's witty observation, ' O learned
Friend,' etc." Pope's " Epistle to Moore " was an early production, and
first published in 1716.

Our fate thou only canst adjourn
   Some few short years, no more!
Ev'n Button's wits to worms shall turn,
   Who maggots were before.   40

TO MR. C., ST. JAMES'S PLACE [1]

Oct. 22.

FEW words aré best; I wish you well:
   Bethel, I'm told, will soon be here;
Some morning walks along the Mall,
   And evening friends will end the year.

If in this interval, between   5
   The falling leaf and coming frost,
You please to see, on Twit'nam green,
   Your friend, your poet, and your host:

For three whole days you here may rest
   From office business, news and strife;   10
And (what most folks would think a jest)
   Want nothing else except your wife.

EPITAPHS

His saltem accumulem donis, et fungar inani
Munere!—VIRG.

[This unavailing gift at least I may bestow.—DRYDEN.]

I

ON CHARLES, EARL OF DORSET

IN THE CHURCH OF WITHYAM IN SUSSEX

DORSET, the grace of Courts, the Muses' pride,
Patron of arts, and judge of Nature, died.
The scourge of pride, though sanctified or great,
Of fops in learning, and of knaves in state:
Yet soft his nature, though severe his lay,   5
His anger moral, and his wisdom gay.

[1] William Cleland, who lived in St. James's Place, where he died in 1741. He wrote, or at least signed, the letter prefacing the 1729 *Dunciad.*

Bless'd satirist! who touch'd the mean so true,
As show'd vice had his hate, and pity too.
Bless'd courtier! who could king and country please,
Yet sacred keep his friendships, and his ease.   10
Bless'd peer! his great forefathers' every grace
Reflecting, and reflected in his race;
Where other BUCKHURSTS, other DORSETS shine,
And patriots still, or poets, deck the line.

II

ON SIR WILLIAM TRUMBULL

ONE OF THE PRINCIPAL SECRETARIES OF STATE TO KING
WILLIAM III., WHO, HAVING RESIGNED HIS PLACE, DIED IN HIS
RETIREMENT AT EASTHAMPSTEAD IN BERKSHIRE, 1716

A PLEASING form; a firm, yet cautious mind;
Sincere, though prudent; constant, yet resign'd:
Honour unchanged, a principle professed,
Fix'd to one side, but moderate to the rest:
An honest courtier, yet a patriot too;   5
Just to his Prince, and to his country true:
Fill'd with the sense of age, the fire of youth,
A scorn of wrangling, yet a zeal for truth;
A generous faith, from superstition free;
A love to peace, and hate of tyranny;   10
Such this man was; who now, from earth removed,
At length enjoys that liberty he loved.

III

ON THE HON. SIMON HARCOURT

ONLY SON OF THE LORD CHANCELLOR HARCOURT; AT THE CHURCH
OF STANTON HARCOURT, IN OXFORDSHIRE, 1720

To this sad shrine, whoe'er thou art! draw near,
Here lies the friend most loved, the son most dear:
Who ne'er knew joy but friendship might divide,
Or gave his father grief but when he died.
    How vain is Reason, Eloquence how weak!   5
If Pope must tell what HARCOURT cannot speak.
Oh let thy once-loved friend inscribe thy stone,
And with a father's sorrows mix his own!

IV

ON JAMES CRAGGS, ESQ.

IN WESTMINSTER ABBEY

JACOBUS CRAGGS,
REGI MAGNÆ BRITANNIÆ A SECRETIS
ET CONSILIIS SANCTIORIBUS,
PRINCIPIS PARITER AC POPULI AMOR ET DELICIÆ;
VIXIT TITULIS ET INVIDIA MAJOR
ANNOS, HEU PAUCOS, XXXV.
OB. FEB. XVI. MDCCXX.

STATESMAN, yet friend to Truth! of soul sincere,
In action faithful, and in honour clear!
Who broke no promise, served no private end,
Who gain'd no title, and who lost no friend;
Ennobled by himself, by all approved,   5
Praised, wept, and honour'd, by the Muse he loved.

V

INTENDED FOR MR. ROWE

IN WESTMINSTER ABBEY

THY reliques, ROWE, to this fair urn we trust,
And sacred, place by DRYDEN's awful dust:
Beneath a rude and nameless stone he lies,[1]
To which thy tomb shall guide inquiring eyes.
Peace to thy gentle shade, and endless rest!   5
Bless'd in thy genius, in thy love too blest!
One grateful woman to thy fame supplies
What a whole thankless land to his denies.

This epitaph, altered by Pope, now stands as follows on the monument in the Abbey to Rowe and his daughter:

Thy reliques, Rowe! to this sad shrine we trust,
And near thy Shakespeare place thy honoured bust,
Oh, next him, skill'd to draw the tender tear,
For never heart felt passion more sincere;
To nobler sentiment to fire the brave,
For never Briton more disdain'd a slave.
Peace to thy gentle shade, and endless rest;
Bless'd in thy genius, in thy love too blest!
And bless'd, that timely from our scene removed,
Thy soul enjoys the liberty it loved.

To these so mourn'd in death, so loved in life!
The childless parent, and the widow'd wife,
With tears inscribes this monumental stone,
That holds their ashes, and expects her own.

[1] The tomb of Dryden was erected on this hint of Pope's by the Duke of Buckingham.

VI

ON MRS. CORBET

WHO DIED OF A CANCER IN HER BREAST

HERE rests a woman, good without pretence,
Bless'd with plain reason, and with sober sense:
No conquests she, but o'er herself, desired;
Nor arts essay'd, but not to be admired.
Passion and Pride were to her soul unknown,   5
Convinced that Virtue only is our own;
So unaffected, so composed a mind;
So firm, yet soft; so strong, yet so refined;
Heaven, as its purest gold, by tortures tried!
The saint sustain'd it, but the woman died.   10

VII

ON THE MONUMENT OF THE HONOURABLE ROBERT DIGBY AND HIS SISTER MARY

ERECTED BY THEIR FATHER THE LORD DIGBY, IN THE CHURCH OF SHERBOURNE IN DORSETSHIRE, 1727

Go! fair example of untainted youth,
Of modest wisdom, and pacific truth:
Composed in sufferings, and in joy sedate,
Good without noise, without pretension great:
Just of thy word, in every thought sincere,   5
Who knew no wish but what the world might hear:
Of softest manners, unaffected mind,
Lover of peace, and friend of human kind:
Go live! for Heaven's eternal year is thine,
Go, and exalt thy moral to divine.   10
   And thou, bless'd maid! attendant on his doom,
Pensive hast follow'd to the silent tomb,
Steer'd the same course to the same quiet shore,
Not parted long, and now to part no more!
Go then, where only bliss sincere is known!   15
Go, where to love and to enjoy are one!
   Yet take these tears, Mortality's relief,
And till we share your joys, forgive our grief:
These little rites, a stone, a verse receive;
'Tis all a father, all a friend can give!   20

VIII

ON SIR GODFREY KNELLER

IN WESTMINSTER ABBEY, 1723

KNELLER, by Heaven and not a master taught,
Whose art was Nature, and whose pictures Thought;
Now for two ages having snatch'd from Fate
Whate'er was beauteous, or whate'er was great,
Lies crown'd with princes, honours, poets' lays,   5
Due to his merit, and brave thirst of praise.
  Living, great Nature fear'd he might outvie
Her works; and dying, fears herself may die.

IX

ON GENERAL HENRY WITHERS

IN WESTMINSTER ABBEY, 1729

HERE, WITHERS, rest! thou bravest, gentlest mind,
Thy country's friend, but more of human kind.
Oh born to arms! Oh worth in youth approved!
Oh soft humanity, in age beloved!
For thee the hardy veteran drops a tear,   5
And the gay courtier feels the sigh sincere.
  WITHERS, adieu! yet not with thee remove
Thy martial spirit, or thy social love!
Amidst corruption, luxury, and rage,
Still leave some ancient virtues to our age;   10
Nor let us say, (those English glories gone)
The last true Briton lies beneath this stone.

X

ON MR. ELIJAH FENTON

AT EASTHAMPSTEAD IN BERKS, 1730

THIS modest stone, what few vain marbles can,
May truly say, Here lies an honest man;
A poet bless'd beyond the poet's fate,
Whom Heaven kept sacred from the proud and great:

Foe to loud praise, and friend to learned ease, 5
Content with science in the vale of peace,
Calmly he look'd on either life, and here
Saw nothing to regret, or there to fear;
From Nature's temperate feast rose satisfied,
Thanked Heaven that he had lived, and that he died. 10

XI

ON MR. GAY

IN WESTMINSTER ABBEY, 1732

Of manners gentle, of affections mild;
In wit, a man; simplicity, a child:
With native humour tempering virtuous rage,
Form'd to delight at once and lash the age:
Above temptation in a low estate, 5
And uncorrupted, ev'n among the great:
A safe companion, and an easy friend,
Unblamed through life, lamented in thy end.
These are thy honours! not that here thy bust
Is mix'd with heroes, or with kings thy dust; 10
But that the worthy and the good shall say,
Striking their pensive bosoms—Here lies GAY.

XII

INTENDED FOR SIR ISAAC NEWTON

IN WESTMINSTER ABBEY

ISAACUS NEWTONUS:
QUEM IMMORTALEM
TESTANTUR TEMPUS, NATURA, CŒLUM:
MORTALEM
HOC MARMOR FATETUR.

Nature and Nature's laws lay hid in night:
God said, Let Newton be! and all was light.

XIII

ON DR. FRANCIS ATTERBURY, BISHOP OF ROCHESTER

WHO DIED IN EXILE AT PARIS, 1732

[His only daughter having expired in his arms, immediately after she arrived in France to see him.]

DIALOGUE

SHE

YES, we have lived—one pang, and then we part!
May Heaven, dear Father! now have all thy heart.
Yet ah! how once we loved, remember still,
Till you are dust like me.

HE

        Dear shade! I will:
Then mix this dust with thine—O spotless ghost!   5
O more than fortune, friends, or country lost!
Is there on earth one care, one wish beside?
Yes—Save my country, Heaven!
                —He said, and died.

XIV

ON EDMUND, DUKE OF BUCKINGHAM

WHO DIED IN THE NINETEENTH YEAR OF HIS AGE, 1735

IF modest youth, with cool reflection crown'd,
And every opening virtue blooming round,
Could save a parent's justest pride from Fate,
Or add one patriot to a sinking state;
This weeping marble had not ask'd thy tear,   5
Or sadly told how many hopes lie here!
The living virtue now had shone approved,
The senate heard him, and his country loved.
Yet softer honours, and less noisy fame
Attend the shade of gentle BUCKINGHAM;   10
In whom a race, for courage famed and art,
Ends in the milder merit of the heart,
And chiefs or sages long to Britain given,
Pays the last tribute of a saint to Heaven.

XV

FOR ONE WHO WOULD NOT BE BURIED IN WESTMINSTER ABBEY

HEROES, and kings! your distance keep:
In peace let one poor poet sleep,
Who never flatter'd folks like you:
Let Horace blush, and Virgil too.

XVI

ON HIMSELF

UNDER this marble, or under this sill,
Or under this turf, or e'en what they will;
Whatever an heir, or a friend in his stead,
Or any good creature shall lay o'er my head,
Lies one who ne'er cared, and still cares not a pin   5
What they said, or may say, of the mortal within;
But who, living and dying, serene still and free,
Trusts in God, that as well as he was, he shall be.

XVII

ON TWO LOVERS STRUCK DEAD BY LIGHTNING

WHEN Eastern lovers feed the funeral fire,
On the same pile the faithful pair expire:
Here pitying Heaven that virtue mutual found,
And blasted both, that it might neither wound.
Hearts so sincere th' Almighty saw well pleased,   5
Sent his own lightning, and the victims seized.

Lord Harcourt, on whose property the unfortunate pair lived,
feared the country people would not understand the above, and
Pope wrote another version:

NEAR THIS PLACE LIE THE BODIES OF
JOHN HEWET AND SARAH DREW,
AN INDUSTRIOUS YOUNG MAN
AND VIRTUOUS MAIDEN OF THIS PARISH;
WHO, BEING AT HARVEST WORK
(WITH SEVERAL OTHERS),
WERE IN ONE INSTANT KILLED BY LIGHTNING,
THE LAST DAY OF JULY, 1718.

THINK not, by rigorous judgment seized,
  A pair so faithful could expire;
Victims so pure Heaven saw well pleased,
  And snatch'd them in celestial fire.

Live well, and fear no sudden fate;   5
  When God calls Virtue to the grave!
Alike 'tis justice soon or late,
  Mercy alike to kill or save.

Virtue unmoved can hear the call,
  And face the flash that melts the ball.   10

THE DUNCIAD

TO DR. JONATHAN SWIFT

BOOK THE FIRST

ARGUMENT

The proposition, the invocation, and the inscription. Then the original of the great empire of Dulness, and cause of the continuance thereof. The college of the goddess in the city, with her private academy for poets in particular; the governors of it, and the four cardinal virtues. Then the poem hastes into the midst of things, presenting her on the evening of a Lord Mayor's day, revolving the long succession of her sons, and the glories past and to come. She fixes her eyes on Bays to be the instrument of that great event which is the subject of the poem. He is described pensive among his books, giving up the cause, and apprehending the period of her empire: after debating whether to betake himself to the church, or to gaming, or to party-writing, he raises an altar of proper books, and (making first his solemn prayer and declaration) purposes thereon to sacrifice all his unsuccessful writings. As the pile is kindled, the goddess, beholding the flame from her seat, flies and puts it out by casting upon it the poem of Thulé. She forthwith reveals herself to him, transports him to her temple, unfolds her arts, and initiates him into her mysteries; then announcing the death of Eusden, the Poet Laureate, anoints him, carries him to court, and proclaims him successor.

THE mighty mother, and her son, who brings
The Smithfield muses to the ear of kings,
I sing. Say you, her instruments, the great!
Call'd to this work by Dulness, Jove, and Fate;
You by whose care, in vain decried, and curst,   5

Still Dunce the second reigns like Dunce the first;
Say, how the goddess bade Britannia sleep,
And pour'd her spirit o'er the land and deep.

    In eldest time, ere mortals writ or read,
Ere Pallas issued from the Thunderer's head,   10
Dulness o'er all possess'd her ancient right,
Daughter of Chaos and eternal Night:
Fate in their dotage this fair idiot gave,
Gross as her sire, and as her mother grave,
Laborious, heavy, busy, bold, and blind,   15
She ruled, in native anarchy, the mind.

    Still her old empire to restore she tries,
For, born a goddess, Dulness never dies.

    O thou! whatever title please thine ear,
Dean, Drapier, Bickerstaff, or Gulliver!   20
Whether thou choose Cervantes' serious air,
Or laugh and shake in Rabelais' easy chair,
Or praise the court, or magnify mankind,
Or thy grieved country's copper chains unbind;
From thy Bœotia though her pow'r retires,   25
Mourn not, my Swift, at aught our realm acquires.
Here pleased behold her mighty wings outspread
To hatch a new Saturnian age of lead.[1]

    Close to those walls[2] where Folly holds her throne,
And laughs to think Monro would take her down,   30
Where o'er the gates, by his famed father's hand,
Great Cibber's brazen, brainless brothers stand;
One cell there is, conceal'd from vulgar eye,
The cave of Poverty and Poetry.
Keen, hollow winds howl through the bleak recess,   35
Emblem of music caused by emptiness.
Hence bards, like Proteus long in vain tied down,
Escape in monsters, and amaze the town.
Hence miscellanies spring, the weekly boast
Of Curll's chaste press, and Lintot's rubric post: 40
Hence hymning Tyburn's elegiac lines,
Hence journals, medleys, merc'ries, magazines:
Sepulchral lies, our holy walls to grace,
And new-year odes, and all the Grub Street race.

    In clouded majesty here Dulness shone;   45
Four guardian virtues, round, support her throne:

[1] The ancient golden age is by poets styled Saturnian; but in the chemical language Saturn is lead.—P.   [2] Bedlam. Two statues by Cibber's father stood at the gates: they were actually of stone.

Fierce champion Fortitude, that knows no fears
Of hisses, blows, or want, or loss of ears:
Calm Temperance, whose blessings those partake
Who hunger and who thirst for scribbling sake: 50
Prudence, whose glass presents th' approaching jail:
Poetic justice, with her lifted scale,
Where, in nice balance, truth with gold she weighs,
And solid pudding against empty praise.
    Here she beholds the chaos dark and deep, 55
Where nameless somethings in their causes sleep,
Till Genial Jacob,[1] or a warm third day,
Call forth each mass, a poem, or a play:
How hints, like spawn, scarce quick in embryo lie,
How new-born nonsense first is taught to cry, 60
Maggots half-form'd in rhyme exactly meet,
And learn to crawl upon poetic feet.
Here one poor word an hundred clenches makes,
And ductile Dulness new meanders takes;
There motley images her fancy strike, 65
Figures ill-pair'd, and similes unlike.
She sees a mob of metaphors advance,
Pleased with the madness of the mazy dance!
How tragedy and comedy embrace;
How farce and epic get a jumbled race; 70
How Time himself stands still at her command,
Realms shift their place, and ocean turns to land.
Here gay Description Egypt glads with show'rs,
Or gives to Zembla fruits, to Barca flow'rs;
Glitt'ring with ice here hoary hills are seen, 75
There painted valleys of eternal green.
In cold December fragrant chaplets blow,
And heavy harvests nod beneath the snow.
    All these, and more, the cloud-compelling queen
Beholds through fogs, that magnify the scene. 80
She, tinsell'd o'er in robes of varying hues,
With self-applause her wild creation views;
Sees momentary monsters rise and fall,
And with her own fool's-colours gilds them all.
    'Twas on the day, when Thorold rich and grave,[2] 85
Like Cimon, triumph'd both on land and wave:

---

[1] "Genial Jacob" was the publisher, Jacob Tonson, who specialised in plays. He had been secretary to the Kit-Cat Club.
[2] Sir George Thorold, Lord Mayor of London, 1720.

(Pomps without guilt, of bloodless swords and maces,
Glad chains, warm furs, broad banners, and broad faces)
Now night descending, the proud scene was o'er,
But lived, in Settle's numbers, one day more.[1]   90
Now mayors and shrieves all hush'd and satiate lay,
Yet eat, in dreams, the custard of the day;
While pensive poets painful vigils keep,
Sleepless themselves to give their readers sleep.
Much to the mindful queen the feast recalls   95
What city swans once sung within the walls;
Much she revolves their arts, their ancient praise,
And sure succession down from Heywood's days.[2]
She saw, with joy, the line immortal run,
Each sire impress'd and glaring in his son: 100
So watchful Bruin forms, with plastic care,
Each growing lump, and brings it to a bear.
She saw old Pryn in restless Daniel shine,[3]
And Eusden eke out Blackmore's endless line;[4]
She saw slow Philips creep like Tate's poor page,[5]   105
And all the mighty mad in Dennis rage.[6]
  In each she marks her image full express'd,
But chief in Bays's monster-breeding breast;[7]
Bays, form'd by Nature stage and town to bless,
And act, and be, a coxcomb with success.   110
Dulness with transport eyes the lively dunce,
Rememb'ring she herself was Pertness once.
Now (shame to Fortune!) an ill run at play
Blank'd his bold visage, and a thin third day:
Swearing and supperless the hero sate,   115
Blasphemed his gods, the dice, and damn'd his fate.
Then gnaw'd his pen, then dash'd it on the ground,
Sinking from thought to thought, a vast profound!
Plunged for his sense, but found no bottom there,
Yet wrote and flounder'd on, in mere despair.   120
Round him much embryo, much abortion lay,
Much future ode, and abdicated play;
Nonsense precipitate, like running lead,

[1] Settle, last official city-poet.
[2] John Heywood, the interlude-writer. (Pope) A confusion with Thomas Heywood.
[3] W. Prynne and Daniel Defoe.
[4] Lawrence Eusden, Poet Laureate, and Sir Richard Blackmore (see Book II.).
[5] Ambrose Philips and Nahum Tate.
[6] John Dennis, Pope's butt and critic.
[7] By Bays, Colley Cibber, Poet Laureate, is meant.

That slipp'd through cracks and zig-zags of the head;
All that on Folly Frenzy could beget,   125
Fruits of dull heat, and sooterkins of wit.
Next, o'er his books his eyes began to roll,
In pleasing memory of all he stole,
How here he sipped, how there he plundered snug,
And sucked all o'er, like an industrious bug.   130
Here lay poor Fletcher's half-eat scenes, and here
The frippery of crucified Molière;
There hapless Shakespeare, yet of Tibbald sore,[1]
Wished he had blotted for himself before.
The rest on outside merit but presume,   135
Or serve (like other fools) to fill a room;
Such with their shelves as due proportion hold,
Or their fond parents dressed in red and gold;
Or where the pictures for the page atone,
And Quarles[2] is saved by beauties not his own.   140
Here swells the shelf with Ogilby the great;[3]
There, stamped with arms, Newcastle shines complete:[4]
Here all his suff'ring brotherhood retire,
And 'scape the martyrdom of jakes and fire:
A Gothic library! of Greece and Rome   145
Well purged, and worthy Settle, Banks, and Broome.[5]
    But, high above, more solid learning shone,
The classics of an age that heard of none;
There Caxton slept, with Wynkyn at his side,[6]
One clasped in wood, and one in strong cow-hide.   150
There saved by spice, like mummies, many a year,
Dry bodies of divinity appear;

[1] Theobald, the editor of Shakespeare, who had criticised Pope's edition.
[2] The pictures illustrating Quarles's *Emblems*.
[3] John Ogilby translated Virgil and Homer, both illustrated, also a magnificent Bible, with prints.
[4] Margaret Cavendish, Duchess of Newcastle. Her works in folio were elegantly bound, and stamped with the ducal arms.
[5] The poet has mentioned these three authors in particular, as they are parallel to our hero in three capacities: (1) Settle was his brother Laureate; only indeed upon half-pay, for the city instead of the court; but equally famous for unintelligible flights in his poems on public occasions, such as shows, birthdays, etc. (2) Banks was his rival in tragedy (though more successful) in one of his tragedies, the *Earl of Essex*, which is yet alive: *Anna Boleyn*, the *Queen of Scots* and *Cyrus the Great* are dead and gone. These he dressed in a sort of beggar's velvet, or a happy mixture of the thick fustian and thin prosaic; exactly imitated in *Perolla and Isidora*, *Cæsar in Egypt* and the *Heroic Daughter*. (3) Broome was a serving-man of Ben Jonson, who once picked up a comedy from his betters, or from some cast scenes of his master, not entirely contemptible.—WARBURTON.
[6] William Caxton and Wynkyn de Worde.

De Lyra [1] there a dreadful front extends,
And here the groaning shelves Philemon [2] bends.
  Of these, twelve volumes, twelve of amplest size,   155
Redeemed from tapers and defrauded pies,
Inspired he seizes; these an altar raise;
An hecatomb of pure unsullied lays
That altar crowns; a folio common-place
Founds the whole pile, of all his works the base;   160
Quartos, octavos, shape the less'ning pyre;
A twisted birthday ode completes the spire.
  Then he: "Great tamer of all human art!
First in my care, and ever at my heart;
Dulness! whose good old cause I yet defend,   165
With whom my muse began, with whom shall end,
E'er since Sir Fopling's periwig [3] was praise,
To the last honours of the Butt [4] and Bays;
O thou! of bus'ness the directing soul!
To this our head like bias to the bowl,   170
Which, as more pond'rous, made its aim more true,
Obliquely waddling to the mark in view:
O! ever gracious to perplexed mankind,
Still spread a healing mist before the mind;
And, lest we err by wit's wild dancing light,   175
Secure us kindly in our native night.
Or, if to wit a coxcomb make pretence,
Guard the sure barrier between that and sense;
Or quite unravel all the reas'ning thread,
And hang some curious cobweb in its stead!   180
As, forced from wind-guns, lead itself can fly,
And pond'rous slugs cut swiftly through the sky;
As clocks to weight their nimble motion owe,
The wheels above urged by the load below:
Me emptiness and dulness could inspire,   185
And were my elasticity and fire.
  Some demon stole my pen (forgive the offence)
And once betrayed me into common sense:

---

[1] De Lyra was a voluminous commentator, who died 1340.—WARTON.
[2] Philemon Holland. "He translated so many books that he might be called translator-general of his age."—WINSTANLY.
[3] The first visible cause of the passion of the town for our hero was a fair, flaxen, full-bottomed periwig, which, he tells us, he wore in his first play of *The Fool in Fashion*. This remarkable periwig usually made its entrance upon the stage in a sedan, brought in by two chairmen, with infinite approbation of the audience.—POPE.
[4] A butt of sack, part of the annual recompense of the Laureate.

Else all my prose and verse were much the same;
This prose on stilts, that poetry fall'n lame. 190
Did on the stage my fops appear confined?
My life gave ampler lessons to mankind.
Did the dead letter unsuccessful prove?
The brisk example never failed to move.
Yet sure had Heav'n decreed to save the state, 195
Heav'n had decreed these works a longer date.
Could Troy be saved by any single hand,
This grey-goose weapon must have made her stand.
What can I now? my Fletcher [1] cast aside,
Take up the Bible, once my better guide? [2] 200
Or tread the path by vent'rous heroes trod,
This box my thunder, this right hand my God?
Or chaired at White's amidst the doctors sit,
Teach oaths to gamesters, and to nobles wit?
Or bidst thou rather party to embrace? 205
(A friend to party thou, and all her race;
'Tis the same rope at different ends they twist;
To dulness Ridpath is as dear as Mist.) [3]
Shall I, like Curtius, desp'rate in my zeal,
O'er head and ears plunge for the commonweal? 210
Or rob Rome's ancient geese of all their glories,
And cackling save the monarchy of Tories?
Hold—to the minister I more incline;
To serve his cause, O queen! is serving thine.
And see! thy very gazetteers [4] give o'er, 215
Even Ralph repents, and Henley writes no more.
What then remains? Ourself. Still, still remain
Cibberian forehead, and Cibberian brain.
This brazen brightness, to the squire so dear;
This polished hardness, that reflects the peer: 220
This arch absurd, that wit and fool delights;
This mess, tossed up of Hockley-hole and White's;
Where dukes and butchers join to wreathe my crown,
At once the bear and fiddle of the town.
"O born in sin, and forth in folly brought! 225

---

[1] Fletcher's plays, to denote a favourite author.

[2] Cibber was sent to Winchester School at an early age with a view to a fellowship at New College.

[3] George Ridpath, author of a Whig paper called the *Flying-Post*; Nathaniel Mist, of a famous Tory paper, *Mist's Weekly Journal*.

[4] A band of ministerial writers who, on the very day their patron quitted his post, laid down their paper, and declared they would never more meddle in politics.—WARBURTON.

Works damned, or to be damned! (your father's fault)
Go, purified by flames ascend the sky,
My better and more Christian progeny!
Unstained, untouched, and yet in maiden sheets;
While all your smutty sisters walk the streets.   230
Ye shall not beg, like gratis-given Bland,[1]
Sent with a pass, and vagrant through the land;
Not sail with Ward, to ape-and-monkey climes,[2]
Where vile Mundungus trucks for viler rhymes:
Not sulphur-tipt, emblaze an ale-house fire;   235
Not wrap up oranges, to pelt your sire!
O! pass more innocent, in infant state,
To the mild limbo of our father Tate:[3]
Or peaceably forgot, at one be blest
In Shadwell's bosom with eternal rest!   240
Soon to that mass of nonsense to return,
Where things destroyed are swept to things unborn."

     With that, a tear (portentous sign of grace!)
Stole from the master of the seven-fold face;
And thrice he lifted high the birthday brand,   245
And thrice he dropt it from his quiv'ring hand;
Then lights the structure, with averted eyes:
The rolling smokes involve the sacrifice.
The opening clouds disclose each work by turns;
Now flames the Cid, and now Perolla burns;[4]   250
Great Cæsar roars, and hisses in the fires;
King John in silence modestly expires;
No merit now the dear Nonjuror[5] claims,
Molière's old stubble in a moment flames.
Tears gushed again, as from pale Priam's eyes   255

[1] It was a practice so to give the *Daily Gazetteer* and ministerial pamphlets (in which this B. was a writer), and send them post free over the kingdom. Bland was Provost of Eton.—WARTON.

[2] "Edward Ward, a voluminous poet in Hudibrastic verse, but best known by the *London Spy* in prose. He has of late years kept a public house in the city (but in a genteel way), and with his wit, humour and good liquor (ale) afforded his guests a pleasurable entertainment, especially those of the high-church party."—JACOB, *Lives of Poets*.

[3] Tate and Shadwell, two predecessors in the laurel.

[4] In the first notes on the *Dunciad* it was said that this author was particularly excellent at tragedy. "This (says he) is as unjust as to say I could not dance on a rope" 'But certain it is that he had attempted to dance on this rope, and fell most shamefully, having produced no less than four tragedies (the names of which the poet preserves in these few lines), the three first of them were fairly printed, acted and damned; the fourth suppressed, in fear of the like treatment.—POPE.

[5] A comedy (by Cibber) threshed out of Molière's *Tartuffe*.—POPE.

When the last blaze sent Ilion to the skies.

Roused by the light, old Dulness heaved the head,
Then snatched a sheet of Thulé [1] from her bed;
Sudden she flies, and whelms it o'er the pyre;
Down sink the flames, and with a hiss expire.   260

Her ample presence fills up all the place;
A veil of fogs dilates her awful face:
Great in her charms! as when on shrieves and may'rs
She looks, and breathes herself into their airs.
She bids him wait her to her sacred dome: 265
Well pleased he entered, and confessed his home.
So spirits ending their terrestrial race
Ascend, and recognise their native place.
This the great mother [2] dearer held than all
The clubs of Quidnuncs, or her own Guildhall: 270
Here stood her opium, here she nursed her owls,
And here she planned th' imperial seat of fools.

Here to her chosen all her works she shows;
Prose swelled to verse, verse loit'ring into prose:
How random thoughts now meaning chance to find,   275
Now leave all memory of sense behind;
How prologues into prefaces decay,
And these to notes are frittered quite away.
How index-learning turns no student pale,
Yet holds the eel of science by the tail: 280
How, with less reading than makes felons scape, [3]
Less human genius than God gives an ape,
Small thanks to France, and none to Rome or Greece,
A past, vamped, future, old, revived, new piece,
'Twixt Plautus, Fletcher, Shakespeare, and Corneille,   285
Can make a Cibber, Tibbald, [4] or Ozell. [5]

The Goddess then, o'er his anointed head,
With mystic words, the sacred opium shed.

---

[1] An unfinished poem of that name, of which one sheet was printed many years ago by Amb. Philips, a northern author. It is a usual method of putting out a fire to cast wet sheets upon it. Some critics have been of opinion that this sheet was of the nature of asbestos, which cannot be consumed by fire: but I rather think it an allegorical allusion to the coldness and heaviness of the writing.—POPE.

[2] *Magna mater*, here applied to dulness. The Quidnuncs, a name given to the ancient members of certain political clubs, who were constantly inquiring *quid nunc ?* what news?—POPE.

[3] Being able to read their " neck verse " before the gallows.

[4] Lewis Tibbald (as pronounced) or Theobald (as written).

[5] John Ozell has obliged the world with many translations of French plays.—POPE.

And lo! her bird (a monster of a fowl,
Something betwixt a Heideggre [1] and owl)   290
Perched on his crown. "All hail! and hail again,
My son: the promised land expects thy reign.
Know, Eusden thirsts no more for sack or praise;
He sleeps among the dull of ancient days;
Safe, where no critics damn, no duns molest,   295
Where wretched Withers,[2] Ward,[3] and Gildon [4] rest,
And high-born Howard,[5] more majestic sire,
With "Fool of Quality" completes the quire.
Thou, Cibber! thou, his laurel shalt support,
Folly, my son, has still a friend at court.   300
Lift up your gates, ye princes, see him come!
Sound, sound, ye viols; be the cat-call dumb!
Bring, bring the madding bay, the drunken vine;
The creeping, dirty, courtly ivy join.
And thou! his aide-de-camp, lead on my sons,   305
Light-armed with points, antitheses, and puns.
Let Bawdry, Billingsgate, my daughters dear,
Support his front, and oaths bring up the rear:
And under his, and under Archer's wing,
Gaming and Grub Street skulk behind the king.[6]   310
   " O! when shall rise a monarch all our own,
And I, a nursing-mother, rock the throne;
'Twixt prince and people close the curtain draw,
Shade him from light, and cover him from law;
Fatten the courtier, starve the learned band,   315
And suckle armies, and dry-nurse the land:
Till senates nod to lullabies divine,
And all be sleep, as at an ode of thine."

[1] A strange bird from Switzerland, and not (as some have supposed) the name of an eminent person who was a man of parts, and as was said of Petronius, *Arbiter Elegantiarum*.—POPE. [Heidegger became manager of the opera-house in London, by which he made £5000 a year.]
[2] George Withers, the poet.
[3] Ward wrote the *London Spy*, and turned *Don Quixote* into Hudibrastic verses.
[4] Charles Gildon, a writer of criticisms and libels, who abused Mr. Pope very scandalously.—POPE.
[5] Hon. Edward Howard, author of the *British Princes* and a great number of wonderful pieces.—POPE.
[6] When the statute against gaming was drawn up, it was represented that the king, by ancient custom, plays at hazard one night in the year; and therefore a clause was inserted with an exception as to that particular. Under this pretence the groom-porter (Archer) had a room appropriated to gaming all the summer the Court was at Kensington, which, his majesty accidentally being acquainted of, with a just indignation prohibited.—POPE.

She ceased. Then swells the chapel-royal throat:
"God save King Cibber!" mounts in every note.   320
Familiar White's, "God save King Colley!" cries;
"God save King Colley!" Drury Lane replies:
To Needham's quick the voice triumphal rode,
But pious Needham [1] dropt the name of God:
Back to the Devil [2] the last echoes roll,   325
And "Coll!" each butcher roars at Hockley Hole.
   So when Jove's block descended from on high
(As sings thy great forefather Ogilby [3])
Loud thunder to its bottom shook the bog,
And the hoarse nation croaked, "God save King Log!"   330

BOOK THE SECOND

ARGUMENT

The king being proclaimed, the solemnity is graced with public games and sports of various kinds; not instituted by the hero, as by Æneas in Virgil, but for greater honour by the goddess in person (in like manner as the games Pythia, Isthmia, etc., were anciently said to be ordained by the gods, and as Thetis herself appearing, according to Homer, *Odyss.* xxiv., proposed the prizes in honour of her son Achilles). Hither flock the poets and critics, attended, as is but just, with their patrons and booksellers. The goddess is first pleased, for her disport, to propose games to the booksellers, and setteth up the phantom of a poet, which they contend to overtake. The races described, with their divers accidents. Next, the game for a poetess. Then follow the exercises for the poets, of tickling, vociferating, diving: The first holds forth the arts and practices of dedicators, the second of disputants and fustian poets, the third of profound, dark, and dirty party-writers. Lastly, for the critics, the goddess proposes (with great propriety) an exercise, not of their parts, but their patience, in hearing the works of two voluminous authors, one in verse and the other in prose, deliberately read without sleeping. The various effects of which, with the several degrees and manners of their operation, are here set forth; till the whole number, not of critics only, but of spectators, actors, and all present, fall asleep; which naturally and necessarily ends the games.

---

[1] A matron of great fame, very religious in her way; whose constant prayer it was that she might "get enough by her profession to leave it off in time and make her peace with God." But her fate was not so happy; for being convicted and set in the pillory she was so ill used by the populace that it put an end to her days.—POPE.

[2] The Devil Tavern, in Fleet Street.

[3] See Ogilby's *Æsop's Fables*, where, in the story of the frogs and their king, this excellent hemistich is to be found.—POPE.

BOOK II

HIGH on a gorgeous seat, that far outshone
Henley's gilt tub,[1] or Fleckno's Irish throne,[2]
Or that where on her Curls the public pours,[3]
All-bounteous, fragrant grains and golden showers,
Great Cibber sate: The proud Parnassian sneer, 5
The conscious simper, and the jealous leer,
Mix in his look: all eyes direct their rays
On him, and crowds turn coxcombs as they gaze:
His peers shine round him with reflected grace:
New edge their dulness, and new bronze their face. 10
So from the sun's broad beam in shallow urns
Heav'ns twinkling sparks draw light, and point their horns.

 Not with more glee, by hands pontific crowned,
With scarlet hats wide-waving circled round,
Rome in her capitol saw Querno sit,[4] 15
Throned on seven hills, the antichrist of wit.

 And now the queen, to glad her sons, proclaims,
By herald hawkers, high heroic games.
They summon all her race: an endless band
Pours forth, and leaves unpeopled half the land, 20
A motley mixture! in long wigs, in bags,
In silks, in crapes, in Garters, and in rags,
From drawing-rooms, from colleges, from garrets,
On horse, on foot, in hacks, and gilded chariots:
All who true dunces in her cause appeared, 25
And all who knew those dunces to reward.

 Amid that area wide they took their stand,
Where the tall May-pole once o'er-looked the Strand.
But now (so Anne and piety ordain)
A church collects the saints of Drury Lane. 30
 With authors, stationers obeyed the call,
(The field of glory is a field for all).

---

[1] The pulpit of a dissenter is usually called a tub; but that of Mr. Orator Henley was covered with velvet, and adorned with gold. He had also a fair altar, and over it this extraordinary inscription, "The Primitive Eucharist."—POPE.

[2] Richard Fleckno was an Irish priest, but had laid aside (as himself expressed it) the mechanic part of priesthood. He printed some plays, poems, letters and travels.—POPE.

[3] Edmund Curl stood in the pillory at Charing Cross.

[4] Camille Querno was of Apulia, who, hearing the great encouragement which Leo X. gave to poets, travelled to Rome with a harp in his hand, and sung to it twenty thousand verses of a poem called *Alexias*.—WARBURTON.

Glory, and gain, th' industrious tribe provoke;
And gentle Dulness ever loves a joke.
A poet's form she placed before their eyes, 35
And bade the nimblest racer seize the prize;
No meagre, muse-rid mope, adust and thin,
In a dun night-gown of his own loose skin;
But such a bulk as no twelve bards could raise,
Twelve starv'ling bards of these degenerate days. 40
All as a partridge plump, full-fed, and fair,
She formed this image of well-bodied air;
With pert flat eyes she windowed well its head:
A brain of feathers, and a heart of lead;
And empty words she gave, and sounding strain, 45
But senseless, lifeless! idol void and vain!
Never was dashed out, at one lucky hit,
A fool, so just a copy of a wit;
So like, that critics said, and courtiers swore,
A wit it was, and called the phantom More.[1] 50

All gaze with ardour: some a poet's name,
Others a sword-knot and laced suit inflame.
But lofty Lintot [2] in the circle rose:
"This prize is mine; who tempt it are my foes;
With me began this genius, and shall end." 55
He spoke: and who with Lintot shall contend?

Fear held them mute. Alone, untaught to fear,
Stood dauntless Curl,[3] "Behold that rival here!
The race by vigour, not by vaunts is won;
So take the hindmost, hell," (he said) and run. 60
Swift as a bard that bailiff leaves behind,
He left huge Lintot and outstripped the wind.
As when a dab-chick waddles through the copse
On feet and wings, and flies, and wades, and hops:

[1] Curl, in his *Key to the Dunciad*, affirmed this to be James Moore Smythe. He wrote *The Rival Modes*, an unsuccessful play.
[2] The action of Mr. Bernard Lintot here imitates that of Dares in Virgil, rising just in this manner to lay hold on a bull. This eminent bookseller printed *The Rival Modes* before-mentioned.—WARBURTON.
[3] We come now to a character of much respect, that of Mr. Edmund Curl. As a plain repetition of great actions is the best praise of them, we shall only say of this eminent man that he carried the trade many lengths beyond what it ever before had arrived at; and that he was the envy and admiration of all his profession. He possessed himself of a command over all authors whatever; he caused them to write what he pleased; they could not call their very names their own. He was not only famous among these; he was taken notice of by the State, the Church and the Law, and received particular marks of distinction from each.—POPE.

So lab'ring on, with shoulders, hands, and head,   65
Wide as a wind-mill all his figure spread,
With arms expanded Bernard rows his state,
And left-legged Jacob [1] seems to emulate.
Full in the middle way there stood a lake,
Which Curl's Corinna [2] chanced that morn to make: 70
(Such was her wont, at early dawn to drop
Her evening cates before her neighbour's shop,)
Here fortuned Curl to slide; loud shout the band,
And " Bernard! Bernard!" rings through all the Strand.
Obscene with filth the miscreant lies bewrayed,   75
Fallen in the plash his wickedness had laid:
Then first (if poets aught of truth declare)
The caitiff vaticide conceived a prayer.

" Hear, Jove! whose name my bards and I adore,
As much at least as any god's, or more;   80
And him and his if more devotion warms,
Down with the Bible, up with the Pope's arms." [3]

`A place there is, betwixt earth, air, and seas,[4]
Where, from Ambrosia, Jove retires for ease.
There in his seat two spacious vents appear,   85
On this he sits, to that he leans his ear,
And hears the various vows of fond mankind;
Some beg an eastern, some a western wind:
All vain petitions, mounting to the sky,
With reams abundant this abode supply: 90
Amused he reads, and then returns the bills
Signed with that Ichor which from gods distils.

In office here fair Cloacina stands,
And ministers to Jove with purest hands.
Forth from the heap she picked her vot'ry's prayer,   95
And placed it next him, a distinction rare!
Oft had the goddess heard her servant's call,
From her black grottos near the temple-wall,
List'ning delighted to the jest unclean
Of link-boys vile, and watermen obscene;   100
Where as he fished her nether realms for wit,

[1] Jacob Tonson, described by Dryden with "two left legs."
[2] This name, it seems, was taken by one Mrs. Thomas, who procured some private letters of Mr. Pope, while almost a boy, to Mr. Cromwell, and sold them without the consent of either of those gentlemen to Curl, who printed them in 12mo, 1727.
[3] The Bible, Curl's sign; the Cross-keys, the Pope's emblem, Lintot's.
[4] See Ozell's translation, 1713, of Tassoni's *La Secchia Rapita*.

She oft had favoured him, and favours yet,
Renewed by ordure's sympathetic force,
As oiled with magic juices for the course,
Vigorous he rises; from the effluvia strong   105
Imbibes new life, and scours and stinks along;
Re-passes Lintot, vindicates the race,
Nor heeds the brown dishonours of his face.

 And now the victor stretched his eager hand,
Where the tall Nothing stood, or seemed to stand;   110
A shapeless shade, it melted from his sight,
Like forms in clouds, or visions of the night.
To seize his papers, Curl, was next thy care;
His papers light fly diverse, tossed in air;
Songs, sonnets, epigrams the winds uplift,   115
And whisk 'em back to Evans, Young, and Swift.[1]
Th' embroidered suit at least he deemed his prey;
That suit an unpaid tailor snatched away,
No rag, no scrap, of all the beau, or wit,
That once so fluttered, and that once so writ.   120

 Heaven rings with laughter. Of the laughter vain,
Dulness, good queen, repeats the jest again.
Three wicked imps of her own Grub Street choir,
She decked like Congreve, Addison, and Prior;
Mears, Warner, Wilkins[2] run: delusive thought!   125
Breval, Bond, Besaleel,[3] the varlets caught.
Curl stretches after Gay, but Gay is gone:
He grasps an empty Joseph[4] for a John;
So Proteus, hunted in a nobler shape,
Became, when seized, a puppy, or an ape.   130

 To him the goddess: "Son! thy grief lay down,
And turn this whole illusion on the town:
As the sage dame, experienced in her trade,
By names of toasts retails each battered jade
(When hapless Monsieur much complains at Paris   135
Of wrongs from Duchesses and Lady Maries);

[1] Dr. Evans, of St. John's College, Oxford, author of the *Apparition*, a satire on Tyndal.

[2] Booksellers, and printers of much anonymous stuff.

[3] Bezaleel Morrice was author of some satires on the translators of Homer, with many other things printed in newspaper.—"Bond, writ a satire against Mr. Pope.—Captain Breval was author of *The Confederates*, an ingenious dramatic performance, to expose Mr. Pope, Mr. Gay, Dr. Arbuthnot, and some ladies of quality," says Curl.—WARBURTON.

[4] Curl printed poems under the name of J. Gay (Joseph Gay) to pass them off for Gay, the poet's. These kinds of cheats were common with him.

Be thine, my stationer! this magic gift;
Cook [1] shall be Prior, and Concanen, Swift:
So shall each hostile name become our own,
And we too boast our Garth and Addison." [2]   140

    With that she gave him (piteous of his case,
Yet smiling at his rueful length of face)
A shaggy tap'stry, [3] worthy to be spread
On Codrus' old, or Dunton's modern bed; [4]
Instructive work! whose wry-mouthed portraiture   145
Displayed the fates her confessors endure.
Earless on high stood unabashed De Foe,
And Tutchin [5] flagrant from the scourge below.
There Ridpath, [6] Roper, cudgelled might ye view;
The very worsted still look'd black and blue.   150
Himself among the storied chiefs he spies, [7]
As, from the blanket, high in air he flies;
And "Oh!" (he cried) "what street, what lane but knows
Our purgings, pumpings, blanketings, and blows?
In ev'ry loom our labours shall be seen,   155
And the fresh vomit run for ever green!"

    See in the circle next, Eliza [8] placed,
Two babes of love close clinging to her waist;
Fair as before her works she stands confessed,

---

[1] The man here specified writ a thing called *The Battle of Poets*, in which Philips and Welsted were the heroes, and Swift and Pope utterly routed. He also published some malevolent things in the British, London and daily journals; and at the same time wrote letters to Mr. Pope protesting his innocence.—WARBURTON.

[2] It must have been particularly agreeable to Pope to celebrate Dr. Garth; both as his constant friend, and as he was his predecessor in this kind of satire. Garth's *Dispensary* attacks the whole body of the apothecaries.—WARBURTON.

[3] A sorry kind of tapestry frequent in old inns, made of worsted or some coarser stuff, like that which is spoken of by Donne—faces as frightful as theirs who whip Christ in old hangings. The imagery woven in it alludes to the mantle of Cloanthus in *Æn.* v.

[4] Of Codrus the poet's bed, see Juvenal, *Sat.* iii. 203, etc.
John Dunton was a broken bookseller and abusive scribbler; he wrote *Neck or Nothing*, a violent satire.—WARBURTON.

[5] John Tutchin, author of some vile verses, and of a weekly paper called the *Observator*: he was sentenced to be whipped through several towns in the west of England, upon which he petitioned King James II. to be hanged.—WARBURTON.

[6] Authors of the *Flying Post* and *Post-boy*, two scandalous papers on different sides, for which they equally and alternately deserved to be cudgelled, and were so.—WARBURTON.

[7] The history of Curl's being tossed in a blanket, and whipped by the scholars of Westminster, is well known.

[8] Eliza Haywood; authoress of some scandalous books.—*Miscellanies.*

In flowers and pearls by bounteous Kirkall[1] dressed, 160
The goddess then: "Who best can send on high
The salient spout, far streaming to the sky;
His be yon Juno of majestic size,
With cow-like udders, and with ox-like eyes,
This China jordan let the chief o'ercome 165
Replenish, not ingloriously, at home."

Osborne[2] and Curl accept the glorious strife,
(Though this his son dissuades, and that his wife),
One on his manly confidence relies;
One on his vigour and superior size. 170
First Osborne leaned against his lettered post;
It rose, and laboured to a curve at most.
So Jove's bright bow displays its watery round,
(Sure sign that no spectator shall be drowned)
A second effort brought but new disgrace: 175
The wild Mæander washed the artist's face;
Thus the small jet, which hasty hands unlock,
Spirts in the gard'ner's eyes who turns the cock,
Not so from shameless Curl; impetuous spread
The stream, and smoking flourished o'er his head, 180
So (famed like thee for turbulence and horns)
Eridanus his humble fountain scorns;
Through half the heavens he pours the exalted urn;
His rapid waters in their passage burn.

Swift as it mounts, all follow with their eyes: 185
Still happy impudence obtains the prize.
Thou triumphest, victor of the high-wrought day,
And the pleased dame, soft smiling, leadest away,
Osborne, through perfect modesty o'ercome,
Crowned with the jordan, walks contented home, 190

But now for authors nobler palms remain;
"Room for my lord!" three jockeys in his train;
Six huntsmen with a shout precede his chair:
He grins, and looks broad nonsense with a stare,
His honour's meaning Dulness thus exprest, 195

---

[1] The name of an engraver.—WARBURTON.

[2] A bookseller in Gray's Inn, very well qualified by his impudence to act this part; and therefore placed here instead of a less deserving predecessor. This man published advertisements for a year together pretending to sell Mr. Pope's subscription books of Homer's *Iliad* at half the price: of which books he had none, but cut to the size of them (which was quarto) the common books in folio, without copperplates, on a worse paper, and never above half the value.—WARBURTON.

This was the Osborne whom Dr. Johnson knocked down with a book.

"He wins this patron, who can tickle best."

He chinks his purse, and takes his seat of state:
With ready quills the dedicators wait;
Now at his head the dext'rous task commence,
And, instant, fancy feels th' imputed sense;   200
Now gentle touches wanton o'er his face,
He struts Adonis, and affects grimace:
Rolli [1] the feather to his ear conveys,
Then his nice taste directs our operas:
Bentley [2] his mouth with classic flattery opes,   205
And the puffed orator bursts out in tropes.
But Welsted [3] most the poet's healing balm
Strives to extract from his soft, giving palm;
Unlucky Welsted! thy unfeeling master,
The more thou ticklest, gripes his fist the faster.   210

While thus each hand promotes the pleasing pain,
And quick sensations skip from vein to vein;
A youth unknown to Phœbus, in despair,
Puts his last refuge all in Heav'n and pray'r.
What force have pious vows! The Queen of Love   215
His sister sends, her vot'ress, from above.
As, taught by Venus, Paris learned the art
To touch Achilles' only tender part;
Secure, through her, the noble prize to carry,
He marches off his grace's secretary.   220

"Now turn to diff'rent sports," (the goddess cries)
"And learn, my sons, the wondrous power of noise,
To move, to raise, to ravish ev'ry heart,
With Shakespeare's nature, or with Jonson's art,
Let others aim: 'tis yours to shake the soul   225
With thunder rumbling from the mustard-bowl. [4]
With horns and trumpets now to madness swell,

---

[1] Paolo Antonio Rolli, an Italian poet, and writer of many operas. He taught Italian to some fine gentlemen, who affected to direct the operas. —WARBURTON.

[2] Not the famous Dr. Richard Bentley, but Thomas Bentley, a small critic, who aped his uncle in a little Horace.—WARBURTON.

[3] Leonard Welsted, author of the *Triumvirate*, or a letter in verse from Palæmon to Celia at Bath, which was meant for a satire on Mr. Pope and some of his friends, about the year 1718.—WARBURTON.

[4] The old way of making thunder and mustard were the same; but since, it is more advantageously performed by troughs of wood with stops in them. Whether Mr. Dennis was the inventor of that improvement, I know not; but it is certain that, being once at a tragedy of a new author, he fell into a great passion at hearing some, and cried, " 'Sdeath! that is my *thunder*."—WARBURTON.

Now sink in sorrows with a tolling bell;
Such happy arts attention can command,
When fancy flags, and sense is at a stand. 230
Improve we these. Three cat-calls be the bribe
Of him, whose chatt'ring shames the monkey tribe:
And his this drum, whose hoarse heroic bass
Drowns the loud clarion of the braying ass."

Now thousand tongues are heard in one loud din; 235
The monkey-mimics rush discordant in;
'Twas chatt'ring, grinning, mouthing, jabb'ring all,
And noise and Norton,[1] brangling and Breval,
Dennis and dissonance, and captious art,
And snip-snap short, and interruption smart, 240
And demonstration thin, and theses thick,
And major, minor, and conclusion quick.
"Hold!" (cried the queen) "a cat-call each shall win:
Equal your merits! equal is your din!
But that this well-disputed game may end, 245
Sound forth, my brayers, and the welkin rend."

As, when the long-eared milky mothers wait
At some sick miser's triple-bolted gate,
For their defrauded, absent foals they make
A moan so loud, that all the guild awake: 250
Sore sighs Sir Gilbert,[2] starting at the bray,
From dreams of millions, and three groats to pay.
So swells each wind-pipe; ass intones to ass;
Harmonic twang! of leather, horn, and brass;
Such as from lab'ring lungs th' enthusiast blows, 255
High sound, attempered to the vocal nose;
Or such as bellow from the deep divine;
There, Webster! pealed thy voice, and Whitfield![3] thine.
But far o'er all, sonorous Blackmore's[4] strain;
Walls, steeples, skies, bray back to him again. 260
In Tott'nham fields, the brethren, with amaze,
Prick all their ears up, and forget to graze;
'Long Chancery Lane retentive rolls the sound,

[1] Norton de Foe, one of the authors of the *Flying Post*. F. Durant Breval,
author of a very extraordinary book of travels and some poems.
[2] Sir Gilbert Heathcote, reputed to be worth £700,000.
[3] The one the writer of a newspaper called the *Weekly Miscellany*, the
other a field preacher.—POPE.
[4] Sir Richard Blackmore, knight, who (as Mr. Dryden expresseth it):
        "Writ to the rumbling of the coach's wheels,"
who produced no less than six epic poems, and many more. 'Tis in this
sense he is styled afterwards the everlasting Blackmore.—POPE.

And courts to courts return it round and round;
Thames wafts it thence to Rufus' roaring hall,[1]   265
And Hungerford re-echoes bawl for bawl.
All hail him victor in both gifts of song,
Who sings so loudly, and who sings so long.

   This labour passed, by Bridewell all descend,
(As morning pray'r and flagellation end)[2]   270
To where Fleet-ditch with disemboguing streams
Rolls the large tribute of dead dogs to Thames,
The king of dykes! than whom no sluice of mud
With deeper sable blots the silver flood.
"Here strip, my children! here at once leap in,   275
Here prove who best can dash through thick and thin,
And who the most in love of dirt excel,
Or dark dexterity[3] of groping well.
Who flings most filth, and wide pollutes around
The stream, be his the weekly journals bound;   280
A pig of lead to him who dives the best;
A peck of coals a-piece shall glad the rest."

   In naked majesty Oldmixon stands,[4]
And Milo-like surveys his arms and hands;
Then, sighing, thus, "And am I now three-score?   285
Ah why, ye gods, should two and two make four?"
He said, and climbed a stranded lighter's height,
Shot to the black abyss, and plunged downright.
The senior's judgment all the crowd admire,
Who but to sink the deeper, rose the higher.   290

   Next Smedley dived,[5] slow circles dimpled o'er
The quaking mud, that closed, and oped no more.
All look, all sigh, and call on Smedley lost;

---

[1] Westminster Hall, built by William Rufus.

[2] It is between eleven and twelve in the morning, after church service, that the criminals are whipped in Bridewell.—This is to mark punctually the time of the day: Homer does it by the circumstance of the judges rising from court, or of the labourer's dinner; our author by one very proper both to the persons and the scene of his poem, which we may remember commenced in the evening of the Lord Mayor's Day: the first book passed in that night; the next morning the games begin in the Strand, thence along Fleet Street (places inhabited by booksellers); then they proceed by Bridewell toward Fleet Ditch, and lastly through Ludgate to the city and the Temple of the Goddess.—POPE.

[3] The three chief qualifications of party-writers: to stick at nothing, to delight in flinging dirt, and to slander in the dark by guess.—POPE.

[4] John Oldmixon, next to Mr. Dennis the most ancient critic of our nation; an unjust censurer of Mr. Addison, in his *Essay on Criticism.*

[5] An Irishman, publisher of a scurrilous weekly paper, the *Whitehall Journal.* He abused Pope and Swift vehemently.

"Smedley" in vain resounds through all the coast.

 Then *essayed;[1] scarce vanished out of sight,   295
He buoys up instant, and returns to light:
He bears no token of the sabler streams,
And mounts far off among the swans of Thames.[2]

 True to the bottom see Concanen[3] creep,
A cold, long-winded native of the deep;   300
If perseverance gain the diver's prize,
Not everlasting Blackmore this denies;
No noise, no stir, no motion canst thou make,
Th' unconscious stream sleeps o'er thee like a lake.

 Next plunged a feeble, but a desp'rate pack,   305
With each a sickly brother at his back:
Sons of a day![4] just buoyant on the flood,
Then numbered with the puppies in the mud.
Ask ye their names? I could as soon disclose
The names of these blind puppies as of those.   310
Fast by, like Niobe, (her children gone)
Sits mother Osborne,[5] stupefied to stone!

 And monumental brass this record bears,
"These are,—ah no! these were, the gazetteers!"

 Not so bold Arnall;[6] with a weight of skull,   315
Furious he dives, precipitately dull.
Whirlpools and storms his circling arm invest.
With all the might of gravitation blest.
No crab more active in the dirty dance,

---

[1] By * it is supposed that Aaron Hill was meant. He wrote *Rinaldo*, the first opera for which Handel composed music in England.

[2] An elegant compliment to Hill. Pope, however, denied that it was meant for him.

[3] Matthew Concanen, an Irishman, bred to the law. He was author of several dull and dead scurrilities in the *British* and *London Journals*, and in a paper called the *Speculatist*.—POPE.

[4] These were daily papers, a number of which, to lessen the expense, were printed one on the back of another.—WARBURTON.

[5] A name assumed by the eldest and gravest of these writers, who at last, being ashamed of his pupils, gave his paper over, and in his age remained silent.—POPE.

[6] William Arnall, bred an attorney, was a perfect genius in this sort of work. He began under twenty with furious party-papers; then succeeded Concanen in the *British Journal*. At the first publication of the *Dunciad*, he prevailed on the author not to give him his due place in it, by a letter professing his detestation of such practices as his predecessor's. But since, by the most unexampled insolence, and personal abuse of several great men, the poet's particular friends, he most amply deserved a niche in the temple of infamy. Witness a paper called the *Free Briton*.—POPE. He was one of Sir Robert Walpole's hired writers, and boasted of the money he received from the Treasury.

Downward to climb, and backward to advance.   320
He brings up half the bottom on his head,
And loudly claims the journals and the lead.
   The plunging prelate, and his pond'rous grace,[1]
With holy envy gave one layman place.
When lo! a burst of thunder shook the flood;   325
Slow rose a form, in majesty of mud;
Shaking the horrors of his sable brows,
And each ferocious feature grim with ooze.
Greater he looks, and more than mortal stares;
Then thus the wonders of the deep declares.   330
   First he relates, how sinking to the chin,
Smit with his mien the mud-nymphs sucked him in:
How young Lutetia, softer than the down,
Nigrina black, and Merdamante brown,
Vied for his love in jetty bowers below,   335
As Hylas fair was ravished long ago.
Then sung, how shown him by the nut-brown maids
A branch of Styx here rises from the shades,
That tinctured as it runs with Lethe's streams,
And wafting vapours from the land of dreams,   340
(As under seas Alpheus' secret sluice
Bears Pisa's off'rings to his Arethuse)
Pours into Thames: and hence the mingled wave
Intoxicates the pert, and lulls the grave:
Here brisker vapours o'er the temple creep,   345
There, all from Paul's to Aldgate drink and sleep.
   Thence to the banks where rev'rend bards repose,
They led him soft; each rev'rend bard arose;
And Milbourn [2] chief, deputed by the rest,
Gave him the cassock, surcingle, and vest.   350
"Receive" (he said) "these robes which once were mine,
Dulness is sacred in a sound divine."
   He ceased, and spread the robe; the crowd confess
The rev'rend Flamen in his lengthened dress.
Around him wide a sable army stand,   355
A low-born, cell-bred, selfish, servile band,
Prompt or to guard or stab, to saint or damn,

---

[1] Bishop Sherlock, whom Bolingbroke attacked for defending the measures of Walpole; and John Potter, Archbishop of Canterbury.

[2] Luke Milbourn, who, when he wrote against Mr. Dryden's *Virgil*, did him justice in printing at the same time his own translations of him, which were intolerable. His manner of writing has a great resemblance with that of the gentlemen of the *Dunciad* against our author.—POPE.

Heav'n's Swiss, who fight for any God, or man.
Through Lud's famed gates, along the well-known Fleet,
Rolls the black troop, and overshades the street;   360
Till show'rs of sermons, characters, essays,
In circling fleeces whiten all the ways:
So clouds, replenished from some bog below,
Mount in dark volumes, and descend in snow.
Here stopt the goddess; and in pomp proclaims   365
A gentler exercise to close the games.
"Ye critics! in whose heads, as equal scales,
I weigh what author's heaviness prevails;
Which most conduce to soothe the soul in slumbers,
My Henley's periods,[1] or my Blackmore's numbers;   370
Attend the trial we propose to make:
If there be man, who o'er such works can wake,
Sleep's all-subduing charms who dares defy,
And boasts Ulysses' ear with Argus' eye;
To him we grant our amplest powers to sit   375
Judge of all present, past, and future wit;
To cavil, censure, dictate, right or wrong;
Full and eternal privilege of tongue."
Three college sophs, and three pert Templars came,
The same their talents, and their tastes the same;   380
Each prompt to query, answer, and debate,
And smit with love of poesy and prate,
The pond'rous books two gentle readers bring;
The heroes sit, the vulgar form a ring.
The clam'rous crowd is hushed with mugs of mum,   385
Till all, tuned equal, send a general hum.
Then mount the clerks, and in one lazy tone
Through the long, heavy, painful page drawl on;
Soft creeping, words on words, the sense compose;
At ev'ry line they stretch, they yawn, they doze.   390
As to soft gales top-heavy pines bow low
Their heads, and lift them as they cease to blow:
Thus oft they rear, and oft the head decline,
As breathe, or pause, by fits, the airs divine.
And now to this side, now to that they nod,   395
As verse, or prose, infuse the drowsy god.
Thrice Budgel aimed to speak,[2] but thrice supprest

[1] The Rev. John Henley, commonly called "Orator Henley."
[2] Famous for his speeches on many occasions about the South Sea scheme, etc. Friend and cousin of Addison, thus a Buttonian. He wrote thirty *Spectators*.

By potent Arthur,[1] knocked his chin and breast.
Toland and Tindal, prompt at priests to jeer,[2]
Yet silent bowed to "Christ's no kingdom here."[3]   400
Who sate the nearest, by the words o'ercome,
Slept first; the distant nodded to the hum.
Then down are rolled the books; stretched o'er them lies
Each gentle clerk, and muttering seals his eyes.
As what a Dutchman plumps into the lakes,   405
One circle first, and then a second makes;
What Dulness dropt among her sons imprest
Like motion, from one circle to the rest;
So from the mid-most the nutation spreads
Round and more round, o'er all the sea of heads.   410
At last Centlivre [4] felt her voice to fail;
Motteux [5] himself unfinished left his tale;
Boyer the state, and Law the stage gave o'er;[6]
Morgan [7] and Mandevil [8] could prate no more;
Norton,[9] from Daniel and Ostrœa sprung,   415
Blessed with his father's front, and mother's tongue,
Hung silent down his never-blushing head;
And all was hushed, as folly's self lay dead.

Thus the soft gifts of sleep conclude the day,
And stretched on bulks, as usual, poets lay.   420
Why should I sing, what bards the nightly muse
Did slumb'ring visit, and convey to stews;
Who prouder marched, with magistrats in state,
To some famed round-house, ever open gate!

---

[1] Blackmore's *Epic Poem*.

[2] Toland, author of the *Atheist's Liturgy*, called Pantheisticon, was a spy in pay to Lord Oxford. Tindal was author of the *Rights of the Christian Church* and *Christianity as Old as the Creation*. He also wrote an abusive pamphlet against Lord Stanhope.—WARBURTON.

[3] This is said by Curl to allude to a sermon of Hoadley, bishop of Bangor. The sermon alluded to was preached before George I. at St. James's, 1717, and went through many editions. It occasioned the Bangorian Controversy. Hoadley had attacked Bishop Atterbury, Pope's dear friend.—WAKEFIELD.

[4] Mrs. Susanna Centlivre, wife to Mr. Centlivre, Yeoman of the Mouth to his Majesty. She writ many plays and a song before she was seven years old. She also writ a ballad against Mr. Pope's *Homer* before he began it.—POPE.

[5] Peter Anthony Motteux, the translator of *Don Quixote*.

[6] A. Boyer, a voluminous compiler of annals, political collections, etc.—William Law, A.M., wrote with great zeal against the stage and wrote the *Serious Call to a Devout and Holy Life*.

[7] A writer against religion.

[8] Author of the *Fable of the Bees*.

[9] Norton Defoe, son of Daniel Defoe. One of the authors of the *Flying Post*.

How Henley lay inspired beside a sink,   425
And to mere mortals seemed a priest in drink:
While others, timely, to the neighb'ring Fleet
(Haunt of the muses) made their safe retreat.

BOOK THE THIRD

ARGUMENT

After the other persons are disposed in their proper places of rest, the goddess transports the king to her temple, and there lays him to slumber with his head on her lap, a position of marvellous virtue, which causes all the visions of wild enthusiasts, projectors, politicians, inamoratas, castle-builders, chemists, and poets. He is immediately carried on the wings of fancy, and led by a mad poetical sibyl to the Elysian shade; where, on the banks of the Lethe, the souls of the dull are dipped by Bavius, before their entrance into this world. There he is met by the ghost of Settle, and by him made acquainted with the wonders of the place, and with those which he himself is destined to perform. He takes him to a mount of vision, from whence he shows him the past triumphs of the empire of Dulness, then the present, and lastly the future: how small a part of the world was ever conquered by science, how soon those conquests were stopped, and those very nations again reduced to her dominion. Then distinguishing the island of Great Britain, shows by what aids, by what persons, and by what degrees it shall be brought to her empire. Some of the persons he causes to pass in review before his eyes, describing each by his proper figure, character, and qualifications. On a sudden the scene shifts, and a vast number of miracles and prodigies appear, utterly surprising and unknown to the king himself, till they are explained to be the wonders of his own reign now commencing. On this subject Settle breaks into a congratulation, yet not unmixed with concern, that his own times were but types of these. He prophesies how first the nation shall be overrun with farces, operas, and shows; how the throne of Dulness shall be advanced over the theatres, and set up even at court; then how her sons shall preside in the seats of arts and sciences: giving a glimpse or Pisgah-sight of the future fulness of her glory, the accomplishment whereof is the subject of the fourth and last book.

BOOK III

But in her temple's last recess enclosed,
On Dulness' lap th' anointed head reposed.
Him close she curtains round with vapours blue,
And soft besprinkles with Cimmerian dew.

Then raptures high the seat of sense o'erflow,   5
Which only heads refined from reason know.
Hence, from the straw where Bedlam's prophet nods,
He hears loud oracles, and talks with gods:
Hence the fool's paradise, the statesman's scheme,
The air-built castle, and the golden dream,   10
The maid's romantic wish, the chemist's flame,[1]
And poet's vision of eternal fame.
   And now, on fancy's easy wings conveyed,
The king descending views the Elysian shade.
A slip-shod sibyl led his steps along,   15
In lofty madness meditating song;
Her tresses staring from poetic dreams,
And never washed, but in Castalia's streams.
Taylor,[2] their better Charon, lends an oar,
(Once swan of Thames, though now he sings no more.)   20
Benlowes,[3] propitious still to blockheads, bows;
And Shadwell nods the poppy [4] on his brows.
Here, in a dusky vale where Lethe rolls,
Old Bavius sits,[5] to dip poetic souls,
And blunt the sense, and fit it for a skull   25
Of solid proof impenetrably dull:
Instant, when dipped, away they wing their flight,
Where Brown and Mears [6] unbar the gates of light,
Demand new bodies, and in calf's array
Rush to the world, impatient for the day.   30
Millions and millions on these banks he views,
Thick as the stars of night or morning dews,
As thick as bees o'er vernal blossoms fly,
As thick as eggs at Ward in pillory.[7]

[1] Alluding to the search for the Philosopher's Stone.
[2] John Taylor, the water-poet.
[3] A country gentleman, famous for his own bad poetry and for patronis-
ing bad poets, as may be seen from many dedications of Quarles and others
to him. Some of these anagrammed his name, Benlowes into Benevolus:
to verify which he spent his whole estate upon them.—POPE.
[4] Shadwell took opium for many years, and died of too large a dose in the
year 1692.—WARBURTON.
[5] Bavius was an ancient poet, celebrated by Virgil for the like cause as
Bays by our author, though not in so Christian-like a manner: for hea-
thenishly it is declared by Virgil of Bavius that he ought to be hated and
detested for his evil works; *Qui Bavium non odit*; whereas we have often
had occasion to observe our poet's great good-nature and mercifulness
through the whole course of this poem.—SCRIBLERUS. POPE.
[6] Booksellers, printers for anybody.
[7] John Ward of Hackney, Esq., member of Parliament, being convicted
of forgery, was first expelled the House, and then sentenced to the pillory
on 17th February, 1727.—POPE.

Wondering he gazed: when lo! a sage appears, 35
By his broad shoulders known, and length of ears,
Known by the band and suit which Settle [1] wore
(His only suit) for twice three years before:
All as the vest, appeared the wearer's frame,
Old in new state, another, yet the same, 40
Bland and familiar as in life, begun
Thus the great father to the greater son.

"Oh, born to see what none can see awake!
Behold the wonders of th' oblivious lake.
Thou, yet unborn, hast touched this sacred shore; 45
The hand of Bavius drenched thee o'er and o'er,
But blind to former, as to future fate,
What mortal knows his pre-existent state?
Who knows how long thy transmigrating soul
Might from Bœotian to Bœotian roll? [2] 50
How many Dutchmen she vouchsafed to thrid?
How many stages through old monks she rid?
And all who since, in mild benighted days,
Mixed the owl's ivy with the poet's bays?
As man's meanders to the vital spring 55
Roll all their tides; then back their circles bring;
Or whirligigs twirled round by skilful swain,
Suck the thread in, then yield it out again:
All nonsense thus, of old or modern date,
Shall in thee centre, from thee circulate. 60
For this our queen unfolds to vision true
Thy mental eye, for thou hast much to view:
Old scenes of glory, times long cast behind
Shall, first recalled, rush forward to thy mind:
Then stretch thy sight o'er all her rising reign, 65
And let the past and future fire thy brain.

"Ascend this hill, whose cloudy point commands
Her boundless empire over seas and lands.
See, round the Poles where keener spangles shine,
Where spices smoke beneath the burning line, 70
(Earth's wide extremes) her sable flag displayed,
And all the nations covered in her shade.

"Far eastward cast thine eye, from whence the sun

---

[1] Elkanah Settle was once a writer in vogue as well as Cibber, both for dramatic poetry and politics.—POPE.
[2] Bœotia was famed for dulness, but it produced Pindar and Epaminondas.

And Orient science their bright course begun:
One god-like monarch [1] all that pride confounds, 75
He, whose long wall the wandering Tartar bounds;
Heavens! what a pile! whole ages perish there,
And one bright blaze turns learning into air.
"Thence to the south extend thy gladdened eyes;
There rival flames with equal glory rise, 80
From shelves to shelves see greedy Vulcan roll,[2]
And lick up all the physic of the soul.
How little, mark! that portion of the ball,
Where, faint at best, the beams of science fall:
Soon as they dawn, from hyperborean skies 85
Embodied dark, what clouds of Vandals rise!
Lo! where Mæotis sleeps, and hardly flows
The freezing Tanais through a waste of snows,
The north by myriads pours her mighty sons,
Great nurse of Goths, of Alans, and of Huns! 90
See Alaric's stern port! the martial frame
Of Genseric! and Attila's dread name!
See the bold Ostrogoths on Latium fall;
See the fierce Visigoths on Spain and Gaul!
See, where the morning gilds the palmy shore, 95
(The soil that arts and infant letters bore)
His conquering tribes th' Arabian prophet [3] draws,
And saving ignorance enthrones by laws.
See Christians, Jews, one heavy Sabbath keep,
And all the Western world believe and sleep. 100
    "Lo! Rome herself, proud mistress now no more
Of arts, but thundering against heathen lore:
Her grey-haired synods damning books unread,
And Bacon trembling for his brazen head.[4]
Padua, with sighs, beholds her Livy burn, 105
And even the antipodes Virgilius mourn.
See the cirque falls, the unpillared temple nods,

---

[1] Chi Ho-am-ti, Emperor of China, the same who built the great wall
between China and Tartary, destroyed all the books and learned men
of that empire.—WARBURTON.

[2] The Caliph, Omar I., having conquered Egypt, caused his general to
burn the Ptolemæan library, on the gates of which was this inscription,
ΨΤΧΗΣ ΙΑΤΡΕΙΟΝ, the physic of the soul.—WARBURTON.

[3] Mahommed.

[4] Friar Bacon, who had a head made of brass, through which, by means
of acoustic pipes, he called his servant, and who was in some danger of
being burned for a magician.

Streets paved with heroes, Tiber choked with gods:
Till Peter's keys some christened Jove adorn,
And Pan to Moses lends his pagan horn;　　　110
See graceless Venus to a virgin turned,
Or Phidias broken, and Apelles burned.

"Behold yon isle, by palmers, pilgrims trod,
Men bearded, bald, cowled, uncowled, shod, unshod,
Peeled, patched, and piebald, Linsey-Wolsey brothers,　115
Grave mummers! sleeveless some, and shirtless others.
That once was Britain—happy! had she seen
No fiercer sons, had Easter never been.
In peace, great goddess, ever be adored;
How keen the war, if Dulness draw the sword!　　120
Thus visit not thy own! on this blest age
Oh spread thy influence, but restrain thy rage!

"And see, my son! the hour is on its way,
That lifts our goddess to imperial sway:
This fav'rite isle, long severed from her reign,　　125
Dove-like, she gathers to her wings again.
Now look through fate! behold the scene she draws!
What aids, what armies to assert her cause!
See all her progeny, illustrious sight!
Behold, and count them, as they rise to light.　　130
As Berecynthia, while her offspring vie
In homage to the mother of the sky,
Surveys around her, in the blest abode,
An hundred sons, and ev'ry son a god:
Not with less glory mighty Dulness crowned　　135
Shall take through Grub Street her triumphant round;
And her Parnassus glancing o'er at once,
Behold an hundred sons, and each a dunce.

"Mark first that youth who takes the foremost place,
And thrusts his person full into your face,　　140
With all thy father's virtues blest, be born!
And a new Cibber shall the stage adorn.[1]

"A second see, by meeker manners known,
And modest as the maid that sips alone;
From the strong fate of drams if thou get free,　　145
Another Durfey, Ward shall sing in thee.
Thee shall each ale-house, thee each gill-house mourn,
And answering gin-shops sourer sighs return.

---

[1] Cibber's son Theophilus. He wrote a ballad opera called *Pattie and Peggy*.

"Jacob, the scourge of grammar, mark with awe,[1]
Nor less revere him, blunderbuss of law.   150
Lo, Popple's brow, tremendous to the town,
Horneck's fierce eye, and Roome's[2] funereal frown.
Lo, sneering Goode,[3] half malice and half whim,
A fiend in glee, ridiculously grim.
Each cygnet sweet, of Bath and Tunbridge race,   155
Whose tuneful whistling makes the waters pass;
Each songster, riddler, every nameless name,
All crowd, who foremost shall be damned to fame.
Some strain in rhyme; the Muses, on their racks,
Scream like the winding of ten thousand jacks: 160
Some free from rhyme or reason, rule or check,
Break Priscian's head, and Pegasus's neck;
Down, down they larum, with impetuous whirl,
The Pindars, and the Miltons of a Curl.

"Silence, ye wolves! while Ralph[4] to Cynthia howls, 165
And makes night hideous—Answer him, ye owls!
"Sense, speech, and measure, living tongues and dead,
Let all give way, and Morris[5] may be read.
Flow, Welsted, flow![6] like thine inspirer, beer,
Though stale, not ripe; though thin, yet never clear;   170
So sweetly mawkish, and so smoothly dull;
Heady, not strong; o'erflowing, though not full.
"Ah, Dennis! Gildon, ah! what ill-starred rage
Divides a friendship long confirmed by age?

[1] This gentleman is son of a maltster of Romsey, bred to the Law, who has diverted himself with poetry. He has writ in prose the *Lives of the Poets*, *Essays*, and many law-books. He very grossly, and unprovoked, abused in that book the author's friend, Mr. Gay.—WARBURTON.

[2] These two were virulent party-writers. The first was Philip Horneck, author of a Billingsgate paper called *The High German Doctor*. Edward Roome was son of an undertaker for funerals in Fleet Street, and writ some of the papers called *Pasquin*. Popple was the author of some vile plays and pamphlets. He published abuses on our author in a paper called the *Prompter*.—WARBURTON.

[3] An ill-natured critic, who writ a satire on our author, called *The Mock Æsop*, and many anonymous libels in newspapers.—WARBURTON.

[4] James Ralph, a name inserted after the first editions, not known to our author till he writ a swearing-piece called *Sawney*, very abusive of Dr. Swift, Mr. Gay and himself. These lines allude to a thing of his entitled *Night*, a poem. This low writer attended his own works with panegyrics in the journals, and once in a particular praised himself high above Mr. Addison. He was wholly illiterate, and knew no language, not even French.

[5] Bezaleel Morrice, see book ii, 126.

[6] See page 142, footnote 3.

Blockheads with reason wicked wits abhor;   175
But fool with fool is barb'rous civil war.
Embrace, embrace, my sons! be foes no more!
Nor glad vile poets with true critics' gore.

"Behold yon pair,[1] in strict embraces joined;
How like in manners, and how like in mind!   180
Equal in wit, and equally polite,
Shall this a *Pasquin*, that a *Grumbler* write;
Like are their merits, like rewards they share,
That shines a consul, this commissioner.

"But who is he, in closet close y-pent,   185
Of sober face, with learned dust besprent?
Right well mine eyes arede[2] the myster wight,
On parchment scraps y-fed, and Wormius hight.[3]
To future ages may thy dulness last,
As thou preservest the dulness of the past!   190

"There, dim in clouds, the poring scholiasts mark,
Wits, who, like owls, see only in the dark.
A lumber-house of books in ev'ry head,
For ever reading, never to be read!

"But, where each science lifts its modern type,   195
Hist'ry his pot, divinity his pipe,
While proud philosophy repines to show,
Dishonest sight! his breeches rent below;
Embrowned with native bronze, lo! Henley stands,[4]
Tuning his voice, and balancing his hands.   200
How fluent nonsense trickles from his tongue!
How sweet the periods, neither said, nor sung!
Still break the benches, Henley! with thy strain,
While Sherlock, Hare, and Gibson[5] preach in vain.
Oh, great restorer of the good old stage,   205

[1] One of these was author of a weekly paper called the *Grumbler*, as the other was concerned in another called *Pasquin*, in which Mr. Pope was abused with the Duke of Buckingham and Bishop of Rochester. They also joined in a piece against his first undertaking to translate the *Iliad*, entitled *Homerides*, by "Sir Iliad Doggrel," printed in 1715.—WARBURTON. They were Thomas Burnet, youngest son of the famous Bishop Burnet, and Colonel Ducket.

[2] Read, or peruse; though sometimes used for counsel.—POPE.

[3] Let not this name, purely fictitious, be conceited to mean the learned Olaus Wormius; much less (as it was unwarrantably foisted into the surreptitious editions) our own antiquary, Mr. Thomas Hearne, who had no way aggrieved our poet, but on the contrary published many curious tracts which he hath to his great contentment perused.—POPE.

[4] Henley the orator.

[5] Bishops of Salisbury, Chichester and London, whose sermons and pastoral letters did honour to their country.—POPE.

Preacher at once, and zany of thy age!
Oh, worthy thou of Egypt's wise abodes,
A decent priest, where monkeys were the gods!
But fate with butchers placed thy priestly stall,
Meek modern faith to murder, hack, and maul;   210
And bade thee live, to crown Britannia's praise,
In Toland's, Tindal's, and Woolston's days.[1]

"Yet oh, my sons, a father's words attend:
(So may the fates preserve the ears you lend)
'Tis yours a Bacon or a Locke to blame,   215
A Newton's genius, or a Milton's flame:
But oh! with One, immortal One dispense;
The source of Newton's light, of Bacon's sense.
Content, each emanation of his fires
That beams on earth, each virtue he inspires,   220
Each art he prompts, each charm he can create,
Whate'er he gives, are giv'n for you to hate.
Persist, by all divine in man unawed,
But, learn, ye dunces! not to scorn your God."

Thus he, for then a ray of reason stole   225
Half through the solid darkness of his soul;
But soon the cloud returned—and thus the sire:
"See now, what Dulness and her sons admire!
See what the charms that smite the simple heart
Not touched by Nature, and not reached by art."   230

His never-blushing head he turned aside,
(Not half so pleased when Goodman prophesied [2])
And looked, and saw a sable sorcerer [3] rise,
Swift to whose hand a wingéd volume flies;
All sudden, gorgons hiss, and dragons glare,   235
And ten-horned fiends and giants rush to war.
Hell rises, Heaven descends, and dance on earth: [4]

[1] Tho. Woolston was an impious madman who wrote in a most insolent style against the miracles of the gospel in the years 1726, etc.—WARBURTON.

[2] Cibber tells us, in his *Life*, that Goodman, at the rehearsal of a play in which he had a part, clapped him on the shoulder and cried, "If he does not make a good actor, I'll be d——d."—"And" (says Mr. Cibber) "I make it a question whether Alexander himself or Charles the Twelfth of Sweden, when at the head of their first victorious armies, could feel a greater transport in their bosoms than I did in mine."—WARBURTON.

[3] Dr. Faustus, the subject of a set of farces which lasted in vogue two or three seasons, in which both play-houses strove to outdo each other for some years. All the extravagances in the sixteen lines following were introduced on the stage, and frequented by persons of the first quality in England to the twentieth and thirtieth time.—WARBURTON.

[4] This monstrous absurdity was actually represented in Tibbald's *Rape of Proserpine*.—WARBURTON.

Gods, imps, and monsters, music, rage, and mirth,
A fire, a jig, a battle, and a ball,
Till one wide conflagration swallows all. 240
    Thence a new world to Nature's laws unknown,
Breaks out refulgent, with a heaven its own:
Another Cynthia her new journey runs,
And other planets circle other suns.
The forests dance, the rivers upward rise, 245
Whales sport in woods, and dolphins in the skies;
And last, to give the whole creation grace,
Lo! one vast egg [1] produces human race.
    Joy fills his soul, joy innocent of thought;
"What power," he cries, "what power these wonders
        wrought?" 250
"Son, what thou seek'st is in thee! look, and find
Each monster meets his likeness in thy mind.
Yet wouldst thou more? in yonder cloud behold,
Whose sarsnet skirts are edged with flamy gold,
A matchless youth! his nod these worlds controls, 255
Wings the red lightning, and the thunder rolls.
Angel of Dulness, sent to scatter round
Her magic charms o'er all unclassic ground:
Yon stars, yon suns, he rears at pleasure higher,
Illumes their light, and sets their flames on fire. 260
Immortal Rich! [2] how calm he sits at ease
'Mid snows of paper, and fierce hail of pease;
And proud his mistress' orders to perform,
Rides in the whirlwind, and directs the storm.
    "But lo! to dark encounter in mid air 265
New Wizards rise; I see my Cibber there!
Booth [3] in his cloudy tabernacle shrined,
On grinning dragons thou shalt mount the wind. [4]
Dire is the conflict, dismal is the din,
Here shouts all Drury, there all Lincoln's Inn; 270
Contending theatres our empire raise,
Alike their labours, and alike their praise.
    "And are these wonders, son, to thee unknown?

[1] In another of these farces Harlequin is hatched upon the stage out of a large egg.—WARBURTON.

[2] John Rich, master of the Theatre Royal in Covent Garden, was the first that excelled this way.—WARBURTON.

[3] Booth was joint manager of Drury Lane with Cibber.

[4] In his *Letter* to Mr. P., Mr. C. solemnly declares this not to be literally true. We hope therefore the reader will understand it allegorically only.
—POPE.

Unknown to thee? these wonders are thy own.[1]
These fate reserved to grace thy reign divine,   275
Foreseen by me, but ah! withheld from mine.
In Lud's old walls though long I ruled, renowned
Far as loud Bow's stupendous bells resound;
Though my own aldermen conferred the bays,
To me committing their eternal praise,   280
Their full-fed heroes, their pacific may'rs,
Their annual trophies,[2] and their monthly wars;
Though long my party[3] built on me their hopes,
For writing pamphlets, and for roasting popes;
Yet lo! in me what authors have to brag on!   285
Reduced at last to hiss in my own dragon.
Avert it, Heaven! that thou, my Cibber, e'er
Should'st wag a serpent-tail in Smithfield fair!
Like the vile straw that's blown about the streets,
The needy poet sticks to all he meets,   290
Coached, carted, trod upon, now loose, now fast,
And carried off in some dog's tail at last.
Happier thy fortunes! like a rolling stone,
Thy giddy dulness still shall lumber on,
Safe in its heaviness, shall never stray,   295
But lick up ev'ry blockhead in the way.
Thee shall the patriot, thee the courtier taste,
And ev'ry year be duller than the last.
Till raised from booths, to theatre, to court,
Her seat imperial Dulness shall transport.   300
Already opera prepares the way,
The sure forerunner of her gentle sway:
Let her thy heart, next drabs and dice, engage,
The third mad passion of thy doting age.
Teach thou the warbling Polypheme[4] to roar,   305

[1] A marvellous line of Theobald; unless the play called *The Double Falsehood* be (as he would have it believed) Shakespeare's.

[2] Annual trophies, on the Lord Mayor's day; and monthly wars in the artillery ground.—WARBURTON.

[3] Settle, like most party-writers, was very uncertain in his political principles. He was employed to hold the pen in the character of a popish successor, but afterwards printed his narrative on the other side. He had managed the ceremony of a famous pope-burning on 17th November, 1680; then became a trooper in King James's army at Hounslow Heath. After the revolution he kept a booth at Bartholomew Fair, where, in the droll called *St. George for England*, he acted in his old age in a dragon of green leather of his own invention; he was at last taken into the Charter House, and there died, aged sixty years.—WARBURTON.

[4] He translated the Italian opera of *Polifemo*; but unfortunately lost the whole jest of the story. The Cyclops asks Ulysses his name, who tells

And scream thyself as none e'er screamed before!
To aid our cause, if Heav'n thou canst not bend,
Hell thou shalt move; for Faustus is our friend:
Pluto with Cato, thou for this shalt join,
And link the Mourning Bride to Proserpine. 310
Grub Street! thy fall should men and gods conspire,
Thy stage shall stand, insure it but from fire.[1]
Another Æschylus appears! prepare
For new abortions, all ye pregnant fair!
In flames, like Semele's,[2] be brought to bed, 315
While op'ning Hell spouts wild-fire at your head,
    " Now, Bavius, take the poppy from thy brow,
And place it here! here all ye heroes bow!
This, this is he, foretold by ancient rhymes:
Th' Augustus born to bring Saturnian times. 320
Signs following signs lead on the mighty year!
See! the dull stars roll round and reappear.
See, see, our own true Phœbus wears the bays!
Our Midas sits Lord Chancellor of plays!
On poets' tombs see Benson's titles writ![3] 325
Lo! Ambrose Philips [4] is preferred for wit!

---

him his name is Noman. After his eye is put out, he roars and calls the brother Cyclops to his aid. They inquire who has hurt him. He answers Noman; whereupon they all go away again. Our ingenious translator made Ulysses answer, " I take no name," whereby all that followed became unintelligible.—POPE.

[1] In the farce of *Proserpine* a cornfield was set on fire; whereupon the other play-house had a barn burnt down for the recreation of the spectators. They also rivalled each other in showing the burnings of hell-fire in *Dr. Faustus*.—POPE.

[2] See Ovid, *Met.* iii.

[3] Benson (surveyor of the buildings to his Majesty King George I.) gave in an idle report to the lords that their house and the painted chamber adjoining were in immediate danger of falling. In favour of this man the famous Sir Christopher Wren, who had been architect to the Crown for above fifty years, who built most of the churches in London, laid the first stone of St. Paul's and lived to finish it, was displaced from his employment at the age of near ninety years.—WARBURTON. Benson erected a monument to Milton in Westminster Abbey, in which his own name is prominent as the founder.

[4] " He was " (saith Mr. Jacob) "one of the wits at Button's and a justice of the peace "; but he hath since met with higher preferment in Ireland. . . . He endeavoured to create some misunderstanding between our author and Mr. Addison, whom also soon after he abused as much. His constant cry was that Mr. Pope was an enemy to the government; and in particular he was the avowed author of a report very industriously spread, that he had a hand in a party-paper called the *Examiner*: a falsehood well known to those yet living who had the direction and publication of it. He proceeded to grosser insults, and hung up a rod at Button's with which he threatened to chastise Pope.—JOHNSON.

See under Ripley rise a new Whitehall,[1]
While Jones' and Boyle's united labours fall;[2]
While Wren with sorrow to the grave descends;
Gay dies unpensioned with a hundred friends;   330
Hibernian politics, O Swift! thy fate;
And Pope's, ten years to comment and translate.[3]
  " Proceed, great days! till learning fly the shore,
Till birch shall blush with noble blood no more,
Till Thames see Eton's sons for ever play,   335
Till Westminster's whole year be holiday,
Till Isis' elders reel, their pupils' sport,
And Alma Mater lie dissolved in port!"
  " Enough! enough!" the raptured monarch cries;
And through the iv'ry gate the vision flies.   340

BOOK THE FOURTH

ARGUMENT

The poet being, in this book, to declare the completion of the prophecies mentioned at the end of the former, makes a new invocation; as the greater poets are wont, when some high and worthy matter is to be sung. He shows the goddess coming in her majesty to destroy order and science, and to substitute the kingdom of the dull upon earth. How she leads captive the sciences and silenceth the muses, and what they be who succeed in their stead. All her children, by a wonderful attraction, are drawn about her, and bear along with them divers others, who promote her empire by connivance, weak resistance, or discouragement of arts; such as half-wits, tasteless admirers, vain pretenders, the flatterers of dunces, or the patrons of them. All these crowd round her; one of

[1] Thomas Ripley. See page 247, footnote 4.
[2] At the time when this poem was written the banqueting house at Whitehall, the church and piazza of Covent Garden, and the palace and chapel of Somerset House, the works of the famous Inigo Jones, had been for many years so neglected as to be in danger of ruin. The portico of Covent Garden church had been just then restored and beautified at the expense of the Earl of Burlington (Richard Boyle); who at the same time, by his publication of the designs of that great master and Palladio, as well as by many noble buildings of his own, revived the true taste of architecture in this kingdom.—WARBURTON.
[3] The author here plainly laments that he was so long employed in translating and commenting. He began the *Iliad* in 1713, and finished it in 1719. The edition of *Shakespeare* (which he undertook merely because nobody else would) took up near two years more in the drudgery of comparing impressions, rectifying the scenery, etc., and the translation of half the *Odyssey* employed him from that time to 1725.—WARBURTON.

them offering to approach her is driven back by a rival; but she commends and encourages both. The first who speak in form are the geniuses of the schools, who assure her of their care to advance her cause, by confining youth to words, and keeping them out of the way of real knowledge. Their address, and her gracious answer; with her charge to them and the universities. The universities appear by their proper deputies, and assure her, that the same method is observed in the progress of education. The speech of Aristarchus on this subject. They are drawn off by a band of young gentlemen returned from travel with their tutors; one of whom delivers to the goddess, in a polite oration, an account of the whole conduct and fruits of their travels: presenting to her at the same time a young nobleman perfectly accomplished. She receives him graciously, and endues him with the happy quality of want of shame. She sees loitering about her a number of indolent persons abandoning all business and duty, and dying with laziness. To these approaches the antiquary Annius, entreating her to make them Virtuosos, and assign them over to him; but Mummius, another antiquary, complaining of his fraudulent proceeding, she finds a method to reconcile their difference. Then enter a troop of people fantastically adorned, offering her strange and exotic presents. Amongst them one stands forth and demands justice on another, who had deprived him of one of the greatest curiosities in nature; but he justifies himself so well that the goddess gives them both her approbation. She recommends to them to find proper employment for the indolents before mentioned, in the study of butterflies, shells, birds' nests, moss, etc., but with particular caution not to proceed beyond trifles, to any useful or extensive views of nature, or of the Author of Nature. Against the last of these apprehensions she is secured by a hearty address from the minute philosophers and freethinkers, one of whom speaks in the name of the rest. The youth, thus instructed and principled, are delivered to her in a body by the hands of Silenus, and then admitted to taste the cup of the Magus, her high priest, which causes a total oblivion of all obligations, divine, civil, moral, or rational. To these her adepts she sends priests, attendants, and comforters of various kinds; confers on them orders and degrees, and then dismissing them with a speech confirming to each his privileges, and telling what she expects from each, concludes with a yawn of extraordinary virtue: the progress and effects whereof on all orders of men, and the consummation of all in the restoration of night and chaos, conclude the poem.

BOOK IV[1]

YET, yet a moment, one dim ray of light
Indulge, dread Chaos, and eternal Night!
Of darkness visible so much be lent,
As half to show, half veil, the deep intent.
Ye pow'rs! whose mysteries restored I sing,   5
To whom Time bears me on his rapid wing,
Suspend a while your force inertly strong,
Then take at once the poet and the song.

  Now flamed the dog-star's unpropitious ray,
Smote ev'ry brain, and withered ev'ry bay;   10
Sick was the sun, the owl forsook his bower,
The moon-struck prophet felt the madding hour:
Then rose the seed of Chaos, and of Night,
To blot out order, and extinguish light,
Of dull and venal a new world to mould,   15
And bring Saturnian days of lead and gold.

  She mounts the throne: her head a cloud concealed,
In broad effulgence all below revealed;
('Tis thus aspiring Dulness ever shines)
Soft on her lap her laureate son reclines.   20

  Beneath her footstool, Science groans in chains,
And Wit dreads exile, penalties, and pains,
There foamed rebellious Logic, gagged and bound,
There, stripped, fair Rhet'ric languished on the ground;
His blunted arms by Sophistry are borne,   25
And shameless Billingsgate her robes adorn.
Morality, by her false guardians drawn,
(Chicane in furs, and Casuistry in lawn,)
Gasps, as they straiten at each end the cord,
And dies when Dulness gives her Page the word.[2]   30

[1] This book may properly be distinguished from the former by the name of the "Greater" *Dunciad*, not so indeed in size, but in subject; and so far contrary to the distinction anciently made of the "Greater" and "Lesser" *Iliad*. But much are they mistaken who imagine this work in any wise inferior to the former, or of any other hand than of our poet; of which I am much more certain than that the *Iliad* itself was the work of Solomon, or the *Batrachomuomachia* of Homer, as Barnes hath affirmed. —BENTLEY. POPE.

[2] There was a judge of this name always ready to hang any man that came in his way, of which he was suffered to give a hundred miserable examples during a long life, even to his dotage.—POPE.

Mad Máthesis [1] alone was unconfined,
Too mad for mere material chains to bind,
Now to pure space lifts her ecstatic stare,
Now running round the circle finds it square.
But held in tenfold bonds the Muses lie,　35
Watched both by Envy's and by Flattery's eye:
There to her heart sad Tragedy addrest
The dagger wont to pierce the tyrant's breast;
But sober History restrained her rage,
And promised vengeance on a barb'rous age.　40
There sunk Thalia, nerveless, cold, and dead,
Had not her sister Satire held her head;
Nor couldst thou, Chesterfield! [2] a tear refuse,
Thou wep'st, and with thee wept each gentle Muse.

　When lo! a harlot form [3] soft sliding by,　45
With mincing step, small voice, and languid eye:
Foreign her air, her robe's discordant pride
In patch-work flutt'ring, and her head aside:
By singing peers upheld on either hand,
She tripped and laughed, too pretty much to stand;　50
Cast on the prostrate Nine a scornful look,
Then thus in quaint recitativo spoke.

　"O Cara! Cara! silence all that train:
Joy to great Chaos! let division reign: [4]
Chromatic tortures soon shall drive them hence,　55
Break all their nerves and fritter all their sense:
One trill shall harmonise joy, grief, and rage,
Wake the dull church, and lull the ranting stage;
To the same notes thy sons shall hum, or snore,

[1] Alluding to the strange conclusions some mathematicians have deduced from their principles concerning the real quantity of matter, the reality of space, etc.—POPE.

[2] This noble person in the year 1737, when the Act was brought into the House of Lords, opposed it in an excellent speech.—POPE.

[3] The attitude given to this phantom represents the nature and genius of the Italian opera; its affected airs, its effeminate sounds, and the practice of patching up these operas with favourite songs, incoherently put together. These things were supported by the subscriptions of the nobility. This circumstance that opera should prepare for the opening of the grand sessions was prophesied of in book iii. ver. 304.—POPE.

[4] Alluding to the false taste of playing tricks in music with numberless divisions, to the neglect of that harmony which conforms to the sense and applies to the passions. Mr. Handel had introduced a great number of hands and more variety of instruments into the orchestra, and employed even drums and cannon to make a fuller chorus; which proved so much too manly for the fine gentlemen of his age, that he was obliged to remove his music into Ireland. After which they were reduced, for want of composers, to practise the patchwork above-mentioned.—POPE.

And all thy yawning daughters cry, "Encore."   60
Another Phœbus, thy own Phœbus, reigns,
Joys in my jigs, and dances in my chains.
But soon, ah soon, rebellion will commence,
If music meanly borrows aid from sense.
Strong in new arms, lo! Giant Handel stands,   65
Like bold Briareus, with a hundred hands;
To stir, to rouse, to shake the soul he comes,
And Jove's own thunders follow Mars's Drums.
Arrest him, empress; or you sleep no more——"
She heard, and drove him to the Hibernian shore.   70
    And now had Fame's posterior trumpet blown,
And all the nations summoned to the throne.
The young, the old, who feel her inward sway,
One instinct seizes, and transports away.
None need a guide, by sure attraction led,   75
And strong impulsive gravity of head;
None want a place, for all their centre found,
Hung to the goddess and cohered around.
Not closer, orb in orb, conglobed are seen
The buzzing bees about their dusky queen.   80
    The gath'ring number as it moves along,
Involves a vast involuntary throng,
Who gently drawn, and struggling less and less,
Roll in her vortex, and her power confess.
Not those alone who passive own her laws,   85
But who, weak rebels, more advance her cause.
Whate'er of dunce in college or in town
Sneers at another in toupee or gown;
Whate'er of mongrel no one class admits,
A wit with dunces, and a dunce with wits.   90
    Nor absent they, no members of her state,
Who pay her homage in her sons, the great;
Who, false to Phœbus, bow the knee to Baal;
Or, impious, preach his word without a call.
Patrons, who sneak from living worth to dead,   95
Withhold the pension, and set up the head;
Or vest dull flatt'ry in the sacred gown;
Or give from fool to fool the laurel crown.
And (last and worst) with all the cant of wit,
Without the soul, the Muse's hypocrite.   100
    There marched the bard and blockhead, side by side,
Who rhymed for hire, and patronised for pride.

Narcissus, praised with all a parson's power,
Looked a white lily sunk beneath a shower.[1]
There moved Montalto [2] with superior air;   105
His stretched-out arm displayed a volume fair;
Courtiers and patriots in two ranks divide,
Through both he passed, and bowed from side to side;
But as in graceful act, with awful eye
Composed he stood, bold Benson [3] thrust him by: 110
On two unequal crutches propped he came,
Milton's on this, on that one Johnston's name.
The decent knight retired with sober rage,
Withdrew his hand, and closed the pompous page.
But (happy for him as the times went then)   115
Appeared Apollo's mayor and aldermen,
On whom three hundred gold-capped youths await,
To lug the pond'rous volume off in state.
    When Dulness, smiling—"Thus revive [4] the wits!
But murder first, and mince them all to bits;   120
As erst Medea (cruel so to save!)
A new edition of old Æson gave;
Let standard authors, thus, like trophies borne,
Appear more glorious as more hacked and torn.
And you, my critics! in the chequered shade,   125
Admire new light through holes yourselves have made.
Leave not a foot of verse, a foot of stone,
A page,[5] a grave, that they can call their own;
But spread, my sons, your glory thin or thick,
On passive paper, or on solid brick.   130
So by each bard an alderman shall sit,[6]

[1] Means Dr. Middleton's laboured encomium on Lord Hervey in his
dedication of the *Life of Cicero.*—WARTON.
[2] Sir Thomas Hanmer, an editor of Shakespeare.—WAKEFIELD.
[3] This man endeavoured to raise himself to fame by erecting monuments,
striking coins, setting up heads and procuring translations of Milton: and
afterwards by as great passion for Arthur Johnston, a Scotch physician's
version of the psalms, of which he printed many fine editions. See more
of him, book iii. ver. 325.—POPE.
[4] The goddess applauds the practice of tacking the obscure names of
persons not eminent in any branch of learning to those of the most dis-
tinguished writers, either by printing editions of their works with im-
pertinent alterations of their text, as in the former instances, or by setting
up monuments disgraced with their own vile names and inscriptions, as
in the latter.—POPE.
[5] *Pagina*, not *pedissequus.* A page of a book; not a servant, follower, or
attendant; no poet having had a page since the death of Mr. Thomas
Durfey.—SCRIBLERUS. (POPE.)
[6] Alluding to the monument erected for Butler by Alderman Barber.—
WARBURTON.

A heavy lord shall hang at ev'ry wit,
And while on fame's triumphal car they ride,
Some slave of mine be pinioned to their side."
    Now crowds on crowds around the goddess press,   135
Each eager to present their first address.
Dunce scorning dunce beholds the next advance,
But fop shows fop superior complaisance.
When lo! a spectre rose, whose index-hand
Held forth the virtue of the dreadful wand;   140
His beavered brow a birchen garland wears,
Dropping with infant's blood, and mother's tears,
O'er every vein a shuddering horror runs;
Eton and Winton shake through all their sons,
All flesh is humbled, Westminster's bold race   145
Shrink, and confess the genius of the place:
The pale boy-senator yet tingling stands,
And holds his breeches close with both his hands.
    Then thus: "Since man from beast by words is known,
Words are man's province, words we teach alone.   150
When reason doubtful, like the Samian letter,[1]
Points him two ways; the narrower is the better.
Placed at the door of learning, youth to guide,
We never suffer it to stand too wide.[2]
To ask, to guess, to know, as they commence,   155
As fancy opens the quick springs of sense,
We ply the memory, we load the brain,
Bind rebel wit, and double chain on chain;
Confine the thought, to exercise the breath;
And keep them in the pale of words till death.   160
Whate'er the talents, or howe'er designed,
We hang one jingling padlock on the mind:
A poet the first day he dips his quill;
And what the last? A very poet still.
Pity! the charm works only in our wall,   165
Lost, lost too soon in yonder house or hall.[3]

---

[1] The letter Y, used by Pythagoras as an emblem of the different roads
to virtue and vice.

    " Et tibi quæ Samios diduxit litera ramos."—*Pers.*
                                 Pope.

[2] This circumstance of the *genius loci* (with that of the index-hand
before) seems to be an allusion to the *Table of Cebes*, where the genius of
human nature points out the road to be pursued by those entering into
life.—Pope.
[3] Westminster Hall and the House of Commons.—Pope.

There truant Wyndham ev'ry muse gave o'er,
There Talbot[1] sunk, and was a wit no more!
How sweet an Ovid, Murray,[2] was our boast!
How many Martials were in Pulteney[3] lost!   170
Else sure some bard, to our eternal praise,
In twice ten thousand rhyming nights and days,
Had reached the work, the All that mortal can;
And South beheld that masterpiece of man."[4]

"Oh" (cried the goddess) "for some pedant reign!   175
Some gentle James, to bless the land again;
To stick the doctor's chair into the throne,
Give law to words, or war with words alone,
Senates and courts with Greek and Latin rule,
And turn the council to a grammar school![5]   180
For sure, if Dulness sees a grateful day,
'Tis in the shade of arbitrary sway.
O! if my sons may learn one earthly thing,
Teach but that one, sufficient for a king;
That which my priests, and mine alone, maintain,   185
Which as it dies, or lives, we fall, or reign:
May you, may Cam and Isis, preach it long!
The Right Divine of kings to govern wrong."

Prompt at the call, around the goddess roll
Broad hats, and hoods, and caps, a sable shoal: 190
Thick and more thick the black blockade extends,
A hundred head of Aristotle's friends.
Nor wert thou, Isis! wanting to the day,
[Though Christchurch long kept prudishly away].[6]
Each staunch Polemic, stubborn as a rock,   195

---

[1] Sir William Wyndham, English statesman; the persistent opponent of Sir Robert Walpole. Charles, Baron Talbot, Lord Chancellor 1733.

[2] The Earl of Mansfield, to whom he addressed an epistle; Chancellor of Great Britain.

[3] William Pulteney, Earl of Bath, who succeeded in depriving Sir Robert Walpole of his place.

[4] Viz. an epigram. The famous Dr. South declared a perfect epigram to be as difficult a performance as an epic poem. And the critics say: "an epic poem is the greatest work human nature is capable of." —Pope.

[5] King James I. delighted in teaching his favourites Latin; and Gondemar, the Spanish ambassador, used to speak false Latin in order to give the king the pleasure of correcting him, thus securing his favour.

[6] This line is doubtless spurious, and foisted in by the impertinence of the editor; and accordingly we have put it between hooks. For I affirm this college came as early as any other by its proper deputies; nor did any college pay homage to dulness in its whole body.—Pope (under Bentley's name). By hooks, Pope means brackets.

Each fierce Logician, still expelling Locke,[1]
Came whip and spur, and dashed through thin and
    thick
On German Crouzaz,[2] and Dutch Burgersdyck.
As many quit the streams that murmuring fall
To lull the sons of Margaret and Clare Hall,[3]   200
Where Bentley late tempestuous wont to sport
In troubled waters, but now sleeps in port.[4]
Before them marched that awful Aristarch;[5]
Ploughed was his front with many a deep remark:
His hat, which never vailed to human pride,   205
Walker[6] with reverence took and laid aside.
Low bowed the rest: he, kingly, did but nod;
So upright Quakers please both man and God.
"Mistress! dismiss that rabble from your throne:
Avaunt—— is Aristarchus[7] yet unknown?   210
Thy mighty scholiast, whose unwearied pains
Made Horace dull, and humbled Milton's strains.
Turn what they will to verse, their toil is vain,
Critics like me[8] shall make it prose again.
Roman and Greek grammarians! know your better: 215
Author of something yet more great than letter;
While towering o'er your alphabet, like Saul,
Stands our Digamma,[9] and o'ertops them all.
'Tis true, on words is still our whole debate,

[1] In the year 1703 there was a meeting of the heads of the University of Oxford to censure Mr. Locke's *Essay on Human Understanding*, and to forbid the reading it. See his letters in the last edition.—POPE.

[2] Author of an abusive commentary on the *Essay on Man*—WARBURTON.

[3] The River Cam running by the walls of these colleges, which are famous for skill in disputation.

[4] Viz. "now retired into harbour, after the tempests that had long agitated his society." So Scriblerus. But the learned Scipio Maffei understands it of a certain wine called Port, from Oporto, a city of Portugal, of which this professor invited him to drink abundantly.—SCIP. MAFF., *De Compotationibus Academicis*. POPE.

[5] The redoubtable Bentley, the Cambridge critic.

[6] John Walker, vice-master of Trinity College, Cambridge, while Bentley was master. He was Bentley's constant friend.

[7] A famous commentator and corrector of Homer, whose name has been frequently used to signify a complete critic.—POPE.

[8] Bentley had much injured Milton by his fancied improvements.—SCRIBLERUS. (POPE.)

[9] Alludes to the boasted restoration of the Æolic Digamma in his long-projected edition of Homer. He calls it *something more than a letter*, from the enormous figure it would make among the other letters, being one gamma set upon the shoulders of another.—POPE.

Disputes of *me* or *te*,[1] of *aut* or *at*,   220
To sound or sink in *cano*, O or A,
Or give up Cicero to C or K.[2]
Let Freind [3] affect to speak as Terence spoke,
And Alsop never but like Horace joke:
For me, what Virgil, Pliny may deny,   225
Manilius or Solinus [4] shall supply:
For Attic phrase in Plato let them seek,
I poach in Suidas [5] for unlicensed Greek,
In ancient sense if any needs will deal,
Be sure I give them fragments, not a meal;   230
What Gellius or Stobæus hashed before,
Or chewed by blind old scholiasts o'er and o'er,
The critic eye, that microscope of wit,
Sees hairs and pores, examines bit by bit:
How parts relate to parts, or they to whole,   235
The body's harmony, the beaming soul,
Are things which Kuster, [6] Burman, Wasse shall see
When man's whole frame is obvious to a flea.

   "Ah, think not, mistress! more true dulness lies
In folly's cap, than wisdom's grave disguise.   240
Like buoys that never sink into the flood,
On learning's surface we but lie and nod.
Thine is the genuine head of many a house,
And much divinity without a νοῦς.

---

[1] It was a serious dispute, about which the learned were much divided, and some treatises written. Had it been about *meum* or *tuum* it could not be more contested than whether at the end of the first Ode of Horace to read *me doctarum hederæ præmia frontium* or *te doctarum hederæ*.—SCRIBLERUS. (POPE.)

[2] Grammatical disputes about the pronunciation of Cicero's name in Greek.

[3] Dr. Robert Freind, master of Westminster School, and canon of Christ Church. Dr. Anthony Alsop, a happy imitator of the Horatian style.—POPE.

[4] Inferior Latin authors. Solinus has been called Pliny's ape. He is supposed to have lived in the third century. His chief work was *Polyhistor*. Manilius wrote a poem on *Astronomy*.

[5] Suidas, a dictionary writer; a collector of impertinent facts and barbarous words; the second, Gellius, a minute critic; the third, Stobæus, an author, who gave his commonplace book to the public, where we happen to find much mincemeat of good old authors.—POPE.

[6] Ludolph Kuster, a German literary critic, who compiled an edition of Suidas in England, and printed it at Cambridge, 1705. That university conferred on him a doctor's degree. Franciscus Burman, Dutch theologian and professor: born 1671, died 1719. Joseph Wasse, English physician and philologist; born 1672, died 1738.

Nor could a Barrow [1] work on every block,[2]   245
Nor has one Atterbury spoiled the flock.
See! still thy own, the heavy cannon roll,
And metaphysic smokes involve the pole.
For thee we dim the eyes and stuff the head
With all such reading as was never read: 250
For thee explain a thing till all men doubt it,
And write about it, goddess, and about it:
So spins the silk-worm small its slender store,
And labours till it clouds itself all o'er.

   "What though we let some better sort of fool   255
Thrid ev'ry science, run through ev'ry school?
Never by tumbler through the hoops was shown
Such skill in passing all, and touching none;
He may indeed (if sober all this time)
Plague with dispute, or persecute with rhyme,   260
We only furnish what he cannot use,
Or wed to what he must divorce, a Muse:
Full in the midst of Euclid dip at once,
And petrify a genius to a dunce;
Or set on metaphysic ground to prance   265
Show all his paces, not a step advance.
With the same cement, ever sure to bind,
We bring to one dead level ev'ry mind.
Then take him to develop, if you can,
And hew the block off,[3] and get out the man.   270
But wherefore waste I words? I see advance
Whore, pupil, and laced governor from France.
Walker! our hat——" nor more he deigned to say,
But, stern as Ajax' spectre, strode away.

   In flowed at once a gay embroidered race,   275
And tittering pushed the pedants off the place:
Some would have spoken, but the voice was drowned
By the French horn, or by the opening hound.
The first came forwards, with as easy mien,

---

[1] Isaac Barrow, Master of Trinity: Francis Atterbury, Dean of Christ Church, both great geniuses and eloquent preachers; one more conversant in the sublime geometry, the other in classical learning; but who equally made it their care to advance the polite arts in their several societies.—POPE.

[2] An allusion to the Latin proverb: " Non ex quovis ligno fit Mercurius."
—WAKEFIELD.

[3] A notion of Aristotle that there was originally in every block of marble a statue which would appear on the removal of the superfluous parts.—POPE.

As if he saw St. James's and the queen. 280
When thus th' attendant orator begun,
" Receive, great empress! thy accomplished son:[1]
Thine from the birth, and sacred from the rod,
A dauntless infant! never scared with God.
The sire saw, one by one, his virtues wake: 285
The mother begged the blessing of a rake.
Thou gavest that ripeness, which so soon began,
And ceased so soon, he ne'er was boy, nor man.
Through school and college, thy kind cloud o'ercast,
Safe and unseen the young Æneas past: 290
Thence bursting glorious, all at once let down,
Stunned with his giddy larum half the town.
Intrepid then, o'er seas and lands he flew:
Europe he saw, and Europe saw him too.
There all thy gifts and graces we display, 295
Thou, only thou, directing all our way!
To where the Seine, obsequious as she runs,
Pours at great Bourbon's feet her silken sons;
Or Tiber, now no longer Roman, rolls,
Vain of Italian arts, Italian souls: 300
To happy convents, bosomed deep in vines,
Where slumber abbots, purple as their wines:
To isles of fragrance, lily-silvered vales,
Diffusing languor in the panting gales:
To lands of singing, or of dancing slaves, 305
Love-whisp'ring woods, and lute-resounding waves.
But chief her shrine where naked Venus keeps,
And Cupids ride the lion of the deeps;[2]
Where, eased of fleets, the Adriatic main
Wafts the smooth eunuch and enamoured swain. 310
Led by my hand, he sauntered Europe round,
And gathered ev'ry vice on Christian ground;
Saw ev'ry court, heard ev'ry king declare
His royal sense of operas or the fair;
The stews and palace equally explored, 315
Intrigued with glory, and with spirit whored:
Tried all *hors-d'œuvres*, all *liqueurs* defined,
Judicious drank, and greatly-daring dined;
Dropped the dull lumber of the Latin store,
Spoiled his own language, and acquired no more; 320
All classic learning lost on classic ground;

[1] The Duke of Kingston.   [2] The winged lion of Venice.

And last turned air, the echo of a sound![1]
See now, half-cured, and perfectly well-bred,
With nothing but a solo in his head;
As much estate, and principle, and wit,   325
As Jansen, Fleetwood, Cibber[2] shall think fit;
Stolen from a duel, followed by a nun,
And, if a borough choose him not, undone;
See, to my country happy I restore
This glorious youth, and add one Venus more.[3]   330
Her too receive, (for her my soul adores)
So may the sons of sons of sons of whores
Prop thine, O empress! like each neighbour throne,
And make a long posterity thy own."
Pleased, she accepts the hero, and the dame   335
Wraps in her veil, and frees from sense of shame.

    Then looked, and saw a lazy, lolling sort,
Unseen at church, at senate, or at court,
Of ever-listless loit'rers, that attend
No cause, no trust, no duty, and no friend.   340
Thee too, my Paridel![4] she marked thee there,
Stretched on the rack of a too easy chair,
And heard thy everlasting yawn confess
The pains and penalties of idleness.
She pitied! but her pity only shed   345
Benigner influence on thy nodding head.

    But Annius,[5] crafty seer, with ebon wand,
And well-dissembled em'rald on his hand,
False as his gems, and cankered as his coins,
Came, crammed with capon, from where Pollio[6] dines.   350
Soft, as the wily fox is seen to creep,

[1] 'Yet less a body than echo itself; for echo reflects sense or words at
least, this gentleman only airs and tunes:
      "Sonus est, qui vivit in illo."—Ovid, *Met.*
                      SCRIBLERUS. (POPE.)

[3] Three eminent managers of plays who, though not governors by pro-
fession, had, each in his way, concerned themselves in the education of
youth.—POPE. The irony lies in "each in his way."
[2] Madame de la Touche, the celebrated mistress of the duke.
[4] The poet seems to speak of this young gentleman with great affection.
The name is taken from Spenser, who gives it to a wandering courtly
squire that travelled about for the same reason for which many young
squires are now fond of travelling, and especially to Paris.—POPE.
[5] The name taken from Annius the Monk of Viterbo, famous for many
impositions and forgeries of ancient manuscripts and inscriptions, which he
was prompted to by mere vanity, but our Annius had a more substantial
motive.—WARBURTON. By Annius was meant Sir Andrew Fountaine.—
WARTON.
[6] Henry Herbert, 9th Earl of Pembroke.

Where bask on sunny banks the simple sheep,
Walk round and round, now prying here, now there,
So he; but pious, whispered first his prayer.

    "Grant, gracious goddess! grant me still to cheat,   355
O may thy cloud still cover the deceit!
Thy choicer mists on this assembly shed,
But pour them thickest on the noble head.
So shall each youth, assisted by our eyes,
See other Cæsars, other Homers rise;   360
Through twilight ages hunt th' Athenian fowl,[1]
Which Chalcis, gods, and mortals call an owl,
Now see an Attys, now a Cecrops [2] clear,
Nay, Mahomet! the pigeon at thine ear;[3]
Be rich in ancient brass, though not in gold,   365
And keep his lares, though his house be sold;
To headless Phœbe his fair bride postpone,
Honour a Syrian prince above his own;
Lord of an Otho, if I vouch it true;
Blest in one Niger, till he knows of two."   370
    Mummius [4] o'erheard him; Mummius, fool-renowned,
Who like his Cheops [5] stinks above the ground,
Fierce as a startled adder, swelled, and said,
Rattling an ancient sistrum at his head:
    "Speakest thou of Syrian princes? [6] traitor base!   375
Mine, goddess! mine is all the hornéd race.
True, he had wit, to make their value rise;
From foolish Greeks to steal them, was as wise;
More glorious yet, from barb'rous hands to keep,
When Sallee rovers chased him on the deep.   380
Then taught by Hermes,[7] and divinely bold,
Down his own throat he risked the Grecian gold,
Received each demi-god, with pious care,
Deep in his entrails—I revered them there,

[1] The owl stamped on the reverse of the ancient money of Athens.
      "Which Chalcis gods, and mortals call an owl,"
is the verse by which Hobbes renders that of Homer.—WARBURTON.
  [2] Cecrops, the first king of Athens, of whom it is hard to suppose any coins extant.—POPE.
  [3] Mahommed professed to receive divine messages from a pigeon.
  [4] This name is not merely an allusion to the mummies he was so fond of, but probably referred to the Roman general of that name, who burned Corinth.—WARBURTON.   Possibly the Earl of Sandwich is meant.
  [5] King of Egypt.
  [6] The strange story following, which may be taken for a fiction of the poet, is justified by a true relation in Spon's *Voyages*.—POPE.
  [7] Hermes or Mercury was the god of thieves.—POPE.

I bought them, shrouded in that living shrine,   385
And, at their second birth, they issue mine."

"Witness, great Ammon! by whose horns I swore," [1]
(Replied soft Annius) "this our paunch before
Still bears them, faithful; and that thus I eat,
Is to refund the medals with the meat.   390
To prove me, goddess! clear of all design,
Bid me with Pollio sup, as well as dine:
There all the learned shall at the labour stand,
And Douglas [2] lend his soft, obstetric hand."

The goddess smiling seemed to give consent;   395
So back to Pollio, hand in hand, they went.

Then thick as locusts black'ning all the ground,
A tribe, with weeds and shells fantastic crowned,
Each with some wondrous gift approached the power,
A nest, a toad, a fungus, or a flower.   400
But far the foremost, two, with earnest zeal
And aspect ardent to the throne appeal.

The first thus opened: "Hear thy suppliant's call,
Great queen, and common mother of us all!
Fair from its humble bed I reared this flower,   405
Suckled, and cheered, with air, and sun, and shower,
Soft on the paper ruff its leaves I spread,
Bright with the gilded button tipped its head;
Then throned in glass, and named it Caroline: [3]
Each maid cried, Charming! and each youth, Divine!   410
Did Nature's pencil ever blend such rays,
Such varied light in one promiscuous blaze?
Now prostrate! dead! behold that Caroline:
No maid cries, Charming! and no youth, Divine!
And lo, the wretch! whose vile, whose insect lust   415
Laid this gay daughter of the spring in dust.
Oh, punish him, or to th' Elysian shades
Dismiss my soul, where no carnation fades!"
He ceased, and wept. With innocence of mien,

---

[1] Jupiter Ammon is called to witness, as the father of Alexander, to whom those kings succeeded, and whose horns they wore on their medals. —Pope.

[2] A physician of great learning and no less taste; above all curious in what related to Horace, of whom he collected every edition, translation and comment, to the number of several hundred volumes.—Warburton. Pope.

[3] An ambitious gardener at Hammersmith caused his favourite flower to be painted on his sign, with this inscription, "This is my Queen Caroline."—Warburton. Pope.

Th' accused stood forth, and thus addressed the queen: 420
  " Of all the enamelled race, whose silv'ry wing
Waves to the tepid zephyrs of the spring,
Or swims along the fluid atmosphere,
Once brightest shined this child of heat and air.
I saw, and started from its vernal bow'r,   425
The rising game, and chased from flow'r to flow'r.
It fled, I followed; now in hope, now pain;
It stopt, I stopt; it moved, I moved again.
At last it fixed, 'twas on what plant it pleased,
And where it fixed, the beauteous bird I seized: 430
Rose or carnation was below my care;
I meddle, goddess! only in my sphere.
I tell the naked fact without disguise,
And, to excuse it, need but show the prize;
Whose spoils this paper offers to your eye,   435
Fair even in death! this peerless butterfly."
  "My sons!" (she answered) "both have done your parts:
Live happy both, and long promote our arts.
But hear a mother, when she recommends
To your fraternal care our sleeping friends.   440
The common soul, of Heav'n's more frugal make,
Serves but to keep fools pert, and knaves awake:
A drowsy watchman, that just gives a knock,
And breaks our rest, to tell us what's o'clock.
Yet by some object ev'ry brain is stirred;   445
The dull may waken to a humming bird;
The most recluse, discreetly opened, find
Congenial matter in the cockle-kind;
The mind, in metaphysics at a loss,
May wander in a wilderness of moss;   450
The head that turns at super-lunar things,
Poised with a tail, may steer on Wilkins' wings.[1]
  "O! would the sons of men once think their eyes
And reason giv'n them but to study flies!
See Nature in some partial narrow shape,   455
And let the Author of the whole escape:
Learn but to trifle, or, who most observe,
To wonder at their Maker, not to serve!"

---

[1] One of the first projectors of the Royal Society, who, among many enlarged and useful notions, entertained the extravagant hope of a possibility to fly to the moon; which has put some volatile geniuses upon making wings for that purpose.—WARBURTON. POPE.

"Be that my task" (replies a gloomy clerk,
Sworn foe to mystery, yet divinely dark;   460
Whose pious hope aspires to see the day
When moral evidence shall quite decay,
And damns implicit faith, and holy lies,
Prompt to impose, and fond to dogmatise:)
"Let others creep by timid steps, and slow,   465
On plain experience lay foundations low,
By common sense to common knowledge bred,
And last, to Nature's cause through Nature led.
All-seeing in thy mists, we want no guide,
Mother of arrogance, and source of pride!   470
We nobly take the high Priori Road,[1]
And reason downward, till we doubt of God;
Make Nature still [2] encroach upon His plan;
And shove Him off as far as e'er we can:
Thrust some mechanic cause into His place;[3]   475
Or bind in matter, or diffuse in space.
Or, at one bound o'erleaping all His laws,
Make God man's image, man the final cause,
Find virtue local, all relation scorn,
See all in self, and but for self be born: 480
Of nought so certain as our reason still,
Of nought so doubtful as of soul and will.
Oh hide the God still more! and make us see
Such as Lucretius drew, a God like thee:
Wrapped up in self, a God without a thought,   485
Regardless of our merit or default.
Or that bright image [4] to our fancy draw,
Which Theocles [5] in raptured vision saw,

[1] Those who, from the effects in this visible world, deduce the Eternal Power and Godhead of the first cause, though they cannot attain to an adequate idea of the Deity, yet discover so much of Him as enables them to see the end of their creation, and the means of their happiness: whereas they who take this high Priori Road (such as Hobbes, Spinoza, Descartes and some better reasoners), for one that goes right ten lose themselves in mists, or ramble after visions, which deprive them of all sight of their end, and mislead them in the choice of wrong means.—WARBURTON. POPE.

[2] This relates to such as being ashamed to assert a mere mechanic cause, and yet unwilling to forsake it entirely, have had recourse to a certain plastic nature, elastic fluid, subtle matter, etc.—WARBURTON. POPE.

[3] The first of these follies is that of Descartes; the second of Hobbes; the third of some succeeding philosophers.—POPE.

[4] Bright image was the title given by the later Platonists to that vision of nature which they had formed out of their own fancy, so bright that they called it Αὐτοπτον Ἀγαλμα, or the self-seen image, i.e. seen by its own light.—SCRIBLERUS. POPE.

[5] The philosopher in Lord Shaftesbury's dialogue The Moralists.

While through poetic scenes the Genius roves,
Or wanders wild in academic groves; 490
That Nature our society adores,
Where Tindal dictates, and Silenus[1] snores.

Roused at his name, up rose the bousy sire,
And shook from out his pipe the seeds of fire;[2]
Then snapped his box, and stroked his belly down, 495
Rosy and rev'rend, though without a gown.
Bland and familiar to the throne he came,
Led up the youth, and called the Goddess dame:
Then thus: "From priest-craft happily set free,
Lo, ev'ry finished son returns to thee: 500
First slave to words, then vassal to a name,
Then dupe to party; child and man the same;
Bounded by Nature, narrowed still by art,
A trifling head, and a contracted heart.
Thus bred, thus taught, how many have I seen, 505
Smiling on all, and smiled on by a queen?[3]
Marked out for honours, honoured for their birth,
To thee the most rebellious things on earth:
Now to thy gentle shadow all are shrunk,
All melted down, in pension, or in punk! 510
So K* so B**[4] sneaked into the grave,
A monarch's half, and half a harlot's slave.
Poor W**[5] nipped in folly's broadest bloom,
Who praises now? his chaplain on his tomb.
Then take them all, oh take them to thy breast! 515
Thy Magus,[6] Goddess! shall perform the rest."

With that, a wizard old his cup extends;
Which whoso tastes, forgets his former friends,
Sire, ancestors, himself. One casts his eyes
Up to a star, and like Endymion dies: 520
A feather, shooting from another's head,
Extracts his brain; and principle is fled;
Lost is his God, his country, ev'rything;
And nothing left but homage to a king!

---

[1] By Silenus he means Thos. Gordon, a violent Whig, the translator of Tacitus, who published the *Independent Whig*.—WARTON.
[2] The Epicurean language, *Semina rerum*, or atoms, Virg., eclog. vi.
   "Semina ignis—semina flammæ."   POPE.
[3] *I.e.* This Queen or Goddess of Dulness.—POPE.
[4] Kent (Duke of) and Berkeley, first Lord of the Admiralty. Both were K.G.s.
[5] Philip, Duke of Wharton, celebrated for his profligacy and eccentricity. He died in exile, 1731.—BOWLES.
[6] The effect of the Magus cup was the reverse of that of Circe.

The vulgar herd turn off to roll with hogs,   525
To run with horses, or to hunt with dogs,
But, sad example! never to escape
Their infamy, still keep the human shape.
But she, good Goddess, sent to ev'ry child
Firm impudence, or stupefaction mild;   530
And straight succeeded, leaving shame no room,
Cibberian forehead, or Cimmerian gloom.

Kind self-conceit to some her glass applies,
Which no one looks in with another's eyes:
But as the flatt'rer or dependant paint,   535
Beholds himself a patriot, chief, or saint.

On others Int'rest her gay liv'ry flings,
Int'rest that waves on party-coloured wings:
Turned to the sun, she casts a thousand dyes,
And, as she turns, the colours fall or rise.   540

Others the siren sisters warble round,
And empty heads console with empty sound.
No more, alas! the voice of fame they hear,
The balm of dulness trickling in their ear.
Great C**, H**, P**, R**, K*, [1]   545
Why all your toils? your sons have learned to sing.
How quick ambition hastes to ridicule!
The sire is made a peer, the son a fool.

On some, a priest succinct in amice white
Attends; all flesh is nothing in his sight!   550
Beeves, at his touch, at once to jelly turn,
And the huge boar is shrunk into an urn:
The board with specious miracles he loads,
Turns hares to larks, and pigeons into toads.
Another (for in all what one can shine?)   555
Explains the *sève* and *verdeur* [2] of the vine.
What cannot copious sacrifice atone?
Thy truffles, Perigord! thy hams, Bayonne!
With French libation, and Italian strain,
Wash Bladen white, and expiate Hays's stain. [3]   560

[1] Cowper, Harcourt, Parker, Raymond, King.
[2] French terms relating to wines.
[3] Bladen—Hays. Names of gamesters. Robert Knight, cashier of the South Sea Company, who fled from England in 1720 (afterwards pardoned in 1742). These lived with the utmost magnificence at Paris, and kept open tables frequented by persons of the first quality of England, and even by princes of the blood of France.—POPE. Colonel Martin Bladen was a man of some literature, and translated Cæsar's *Commentaries*. I never could learn that he had offended Pope. He was uncle to William Collins, the poet, whom he left an estate.—WARTON.

Knight lifts the head, for what are crowds undone,
To three essential partridges in one?
Gone every blush, and silent all reproach,
Contending princes mount them in their coach.

Next, bidding all draw near on bended knees, 565
The queen confers her titles and degrees.
Her children first of more distinguished sort,
Who study Shakespeare at the Inns of Court,[1]
Impale a glow-worm, or vertù profess,
Shine in the dignity of F.R.S. 570
Some, deep Freemasons, join the silent race
Worthy to fill Pythagoras's place:
Some botanists, or florists at the least,
Or issue members of an annual feast.
Nor past the meanest unregarded, one 575
Rose a Gregorian, one a Gormogon.[2]
The last, not least in honour or applause,
Isis and Cam made doctors of her laws.

Then, blessing all, "Go, children of my care!
To practice now from theory repair. 580
All my commands are easy, short, and full:
My sons! be proud, be selfish, and be dull.
Guard my prerogative, assert my throne:
This nod confirms each privilege your own.
The cap and switch be sacred to his grace; 585
With staff and pumps the marquis lead the race;
From stage to stage the licensed earl may run,
Paired with his fellow-charioteer, the sun;
The learned baron butterflies design,
Or draw to silk Arachne's subtle line;[3] 590
The judge to dance his brother sergeant call;[4]
The senator at cricket urge the ball;
The bishop stow (pontific luxury!)
An hundred souls of turkeys in a pie;
The sturdy squire to Gallic masters stoop, 595
And drown his lands and manors in a soupe.
Others import yet nobler arts from France,

[1] Including perhaps Thomas Edwards who later (1748) attacked Warburton in his entertaining *The Canons of Criticism*.
[2] A sort of lay brothers, slips from the roots of the Freemasons.—POPE.
[3] This is one of the most ingenious employments assigned, and therefore recommended only to peers of learning. Of weaving stockings of the webs of spiders, see the *Philosophical Transactions*.—WARBURTON. POPE.
[4] Alluding, perhaps, to that ancient and solemn dance intituled *A Call of Sergeants*.—POPE.

Teach kings to fiddle, and make senates dance,
Perhaps more high some daring son may soar,
Proud to my list to add one monarch more!   600
And nobly conscious, princes are but things
Born for first ministers, as slaves for kings.
Tyrant supreme! shall three estates command,
And make one mighty Dunciad of the land!"

   More she had spoke, but yawned—All Nature nods: 605
What mortal can resist the yawn of Gods?
Churches and chapels instantly it reached;
(St. James's first, for leaden G—— preached)[1]
Then catched the schools; the hall scarce kept awake;
The convocation gaped, but could not speak: 610
Lost was the nation's sense, nor could be found,
While the long solemn unison went round:
Wide, and more wide, it spread o'er all the realm;
Even Palinurus[2] nodded at the helm:
The vapour mild o'er each committee crept;   615
Unfinished treaties in each office slept;
And chiefless armies dozed out the campaign;
And navies yawned for orders on the main.

   O Muse! relate, (for you can tell alone
Wits have short memories, and dunces none,)   620
Relate, who first, who last resigned to rest;
Whose heads she partly, whose completely, blest;
What charms could faction, what ambition lull,
The venal quiet, and entrance the dull;
Till drowned was sense, and shame, and right, and wrong—
O sing, and hush the nations with thy song!   626

    .   .   .   .   .

   In vain, in vain—the all-composing hour
Resistless falls: the Muse obeys the pow'r.
She comes! she comes! the sable throne behold
Of Night primeval and of Chaos old!   630
Before her, fancy's gilded clouds decay,
And all its varying rainbows die away.
Wit shoots in vain its momentary fires,
The meteor drops, and in a flash expires.
As one by one, at dread Medea's strain,   635

[1] Dr. Gilbert, Archbishop of York, who had attacked Dr. King of Oxford,
whom Pope much respected.—WARTON.
[2] Palinurus was the pilot of Aeneas, who fell into the sea when sleeping
at the helm. Sir Robert Walpole is here meant.

The sick'ning stars fade off th' ethereal plain;
As Argus' eyes by Hermes' wand opprest,
Closed one by one to everlasting rest;
Thus at her felt approach, and secret might,
Art after art goes out, and all is night,   640
See skulking Truth to her old cavern fled,
Mountains of casuistry heaped o'er her head!
Philosophy, that leaned on Heaven before,
Shrinks to her second cause, and is no more.
Physic of metaphysic begs defence,   645
And metaphysic calls for aid on sense!
See mystery to mathematics fly!
In vain! they gaze, turn giddy, rave, and die.
Religion blushing veils her sacred fires,
And unawares morality expires.   650
Nor public flame, nor private, dares to shine,
Nor human spark is left, nor glimpse divine!
Lo! thy dread empire, Chaos! is restored;
Light dies before thy uncreating word;
Thy hand, great Anarch! lets the curtain fall,   655
And universal darkness buries all.

ESSAY ON MAN

EPISTLE I

ARGUMENT

OF THE NATURE AND STATE OF MAN WITH RESPECT TO THE UNIVERSE

Of man in the abstract.—I. That we can judge only with regard
to our own system, being ignorant of the relation of systems and
things, ver. 17, etc. II. That man is not to be deemed imperfect,
but a being suited to his place and rank in the creation, agreeable
to the general order of things, and conformable to ends and rela-
tions to him unknown, ver. 35, etc. III. That it is partly upon his
ignorance of future events, and partly upon the hope of a future
state, that all his happiness in the present depends, ver. 77, etc.
IV. The pride of aiming at more knowledge, and pretending to
more perfection, the cause of man's error and misery. The impiety
of putting himself in the place of God, and judging of the fitness or

unfitness, perfection or imperfection, justice or injustice, of His
dispensations, ver. 113, etc.   V. The absurdity of conceiting himself
the final cause of the creation, or expecting that perfection in the
moral world which is not in the natural, ver. 131, etc.   VI. The
unreasonableness of his complaints against Providence, while on
the one hand he demands the perfections of the angels and on the
other the bodily qualifications of the brutes; though to possess
any of the sensitive faculties in a higher degree would render
him miserable, ver. 173, etc.   VII. That throughout the whole
visible world an universal order and gradation in the sensual and
mental faculties is observed, which causes a subordination of
creature to creature, and of all creatures to Man.   The gradations
of sense, instinct, thought, reflection, reason; that reason alone
countervails all the other faculties, ver. 207.   VIII. How much
farther this order and subordination of living creatures may ex-
tend above and below us; were any part of which broken, not
that part only, but the whole connected creation, must be
destroyed, ver. 233.   IX. The extravagance, madness, and pride
of such a desire, ver. 259.   X. The consequence of all the absolute
submission due to Providence, both as to our present and future
state, ver. 281, etc., to the end.

AWAKE, my St. John! leave all meaner things
To low ambition and the pride of kings.
Let us (since life can little more supply
Than just to look about us, and to die)
Expatiate free o'er all this scene of man;   5
A mighty maze! but not without a plan:
A wild, where weeds and flowers promiscuous shoot;
Or garden, tempting with forbidden fruit.
Together let us beat this ample field,
Try what the open, what the covert yield!   10
The latent tracts, the giddy heights explore
Of all who blindly creep, or sightless soar;
Eye Nature's walks, shoot folly as it flies,
And catch the manners living as they rise:
Laugh where we must, be candid where we can;   15
But vindicate the ways of God to man.

    I. Say first, of God above, or man below,
What can we reason, but from what we know?
Of man, what see we but his station here,
From which to reason, or to which refer?   20
Through worlds unnumbered, though the God be known,
'Tis ours to trace Him only in our own.
He, who through vast immensity can pierce,
See worlds on worlds compose one universe,
Observe how system into system runs,   25

What other planets circle other suns,
What varied being peoples every star,
May tell why Heaven has made us as we are,
But of this frame the bearings and the ties,
The strong connections, nice dependencies, 30
Gradations just, has thy pervading soul
Look'd through? or can a part contain the whole?

   Is the great chain, that draws all to agree,
And drawn, supports, upheld by God or thee?
   II. Presumptuous man! the reason wouldst thou find, 35
Why form'd so weak, so little, and so blind?
First, if thou canst, the harder reason guess,
Why form'd no weaker, blinder, and no less?
Ask of thy mother earth, why oaks are made
Taller and stronger than the weeds they shade? 40
Or ask of yonder argent fields above,
Why Jove's satellites are less than Jove?
   Of systems possible, if 'tis confess'd,
That Wisdom infinite must form the best,
Where all must full, or not coherent be, 45
And all that rises, rise in due degree;
Then in the scale of reas'ning life, 'tis plain,
There must be, somewhere, such a rank as man:
And all the question (wrangle e'er so long)
Is only this, if God has placed him wrong? 50
   Respecting man, whatever wrong we call,
May, must be right, as relative to all.
In human works, though labour'd on with pain,
A thousand movements scarce one purpose gain;
In God's, one single can its end produce; 55
Yet serves to second too, some other use,
So man, who here seems principal alone,
Perhaps acts second to some sphere unknown,
Touches some wheel, or verges to some goal;
'Tis but a part we see, and not a whole. 60
   When the proud steed shall know why man restrains
His fiery course, or drives him o'er the plains;
When the dull ox, why now he breaks the clod,
Is now a victim, and now Egypt's god:
Then shall man's pride and dulness comprehend 65
His actions', passions', being's use and end;
Why doing, suff'ring, check'd, impell'd; and why
This hour a slave, the next a deity.

Then say not man's imperfect, Heaven in fault;
Say rather, man's as perfect as he ought: 70
His knowledge measured to his state and place;
His time a moment, and a point his space.
If to be perfect in a certain sphere,
What matter, soon or late, or here or there?
The blest to-day is as completely so,   75
As who began a thousand years ago.
    III. Heaven from all creatures hides the book of Fate,
All but the page prescribed, their present state:
From brutes what men, from men what spirits know:
Or who could suffer being here below?   80
The lamb thy riot dooms to bleed to-day,
Had he thy reason, would he skip and play?
Pleased to the last, he crops the flowery food,
And licks the hand just raised to shed his blood.
Oh blindness to the future! kindly given,   85
That each may fill the circle mark'd by Heaven:
Who sees with equal eye, as God of all,
A hero perish, or a sparrow fall,
Atoms or systems into ruin hurl'd,
And now a bubble burst, and now a world.   90
    Hope humbly then; with trembling pinions soar;
Wait the great teacher, Death; and God adore.
What future bliss, He gives not thee to know,
But gives that hope to be thy blessing now.
Hope springs eternal in the human breast: 95
Man never Is, but always To be blest.
The soul, uneasy, and confined from home,
Rests and expatiates in a life to come.
    Lo, the poor Indian! whose untutor'd mind
Sees God in clouds, or hears Him in the wind;   100
His soul, proud Science never taught to stray
Far as the solar-walk, or milky-way;
Yet simple Nature to his hope has given,
Behind the cloud-topp'd hill, and humbler Heaven,
Some safer world in depth of woods embraced,   105
Some happier island in the watery waste,
Where slaves once more their native land behold,
No fiends torment, no Christians thirst for gold.
To Be, contents his natural desire,
He asks no angel's wings, no seraph's fire;   110
But thinks, admitted to that equal sky,

His faithful dog shall bear him company.
    IV. Go, wiser thou! and in thy scale of sense,
Weigh thy opinion against Providence;
Call imperfection what thou fanciest such, 115
Say, here He gives too little, there too much:
Destroy all creatures for thy sport or gust,
Yet cry, If man's unhappy, God's unjust;
If man alone engross not Heaven's high care,
Alone made perfect here, immortal there: 120
Snatch from His hand the balance and the rod,
Re-judge His justice, be the god of God.
In pride, in reas'ning pride, our error lies;
All quit their sphere, and rush into the skies.
Pride still is aiming at the blest abodes, 125
Men would be angels, angels would be gods.
Aspiring to be gods, if angels fell,
Aspiring to be angels, men rebel:
And who but wishes to invert the laws
Of Order, sins against the Eternal Cause. 130
    V. Ask for what end the Heavenly bodies shine—
Earth for whose use? Pride answers, "'Tis for mine:
For me kind Nature wakes her genial power,
Suckles each herb, and spreads out ev'ry flower;
Annual for me, the grape, the rose renew, 135
The juice nectareous, and the balmy dew;
For me, the mine a thousand treasures brings;
For me, health gushes from a thousand springs;
Seas roll to waft me, suns to light me rise;
My footstool earth, my canopy the skies." 140
    But errs not Nature from this gracious end,
From burning suns when livid deaths descend,
When earthquakes swallow, or when tempests sweep
Towns to one grave, whole nations to the deep?
"No, ('tis replied) the first Almighty Cause 145
Acts not by partial, but by gen'ral laws;
The exceptions few: some change since all began:
And what created perfect?"—Why then man?
If the great end be human happiness,
Then Nature deviates; and can man do less? 150
As much that end a constant course requires
Of showers and sunshine, as of man's desires;
As much eternal springs and cloudless skies,
As men for ever temperate, calm, and wise.

If plagues or earthquakes break not Heaven's design,   155
Why then a Borgia, or a Catiline?
Who knows but He, whose hand the lightning forms,
Who heaves old Ocean, and who wings the storms;
Pours fierce ambition in a Cæsar's mind,
Or turns young Ammon loose to scourge mankind?   160
From pride, from pride, our very reas'ning springs;
Account for moral as for natural things:
Why charge we Heaven in those, in these acquit?
In both, to reason right, is to submit.

Better for us, perhaps, it might appear,   165
Were there all harmony, all virtue here;
That never air or ocean felt the wind,
That never passion discomposed the mind.
But all subsists by elemental strife;
And passions are the elements of life.   170
The general order, since the whole began,
Is kept by Nature, and is kept in man.

VI. What would this man? Now upward will he soar,
And little less than angel, would be more;
Now looking downwards, just as grieved appears,   175
To want the strength of bulls, the fur of bears.
Made for his use all creatures if he call,
Say what their use, had he the powers of all?
Nature to these, without profusion, kind,
The proper organs, proper powers assign'd;   180
Each seeming want compensated of course,
Here with degrees of swiftness, there of force;
All in exact proportion to the state;
Nothing to add, and nothing to abate.
Each beast, each insect, happy in its own: 185
Is Heaven unkind to man, and man alone?
Shall he alone, whom rational we call,
Be pleased with nothing, if not blest with all?

The bliss of man (could pride that blessing find)
Is not to act or think beyond mankind;   190
No powers of body or of soul to share,
But what his Nature and his state can bear.
Why has not man a microscopic eye?
For this plain reason, man is not a fly.
Say what the use, were finer optics given,   195
To inspect a mite, not comprehend the heaven?
Or touch, if trembling alive all o'er,

To smart and agonise at every pore?
Or quick effluvia darting through the brain,
Die of a rose in aromatic pain? 200
If Nature thunder'd in his opening ears,
And stunn'd him with the music of the spheres,
How would he wish that Heaven had left him still
The whisp'ring zephyr, and the purling rill?
Who finds not Providence all good and wise, 205
Alike in what it gives and what denies?
   VII. Far as creation's ample range extends,
The scale of sensual, mental powers ascends:
Mark how it mounts to man's imperial race,
From the green myriads in the peopled grass: 210
What modes of sight betwixt each wide extreme,
The mole's dim curtain, and the lynx's beam:
Of smell, the headlong lioness between,[1]
And hound sagacious on the tainted green:
Of hearing, from the life that fills the flood, 215
To that which warbles through the vernal wood?
The spider's touch, how exquisitely fine!
Feels at each thread, and lives along the line:
In the nice bee, what sense so subtly true
From poisonous herbs extract the healing dew? 220
How instinct varies in the grov'ling swine,
Compared, half-reasoning elephant, with thine!
'Twixt that, and reason, what a nice barrier?
For ever separate, yet for ever near!
Remembrance and reflection, how allied; 225
What thin partitions sense from thought divide;[2]
And middle natures, how they long to join,
Yet never pass the insuperable line!
Without this just gradation could they be
Subjected, these to those, or all to thee? 230
The powers of all subdued by thee alone,
Is not thy reason all these powers in one?
   VIII. See, through this air, this ocean, and this earth,

[1] The manner of the lions hunting their prey in the deserts of Africa is this: At their first going out in the night-time they set up a loud roar, and then listen to the noise made by the beasts in their flight, pursuing them by the ear and not by the nostril. It is probable that the story of the jackal's hunting for the lion was occasioned by observation of this defect of scent in that terrible animal.

[2] Taken from Dryden's *Absalom and Achitophel*:

    " Great wits are sure to madness near allied,
      And thin partitions do their bounds divide."

All matter quick, and bursting into birth.
Above, how high, progressive life may go!   235
Around, how wide! how deep extend below!
Vast chain of being! which from God began,
Natures ethereal, human, angel, man,
Beast, bird, fish, insect, what no eye can see,
No glass can reach; from infinite to thee,   240
From thee to nothing.—On superior powers
Were we to press, inferior might on ours;
Or in the full creation leave a void,
Where, one step broken, the great scale's destroy'd:
From Nature's chain whatever link you strike,   245
Tenth, or ten thousandth, breaks the chain alike.
    And, if each system in gradation roll
Alike essential to the amazing whole,
The least confusion but in one, not all
That system only, but the whole must fall.   250
Let earth, unbalanced, from her orbit fly,
Planets and suns run lawless through the sky;
Let ruling angels from their spheres be hurl'd,
Being on being wreck'd, and world on world;
Heaven's whole foundations to their centre nod,   255
And Nature tremble to the throne of God.
All this dread order break—for whom? for thee?
Vile worm!—oh madness! pride! impiety!
    IX. What if the foot, ordain'd the dust to tread,
Or hand, to toil, aspired to be the head?   260
What if the head, the eye, or ear repined
To serve mere engines to the ruling mind?
Just as absurd for any part to claim
To be another, in this general frame;
Just as absurd, to mourn the tasks or pains   265
The great Directing Mind of all ordains.
    All are but parts of one stupendous whole,
Whose body Nature is, and God the soul;
That, changed through all, and yet in all the same;
Great in the earth, as in the ethereal frame;   270
Warms in the sun, refreshes in the breeze,
Glows in the stars, and blossoms in the trees;
Lives through all life, extends through all extent;
Spreads undivided, operates unspent!
Breathes in our soul, informs our mortal part,   275
As full, as perfect, in a hair as heart;

As full, as perfect in vile man that mourns,
As the rapt seraph that adores and burns:
To him no high, no low, no great, no small;
He fills, He bounds, connects, and equals all.   280
  X. Cease then, nor order imperfection name:
Our proper bliss depends on what we blame.
Know thy own point: this kind, this due degree
Of blindness, weakness, Heaven bestows on thee.
Submit, in this, or any other sphere,   285
Secure to be as blest as thou canst bear:
Safe in the hand of one Disposing Power,
Or in the natal, or the mortal hour.
All Nature is but art, unknown to thee
All chance, direction, which thou canst not see;   290
All discord, harmony not understood;
All partial evil, universal good:
And, spite of pride, in erring reason's spite,
One truth is clear, Whatever is, is right.

EPISTLE II

ARGUMENT

OF THE NATURE AND STATE OF MAN WITH RESPECT TO HIMSELF AS AN INDIVIDUAL

I. The business of Man not to pry into God, but to study himself.
His middle nature: his powers and frailties, ver. 1 to 19. The limits
of his capacity, ver. 19, etc. II. The two principles of man, self-
love and reason, both necessary, ver. 53, etc. Self-love the stronger,
and why, ver. 67, etc. Their end the same, ver. 81, etc. III. The
passions, and their use, ver. 93 to 130. The predominant passion,
and its force, ver. 132 to 160. Its necessity in directing men to
different purposes, ver. 165, etc. Its providential use, in fixing our
principle and ascertaining our virtue, ver. 177. IV. Virtue and vice
joined in our mixed nature; the limits near, yet the things separate
and evident: what is the office of reason, ver. 202 to 216. V. How
odious vice in itself, and how we deceive ourselves into it, ver. 217.
VI. That, however, the ends of Providence and general good are
answered in our passions and imperfections, ver. 238, etc. How
usefully these are distributed to all orders of men, ver. 241. How
useful they are to society, ver. 251. And to individuals, ver. 263.
In every state, and every age of life, ver. 273, etc.

Know then thyself, presume not God to scan,
The proper study of mankind is man.
Placed on this isthmus of a middle state,
A being darkly wise, and rudely great:

With too much knowledge for the sceptic side,   5
With too much weakness for the stoic's pride,
He hangs between; in doubt to act, or rest;
In doubt to deem himself a god, or beast;
In doubt his mind or body to prefer;
Born but to die, and reasoning but to err;   10
Alike in ignorance, his reason such,
Whether he thinks too little, or too much:
Chaos of Thought and Passion, all confused;
Still by himself abused or disabused;
Created half to rise, and half to fall;   15
Great lord of all things, yet a prey to all;
Sole judge of truth, in endless error hurl'd:
The glory, jest, and riddle of the world!

   Go, wondrous creature! mount where Science guides,
Go, measure earth, weigh air, and state the tides;   20
Instruct the planets in what orbs to run,
Correct old Time, and regulate the sun;[1]
Go, soar with Plato to th' empyreal sphere,
To the first good, first perfect, and first fair;
Or tread the mazy round his followers trod,   25
And quitting sense call imitating God;
As Eastern priests in giddy circles run,
And turn their heads to imitate the sun.
Go, teach Eternal Wisdom how to rule—
Then drop into thyself, and be a fool!   30

   Superior beings, when of late they saw
A mortal man unfold all Nature's law,
Admired such wisdom in an earthly shape,
And show'd a Newton as we show an ape.

   Could he, whose rules the rapid comet bind,   35
Describe or fix one movement of his mind?
Who saw its fires here rise, and there descend,
Explain his own beginning, or his end?
Alas what wonder! Man's superior part
Uncheck'd may rise, and climb from art to art;   40
But when his own great work is but begun,
What reason weaves, by passion is undone.

   Trace Science then, with modesty thy guide;

[1] " This alludes to Sir Isaac Newton's *Grecian Chronology*, which he reformed on those two sublime conceptions: the difference between the reigns of kings and the generations of men; and the position of the colures of the equinoxes and solstices at the time of the Argonautic expedition."— WARBURTON.

First strip off all her equipage of pride;
Deduct but what is vanity or dress,   45
Or learning's luxury, or idleness;
Or tricks to show the stretch of human brain,
Mere curious pleasure, or ingenious pain;
Expunge the whole, or lop the excrescent parts
Of all our vices have created arts;   50
Then see how little the remaining sum,
Which served the past, and must the times to come!
   II. Two principles in human nature reign;
Self-love, to urge, and Reason, to restrain;
Nor this a good, nor that a bad we call,   55
Each works its end, to move or govern all:
And to their proper operation still,
Ascribe all good; to their improper, ill.
  Self-love, the spring of motion, acts the soul;
Reason's comparing balance rules the whole.   60
Man, but for that, no action could attend,
And, but for this, were active to no end:
Fix'd like a plant on his peculiar spot,
To draw nutrition, propagate, and rot:
Or, meteor-like, flame lawless through the void,   65
Destroying others, by himself destroy'd.
Most strength the moving principle requires;
Active its task, it prompts, impels, inspires.
Sedate and quiet the comparing lies,
Form'd but to check, deliberate, and advise.   70
Self-love, still stronger, as its objects nigh;
Reason's at distance, and in prospect lie:
That sees immediate good by present sense;
Reason, the future and the consequence.
Thicker than arguments, temptations throng,   75
At best more watchful this, but that more strong.
The action of the stronger to suspend
Reason still use, to reason still attend.
Attention, habit, and experience gains;
Each strengthens reason, and self-love restrains.   80
Let subtle schoolmen teach these friends to fight,
More studious to divide than to unite;
And grace and virtue, sense and reason split,
With all the rash dexterity of wit.
Wits, just like fools, at war about a name,   85
Have full as oft no meaning, or the same.

Self-love and reason to one end aspire,
Pain their aversion, pleasure their desire;
But greedy that its object would devour,
This taste the honey, and not wound the flower: 90
Pleasure, or wrong or rightly understood,
Our greatest evil, or our greatest good.

    III. Modes of self-love the passions we may call:
'Tis real good, or seeming, moves them all:
But since not every good we can divide,   95
And reason bids us for our own provide;
Passions, though selfish, if their means be fair,
'List under reason, and deserve her care:
Those that imparted court a nobler aim,
Exalt their kind, and take some virtue's name.   100

    In lazy apathy let Stoics boast
Their virtue fix'd; 'tis fix'd as in a frost;
Contracted all, retiring to the breast;
But strength of mind is exercise, not rest:
The rising tempest puts in act the soul,   105
Parts it may ravage, but preserves the whole.
On life's vast ocean diversely we sail,
Reason the card, but passion is the gale;[1]
Nor God alone in the still calm we find,
He mounts the storm, and walks upon the wind.   110

    Passions, like elements, though born to fight,
Yet, mix'd and soften'd, in His work unite:
These 'tis enough to temper and employ;
But what composes man, can man destroy?
Suffice that reason keep to Nature's road,   115
Subject, compound them, follow her and God.
Love, hope, and joy, fair pleasure's smiling train,
Hate, fear, and grief, the family of pain,
These mix'd with art, and to due bounds confined,
Make and maintain the balance of the mind: 120
The lights and shades, whose well-accorded strife
Gives all the strength and colour of our life.

    Pleasures are ever in our hands or eyes;
And when in act, they cease; in prospect, rise:
Present to grasp, and future still to find,   125
The whole employ of body and of mind.
All spread their charms, but charm not all alike;

[1] The idea is in Bacon.—"The mind would be temperate and stayed, if the affections, *as winds*, did not put it into tumult."—BOWLES.

On different senses, different objects strike;
Hence different passions more or less inflame,
As strong or weak, the organs of the frame; 130
And hence one master passion in the breast,
Like Aaron's serpent, swallows up the rest.
 As man, perhaps, the moment of his breath
Receives the lurking principle of death;
The young disease, that must subdue at length, 135
Grows with his growth, and strengthens with his strength;
So, cast and mingled with his very frame,
The mind's disease, its ruling passion came;
Each vital humour which should feed the whole,
Soon flows to this, in body and in soul: 140
Whatever warms the heart, or fills the head,
As the mind opens, and its functions spread,
Imagination plies her dangerous art,
And pours it all upon the peccant part.
Nature its mother, habit is its nurse; 145
Wit, spirit, faculties, but make it worse;
Reason itself but gives it edge and power;
As Heaven's blest beam turns vinegar more sour.
We, wretched subjects though to lawful sway,
In this weak queen some favourite still obey: 150
Ah! if she lend not arms as well as rules,
What can she more than tell us we are fools?
Teach us to mourn our nature, not to mend,
A sharp accuser, but a helpless friend!
Or from a judge turn pleader, to persuade 155
The choice we make, or justify it made;
Proud of an easy conquest all along,
She but removes weak passions for the strong:
So, when small humours gather to a gout,
The doctor fancies he has driven them out. 160
 Yes, Nature's road must ever be preferr'd;
Reason is here no guide, but still a guard;
'Tis hers to rectify, not overthrow,
And treat this passion more as friend than foe:
A mightier power the strong direction sends, 165
And several men impels to several ends:
Like varying winds, by other passions toss'd,
This drives them constant to a certain coast.
Let power or knowledge, gold or glory please,
Or (oft more strong than all) the love of ease; 170

Through life 'tis follow'd, even at life's expense;
The merchant's toil, the sage's indolence,
The monk's humility, the hero's pride,
All, all alike find reason on their side.

    The eternal art educing good from ill,   175
Grafts on this passion our best principle:
'Tis thus the mercury of man is fix'd,
Strong grows the virtue with his nature mix'd;
The dross cements what else were too refined,
And in one interest body acts with mind.   180

    As fruits, ungrateful to the planter's care,
On savage stocks inserted learn to bear;
The surest virtues thus from passions shoot,
Wild Nature's vigour working at the root.
What crops of wit and honesty appear   185
From spleen, from obstinacy, hate, or fear!
See anger, zeal and fortitude supply;
Even av'rice, prudence; sloth, philosophy;
Lust, through some certain strainers well refined,
Is gentle love, and charms all womankind;   190
Envy, to which the ignoble mind's a slave,
Is emulation in the learn'd or brave;
Nor virtue, male or female, can we name,
But what will grow on pride, or grow on shame.

    Thus Nature gives us (let it check our pride)   195
The virtue nearest to our vice allied:
Reason the bias turns to good from ill,
And Nero reigns a Titus, if he will.
The fiery soul abhorr'd in Catiline,
In Decius charms, in Curtius is divine: 200
The same ambition can destroy or save,
And makes a patriot as it makes a knave.

    IV. This light and darkness in our chaos join'd,
What shall divide? The God within the mind.[1]

    Extremes in Nature equal ends produce,   205
In man they join to some mysterious use;
Though each by turns the other's bounds invade,
As, in some well-wrought picture, light and shade,
And oft so mix, the difference is too nice
Where ends the virtue or begins the vice.   210
    Fools! who from hence into the notion fall
That vice or virtue there is none at all.

          [1] A Platonic phrase for conscience.

If white and black blend, soften, and unite
A thousand ways, is there no black or white?
Ask your own heart, and nothing is so plain; 215
'Tis to mistake them, costs the time and pain.
    V. Vice is a monster of so frightful mien,
As, to be hated, needs but to be seen;
Yet seen too oft, familiar with her face,
We first endure, then pity, then embrace. 220
But where the extreme of vice, was ne'er agreed:
Ask where's the north? at York, 'tis on the Tweed;
In Scotland, at the Orcades; and there,
At Greenland, Zembla, or the Lord knows where.
No creature owns it in the first degree, 225
But thinks his neighbour farther gone than he:
Even those who dwell beneath its very zone,
Or never feel the rage, or never own;
What happier natures shrink at with affright,
The hard inhabitant contends is right. 230
    VI. Virtuous and vicious every man must be,
Few in the extreme, but all in the degree;
The rogue and fool by fits is fair and wise;
And even the best by fits what they despise.
'Tis but by parts we follow good or ill; 235
For, vice or virtue, self directs it still;
Each individual seeks a several goal;
But Heaven's great view is one, and that the whole,
That counter-works each folly and caprice;
That disappoints the effect of every vice; 240
That, happy frailties to all ranks applied:
Shame to the virgin, to the matron pride,
Fear to the statesman, rashness to the chief;
To kings presumption, and to crowds belief:
That, virtue's ends from vanity can raise, 245
Which seeks no interest, no reward but praise;
And build on wants, and on defects of mind,
The joy, the peace, the glory of mankind.
    Heaven forming each on other to depend,
A master, or a servant, or a friend, 250
Bids each on other for assistance call,
Till one man's weakness grows the strength of all.
Wants, frailties, passions, closer still ally
The common interest, or endear the tie.
To these we owe true friendship, love sincere, 255

Each homefelt joy that life inherits here;
Yet from the same we learn, in its decline,
Those joys, those loves, those interests to resign;
Taught half by reason, half by mere decay,
To welcome death, and calmly pass away.   260

  Whate'er the passion, knowledge, fame, or pelf,
Not one will change his neighbour with himself.
The learn'd is happy Nature to explore,
The fool is happy that he knows no more;
The rich is happy in the plenty given,   265
The poor contents him with the care of Heaven.
See the blind beggar dance, the cripple sing,
The sot a hero, lunatic a king;
The starving chemist in his golden views
Supremely blest, the poet in his muse.   270
See some strange comfort every state attend,
And pride bestow'd on all, a common friend:
See some fit passion every age supply,
Hope travels through, nor quits us when we die.

  Behold the child, by Nature's kindly law,   275
Pleased with a rattle, tickled with a straw:
Some livelier plaything gives his youth delight,
A little louder, but as empty quite:
Scarfs, garters, gold, amuse his riper stage,
And beads and prayer-books are the toys of age: 280
Pleased with this bauble still, as that before;
Till tired he sleeps, and life's poor play is o'er.
Meanwhile opinion gilds with varying rays
Those painted clouds that beautify our days;
Each want of happiness by hope supplied,   285
And each vacuity of sense by pride:
These build as fast as knowledge can destroy;
In folly's cup still laughs the bubble, joy;
One prospect lost, another still we gain;
And not a vanity is given in vain;   290
Even mean self-love becomes, by force divine,
The scale to measure others' wants by thine.
See! and confess, one comfort still must rise;
'Tis this,—though man's a fool, yet God is wise.

EPISTLE III

ARGUMENT

OF THE NATURE AND STATE OF MAN WITH RESPECT TO SOCIETY

HERE then we rest: "The Universal Cause
Acts to one end, but acts by various laws."
In all the madness of superfluous health,
The trim of pride, the impudence of wealth,
Let this great truth be present night and day;   5
But most be present if we preach or pray.
    Look round our world; behold the chain of love
Combining all below and all above.
See plastic Nature working to this end,
The single atoms each to other tend,   10
Attract, attracted to, the next in place
Form'd and impell'd its neighbour to embrace.
See Matter next, with various life endued,
Press to one centre still, the general good.
See dying vegetables life sustain,[1]   15
See life dissolving vegetate again:
All forms that perish other forms supply;
(By turns we catch the vital breath, and die)
Like bubbles on the sea of Matter borne,
They rise, they break, and to that sea return.   20
Nothing is foreign: parts relate to whole;

[1] Taken from Shaftesbury's *The Moralists*.

One all-extending, all-preserving soul
Connects each being, greatest with the least;
Made beast in aid of man, and man of beast;
All served, all serving: nothing stands alone: 25
The chain holds on, and where it ends, unknown.

Has God, thou fool! work'd solely for thy good,
Thy joy, thy pastime, thy attire, thy food?
Who for thy table feeds the wanton fawn,
For him as kindly spread the flowery lawn: 30
Is it for thee the lark ascends and sings?
Joy tunes his voice, joy elevates his wings.
Is it for thee the linnet pours his throat?
Loves of his own and raptures swell the note.
The bounding steed you pompously bestride   35
Shares with his lord the pleasure and the pride.
Is thine alone the seed that strews the plain?
The birds of heaven shall vindicate their grain.
Thine the full harvest of the golden year?
Part pays, and justly, the deserving steer: 40
The hog, that ploughs not, nor obeys thy call,
Lives on the labours of this lord of all.

Know, Nature's children all divide her care;
The fur that warms a monarch warm'd a bear.
While man exclaims, "See all things for my use!"   45
"See man for mine!" replies a pamper'd goose:[1]
And just as short of reason he must fall,
Who thinks all made for one, not one for all.

Grant that the powerful still the weak control;
Be man the wit and tyrant of the whole: 50
Nature that tyrant checks; he only knows,
And helps, another creature's wants and woes.
Say, will the falcon, stooping from above,
Smit with her varying plumage, spare the dove?
Admires the jay the insect's gilded wings?   55
Or hears the hawk when Philomela sings?
Man cares for all: to birds he gives his woods,
To beasts his pastures, and to fish his floods;
For some his interest prompts him to provide,

[1] Taken from Peter Charron. A passage in one of Gay's *Fables* may have
first suggested the illustration to Pope:

> " When with huge figs the branches bend,
> When clusters from the vine depend,
> The snail looks round on flower and tree,
> And cries, ' All these were made for me!' "

For more his pleasure, yet for more his pride: 60
All feed on one vain patron, and enjoy
The extensive blessing of his luxury.
That very life his learned hunger craves,
He saves from famine, from the savage saves:
Nay, feasts the animal he dooms his feast, 65
And. till he ends the being, makes it bless'd;
Which sees no more the stroke, or feels the pain,
Than favour'd man by touch ethereal slain.[1]
The creature had his feast of life before;
Thou too must perish when thy feast is o'er! 70
   To each unthinking being, Heaven, a friend,
Gives not the useless knowledge of its end:
To man imparts it; but with such a view
As, while he dreads it, makes him hope it too:
The hour conceal'd, and so remote the fear, 75
Death still draws nearer, never seeming near.
Great standing miracle! that Heaven assign'd
Its only thinking thing this turn of mind.
   II. Whether with reason or with instinct blest,
Know, all enjoy that power which suits them best; 80
To bliss alike by that direction tend,
And find the means proportion'd to their end.
Say, where full instinct is the unerring guide,
What pope or council can they need beside?
Reason, however able, cool at best, 85
Cares not for service, or but serves when press'd,
Stays till we call, and then not often near;
But honest instinct comes a volunteer,
Sure never to o'ershoot, but just to hit;
While still too wide or short is human wit; 90
Sure by quick nature happiness to gain,
Which heavier reason labours at in vain.
This too serves always, reason never long;
One must go right, the other may go wrong.
See then the acting and comparing powers 95
One in their nature, which are two in ours;
And reason raise o'er instinct as you can,
In this 'tis God directs, in that 'tis man.
   Who taught the nations of the field and wood

[1] Several of the ancients, and many of the Orientals since, esteemed those who were struck by lightning as sacred persons, and the particular favourites of Heaven.—POPE.

To shun their poison, and to choose their food?   100
Prescient, the tides or tempests to withstand,
Build on the wave, or arch beneath the sand?
Who made the spider parallels design,
Sure as De Moivre, without rule or line?
Who bade the stork, Columbus-like, explore   105
Heavens not his own, and worlds unknown before?
Who calls the council, states the certain day,
Who forms the phalanx, and who points the way?
   III. God, in the nature of each being, founds
Its proper bliss, and sets its proper bounds: 110
But as He framed a whole, the whole to bless,
On mutual wants built mutual happiness:
So from the first eternal Order ran,
And creature link'd to creature, man to man.
Whate'er of life all-quick'ning ether keeps,   115
Or breathes through air, or shoots beneath the deeps,
Or pours profuse on earth, one nature feeds
The vital flame, and swells the genial seeds.
Not man alone, but all that roam the wood,
Or wing the sky, or roll along the flood,   120
Each loves itself, but not itself alone,
Each sex desires alike, till two are one.
Nor ends the pleasure with the fierce embrace:
They love themselves, a third time, in their race.
Thus beast and bird their common charge attend,   125
The mothers nurse it, and the sires defend;
The young dismiss'd to wander earth or air,
There stops the instinct, and there ends the care;
The link dissolves, each seeks a fresh embrace,
Another love succeeds, another race.   130
A longer care man's helpless kind demands;
That longer care contracts more lasting bands:
Reflection, reason, still the ties improve,
At once extend the interest, and the love:
With choice we fix, with sympathy we burn;   135
Each virtue in each passion takes its turn;
And still new needs, new helps, new habits rise,
That graft benevolence on charities.
Still as one brood, and as another rose,
These natural love maintain'd, habitual those: 140
The last, scarce ripen'd into perfect man,
Saw helpless him from whom their life began:

Memory and forecast just returns engage,
That pointed back to youth, this on to age;
While pleasure, gratitude, and hope combined, 145
Still spread the interest and preserved the kind.
    IV. Nor think, in Nature's state they blindly trod;
The state of Nature was the reign of God:
Self-love and social at her birth began,
Union the bond of all things, and of man. 150
Pride then was not; nor arts, that pride to aid;
Man walk'd with beast, joint tenant of the shade;
The same his table, and the same his bed;
No murder clothed him, and no murder fed.
In the same temple, the resounding wood, 155
All vocal beings hymn'd their equal God:
The shrine with gore unstain'd, with gold undress'd,
Unbribed, unbloody, stood the blameless priest:
Heaven's attribute was universal care,
And man's prerogative, to rule, but spare. 160
Ah! how unlike the man of times to come!
Of half that live the butcher and the tomb;
Who, foe to Nature, hears the general groan,
Murders their species, and betrays his own.
But just disease to luxury succeeds, 165
And every death its own avenger breeds;
The fury-passions from that blood began,
And turn'd on man, a fiercer savage, man.
    See him from Nature rising slow to Art!
To copy instinct then was reason's part; 170
Thus then to man the voice of Nature spake:
"Go, from the creatures thy instructions take:
Learn from the birds what food the thickets yield;
Learn from the beasts the physic of the field;
Thy arts of building from the bee receive; 175
Learn of the mole to plough, the worm to weave;
Learn of the little nautilus to sail,
Spread the thin oar, and catch the driving gale.
Here too all forms of social union find,
And hence let reason, late, instruct mankind: 180
Here subterranean works and cities see;
There towns aerial on the waving tree.
Learn each small people's genius, policies,
The ants' republic, and the realm of bees;
How those in common all their wealth bestow, 185

And anarchy without confusion know;
And these for ever, though a monarch reign,
Their separate cells and properties maintain.
Mark what unvaried laws preserve each state,
Laws wise as Nature, and as fix'd as fate. 190
In vain thy reason finer webs shall draw,
Entangle Justice in her net of law,
And right, too rigid, harden into wrong;
Still for the strong too weak, the weak too strong.
Yet go! and thus o'er all the creatures sway, 195
Thus let the wiser make the rest obey:
And for those arts mere instinct could afford,
Be crown'd as monarchs, or as gods adored."
    V. Great Nature spoke; observant men obey'd;
Cities were built, societies were made: 200
Here rose one little state; another near
Grew by like means, and join'd, through love or fear.
Did here the trees with ruddier burdens bend,
And there the streams in purer rills descend?
What war could ravish, commerce could bestow, 205
And he return'd a friend, who came a foe.
Converse and love mankind might strongly draw,
When love was liberty, and nature law.[1]
Thus states were form'd; the name of king unknown,
Till common interest placed the sway in one. 210
'Twas virtue only (or in arts or arms,
Diffusing blessings, or averting harms),
The same which in a sire the sons obey'd,
A prince the father of a people made.
    VI. Till then, by Nature crown'd, each patriarch sate, 215
King, priest, and parent of his growing state;
On him, their second Providence, they hung,
Their law his eye, their oracle his tongue.
He from the wondering furrow call'd the food,
Taught to command the fire, control the flood, 220
Draw forth the monsters of the abyss profound,
Or fetch the aerial eagle to the ground.
Till drooping, sickening, dying, they began
Whom they revered as God to mourn as man:
Then, looking up from sire to sire, explored 225
One great first Father, and that first adored.
Or plain tradition that this all begun,

[1] Copied from the poet's own epistle of " Eloisa," ver. 92.

Convey'd unbroken faith from sire to son;
The worker from the work distinct was known,
And simple reason never sought but one: 230
Ere wit oblique had broke that steady light,
Man, like his Maker, saw that all was right;
To virtue, in the paths of pleasure trod,
And own'd a Father when he own'd a God.
Love, all the faith and all the allegiance then;   235
For Nature knew no right divine in men,
No ill could fear in God; and understood
A sovereign Being, but a sovereign good:
True faith, true policy, united ran,
That was but love of God, and this of man.   240
    Who first taught souls enslaved, and realms undone,
The enormous faith of many made for one;
That proud exception to all Nature's laws,
To invert the world, and counter-work its cause?
Force first made conquest, and that conquest, law;   245
Till Superstition taught the tyrant awe,
Then shared the tyranny, then lent it aid,
And gods of conquerors, slaves of subjects made:
She midst the lightning's blaze, and thunder's sound,
When rock'd the mountains, and when groan'd the ground, 250
She taught the weak to bend, the proud to pray,
To power unseen, and mightier far than they:
She, from the rending earth and bursting skies,
Saw gods descend, and fiends infernal rise:
Here fix'd the dreadful, there the blest abodes: 255
Fear made her devils, and weak hope her gods;
Gods partial, changeful, passionate, unjust,
Whose attributes were rage, revenge, or lust;
Such as the souls of cowards might conceive,
And, form'd like tyrants, tyrants would believe.   260
Zeal then, not charity, became the guide;
And hell was built on spite, and heaven on pride.
Then sacred seem'd the ethereal vault no more;
Altars grew marble then, and reek'd with gore:
Then first the flamen tasted living food;   265
Next his grim idol smear'd with human blood;
With Heaven's own thunders shook the world below,
And play'd the god an engine on his foe.
    So drives self-love through just and through unjust,
To one man's power, ambition, lucre, lust: 270

The same self-love, in all, becomes the cause
Of what restrains him, government and laws.
For, what one likes, if others like as well,
What serves one will, when many wills rebel?
How shall he keep, what, sleeping or awake,   275
A weaker may surprise, a stronger take?
His safety must his liberty restrain:
All join to guard what each desires to gain.
Forced into virtue thus, by self-defence,
Even kings learn'd justice and benevolence: 280
Self-love forsook the path it first pursued,
And found the private in the public good.

'Twas then the studious head or generous mind,
Follower of God, or friend of human kind,
Poet or patriot, rose but to restore   285
The faith and moral Nature gave before;
Relumed her ancient light, not kindled new,
If not God's image, yet his shadow drew;
Taught power's due use to people and to kings,
Taught nor to slack, nor strain its tender strings,   290
The less, or greater, set so justly true,
That touching one must strike the other too:
Till jarring interests of themselves create
The according music of a well-mix'd state.
Such is the world's great harmony, that springs   295
From order, union, full consent of things:
Where small and great, where weak and mighty, made
To serve, not suffer—strengthen, not invade;
More powerful each as needful to the rest,
And, in proportion as it blesses, blest;   300
Draw to one point, and to one centre bring
Beast, man, or angel, servant, lord, or king.

For forms of government let fools contest:
Whate'er is best administer'd is best:
For modes of faith, let graceless zealots fight;   305
His can't be wrong whose life is in the right;[1]
In faith and hope the world will disagree,
But all mankind's concern is charity:
All must be false that thwart this one great end:
And all of God that bless mankind or mend.   310

---

[1] "His faith, perhaps, in some nice tenets might
     Be wrong; his life, I'm sure, was in the right."
                                   COWLEY on Crashaw.

Man, like the generous vine, supported lives:
The strength he gains is from the embrace he gives.
On their own axis as the planets run,
Yet make at once their circle round the sun;
So two consistent motions act the soul;
And one regards itself, and one the whole.

    Thus God and Nature link'd the general frame,
And bade self-love and social be the same.

315

EPISTLE IV

ARGUMENT

OF THE NATURE AND STATE OF MAN WITH RESPECT TO HAPPINESS

I. False notions of happiness, philosophical and popular, answered from ver. 19 to 27. II. It is the end of all men, and attainable by all, ver. 29. God intends happiness to be equal; and to be so it must be social, since all particular happiness depends on general, and since He governs by general, not particular, laws, ver. 35. As it is necessary for order, and the peace and welfare of society, that external goods should be unequal, happiness is not made to consist in these, ver. 51. But notwithstanding that inequality, the balance of happiness among mankind is kept even by Providence by the two passions of hope and fear, ver. 70. III. What the happiness of individuals is, as far as is consistent with the constitution of this world; and that the good man has here the advantage, ver. 77. The error of imputing to virtue what are only the calamities of Nature or of Fortune, ver. 94. IV. The folly of expecting that God should alter His general laws in favour of particulars, ver. 121. V. That we are not judges who are good; but that, whoever they are, they must be happiest, ver. 131, etc. VI. That external goods are not the proper rewards, but often inconsistent with, or destructive of virtue, ver. 167. That even these can make no man happy without virtue: instanced in riches, ver. 185. Honours, ver. 193. Nobility, ver. 205. Greatness, ver. 217. Fame, ver. 237. Superior talents, ver. 259, etc. With pictures of human infelicity in men possessed of them all, ver. 269, etc. VII. That virtue only constitutes a happiness whose object is universal, and whose prospect eternal, ver. 309. That the perfection of virtue and happiness consists in a conformity to the order of Providence here, and a resignation to it here and hereafter, ver. 326, etc.

OH Happiness! our being's end and aim!
Good, pleasure, ease, content! whate'er thy name:
That something still which prompts the eternal sigh,
For which we bear to live, or dare to die,

Which still so near us, yet beyond us lies, 5
O'erlook'd, seen double, by the fool and wise.
Plant of celestial seed! if dropp'd below,
Say, in what mortal soil thou deign'st to grow?
Fair opening to some court's propitious shine,
Or deep with diamonds in the flaming mine? 10
Twined with the wreaths Parnassian laurels yield,
Or reap'd in iron harvests of the field?
Where grows? where grows it not? If vain our toil,
We ought to blame the culture, not the soil:
Fix'd to no spot is happiness sincere, 15
'Tis nowhere to be found, or everywhere:
'Tis never to be bought, but always free,
And, fled from monarchs, St. John! dwells with thee.

Ask of the learn'd the way? the learn'd are blind;
This bids to serve, and that to shun, mankind; 20
Some place the bliss in action, some in ease,
Those call it pleasure, and contentment these;
Some, sunk to beasts, find pleasure end in pain;
Some, swell'd to gods, confess even virtue vain;
Or, indolent, to each extreme they fall, 25
To trust in everything, or doubt of all.

Who thus define it, say they more or less
Than this, that happiness is happiness?

II. Take Nature's path, and mad opinions leave;
All states can reach it, and all heads conceive; 30
Obvious her goods, in no extreme they dwell;
There needs but thinking right, and meaning well;
And, mourn our various portions as we please,
Equal is common sense and common ease.

Remember, man, "The Universal Cause 35
Acts not by partial, but by general laws";
And makes what happiness we justly call
Subsist, not in the good of one, but all.
There's not a blessing individuals find,
But some way leans and hearkens to the kind: 40
No bandit fierce, no tyrant mad with pride,
No cavern'd hermit, rests self-satisfied:
Who most to shun or hate mankind pretend,
Seek an admirer, or would fix a friend:
Abstract what others feel, what others think, 45
All pleasures sicken, and all glories sink;
Each has his share; and who would more obtain,

Shall find the pleasure pays not half the pain.

Order is Heaven's first law; and, this confess'd,
Some are, and must be, greater than the rest, 50
More rich, more wise; but who infers from hence
That such are happier, shocks all common sense.
Heaven to mankind impartial we confess,
If all are equal in their happiness:
But mutual wants this happiness increase; 55
All nature's difference keeps all nature's peace.
Condition, circumstance, is not the thing;
Bliss is the same in subject or in king,
In who obtain defence, or who defend,
In him who is, or him who finds a friend: 60
Heaven breathes through every member of the whole
One common blessing, as one common soul.
But fortune's gifts, if each alike possess'd,
And each were equal, must not all contest?
If then to all men happiness was meant, 65
God in externals could not place content.

Fortune her gifts may variously dispose,
And these be happy call'd, unhappy those;
But Heaven's just balance equal will appear,
While those are placed in hope, and these in fear: 70
Not present good or ill, the joy or curse,
But future views of better or of worse.

Oh sons of earth! attempt ye still to rise,
By mountains piled on mountains, to the skies?
Heaven still with laughter the vain toil surveys, 75
And buries madmen in the heaps they raise.
III. Know, all the good that individuals find,
Or God and Nature meant to mere mankind,
Reason's whole pleasure, all the joys of sense,
Lie in three words—health, peace, and competence. 80
But health consists with temperance alone;
And peace, O Virtue! peace is all thy own.
The good or bad the gifts of fortune gain;
But these less taste them as they worse obtain.
Say, in pursuit of profit or delight, 85
Who risk the most, that take wrong means, or right?
Of vice or virtue, whether blest or curst,
Which meets contempt, or which compassion first?
Count all the advantage prosperous vice attains,
'Tis but what virtue flies from and disdains: 90

And grant the bad what happiness they would,
One they must want, which is, to pass for good.
Oh blind to truth, and God's whole scheme below,
Who fancy bliss to vice, to virtue woe!
Who sees and follows that great scheme the best, 95
Best knows the blessing, and will most be blest.
But fools, the good alone unhappy call,
For ills or accidents that chance to all.
See Falkland dies, the virtuous and the just![1]
See godlike Turenne prostrate on the dust![2] 100
See Sidney bleeds amid the martial strife![3]
Was this their virtue, or contempt of life?
Say, was it virtue, more though Heaven ne'er gave,
Lamented Digby! sunk thee to the grave?
Tell me, if virtue made the son expire,[4] 105
Why, full of days and honour, lives the sire?
Why drew Marseilles' good bishop purer breath,
When nature sicken'd, and each gale was death?[5]
Or why so long (in life if long can be)
Lent Heaven a parent to the poor and me?[6] 110
    What makes all physical or moral ill?
There deviates nature, and here wanders will.
God sends not ill; if rightly understood,
Or partial ill is universal good,
Or change admits, or nature lets it fall, 115
Short, and but rare, 'till man improved it all.
We just as wisely might of Heaven complain
That righteous Abel was destroy'd by Cain,
As that the virtuous son is ill at ease
When his lewd father gave the dire disease. 120

[1] Lucius Cary, the second Viscount Falkland. He was learned, eloquent, and high-minded, but probably better fitted for speculation than action. His first public services were on the side of the Parliament, but he afterwards embraced the cause of Charles, and died in battle, a volunteer, at Newbury, in 1643, aged thirty-four.

[2] Marshal Turenne was killed by a cannon shot, 27th July, 1675, near the village of Saltyback.

[3] Sir Philip Sidney, the flower of the English nobility, in the chivalrous and romantic reign of Elizabeth, was mortally wounded in a victorious action near Zutphen, and died on 17th October, 1586.

[4] See Pope's epitaph on the Hon. Robert Digby, who died in 1726.

[5] The celebrated Bishop of Marseilles, M. de Belsunce, distinguished himself in a particular manner by his intrepid zeal and philanthropy during the time of the great plague in Marseilles, in 1720. The bishop lived till 1755.

[6] Pope's mother died the same year, 1733, that this fourth epistle was published. She was in her ninety-second year.

IV. Think we, like some weak prince, the Eternal Cause
Prone for His favourites to reverse His laws?
Shall burning Ætna, if a sage requires,[1]
Forget to thunder, and recall her fires?
On air or sea new motions be impress'd,   125
Oh blameless Bethel! to relieve thy breast?[2]
When the loose mountain trembles from on high,
Shall gravitation cease if you go by?
Or some old temple, nodding to its fall,
For Chartres' head reserve the hanging wall?   130
    V. But still this world (so fitted for the knave)
Contents us not. A better shall we have?
A kingdom of the just then let it be:
But first consider how those just agree.
The good must merit God's peculiar care!   135
But who but God can tell us who they are?
One thinks on Calvin Heaven's own spirit fell·
Another deems him instrument of hell;
If Calvin feel Heaven's blessing, or its rod,
This cries, There is, and that, There is no God.   140
What shocks one part will edify the rest,
Nor with one system can they all be blest.
The very best will variously incline,
And what rewards your virtue, punish mine.
Whatever is, is right.—This world, 'tis true,   145
Was made for Cæsar—but for Titus too;
And which more blest? who chain'd his country, say,
Or he whose virtue sigh'd to lose a day?
    "But sometimes virtue starves, while vice is fed."
What then? is the reward of virtue bread?   150
That, vice may merit, 'tis the price of toil;
The knave deserves it, when he tills the soil,
The knave deserves it, when he tempts the main,
Where folly fights for kings, or dives for gain.
The good man may be weak, be indolent;   155
Nor is his claim to plenty, but content.
But grant him riches, your demand is o'er?
"No—shall the good want health, the good want power?"
Add health and power, and every earthly thing,

[1] Alluding to the fate of the elder Pliny, who, being at Misenum during the great eruption of Vesuvius, in the first year of Titus, and being anxious to make observations on the phenomenon, incautiously exposed himself, and was suffocated. Or possibly Empedocles.

[2] Hugh Bethel, Esq., the poet's friend, who was afflicted with asthma.

"Why bounded power? why private? why no king?" 160
Nay, why external for internal given?
Why is not man a god, and earth a heaven?
Who ask and reason thus will scarce conceive
God gives enough while He has more to give;
Immense the power, immense were the demand; 165
Say, at what part of nature will they stand?
    VI. What nothing earthly gives, or can destroy,
The soul's calm sunshine, and the heartfelt joy,
Is virtue's prize: a better would you fix?
Then give humility a coach and six, 170
Justice a conqueror's sword, or truth a gown,
Or public spirit its great cure, a crown.
Weak, foolish man! will Heaven reward us there
With the same trash mad mortals wish for here?
The boy and man an individual makes, 175
Yet sigh'st thou now for apples and for cakes?
Go, like the Indian, in another life
Expect thy dog, thy bottle, and thy wife;
As well as dream such trifles are assign'd,
As toys and empires, for a godlike mind. 180
Rewards, that either would to virtue bring
No joy, or be destructive of the thing:
How oft by these at sixty are undone
The virtues of a saint at twenty-one!
To whom can riches give repute, or trust, 185
Content, or pleasure, but the good and just?
Judges and senates have been bought for gold,
Esteem and love were never to be sold.
O fool! to think God hates the worthy mind,
The lover and the love of human kind, 190
Whose life is healthful, and whose conscience clear,
Because he wants a thousand pounds a year.
    Honour and shame from no condition rise:
Act well your part; there all the honour lies.
Fortune in men has some small difference made, 195
One flaunts in rags, one flutters in brocade;
The cobbler apron'd, and the parson gown'd,
The friar hooded, and the monarch crown'd.
"What differ more (you cry) than crown and cowl?"
I'll tell you, friend! a wise man and a fool. 200
You'll find, if once the monarch acts the monk,
Or, cobbler-like, the parson will be drunk,

Worth makes the man, and want of it the fellow:
The rest is all but leather or prunella.

    Stuck o'er with titles and hung round with strings,   205
That thou may'st be by kings or whores of kings,
Boast the pure blood of an illustrious race,
In quiet flow from Lucrece to Lucrece:
But by your father's worth if yours you rate,
Count me those only who were good and great.   210
Go! if your ancient but ignoble blood
Has crept through scoundrels ever since the flood,
Go! and pretend your family is young;
Nor own your fathers have been fools so long.
What can ennoble sots, or slaves, or cowards?   215
Alas! not all the blood of all the Howards.

    Look next on greatness; say where greatness lies.
Where, but among the heroes and the wise?
Heroes are much the same, the point's agreed,
From Macedonia's madman to the Swede;[1]
The whole strange purpose of their lives to find   220
Or make an enemy of all mankind!
Not one looks backward, onward still he goes,
Yet ne'er looks forward farther than his nose.
No less alike the politic and wise;   225
All sly slow things, with circumspective eyes:
Men in their loose unguarded hours they take,
Not that themselves are wise, but others weak.
But grant that those can conquer, these can cheat;
'Tis phrase absurd to call a villain great: 230
Who wickedly is wise, or madly brave,
Is but the more a fool, the more a knave.
Who noble ends by noble means obtains,
Or failing, smiles in exile or in chains,
Like good Aurelius let him reign, or bleed   235
Like Socrates,[2] that man is great indeed.

    What's fame? A fancied life in others' breath,
A thing beyond us, even before our death.
Just what you hear, you have, and what's unknown
The same (my lord) if Tully's, or your own.   240
All that we feel of it begins and ends
In the small circle of our foes or friends;

---

[1] Alexander, and Charles XII. of Sweden.
[2] There is certainly an impropriety in the use of the word "bleed" in the case of Socrates, who died by the poison of hemlock.

To all beside as much an empty shade
An Eugene living,[1] as a Cæsar dead;
Alike or when, or where, they shone, or shine,   245
Or on the Rubicon, or on the Rhine.
A wit's a feather, and a chief's a rod;
An honest man's the noblest work of God.
Fame but from death a villain's name can save,
As Justice tears his body from the grave!   250
When what to oblivion better were resign'd
Is hung on high to poison half mankind.
All fame is foreign, but of true desert;
Plays round the head, but comes not to the heart:
One self-approving hour whole years outweighs   255
Of stupid starers, and of loud huzzas;
And more true joy Marcellus exiled feels,
Than Cæsar with a senate at his heels.

   In parts superior what advantage lies?
Tell (for you can) what is it to be wise?   260
'Tis but to know how little can be known;
To see all others' faults and feel our own:
Condemn'd in business or in arts to drudge,
Without a second or without a judge:
Truths would you teach, or save a sinking land?   265
All fear, none aid you, and few understand.
Painful pre-eminence![2] yourself to view
Above life's weakness, and its comforts too.

   Bring then these blessings to a strict account;
Make fair deductions; see to what they mount: 270
How much of other each is sure to cost;
How each for other oft is wholly lost;
How inconsistent greater goods with these;
How sometimes life is risk'd, and always ease:
Think, and if still the things thy envy call,   275
Say, wouldst thou be the man to whom they fall?
To sigh for ribands if thou art so silly,
Mark how they grace Lord Umbra or Sir Billy.
Is yellow dirt the passion of thy life?
Look but on Gripus or on Gripus' wife.   280
If parts allure thee, think how Bacon shined,
The wisest, brightest, meanest of mankind:

[1] Prince Eugene died three years afterwards at Vienna, 10th April, 1736.
[2] An expression in Addison's *Cato*.

Or, ravish'd with the whistling of a name,[1]
See Cromwell, damn'd to everlasting fame!
If all, united, thy ambition call, 285
From ancient story, learn to scorn them all.
There, in the rich, the honour'd, famed, and great,
See the false scale of happiness complete!
In hearts of kings, or arms of queens, who lay,
How happy those to ruin, these betray. 290
Mark by what wretched steps their glory grows,[2]
From dirt and sea-weed as proud Venice rose;
In each how guilt and greatness equal ran,
And all that raised the hero sunk the man:
Now Europe's laurels on their brows behold, 295
But stain'd with blood, or ill exchanged for gold:
Then see them broke with toils, or sunk in ease,
Or infamous for plunder'd provinces.
Oh wealth ill-fated! which no act of fame
E'er taught to shine, or sanctified from shame! 300
What greater bliss attends their close of life?
Some greedy minion, or imperious wife,
The trophied arches, storied halls invade,
And haunt their slumbers in the pompous shade.
Alas! not dazzled with their noontide ray, 305
Compute the morn and evening to the day:
The whole amount of that enormous fame,
A tale that blends their glory with their shame!
    VII. Know then this truth (enough for man to know),
"Virtue alone is happiness below." 310
The only point where human bliss stands still,
And tastes the good without the fall to ill;
Where only merit constant pay receives,
Is blest in what it takes and what it gives;
The joy unequall'd, if its end it gain, 315
And if it lose, attended with no pain:
Without satiety, though e'er so bless'd,
And but more relish'd as the more distress'd:
The broadest mirth unfeeling folly wears,
Less pleasing far than virtue's very tears: 320
Good, from each object, from each place acquired,
For ever exercised, yet never tired;

[1] Charm'd with the foolish whistlings of a name.—COWLEY.
[2] This striking passage is a satire on the Duke and Duchess of Marlborough.

Never elated while one man's oppress'd;
Never dejected while another's bless'd;
And where no wants, no wishes can remain,   325
Since but to wish more virtue, is to gain.
    See the sole bliss Heaven could on all bestow;
Which who but feels can taste, but thinks can know.
Yet poor with fortune, and with learning blind,
The bad must miss, the good, untaught, will find;   330
Slave to no sect, who takes no private road,
But looks through Nature up to Nature's God:
Pursues that chain which links the immense design,
Joins Heaven and earth, and mortal and divine;
Sees that no being any bliss can know,   335
But touches some above, and some below;
Learns, from this union of the rising whole,
The first, last purpose of the human soul;
And knows where faith, law, morals, all began,
All end, in love of God, and love of man.   340
For him alone, hope leads from goal to goal,
And opens still, and opens on his soul;
Till lengthen'd on to faith, and unconfined,
It pours the bliss that fills up all the mind.
He sees why nature plants in man alone   345
Hope of known bliss, and faith in bliss unknown:
(Nature, whose dictates to no other kind
Are given in vain, but what they seek they find;)
Wise is her present; she connects in this
His greatest virtue with his greatest bliss;   350
At once his own bright prospect to be blest,
And strongest motive to assist the rest.
    Self-love thus push'd to social, to divine,
Gives thee to make thy neighbour's blessing thine.
Is this too little for the boundless heart?   355
Extend it, let thy enemies have part:
Grasp the whole worlds of reason, life, and sense,
In one close system of benevolence:
Happier as kinder, in whate'er degree,
And height of bliss but height of charity.   360
    God loves from whole to parts: but human soul
Must rise from individual to the whole.
Self-love but serves the virtuous mind to wake,
As the small pebble stirs the peaceful lake;
The centre moved, a circle straight succeeds,   365

Another still, and still another spreads;
Friend, parent, neighbour, first it will embrace;
His country next; and next all human race;
Wide and more wide, the o'erflowings of the mind
Take every creature in, of every kind;　　　　370
Earth smiles around, with boundless bounty blest,
And Heaven beholds its image in his breast.

  Come, then, my friend! my genius! come along;
Oh master of the poet and the song!
And while the Muse now stoops, or now ascends,　　375
To man's low passions, or their glorious ends,
Teach me, like thee, in various nature wise,
To fall with dignity, with temper rise;
Form'd by thy converse happily to steer
From grave to gay, from lively to severe;　　　　380
Correct, with spirit; eloquent, with ease;
Intent to reason, or polite to please.
Oh! while along the stream of time thy name
Expanded flies, and gathers all its fame;
Say, shall my little bark attendant sail,　　　　385
Pursue the triumph, and partake the gale?
When statesmen, heroes, kings, in dust repose,
Whose sons shall blush their fathers were thy foes,
Shall then this verse to future age pretend
Thou wert my guide, philosopher, and friend?　　390
That, urged by thee, I turn'd the tuneful art
From sounds to things, from fancy to the heart;
For Wit's false mirror held up Nature's light;
Show'd erring Pride,—Whatever is, is right!
That reason, passion, answer one great aim;　　395
That true self-love and social are the same;
That virtue only makes our bliss below;
And all our knowledge is,—Ourselves to know.

THE UNIVERSAL PRAYER

DEO OPT. MAX.

FATHER of all! in every age,
  In every clime adored,
By saint, by savage, and by sage,
  Jehovah, Jove, or Lord!

Thou great First Cause, least understood,   5
  Who all my sense confined
To know but this, that Thou art good,
  And that myself am blind;

Yet gave me, in this dark estate,
  To see the good from ill;   10
And, binding nature fast in fate,
  Left free the human will.

What conscience dictates to be done,
  Or warns me not to do,
This teach me more than hell to shun,   15
  That more than heaven pursue.

What blessings Thy free bounty gives
  Let me not cast away;
For God is paid when man receives;
  To enjoy is to obey.   20

Yet not to earth's contracted span
  Thy goodness let me bound,
Or think Thee Lord alone of man,
  When thousand worlds are round:

Let not this weak, unknowing hand   25
  Presume Thy bolts to throw,
And deal damnation round the land
  On each I judge Thy foe.

If I am right, Thy grace impart,
　Still in the right to stay;
If I am wrong, oh teach my heart
　To find that better way!　　　　　　30

Save me alike from foolish pride,
　Or impious discontent,
At aught Thy wisdom has denied,
　Or aught Thy goodness lent.　　　　35

Teach me to feel another's woe,
　To hide the fault I see;
That mercy I to others show
　That mercy show to me.　　　　　　40

Mean though I am, not wholly so
　Since quicken'd by Thy breath;
Oh lead me, wheresoe'er I go,
　Through this day's life or death!

This day be bread and peace my lot:　45
　All else beneath the sun,
Thou know'st if best bestow'd or not,
　And let Thy will be done.

To Thee, whose temple is all space,
　Whose altar, earth, sea, skies!
One chorus let all Being raise!　　　50
　All Nature's incense rise!

MORAL ESSAYS

IN FOUR EPISTLES TO SEVERAL PERSONS

> Est brevitate opus, ut currat sententia, neu se
> Impediat verbis lassas onerantibus aures:
> Et sermone opus est modò tristi, sæpe jocoso,
> Defendente vicem modò Rhetoris atque Poetæ,
> Interdum urbani, parcentis viribus, atque
> Extenuantis eas consultò.—HORACE.

> [Close be your language; let your sense be clear,
> Nor with a weight of words fatigue the ear;
> From grave to jovial you must change with art,
> Now play the critic's, now the poet's part;
> In raillery assume a graver air,
> Discreetly hide your strength, your vigour spare;
> For ridicule shall frequently prevail,
> And cut the knot when graver reasons fail.—FRANCIS.]

EPISTLE I

TO SIR RICHARD TEMPLE, LORD COBHAM

ARGUMENT

OF THE KNOWLEDGE AND CHARACTERS OF MEN

I. That it is not sufficient for this knowledge to consider Man in the abstract: books will not serve the purpose, nor yet your own experience singly, ver. 1. General maxims, unless they be formed upon both, will be but notional, ver. 10. Some peculiarity in every man, characteristic to himself, yet varying from himself, ver. 15. Difficulties arising from our own passions, fancies, faculties, etc., ver. 31. The shortness of life to observe in, and the uncertainty of the principles of action in men to observe by, ver. 37, etc. Our own principle of action often hid from ourselves, ver. 41. Some few characters plain, but in general confounded, dissembled, or inconsistent, ver. 51. Unimaginable weaknesses in the greatest, ver. 69, etc. The same man utterly different in different places and seasons, ver. 71. Nothing constant and certain but God and Nature, ver. 95. No judging of the motives from the actions; the same actions proceeding from contrary motives, and the same motives influencing contrary actions, ver. 100. II. Yet to form characters we can only take the strongest actions of a man's life and try to make them agree: the utter uncertainty of this, from nature itself and from policy, ver. 120. Characters given according to the rank of men of the world, ver. 135. And some reason for it, ver. 140. Education alters the nature, or at least character, of many, ver. 149. Actions, passions, opinions, manners, humours, or principles, all subject to change. No judging by nature, from ver. 158 to

YES, you despise the man to books confined,
Who from his study rails at human kind;
Though what he learns he speaks, and may advance
Some general maxims, or be right by chance.
The coxcomb bird, so talkative and grave,   5
That from his cage cries cuckold, whore, and knave,
Though many a passenger he rightly call,
You hold him no philosopher at all.
   And yet the fate of all extremes is such,
Men may be read, as well as books, too much.   10
To observations which ourselves we make,
We grow more partial for the observer's sake;
To written wisdom, as another's, less:
Maxims are drawn from notions, those from guess.
There's some peculiar in each leaf and grain,   15
Some unmark'd fibre, or some varying vein:
Shall only man be taken in the gross?
Grant but as many sorts of mind as moss.[1]
   That each from other differs, first confess;
Next, that he varies from himself no less;   20
Add Nature's, custom's, reason's, passion's strife,
And all opinion's colours cast on life.
   Our depths who fathoms, or our shallows finds,
Quick whirls, and shifting eddies, of our minds?
On human actions reason though you can,   25
It may be reason, but it is not man:
His principle of action once explore,
That instant 'tis his principle no more.
Like following life through creatures you dissect,
You lose it in the moment you detect.   30
   Yet more; the difference is as great between
The optics seeing as the objects seen.
All manners take a tincture from our own;
Or come discolour'd through our passions shown.

[1] There are above three hundred sorts of moss observed by naturalists.
—POPE.

Or fancy's beam enlarges, multiplies, 35
Contracts, inverts, and gives ten thousand dyes.
    Nor will life's stream for observation stay,
It hurries all too fast to mark their way:
In vain sedate reflections we would make,
When half our knowledge we must snatch, not take. 40
Oft in the passions' wild rotation toss'd,
Our spring of action to ourselves is lost:
Tired, not determined, to the last we yield,
And what comes then is master of the field.
As the last image of that troubled heap, 45
When sense subsides, and fancy sports in sleep
(Though past the recollection of the thought),
Becomes the stuff of which our dream is wrought;
Something as dim to our internal view
Is thus, perhaps, the cause of most we do. 50
    True, some are open, and to all men known;
Others so very close, they're hid from none
(So darkness strikes the sense no less than light):
Thus gracious Chandos [1] is beloved at sight;
And every child hates Shylock, though his soul 55
Still sits at squat, and peeps not from its hole;
At half mankind when generous Manly [2] raves,
All know 'tis virtue, for he thinks them knaves:
When universal homage Umbra [3] pays,
All see 'tis vice, and itch of vulgar praise. 60
When flattery glares, all hate it in a queen,
While one there is who charms us with his spleen. [4]
    But these plain characters we rarely find;
Though strong the bent, yet quick the turns of mind:
Or puzzling contraries confound the whole; 65
Or affectations quite reverse the soul.
The dull, flat falsehood serves for policy;
And, in the cunning, truth itself's a lie:
Unthought-of frailties cheat us in the wise;
The fool lies hid in inconsistencies. 70
    See the same man, in vigour, in the gout;
Alone, in company; in place, or out;
Early at business, and at hazard late;

[1] James Brydges, first Duke of Chandos.
[2] In Wycherley's comedy, *The Plain Dealer*.
[3] Probably Walter Carey, a Whig official. See "Umbra" in the Miscellanies.
[4] Swift.

Mad at a fox-chase, wise at a debate;
Drunk at a borough, civil at a ball;
Friendly at Hackney, faithless at Whitehall. 75
   Catius [1] is ever moral, ever grave,
Thinks who endures a knave is next a knave,
Save just at dinner—then prefers, no doubt,
A rogue with venison to a saint without. 80
   Who would not praise Patricio's high desert, [2]
His hand unstain'd, his uncorrupted heart,
His comprehensive head all interests weigh'd,
All Europe saved, yet Britain not betray'd?
He thanks you not, his pride is in piquet, 85
Newmarket fame and judgment at a bet.
   What made (say Montaigne, or more sage Charron!)
Otho a warrior, Cromwell a buffoon?
A perjured prince a leaden saint revere, [3]
A godless regent tremble at a star? [4] 90
The throne a bigot keep, a genius quit, [5]
Faithless through piety, and duped through wit?
Europe a woman, child, or dotard rule, [6]
And just her wisest monarch made a fool?
   Know, God and Nature only are the same: 95
In man, the judgment shoots at flying game;
A bird of passage! gone as soon as found,
Now in the moon, perhaps, now under ground.
   II. In vain the sage, with retrospective eye,
Would from the apparent *what* conclude the *why*, 100
Infer the motive from the deed, and show
That what we chanced was what we meant to do.
Behold! if fortune or a mistress frowns,
Some plunge in business, others shave their crowns:
To ease the soul of one oppressive weight, 105
This quits an empire, that embroils a state:

---

[1] Charles Dartineuf, a noted epicure.
[2] Sidney, Earl of Godolphin.
[3] Louis XI. of France wore in his hat a leaden image of the Virgin Mary, which when he swore by he feared to break his oath.
[4] Philip Duke of Orleans, Regent of France in the minority of Louis XV., superstitious in judicial astrology, though an unbeliever in all religion.
[5] Philip V. of Spain who, after renouncing the throne for religion, resumed it to gratify his queen; and Victor Amadeus II., King of Sardinia, who resigned the crown, and, trying to reassume it, was imprisoned till his death.
[6] The Czarina, the King of France, the Pope, and the above-mentioned King of Sardinia.

The same adust complexion has impell'd
Charles to the convent, Philip to the field.[1]
　　Not always actions show the man; we find
Who does a kindness, is not therefore kind:　　　　　110
Perhaps prosperity becalm'd his breast,
Perhaps the wind just shifted from the east:
Not therefore humble he who seeks retreat,
Pride guides his steps, and bids him shun the great:
Who combats bravely is not therefore brave,　　　　115
He dreads a death-bed like the meanest slave:
Who reasons wisely is not therefore wise,
His pride in reasoning, not in acting lies.
　　But grant that actions best discover man;
Take the most strong, and sort them as you can:　　120
The few that glare, each character must mark,
You balance not the many in the dark.
What will you do with such as disagree?
Suppress them, or miscall them policy?
Must then at once (the character to save)　　　　　125
The plain rough hero turn a crafty knave?
Alas! in truth the man but changed his mind,
Perhaps was sick, in love, or had not dined.
Ask why from Britain Cæsar would retreat?
Cæsar himself might whisper he was beat.　　　　　130
Why risk the world's great empire for a punk?[2]
Cæsar perhaps might answer he was drunk.
But, sage historians! 'tis your task to prove
One action, conduct; one, heroic love.
　　'Tis from high life high characters are drawn,　　135
A saint in crape is twice a saint in lawn:
A judge is just, a chancellor juster still;
A gownman, learn'd; a bishop, what you will;
Wise, if a minister; but, if a king,
More wise, more learn'd, more just, more everything.　140
Court-virtues bear, like gems, the highest rate,
Born where Heaven's influence scarce can penetrate:
In life's low vale, the soil the virtues like,
They please as beauties, here as wonders strike.
Though the same sun with all diffusive rays　　　　145

---

[1] Warburton remarks on this line: " The *atrabilaire* complexion of
Philip II. is well known, but not so well that he derived it from his father,
Charles V."
[2] Cleopatra.

Blush in the rose, and in the diamond blaze,
We prize the stronger effort of his power,
And justly set the gem above the flower.

'Tis education forms the common mind,
Just as the twig is bent, the tree's inclined.   150
Boastful and rough, your first son is a squire;
The next a tradesman, meek, and much a liar:
Tom struts a soldier, open, bold, and brave;
Will sneaks a scrivener, an exceeding knave.
Is he a Churchman? then he's fond of power: 155
A Quaker? sly: a Presbyterian? sour:
A smart free-thinker? all things in an hour.

Ask men's opinions: Scoto now shall tell [1]
How trade increases, and the world goes well;
Strike off his pension, by the setting sun,   160
And Britain, if not Europe, is undone.

That gay free-thinker, a fine talker once,
What turns him now a stupid silent dunce?
Some god, or spirit, he has lately found;
Or chanced to meet a minister that frown'd.   165

Judge we by nature? Habit can efface,
Interest o'ercome, or policy take place:
By actions? those uncertainty divides;
By passions? these dissimulation hides:
Opinions? they still take a wider range: 170
Find, if you can, in what you cannot change.

Manners with fortunes, humours turn with climes,
Tenets with books, and principles with times.

III. Search then the RULING PASSION: there, alone,
The wild are constant, and the cunning known;   175
The fool consistent, and the false sincere;
Priests, princes, women, no dissemblers here.
This clue once found unravels all the rest,
The prospect clears, and WHARTON stands confess'd.

WHARTON! the scorn and wonder of our days,   180
Whose ruling passion was the lust of praise:
Born with whate'er could win it from the wise,
Women and fools must like him, or he dies:
Though wondering senates hung on all he spoke,
The club must hail him master of the joke.   185
Shall parts so various aim at nothing new?

---

[1] In the first edition: " J——n now shall tell "; meaning, perhaps, Johnston the Scottish Secretary, afterwards Lord Register.

He'll shine a Tully and a Wilmot too.[1]
Then turns repentant, and his God adores
With the same spirit that he drinks and whores;
Enough if all around him but admire,　　　　　　190
And now the punk applaud, and now the friar.
Thus with each gift of Nature and of art,
And wanting nothing but an honest heart;
Grown all to all, from no one vice exempt,
And most contemptible, to shun contempt;　　　195
His passion still, to covet general praise,
His life, to forfeit it a thousand ways;
A constant bounty which no friend has made;
An angel tongue, which no man can persuade;
A fool, with more of wit than half mankind,　　200
Too rash for thought, for action too refined;
A tyrant to the wife his heart approves;
A rebel to the very king he loves;
He dies, sad outcast of each Church and State,
And, harder still! flagitious, yet not great.　　205
Ask you why WHARTON broke through every rule?
'Twas all for fear the knaves should call him fool.

Nature well known, no prodigies remain,
Comets are regular, and WHARTON plain.

Yet, in this search, the wisest may mistake,　　210
If second qualities for first they take.
When Catiline by rapine swell'd his store;
When Cæsar made a noble dame a whore;[2]
In this the lust, in that the avarice,
Were means, not ends; ambition was the vice.　215
That very Cæsar born in Scipio's days,
Had aim'd, like him, by chastity, at praise.
Lucullus, when frugality could charm,
Had roasted turnips in the Sabine farm.
In vain the observer eyes the builder's toil,　　220
But quite mistakes the scaffold for the pile.

In this one passion man can strength enjoy,
As fits give vigour, just when they destroy.
Time, that on all things lays his lenient hand,
Yet tames not this; it sticks to our last sand.　225
Consistent in our follies and our sins,
Here honest Nature ends as she begins.

---

[1] John Wilmot, Earl of Rochester.
[2] The sister of Cato and the mother of Brutus.

Old politicians chew on wisdom past,
And totter on in business to the last;
As weak, as earnest, and as gravely out,   230
As sober Lanesborough dancing in the gout.[1]
  Behold a reverend sire, whom want of grace
Has made the father of a nameless race,
Shoved from the wall perhaps, or rudely press'd
By his own son, that passes by unbless'd: 235
Still to his wench he crawls on knocking knees,
And envies every sparrow that he sees.
  A salmon's belly, Helluo, was thy fate;
The doctor call'd, declares all help too late:
"Mercy! (cries Helluo) mercy on my soul!   240
Is there no hope?—alas!—then bring the jole."
  The frugal crone, whom praying priests attend,
Still strives to save the hallow'd taper's end,
Collects her breath, as ebbing life retires,
For one puff more, and in that puff expires.[2]   245
  "Odious! in woollen! 'twould a saint provoke
(Were the last words that poor Narcissa spoke):[3]
No, let a charming chintz and Brussels lace
Wrap my cold limbs, and shade my lifeless face:
One would not, sure, be frightful when one's dead—   250
And—Betty—give this cheek a little red."
  The courtier smooth, who forty years had shined
An humble servant to all human kind,
Just brought out this, when scarce his tongue could stir,
"If—where I'm going—I could serve you, sir?"   255
  "I give and I devise (old Euclio said,
And sigh'd) my lands and tenements to Ned."
"Your money, sir?"—"My money, sir, what all?
Why,—if I must—(then wept) I give it Paul."
"The manor, sir?"—"The manor! hold (he cried),   260
Not that—I cannot part with that!"—and died.[4]
  And you, brave COBHAM, to the latest breath,

---

[1] An ancient nobleman who, though disabled by the gout, demanded an audience of the queen upon the death of Prince George of Denmark, to advise her to preserve her health and dispel her grief by dancing. Died at Dublin, 1736.

[2] Warburton states that this fact was told the poet of a lady at Paris.

[3] Founded on fact, though the author had the goodness not to mention the name of a very celebrated actress. It was Mrs. Oldfield he meant.

[4] Said to have been Sir Charles Duncombe, the "City Knight," who had been a rich goldsmith in Lombard Street. Warton says that Sir William Bateman "used those very words" assigned to Euclio on his death-bed.

Shall feel your ruling passion strong in death:
Such in those moments as in all the past,
"Oh, save my country, Heaven!" shall be your last.   265

EPISTLE II

TO A LADY

ARGUMENT

OF THE CHARACTERS OF WOMEN

The lady to whom this Epistle is addressed was the poet's
cherished friend, Martha Blount, who had then arrived at the sober
age of forty-five. Her poet was two years older. Prefixed to the
first edition of the poem in 1735 was the following

" ADVERTISEMENT

" The author being very sensible how particular a tenderness is
due to the female sex, and, at the same time, how little they show
to each other, declares, upon his honour, that no one character is
drawn from the life in this Epistle. It would otherwise be most
improperly inscribed to a lady who, of all the women he knows, is
the last that would be entertained at the expense of another."

The characters of Philomedé, Atossa, and Chloe were added—
though not published till after Pope's death—in the edition which,
with the assistance of Warburton, he had prepared for the press.
The Epistle was thus extended from 200 to 292 lines.

NOTHING so true as what you once let fall:
"Most women have no characters at all."
Matter too soft a lasting mark to bear,
And best distinguish'd by black, brown, or fair.
    How many pictures of one nymph we view,   5
All how unlike each other, all how true!
Arcadia's Countess, here, in ermin'd pride,
Is there, Pastora by a fountain side.
Here Fannia, leering on her own good man,
And there, a naked Leda with a swan.   10
Let then the fair one beautifully cry
In Magdalen's loose hair and lifted eye,
Or dress'd in smiles of sweet Cecilia shine,
With simpering angels, palms, and harps divine;
Whether the charmer sinner it, or saint it,   15
If folly grow romantic, I must paint it.
    Come, then, the colours and the ground prepare!
Dip in the rainbow, trick her off in air;
Choose a firm cloud before it fall, and in it

Catch, ere she change, the Cynthia of this minute,   20
   Rufa, whose eye quick glancing o'er the park
Attracts each light gay meteor of a spark,
Agrees as ill with Rufa studying Locke,
As Sappho's diamonds with her dirty smock;
Or Sappho at her toilet's greasy task,   25
With Sappho fragrant at an evening mask:[1]
So morning insects, that in muck begun,
Shine, buzz, and fly-blow in the setting sun.
   How soft is Silia! fearful to offend;
The frail one's advocate, the weak one's friend,   30
To her, Calista proved her conduct nice;
And good Simplicius asks of her advice.
Sudden, she storms! she raves! You tip the wink,
But spare your censure—Silia does not drink.
All eyes may see from what the change arose,   35
All eyes may see—a pimple on her nose.
   Papillia, wedded to her amorous spark,
Sighs for the shades—"How charming is a park!"
A park is purchased, but the fair he sees
All bathed in tears—"Oh odious, odious trees!"   40
   Ladies, like variegated tulips, show,
'Tis to their changes half their charms we owe;
Fine by defect, and delicately weak,
Their happy spots the nice admirer take.
'Twas thus Calypso once each heart alarm'd,   45
Awed without virtue, without beauty charm'd;
Her tongue bewitch'd as oddly as her eyes,
Less wit than mimic, more a wit than wise;
Strange graces still, and stranger flights she had,
Was just not ugly, and was just not mad;   50
Yet ne'er so sure our passion to create,
As when she touch'd the brink of all we hate.
   Narcissa's nature, tolerably mild,
To make a wash would hardly stew a child;
Has e'en been proved to grant a lover's prayer,
And paid a tradesman once, to make him stare;   55
Gave alms at Easter, in a Christian trim,
And made a widow happy for a whim.
Why then declare good-nature is her scorn,
When 'tis by that alone she can be borne?   60

[1] Supposed to glance at Lady Mary Wortley Montagu (whose negligence in dress is often coarsely alluded to by Pope and Walpole).

Why pique all mortals, yet affect a name?
A fool to pleasure, yet a slave to fame:
Now deep in Taylor and the Book of Martyrs,
Now drinking citron with his grace and Chartres:
Now conscience chills her, and now passion burns;   65
And atheism and religion take their turns;
A very heathen in the carnal part,
Yet still a sad, good Christian at her heart,
    See Sin in state, majestically drunk;
Proud as a peeress, prouder as a punk;   70
Chaste to her husband, frank to all beside,
A teeming mistress, but a barren bride.
What then? let blood and body bear the fault,
Her head's untouch'd, that noble seat of thought:
Such this day's doctrine—in another fit   75
She sins with poets through pure love of wit,
What has not fired her bosom or her brain?
Cæsar and Tall-boy, Charles and Charlemagne.[1]
As Helluo, late dictator of the feast,
The nose of *haut-goût* and the tip of taste,   80
Critiqued your wine, and analysed your meat,
Yet on plain pudding deign'd at home to eat:
So Philomedé, lecturing all mankind
On the soft passion, and the taste refined,
The address, the delicacy—stoops at once,   85
And makes her hearty meal upon a dunce,
    Flavia's a wit, has too much sense to pray;
To toast our wants and wishes is her way;
Nor asks of God, but of her stars, to give
The mighty blessing, "While we live, to live."   90
Then all for death, that opiate of the soul!
Lucretia's dagger, Rosamonda's bowl.
Say, what can cause such impotence of mind?
A spark too fickle, or a spouse too kind.
Wise wretch! with pleasures too refined to please;   95
With too much spirit to be e'er at ease;
With too much quickness ever to be taught;
With too much thinking to have common thought;
You purchase pain with all that joy can give,
And die of nothing but a rage to live.   100
    Turn then from wits; and look on Simo's mate,
No ass so meek, no ass so obstinate.

[1] Tall-boy was a character in a comedy called *The Jovial Crew.*

Or her that owns her faults, but never mends,
Because she's honest, and the best of friends,
Or her whose life the church and scandal share, 105
For ever in a passion or a prayer.
Or her who laughs at hell, but (like her grace) [1]
Cries, "Ah! how charming if there's no such place!"
Or who in sweet vicissitude appears
Of mirth and opium, ratafia and tears, 110
The daily anodyne, and nightly draught,
To kill those foes to fair ones, time and thought.
Woman and fool are two hard things to hit;
For true no-meaning puzzles more than wit.

But what are these to great Atossa's mind? [2] 115
Scarce once herself, by turns all womankind!
Who, with herself, or others, from her birth
Finds all her life one warfare upon earth:
Shines in exposing knaves and painting fools,
Yet is whate'er she hates and ridicules. 120
No thought advances, but her eddy brain
Whisks it about, and down it goes again.
Full sixty years the world has been her trade,
The wisest fool much time has ever made.
From loveless youth to unrespected age, 125
No passion gratified, except her rage,
So much the fury still outran the wit,
The pleasure miss'd her, and the scandal hit.
Who breaks with her, provokes revenge from hell,
But he's a bolder man who dares be well. 130
Her every turn with violence pursued,
No more a storm her hate than gratitude:
To that each passion turns, or soon or late;
Love, if it makes her yield, must make her hate.
Superiors? death! and equals? what a curse! 135
But an inferior not dependant? worse!
Offend her, and she knows not to forgive;
Oblige her, and she'll hate you while you live:
But die, and she'll adore you—then the bust
And temple rise—then fall again to dust. 140
Last night, her lord was all that's good and great;
A knave this morning, and his will a cheat.

[1] Perhaps the Duchess of Montagu, Lady Mary Churchill, youngest daughter of the Duke of Marlborough.
[2] Atossa is mentioned in Herodotus, and said to be a follower of Sappho. Pope's Atossa was Katherine, Duchess of Buckinghamshire.

Strange! by the means defeated of the ends,
By spirit robbed of power, by warmth of friends,
By wealth of followers! without one distress,   145
Sick of herself, through very selfishness!
Atossa, cursed with every granted prayer,
Childless with all her children, wants an heir.
To heirs unknown descends the unguarded store,
Or wanders, heaven-directed, to the poor.   150

　　Pictures like these, dear Madam, to design,
Ask no firm hand, and no unerring line;
Some wandering touches, some reflected light,
Some flying stroke alone can hit them right:
For how should equal colours do the knack?   155
Cameleons who can paint in white and black?
　　"Yet Chloe sure was form'd without a spot."—
Nature in her then err'd not, but forgot.
"With every pleasing, every prudent part,
Say, what can Chloe want?"—She wants a heart.   160
She speaks, behaves, and acts, just as she ought,
But never, never reached one generous thought.
Virtue she finds too painful an endeavour,
Content to dwell in decencies for ever.
So very reasonable, so unmoved,   165
As never yet to love, or to be loved.
She, while her lover pants upon her breast,
Can mark the figures on an Indian chest;
And when she sees her friend in deep despair,
Observes how much a chintz exceeds mohair!   170
Forbid it, Heaven, a favour or a debt
She e'er should cancel—but she may forget.
Safe is your secret still in Chloe's ear;
But none of Chloe's shall you ever hear.
Of all her dears she never slander'd one,   175
But cares not if a thousand are undone.
Would Chloe know if you're alive or dead?
She bids her footman put it in her head.[1]
Chloe is prudent—would you too be wise?
Then never break your heart when Chloe dies.   180

　　One certain portrait may (I grant) be seen,
Which Heaven has varnish'd out, and made a queen:

------

[1] Warton says that Pope, being at dinner one day with Mrs. Howard, afterwards Countess of Suffolk—the Chloe of the poem—heard her order her footman to put her in mind to send to know how Mrs. Blount, who was ill, had passed the night.

The same for ever! and described by all
With truth and goodness, as with crown and ball.
Poets heap virtues, painters gems, at will,   185
And show their zeal, and hide their want of skill.
'Tis well—but artists! who can paint or write,
To draw the naked is your true delight.
That robe of quality so struts and swells,
None see what parts of nature it conceals: 190
The exactest traits of body or of mind,
We owe to models of an humble kind.
If Queensberry to strip there's no compelling,
'Tis from a handmaid we must take a Helen.
From peer or bishop 'tis no easy thing   195
To draw the man who loves his God or king:
Alas! I copy (or my draught would fail)
From honest Mahomet, or plain Parson Hale.
    But grant, in public, men sometimes are shown,
A woman's seen in private life alone: 200
Our bolder talents in full light display'd;
Your virtues open fairest in the shade.
Bred to disguise, in public 'tis you hide;
There, none distinguish 'twixt your shame or pride,
Weakness or delicacy; all so nice,   205
That each may seem a virtue or a vice.
    In men we various ruling passions find;
In women, two almost divide the kind;
Those, only fix'd, they first or last obey,
The love of pleasure, and the love of sway.   210
    That, Nature gives; and where the lesson taught
Is but to please, can pleasure seem a fault?
Experience, this; by man's oppression cursed,
They seek the second not to lose the first.
    Men, some to business, some to pleasure take;   215
But every woman is at heart a rake:
Men, some to quiet, some to public strife;
But every lady would be queen for life.
    Yet mark the fate of a whole sex of queens!
Power all their end, but beauty all the means: 220
In youth they conquer with so wild a rage,
As leaves them scarce a subject in their age:
For foreign glory, foreign joy, they roam;
No thought of peace or happiness at home.
But wisdom's triumph is well-timed retreat,   225

As hard a science to the fair as great!
Beauties, like tyrants, old and friendless grown,
Yet hate repose, and dread to be alone.
Worn out in public, weary every eye,
Nor leave one sigh behind them when they die.   230
    Pleasures the sex, as children birds, pursue,
Still out of reach, yet never out of view;
Sure, if they catch, to spoil the toy at most,
To covet flying, and regret when lost:
At last, to follies youth could scarce defend,   235
It grows their age's prudence to pretend;
Ashamed to own they gave delight before,
Reduced to feign it, when they give no more:
As hags hold sabbaths, less for joy than spite,
So these their merry, miserable night;   240
Still round and round the ghosts of beauty glide,
And haunt the places where their honour died.
    See how the world its veterans rewards!
A youth of frolics, an old age of cards;
Fair to no purpose, artful to no end,   245
Young without lovers, old without a friend;
A fop their passion, but their prize a sot,
Alive, ridiculous, and dead, forgot![1]
    Ah, friend! to dazzle let the vain design;
To raise the thought and touch the heart be thine!   250
That charm shall grow, while what fatigues the ring,[2]
Flaunts and goes down, an unregarded thing:
So when the sun's broad beam has tired the sight,
All mild ascends the moon's more sober light,
Serene in virgin modesty she shines,   255
And unobserved the glaring orb declines.
    Oh! bless'd with temper, whose unclouded ray
Can make to-morrow cheerful as to-day;
She who can love a sister's charms, or hear[3]
Sighs for a daughter with unwounded ear;   260
She who ne'er answers till a husband cools,
Or, if she rules him, never shows she rules;
Charms by accepting, by submitting sways,

[1] The six lines, v. 243–248, originally formed part of the poem addressed to Martha Blount on her birthday, and published in the *Miscellanies*.
[2] The ring or circle in Hyde Park was a place of fashionable resort from the time of Charles I. to that of George II., when it was partly destroyed by the formation of the Serpentine river.
[3] The sister was Teresa Blount, two years older than Martha.

Yet has her humour most when she obeys;
Let fops or fortune fly which way they will,   265
Disdains all loss of tickets, or codille;
Spleen, vapours, or small-pox, above them all,
And mistress of herself, though China fall.[1]
  And yet, believe me, good as well as ill,
Woman's at best a contradiction still.   270
Heaven, when it strives to polish all it can
Its last best work, but forms a softer man;
Picks from each sex, to make the favourite blest,
Your love of pleasure, our desire of rest:
Blends, in exception to all general rules,   275
Your taste of follies, with our scorn of fools:
Reserve with frankness, art with truth allied,
Courage with softness, modesty with pride;
Fix'd principles, with fancy ever new;
Shakes all together, and produces—you!   280
  Be this a woman's fame; with this unblest,
Toasts live a scorn, and queens may die a jest.
This Phœbus promised (I forget the year)
When those blue eyes first open'd on the sphere;
Ascendant Phœbus watch'd that hour with care,   285
Averted half your parents' simple prayer;
And gave you beauty, but denied the pelf
That buys your sex a tyrant o'er itself.
The generous god, who wit and gold refines,
And ripens spirits as he ripens mines,   290
Kept dross for duchesses, the world shall know it,
To you gave sense, good humour, and a poet.

[1] The allusion to the fall of China is taken from Addison in *The Lover*. The *tickets* were lottery tickets, in which Pope and Miss Blount dabbled occasionally.

EPISTLE III[1]

TO ALLEN, LORD BATHURST

ARGUMENT

OF THE USE OF RICHES

That it is known to few, most falling into one of the extremes,
avarice or profusion, ver. 1, etc. The point discussed, whether the
invention of money has been more commodious or pernicious to
mankind, ver. 21 to 77. That riches, either to the avaricious or the
prodigal, cannot afford happiness, scarcely necessaries, ver. 89 to 160.
That avarice is an absolute frenzy, without an end or purpose, ver.
113, etc., 152. Conjectures about the motives of avaricious men,
ver. 121 to 153. That the conduct of men, with respect to riches,
can only be accounted for by the order of Providence, which works
the general good out of extremes, and brings all to its great end by
perpetual revolutions, ver. 161 to 178. How a miser acts upon
principles which appear to him reasonable, ver. 179. How a prodigal
does the same, ver. 199. The due medium and true use of riches,
ver. 219. The Man of Ross, ver. 250. The fate of the profuse and
the covetous, in two examples: both miserable in life and in death,
ver. 300, etc. The story of Sir Balaam, ver. 339 to the end.

> *P.* Who shall decide, when doctors disagree,
> And soundest casuists doubt, like you and me?
> You hold the word, from Jove to Momus given,
> That man was made the standing jest of Heaven:
> And gold but sent to keep the fools in play,   5
> For some to heap, and some to throw away.
>
> But I, who think more highly of our kind
> (And, surely, Heaven and I are of a mind),
> Opine that Nature, as in duty bound,
> Deep hid the shining mischief underground: 10
> But when by man's audacious labour won,
> Flamed forth this rival to its sire, the sun,

---

[1] This Epistle was written (in 1732) after a violent outcry against Pope,
on a supposition that he had ridiculed a worthy nobleman merely for his
wrong taste. He justified himself upon that article in a letter to the Earl
of Burlington; at the end of which are these words: " I have learnt that
there are some who would rather be wicked than ridiculous; and therefore
it may be safer to attack vices than follies. I will therefore leave my betters
in the quiet possession of their idols, their groves and their high places;
and change my subject from their pride to their meanness, from their
vanities to their miseries; and, as the only certain way to avoid mis-
constructions, to lessen offence, and not to multiply ill-natured appli-
cations, I may probably, in my next, make use of real names instead of
fictitious ones."

Then careful Heaven supplied two sorts of men,
To squander these, and those to hide again.

    Like doctors thus, when much dispute has pass'd,   15
We find our tenets just the same at last,
Both fairly owning, riches, in effect,
No grace of Heaven or token of the elect;
Given to the fool, the mad, the vain, the evil,
To Ward, to Waters, Chartres, and the Devil.[1]   20

    B. What Nature wants, commodious gold bestows,
'Tis thus we eat the bread another sows.

    P. But how unequal it bestows, observe,
'Tis thus we riot, while who sow it starve:
What Nature wants (a phrase I much distrust)   25
Extends to luxury, extends to lust:
Useful, I grant, it serves what life requires,
But dreadful, too, the dark assassin hires.

    B. Trade it may help, society extend:

    P. But lures the pirate, and corrupts the friend.   30

    B. It raises armies in a nation's aid:

    P. But bribes a senate, and the land's betray'd,
In vain may heroes fight, and patriots rave;
If secret gold sap on from knave to knave.
Once, we confess, beneath the patriot's cloak,[2]   35
From the crack'd bag the dropping guinea spoke,
And, jingling down the back-stairs, told the crew,
"Old Cato is as great a rogue as you."
Blest paper-credit! last and best supply!
That lends corruption lighter wings to fly!   40
Gold imp'd by thee, can compass hardest things,

---

[1] John Ward of Hackney, member of Parliament, being prosecuted by the Duchess of Buckingham, and convicted of forgery, was first expelled the House, and then stood in the pillory on 17th March, 1727.

Fr. Chartres, a man infamous for all manner of vices. When he was an ensign in the army, he was drummed out of the regiment for a cheat. His house was a perpetual bawdy-house. He was twice condemned for rapes, and pardoned; but the last time not without imprisonment in Newgate, and large confiscations. He died in Scotland in 1731, aged sixty-two.

Mr. Waters, the third of these worthies, was a man no way resembling the former in his military, but extremely so in his civil capacity; his great fortune having been raised by the like diligent attendance on the necessities of others. See also note 4, p. 238.

[2] In the reign of William III. an unsuspected old patriot, coming out at the back-door from having been closeted by the king, where he had received a large bag of guineas, the bursting of the bag discovered his business there.

Sir Christopher Musgrave, who, Burnet says, had £12,000 from King William III.

Can pocket states, can fetch or carry kings; [1]
A single leaf shall waft an army o'er,
Or ship off senates to some distant shore; [2]
A leaf, like Sibyl's, scatter to and fro   45
Our fates and fortunes, as the wind shall blow:
Pregnant with thousands flits the scrap unseen,
And silent sells a king, or buys a queen,
   Oh! that such bulky bribes as all might see,
Still, as of old, incumber'd villainy!   50
Could France or Rome divert our brave designs,
With all their brandies, or with all their wines?
What could they more than knights and 'squires confound,
Or water all the quorum ten miles round?
A statesman's slumbers how this speech would spoil!   55
"Sir, Spain has sent a thousand jars of oil;
Huge bales of British cloth blockade the door:
A hundred oxen at your levée roar."
   Poor avarice one torment more would find;
Nor could profusion squander all in kind.   60
Astride his cheese Sir Morgan might we meet;
And Worldly crying coals from street to street, [3]
Whom, with a wig so wild, and mien so mazed,
Pity mistakes for some poor tradesman crazed.
Had Colepepper's whole wealth been hops and hogs, [4]   65
Could he himself have sent it to the dogs?
His Grace will game: to White's a bull be led, [5]
With spurning heels and with a butting head.
To White's be carried, as to ancient games,
Fair coursers, vases, and alluring dames.   70
Shall then Uxorio, if the stakes he sweep, [6]
Bear home six whores, and make his lady weep?

[1] In our author's time many princes had been sent about the world, and great changes of kings projected in Europe. The Partition Treaty had disposed of Spain; France had set up a king for England, who was sent to Scotland, and back again; King Stanislaus was sent to Poland, and back again; the Duke of Anjou was sent to Spain, and Don Carlos to Italy.

[2] Alludes to several ministers, counsellors and patriots banished in our time to Siberia, and to that more glorious fate of the Parliament of Paris, banished to Pontoise in the year 1720.

[3] Some misers of great wealth, proprietors of the coal-mines, had entered at this time into an association to keep up coals to an extravagant price.

[4] Sir William Colepepper, Bart., a person of an ancient family and ample fortune, who, after ruining himself at the gaming-table, passed the rest of his days in sitting there to see the ruin of others; preferring to subsist upon borrowing and begging, rather than to enter into any reputable method of life, and refusing a post in the army which was offered him.

[5] White's Club-house, in St. James's Street.

[6] The Earl of Bristol.

Or soft Adonis, so perfumed and fine,[1]
Drive to St. James's a whole herd of swine?
Oh filthy check on all industrious skill,   75
To spoil the nation's last great trade, Quadrille!
Since then, my lord, on such a world we fall,
What say you? *B.* Say? Why, take it, gold and all.
   P. What riches give us, let us then inquire:
Meat, fire, and clothes. *B.* What more? *P.* Meat, clothes,
     and fire.   80
Is this too little? would you more than live?
Alas! 'tis more than Turner finds they give.[2]
Alas! 'tis more than (all his visions past)
Unhappy Wharton, waking, found at last![3]
What can they give? to dying Hopkins, heirs;[4]   85
To Chartres, vigour; Japhet,[5] nose and ears?
Can they in gems bid pallid Hippia glow,
In Fulvia's buckle ease the throbs below;
Or heal, old Narses, thy obscener ail,
With all the embroidery plaster'd at thy tail?   90
They might (were Harpax not too wise to spend)
Give Harpax' self the blessing of a friend;
Or find some doctor that would save the life
Of wretched Shylock, spite of Shylock's wife:
But thousands die, without or this or that,   95
Die, and endow a college, or a cat.[6]
To some, indeed, Heaven grants the happier fate,
To enrich a bastard, or a son they hate.
   Perhaps you think the poor might have their part;

---

[1] Lord Hervey, son of the Earl of Bristol.

[2] One who, being possessed of three hundred thousand pounds, laid down his coach because interest was reduced from five to four per cent., and then put seventy thousand into the Charitable Corporation for better interest; which sum having lost, he took it so much to heart that he kept his chamber ever after.

Richard Turner, usually called "Plum Turner." He had been a Turkey merchant. Died 8th February, 1733.

[3] A nobleman of great qualities, but as unfortunate in the application of them as if they had been vices and follies. See his character in the First Epistle.

[4] A citizen whose rapacity obtained him the name of Vulture Hopkins. He died worth three hundred thousand pounds, which he would give to no person living, but left it so as not to be inherited till after the second generation; but the Chancery afterwards set aside the will.

[5] Japhet Crook, alias Sir Peter Stranger, was punished with the loss of those parts for having forged a conveyance of an estate to himself, upon which he took up several thousand pounds.

[6] A famous duchess of R[ichmond] in her last will left considerable legacies and annuities to her cats.

Bond damns the poor, and hates them from his heart:[1] 100
The grave Sir Gilbert holds it for a rule
That every man in want is knave or fool:
"God cannot love (says Blunt, with tearless eyes)
The wretch he starves"—and piously denies:
But the good bishop, with a meeker air, 105
Admits, and leaves them, Providence's care.

    Yet to be just to these poor men of pelf,
Each does but hate his neighbour as himself:
Damn'd to the mines, an equal fate betides
The slave that digs it, and the slave that hides. 110

    B. Who suffer thus, mere charity should own,
Must act on motives powerful, though unknown.

    P. Some war, some plague, or famine, they foresee,
Some revelation hid from you and me.
Why Shylock wants a meal, the cause is found, 115
He thinks a loaf will rise to fifty pound.
What made directors cheat in South Sea year?
To live on venison when it sold so dear.[2]
Ask you why Phryne the whole auction buys?
Phryne foresees a general excise.[3] 120
Why she and Sappho raise that monstrous sum?
Alas! they fear a man will cost a plum.

    Wise Peter [4] sees the world's respect for gold,
And therefore hopes this nation may be sold:
Glorious ambition! Peter, swell thy store, 125
And be what Rome's great Didius was before.[5]

[1] In the year 1730 a corporation was established to lend money to the poor upon pledges, by the name of the Charitable Corporation; but the whole was turned only to a method of enriching particular people to the ruin of such numbers that it became a parliamentary concern to endeavour the relief of those sufferers, and three of the managers, who were members of the House, were expelled. By the report of the committee appointed to inquire into that iniquitous affair, it appears that when it was objected to the intended removal of the office, that the poor, for whose use it was erected, would be hurt by it, Dennis Bond, one of the directors, replied, " Damn the poor."

Bond was long in Parliament, and represented successively the boroughs of Dorchester, Corfe Castle and Poole. He died 30th January, 1746–7. Sir Gilbert, in the next line, is Sir Gilbert Heathcote.

[2] In the South Sea year the price of a haunch of venison was from three to five pounds.

[3] Many people, about the year 1733, had a conceit that such a thing was intended.

[4] Peter Walter, a dexterous attorney.

[5] A Roman lawyer, so rich as to purchase the empire when it was set to sale upon the death of Pertinax.

The crown of Poland,[1] venal twice an age,
To just three millions stinted modest Gage;
But nobler scenes Maria's dreams unfold,
Hereditary realms, and worlds of gold.   130
Congenial souls! whose life one avarice joins,
And one fate buries in the Asturian mines.

    Much-injured Blunt![2] why bears he Britain's hate?
A wizard told him in these words our fate:
"At length corruption, like a general flood   135
(So long by watchful ministers withstood),
Shall deluge all; and avarice creeping on,
Spread like a low-born mist, and blot the sun;
Statesman and patriot ply alike the stocks,
Peeress and butler share alike the box,   140
And judges job, and bishops bite the town,
And mighty dukes pack cards for half-a-crown.
See Britain sunk in lucre's sordid charms,
And France revenged on Anne's and Edward's arms!"
'Twas no court-badge, great scrivener, fired thy brain, 145
Nor lordly luxury, nor city gain:
No, 'twas thy righteous end, ashamed to see
Senates degenerate, patriots disagree;
And, nobly wishing party-rage to cease,
To buy both sides, and give thy country peace.   150
    "All this is madness," cries a sober sage:
But who, my friend, has reason in his rage?
"The ruling passion, be it what it will,
The ruling passion conquers reason still."
Less mad the wildest whimsey we can frame,   155
Than e'en that passion, if it has no aim;
For though such motives folly you may call,
The folly's greater to have none at all.
    Hear then the truth: "'Tis Heaven each passion sends,
And different men directs to different ends.   160

[1] The two persons here mentioned were of quality, each of whom in the Mississipi despised to realise above three hundred thousand pounds; the gentleman with a view to the purchase of the crown of Poland, the lady on a vision of the like royal nature. They retired into Spain, where they were still in search of gold in the mines of the Asturias.

[2] Sir John Blunt, one of the first projectors of the South Sea Company, and afterwards one of the directors. Also one of those who suffered most severely by the bill of pains and penalties on the said directors. Whether he did really credit the prophecy here mentioned is not certain, but it was constantly in this very style he declaimed against the corruption and luxury of the age, the partiality of parliaments, and the misery of party-spirit. Died 1732.

Extremes in Nature equal good produce,
Extremes in man concur to general use."
Ask we what makes one keep, and one bestow?
That power who bids the ocean ebb and flow,
Bids seed-time, harvest, equal course maintain,   165
Through reconciled extremes of drought and rain,
Builds life on death, on change duration founds,
And gives the eternal wheels to know their rounds.

Riches, like insects, when concealed they lie,
Wait but for wings, and in their season fly.   170
Who sees pale Mammon pine amidst his store,
Sees but a backward steward for the poor;
This year a reservoir, to keep and spare;
The next, a fountain, spouting through his heir,
In lavish streams to quench a country's thirst,   175
And men and dogs shall drink him till they burst.

Old Cotta shamed his fortune and his birth,
Yet was not Cotta void of wit or worth:
What though (the use of barbarous spits forgot)
His kitchen vied in coolness with his grot?   180
His court with nettles, moats with cresses stored,
With soups unbought and salads blessed his board? [1]
If Cotta lived on pulse, it was no more
Than Brahmins, saints, and sages did before;
To cram the rich was prodigal expense,   185
And who would take the poor from Providence?
Like some lone Chartreux stands the good old hall,
Silence without, and fasts within the wall;
No raftered roofs with dance and tabor sound,
No noontide bell invites the country round: 190
Tenants with sighs the smokeless towers survey,
And turn the unwilling steeds another way:
Benighted wanderers, the forest o'er,
Curse the saved candle and unopening door;
While the gaunt mastiff growling at the gate   195
Affrights the beggar whom he longs to eat.

Not so his son; he mark'd this oversight,
And then mistook reverse of wrong for right.
(For what to shun will no great knowledge need,
But what to follow is a task indeed.)   200
Yet sure, of qualities deserving praise,
More go to ruin fortunes than to raise.

[1] " ——dapibus mensas onerabat inemptis."—VIRGIL.

What slaughter'd hecatombs, what floods of wine,
Fill the capacious 'squire and deep divine!
Yet no mean motives this profusion draws,   205
His oxen perish in his country's cause;
'Tis GEORGE and LIBERTY that crowns the cup,
And zeal for that great House which eats him up.
The woods recede around the naked seat,
The sylvans groan—no matter—for the fleet: 210
Next goes his wool, to clothe our valiant bands;
Last, for his country's love, he sells his lands.
To town he comes, completes the nation's hope,
And heads the bold train-bands, and burns a pope.
And shall not Britain now reward his toils,   215
Britain, that pays her patriots with her spoils?
In vain at Court the bankrupt pleads his cause,
His thankless country leaves him to her laws.

    The sense to value riches, with the art
To enjoy them, and the virtue to impart,   220
Not meanly, nor ambitiously pursued,
Not sunk by sloth, not raised by servitude;
To balance fortune by a just expense,
Join with economy, magnificence;
With splendour, charity; with plenty, health;   225
Oh, teach us, Bathurst! yet unspoil'd by wealth!
That secret rare, between the extremes to move
Of mad good-nature and of mean self-love.
    B. To worth or want well weigh'd, be bounty given,
And ease, or emulate, the care of Heaven   230
(Whose measure full o'erflows on human race);
Mend Fortune's fault, and justify her grace.
Wealth in the gross is death, but life, diffused;
As poison heals, in just proportion used:
In heaps, like ambergris, a stink it lies,   235
But, well dispersed, is incense to the skies.
    P. Who starves by nobles, or with nobles eats?
The wretch that trusts them, and the rogue that cheats.
Is there a lord who knows a cheerful noon
Without a fiddler, flatterer, or buffoon?   240
Whose table wit or modest merit share,
Unelbow'd by a gamester, pimp, or player?
Who copies yours, or Oxford's better part,[1]

[1] Edwin Harley, Earl of Oxford, the son of Robert, created Earl of Oxford and Earl Mortimer by Queen Anne. Died 1741. He left behind him one of the most noble libraries in Europe.

To ease the oppress'd, and raise the sinking heart?
Where'er he shines, oh Fortune, gild the scene,　　245
And angels guard him in the golden mean!
There English bounty yet awhile may stand,
And honour linger ere it leaves the land.
　　But all our praises why should lords engross?
Rise, honest Muse! and sing the Man of Ross: [1]　　250
Pleased Vaga echoes through her winding bounds,
And rapid Severn hoarse applause resounds.
Who hung with woods yon mountain's sultry brow?
From the dry rock who bade the waters flow?
Not to the skies in useless columns toss'd,　　255
Or in proud falls magnificently lost,
But clear and artless, pouring through the plain
Health to the sick, and solace to the swain.
Whose causeway parts the vale with shady rows?
Whose seats the weary traveller repose?　　260
Who taught that heaven-directed spire to rise?
"The Man of Ross," each lisping babe replies.
Behold the market-place with poor o'erspread!
The Man of Ross divides the weekly bread:
He feeds yon almshouse, neat, but void of state,　　265
Where Age and Want sit smiling at the gate;
Him portion'd maids, apprenticed orphans bless'd,
The young who labour, and the old who rest.
Is any sick? the Man of Ross relieves,
Prescribes, attends, the medicine makes, and gives.　　270
Is there a variance? enter but his door,
Balk'd are the courts, and contest is no more.
Despairing quacks with curses fled the place,
And vile attorneys, now an useless race.
　　B. Thrice happy man! enabled to pursue　　275
What all so wish, but want the power to do!
Oh say, what sums that generous hand supply?
What mines to swell that boundless charity?
　　P. Of debts and taxes, wife and children clear,
This man possess'd—five hundred pounds a year!　　280
Blush, Grandeur, blush! proud courts, withdraw your blaze!
Ye little stars, hide your diminish'd rays.
　　B. And what? no monument, inscription, stone?
His race, his form, his name almost unknown?

[1] John Kyrle. Died 1724, aged 90, and lies interred in the chancel of
the church of Ross, in Herefordshire.

P. Who builds a church to God, and not to fame, 285
Will never mark the marble with his name:
Go, search it there, where to be born, and die,
Of rich and poor makes all the history;[1]
Enough that Virtue fill'd the space between;
Proved, by the ends of being, to have been.   290
When Hopkins dies, a thousand lights attend
The wretch, who living saved a candle's end;
Shouldering God's altar a vile image stands,
Belies his features, nay extends his hands;
That livelong wig which Gorgon's self might own,   295
Eternal buckle takes in Parian stone.
Behold what blessings wealth to life can lend!
And see what comfort it affords our end.
In the worst inn's worst room, with mat half-hung,
The floors of plaster, and the walls of dung,   300
On once a flock-bed, but repair'd with straw,
With tape-tied curtains never meant to draw,
The George and Garter dangling from that bed
Where tawdry yellow strove with dirty red,
Great Villiers lies,[2]—alas! how changed from him,   305
That life of pleasure, and that soul of whim!
Gallant and gay, in Cliveden's proud alcove,[3]
The bower of wanton Shrewsbury and love;[4]
Or just as gay, at council, in a ring
Of mimick'd statesmen, and their merry King,   310
No wit to flatter left of all his store!
No fool to laugh at, which he valued more.
There, victor of his health, of fortune, friends,
And fame, this lord of useless thousands ends.

    His Grace's fate sage Cutler could foresee,   315
And well (he thought) advised him, "Live like me."
As well his Grace replied, "Like you, Sir John?
That I can do, when all I have is gone."
Resolve me, Reason, which of these is worse,
Want with a full, or with an empty purse?   320
Thy life more wretched, Cutler, was confess'd,

[1] The parish register.
[2] George Villiers, second Duke of Buckingham, yet more famous for his vices than his misfortunes, having been possessed of about £50,000 a year, died, 1687, in a remote inn in Yorkshire, reduced to the utmost misery.
[3] A palace on the banks of the Thames, built by the Duke of Buckingham.
[4] The Countess of Shrewsbury. Her husband was killed by the Duke of Buckingham in a duel; and it has been said that during the combat she held the duke's horses, in the habit of a page.

Arise, and tell me, was thy death more bless'd?
Cutler saw tenants break, and houses fall;
For very want he could not build a wall.
His only daughter in a stranger's power;   325
For very want he could not pay a dower.
A few grey hairs his reverend temples crowned;
'Twas very want that sold them for two pound.
What e'en denied a cordial at his end,
Banish'd the doctor, and expell'd the friend?   330
What but a want, which you perhaps think mad,
Yet numbers feel—the want of what he had!
Cutler and Brutus, dying, both exclaim,
"Virtue! and Wealth! what are ye but a name!"
    Say, for such worth are other worlds prepared?   335
Or are they both in this their own reward?
A knotty point! to which we now proceed.
But you are tired—I'll tell a tale. _B._ Agreed.
    _P._ Where London's column, pointing at the skies[1]
Like a tall bully, lifts the head and lies;   340
There dwelt a citizen of sober fame,
A plain good man, and Balaam was his name;
Religious, punctual, frugal, and so forth;
His word would pass for more than he was worth.
One solid dish his week-day meal affords,   345
An added pudding solemnised the Lord's:
Constant at Church and 'Change; his gains were sure,
His givings rare, save farthings to the poor.
The Devil was piqued such saintship to behold,
And longed to tempt him, like good Job of old: 350
But Satan now is wiser than of yore,
And tempts by making rich, not making poor.
    Roused by the Prince of Air, the whirlwinds sweep
The surge, and plunge his father in the deep;
Then full against his Cornish lands they roar,[2]   355
And two rich shipwrecks bless the lucky shore.
    Sir Balaam now, he lives like other folks,
He takes his chirping pint, and cracks his jokes:

[1] The Monument, in memory of the fire of London, with an inscription importing that city to have been burnt by the Papists, which was erased in the reign of James II., re-cut in the reign of William III., and erased again in the reign of William IV. (1831).

[2] In Cornwall, when a ship happened to be stranded there, the inhabitants have been known to bore holes in it to prevent its getting off; to plunder, and sometimes even to massacre, the people.

"Live like yourself," was soon my Lady's word;
And lo! two puddings smoked upon the board.   360
    Asleep and naked as an Indian lay,
An honest factor stole a gem away:
He pledged it to the knight, the knight had wit,
So kept the diamond,[1] and the rogue was bit.
Some scruple rose, but thus he eased his thought: 365
"I'll now give sixpence where I gave a groat;
Where once I went to church, I'll now go twice;
And am so clear too of all other vice."
    The Tempter saw his time; the work he plied;
Stocks and subscriptions pour on every side,   370
Till all the demon makes his full descent
In one abundant shower of cent. per cent.;
Sinks deep within him, and possesses whole,
Then dubs Director, and secures his soul.
    Behold Sir Balaam now a man of spirit,   375
Ascribes his gettings to his parts and merit;
What late he call'd a blessing, now was wit,
And God's good Providence, a lucky hit.
Things change their titles, as our manners turn:
His counting-house employ'd the Sunday morn: 380
Seldom at Church ('twas such a busy life),
But duly sent his family and wife.
There (so the Devil ordain'd) one Christmastide
My good old lady catch'd a cold, and died.
    A nymph of quality admires our knight;   385
He marries, bows at Court, and grows polite:
Leaves the dull cits, and joins (to please the fair)
The well-bred cuckolds in St. James's air:
First, for his son a gay commission buys,
Who drinks, whores, fights, and, in a duel, dies: 390
His daughter flaunts a viscount's tawdry wife;
She bears a coronet, and pox, for life.
In Britain's senate he a seat obtains,
And one more pensioner St. Stephen gains.[2]
My lady falls to play: so bad her chance,   395
He must repair it; takes a bribe from France;
The House impeach him; Coningsby harangues;

---

[1] Pope was supposed to allude here to the Pitt diamond, a gem brought to this country by Thomas Pitt, Governor of Madras, about 1700. The report that Mr. Pitt had obtained this diamond by dishonourable means was very general.

[2] " ——atque unum civem donare Sibyllæ."—JUVENAL.

The Court forsake him—and Sir Balaam hangs.
Wife, son, and daughter, Satan! are thy own,
His wealth, yet dearer, forfeit to the Crown: 400
The Devil and the King divide the prize,
And sad Sir Balaam curses God, and dies

EPISTLE IV

TO RICHARD BOYLE, EARL OF BURLINGTON

ARGUMENT

OF THE USE OF RICHES

The vanity of expense in people of wealth and quality. The abuse
of the word taste, ver. 13. That the first principle and foundation
in this, as in everything else, is good sense, ver. 39. The chief proof
of it is to follow Nature, even in works of mere luxury and elegance.
Instanced in architecture and gardening, where all must be adapted
to the genius and use of the place, and the beauties not forced into
it, but resulting from it, ver. 47. How men are disappointed in their
most expensive undertakings for want of this true foundation,
without which nothing can please long, if at all; and the best
examples and rules will be but perverted into something burden-
some or ridiculous, ver. 65, etc., to 98. A description of the false
taste of magnificence; the first grand error of which is to imagine
that greatness consists in the size and dimensions, instead of the
proportion and harmony of the whole, ver. 99; and the second,
either in joining together parts incoherent, or too minutely resem-
bling, or in the repetition of the same too frequently, ver. 105, etc.
A word or two of false taste in books, in music, in painting, even in
preaching and prayer, and lastly in entertainments, ver. 133, etc.
Yet Providence is justified in giving wealth to be squandered in
this manner, since it is dispersed to the poor and laborious part of
mankind, ver. 169 (recurring to what is laid down in the *Essay on
Man*, Epistle II., and in the epistle preceding, ver .159, etc.). What
are the proper objects of magnificence, and a proper field for the
expense of great men, ver. 177, etc.; and finally, the great and
public works which become a prince, ver. 191 to the end.

'TIS strange, the miser should his cares employ
To gain those riches he can ne'er enjoy:
Is it less strange, the prodigal should waste
His wealth to purchase what he ne'er can taste?
Not for himself he sees, or hears, or eats;   5
Artists must choose his pictures, music, meats:

He buys for Topham [1] drawings and designs,
For Pembroke statues, dirty gods, and coins; [2]
Rare monkish manuscripts for Hearne alone,
And books for Mead, and butterflies for Sloane. [3]   10
Think we all these are for himself? no more
Than his fine wife, alas! or finer whore.

For what has Virro painted, built, and planted?
Only to show how many tastes he wanted.
What brought Sir Visto's ill-got wealth to waste?   15
Some demon whisper'd, "Visto! have a taste."
Heaven visits with a taste the wealthy fool,
And needs no rod but Ripley with a rule. [4]
See! sportive Fate, to punish awkward pride,
Bids Bubo build, [5] and sends him such a guide: 20
A standing sermon, at each year's expense,
That never coxcomb reach'd magnificence!

You show us Rome was glorious, not profuse, [6]
And pompous buildings once were things of use,
Yet shall (my lord) your just, your noble rules   25
Fill half the land with imitating fools;
Who random drawings from your sheets shall take,
And of one beauty many blunders make;
Load some vain church with old theatric state,
Turn arcs of triumph to a garden-gate;   30
Reverse your ornaments, and hang them all
On some patch'd dog-hole eked with ends of wall;
Then clap four slices of pilaster on 't,
That, laced with bits of rustic, makes a front.
Shall call the winds through long arcades to roar,   35

[1] A gentleman famous for a judicious collection of drawings.

[2] Thomas, eighth Earl of Pembroke, collected the statues and medals at Wilton, the magnificent seat of the family. His successor, Earl Henry, added materially to the decoration of the mansion.

[3] Two eminent physicians; the one had an excellent library, the other the finest collection in Europe of natural curiosities. Dr. Mead's books, alluded to by the poet, consisted of about 10,000 volumes, which, with his valuable collection of medals and paintings, were sold by auction after his death in 1754. Sir Hans Sloane's collection was fortunately preserved. Died in 1752.

[4] A carpenter, employed by a first minister, who raised him to an architect and made him Comptroller of the Board of Works. Ripley was the architect of Houghton, the residence of Sir R. Walpole, in Norfolk, and of Woolterton, the house of the elder Horace Walpole. He also designed the front of the Admiralty. He owed the commencement of his success in life to the fact of his marrying a servant of Sir R. Walpole's. Died 1758.

[5] Bubo, Bubb Dodington, Lord Melcombe. He completed Eastbury.

[6] The Earl of Burlington was then publishing the *Designs* of Inigo Jones and the *Antiquities of Rome* by Palladio.

Proud to catch cold at a Venetian door;
Conscious they act a true Palladian part,
And, if they starve, they starve by rules of art.
　Oft have you hinted to your brother peer
A certain truth, which many buy too dear: 40
Something there is more needful than expense,
And something previous even to taste—'tis sense:
Good sense, which only is the gift of Heaven,
And, though no science, fairly worth the seven:
A light, which in yourself you must perceive;   45
Jones and Le Nôtre have it not to give.[1]
　To build, to plant, whatever you intend,
To rear the column, or the arch to bend,
To swell the terrace, or to sink the grot,
In all, let Nature never be forgot,   50
But treat the goddess like a modest fair,
Nor over-dress, nor leave her wholly bare;
Let not each beauty everywhere be spied,
Where half the skill is decently to hide.
He gains all points, who pleasingly confounds,   55
Surprises, varies, and conceals the bounds.
　Consult the genius of the place in all;
That tells the waters or to rise or fall;
Or helps the ambitious hill the heavens to scale,
Or scoops in circling theatres the vale;   60
Calls in the country, catches opening glades,
Joins willing woods, and varies shades from shades;
Now breaks, or now directs, the intending lines;
Paints, as you plant, and, as you work, designs.
Still follow sense, of every art the soul,   65
Parts answering parts shall slide into a whole,
Spontaneous beauties all around advance,
Start ev'n from difficulty, strike from chance;
Nature shall join you; Time shall make it grow
A work to wonder at—perhaps a Stowe.[2]   70
　Without it, proud Versailles! thy glory falls;
And Nero's terraces desert their walls:
The vast parterres a thousand hands shall make,

---

[1] Inigo Jones, the celebrated architect, and M. Le Nôtre, the designer of the best gardens in France. Le Nôtre is said to have been engaged by Charles II. to aid in laying out and improving St. James's Park, London.
[2] The seat and gardens of the Lord Viscount Cobham, in Buckinghamshire.

Lo! Cobham comes, and floats them with a lake:
Or cut wide views through mountains to the plain,[1]   75
You'll wish your hill or shelter'd seat again.
Even in an ornament its place remark,
Nor in an hermitage set Dr. Clarke.[2]
Behold Villario's ten years' toil complete;
His quincunx darkens, his espaliers meet;   80
The wood supports the plain, the parts unite,
And strength of shade contends with strength of light;
A waving glow the bloomy beds display,
Blushing in bright diversities of day,
With silver-quivering rills meander'd o'er—   85
Enjoy them, you! Villario can no more:
Tired of the scene parterres and fountains yield,
He finds at last he better likes a field.

Through his young woods how pleased Sabinus stray'd,
Or sate delighted in the thickening shade,   90
With annual joy the reddening shoots to greet,
Or see the stretching branches long to meet!
His son's fine taste an opener vista loves,
Foe to the Dryads of his father's groves;
One boundless green, or flourish'd carpet views,   95
With all the mournful family of yews:
The thriving plants, ignoble broomsticks made,
Now sweep those alleys they were born to shade.

At Timon's villa let us pass a day,[3]
Where all cry out, "What sums are thrown away!"   100
So proud, so grand: of that stupendous air,
Soft and agreeable come never there.
Greatness, with Timon, dwells in such a draught
As brings all Brobdignag before your thought.
To compass this, his building is a town,   105
His pond an ocean, his parterre a down:
Who but must laugh, the master when he sees,
A puny insect, shivering at a breeze!
Lo, what huge heaps of littleness around!

[1] This was done in Hertfordshire by a wealthy citizen, at the expense of above £5,000, by which means (merely to overlook a dead plain) he let in the north wind upon his house and parterre, which were before adorned and defended by beautiful woods. The citizen was Benjamin Styles.
[2] Dr. S. Clarke's bust, placed by the queen in the Hermitage, while the doctor duly frequented the court.
[3] No longer supposed to be a satire on the Duke of Chandos's seat of Canons, destroyed in 1747. It is a composite picture.

The whole, a labour'd quarry above ground,[1]   110
Two cupids squirt before: a lake behind
Improves the keenness of the northern wind.
His gardens next your admiration call,
On every side you look, behold the wall!
No pleasing intricacies intervene,   115
No artful wildness to perplex the scene:
Grove nods at grove, each alley has a brother,
And half the platform just reflects the other.
The suffering eye inverted Nature sees,
Trees cut to statues, statues thick as trees;   120
With here a fountain, never to be play'd;
And there a summer-house, that knows no shade:
Here Amphitrite sails through myrtle bowers;
There gladiators fight, or die in flowers;[2]
Unwater'd see the drooping sea-horse mourn,   125
And swallows roost in Nilus' dusty urn.

My Lord advances with majestic mien,
Smit with the mighty pleasure to be seen:
But soft—by regular approach—not yet—
First through the length of yon hot terrace sweat;   130
And when up ten steep slopes you've dragg'd your thighs,
Just at his study-door he'll bless your eyes.

His study! with what authors is it stored?
In books, not authors, curious is my Lord;
To all their dated backs he turns you round;   135
These Aldus printed, those Du Sueïl has bound.
Lo, some are vellum, and the rest as good
For all his Lordship knows, but they are wood.
For Locke or Milton 'tis in vain to look,
These shelves admit not any modern book.   140

And now the chapel's silver bell you hear,
That summons you to all the pride of prayer:
Light quirks of music, broken and uneven,
Make the soul dance upon a jig to Heaven.
On painted ceilings you devoutly stare,[3]   145
Where sprawl the saints of Verrio or Laguerre,[4]

---

[1] This phrase Pope applies in one of his letters to Blenheim House. The *heaviness* of Blenheim was often brought against Vanbrugh, its architect.
[2] The two statues of the *Gladiator pugnans* and *Gladiator moriens*.
[3] Painting of naked figures in churches, etc., has obliged some Popes to put draperies on some of those of the best masters.
[4] Verrio (Antonio) painted many ceilings, etc., at Windsor, Hampton Court, etc., and Laguerre at Blenheim Castle and other places.

Or gilded clouds in fair expansion lie,
And bring all Paradise before your eye.
To rest, the cushion and soft dean invite,
Who never mentions Hell to ears polite.[1]   150
    But hark! the chiming clocks to dinner call;
A hundred footsteps scrape the marble hall:
The rich buffet well-coloured serpents grace,
And gaping Tritons spew to wash your face.
Is this a dinner? this a genial room?   155
No, 'tis a temple, and a hecatomb.
A solemn sacrifice, perform'd in state,
You drink by measure, and to minutes eat.
So quick retires each flying course, you'd swear
Sancho's dread doctor and his wand were there.[2]   160
Between each act the trembling salvers ring,
From soup to sweet-wine, and God bless the king.
In plenty starving, tantalised in state,
And complaisantly help'd to all I hate,
Treated, caress'd, and tired, I take my leave,   165
Sick of his civil pride from morn to eve;
I curse such lavish cost, and little skill,
And swear no day was ever pass'd so ill.
    Yet hence the poor are clothed, the hungry fed;
Health to himself, and to his infants bread,   170
The labourer bears: what his hard heart denies,
His charitable vanity supplies.
    Another age shall see the golden ear
Imbrown the slope, and nod on the parterre,
Deep harvest bury all his pride has plann'd,   175
And laughing Ceres reassume the land.[3]
    Who then shall grace, or who improve the soil?—
Who plants like Bathurst, or who builds like Boyle.
'Tis use alone that sanctifies expense,
And splendour borrows all her rays from sense.   180
    His father's acres who enjoys in peace,
Or makes his neighbours glad, if he increase:

[1] A reverend dean, preaching at court, threatened the sinner with punishment in a "place which he thought it not decent to name in so polite an assembly."
[2] See *Don Quixote*, chap. xlvii.
[3] On this passage Warburton remarked: "Had the poet lived three years longer, he had seen this prophecy fulfilled." He shared a common error in believing that Timon's Villa and the Duke of Chandos's seat of Canons were the same. Canons was pulled down three years after Pope's death, and the parterres again reverted to arable land.

Whose cheerful tenants bless their yearly toil,
Yet to their lord owe more than to the soil;
Whose ample lawns are not ashamed to feed   185
The milky heifer and deserving steed;
Whose rising forests, not for pride or show,
But future buildings, future navies grow:
Let his plantations stretch from down to down,
First shade a country, and then raise a town.   190
    You too proceed! make falling arts your care,
Erect new wonders, and the old repair;
Jones and Palladio to themselves restore,
And be whate'er Vitruvius was before:
'Till kings call forth the ideas of your mind [1]   195
(Proud to accomplish what such hands design'd),
Bid harbours open, public ways extend,
Bid temples, worthier of the god, ascend;
Bid the broad arch the dangerous flood contain,
The mole projected break the roaring main;   200
Back to his bounds their subject sea command,
And roll obedient rivers through the land;
These honours Peace to happy Britain brings,
These are imperial works, and worthy kings.

SATIRES

EPISTLE TO DR. ARBUTHNOT

OR, PROLOGUE TO THE SATIRES

Neque sermonibus vulgi dederis te, nec in præmiis humanis spem posueris
rerum tuarum; suis te oportet illecebris ipsa virtus trahat ad verum decus.
Quid de te alii loquantur, ipsi videant, sed loquentur tamen.—CICERO.

[And do not yield yourself up to the speeches of the vulgar, nor in your
affairs place hope in human rewards: virtue ought to draw you to true
glory by its own allurements. Why should others speak of you? Let them
study themselves—yet they will speak.]

ADVERTISEMENT

This paper is a sort of bill of complaint, begun many years since,
and drawn up by snatches, as the several occasions offered. I had
no thoughts of publishing it, till it pleased some persons of rank
and fortune (the authors of *Verses to the Imitator of Horace*, and of

[1] This poem was published in the year 1732, when some of the new-built
churches, by the Act of Queen Anne, were ready to fall, being founded
in boggy land.

an *Epistle to a Doctor of Divinity from a Nobleman at Hampton Court*)
to attack, in a very extraordinary manner, not only my writings
(of which, being public, the public is judge), but my person, morals,
and family, whereof, to those who know me not, a truer information
may be requisite.   Being divided between the necessity to say
something of myself and my own laziness to undertake so awkward
a task, I thought it the shortest way to put the last hand to this
Epistle.   If it have anything pleasing, it will be that by which I
am most desirous to please, the truth and the sentiment; and if
anything offensive, it will be only to those I am least sorry to offend,
the vicious or the ungenerous.

Many will know their own pictures in it, there being not a cir-
cumstance but what is true; but I have for the most part spared
their names, and they may escape being laughed at if they please.

I would have some of them know it was owing to the request of
the learned and candid friend to whom it is inscribed that I make
not as free use of theirs as they have done of mine.   However, I
shall have this advantage and honour on my side, that whereas, by
their proceeding, any abuse may be directed at any man, no injury
can possibly be done by mine, since a nameless character can never
be found out but by its truth and likeness.

> *P.* SHUT, shut the door, good John![1] fatigued, I said;
> Tie up the knocker, say I'm sick, I'm dead.
> The Dog-star rages! nay 'tis past a doubt,
> All Bedlam, or Parnassus, is let out:
> Fire in each eye, and papers in each hand,   5
> They rave, recite, and madden round the land.
>
>   What walls can guard me, or what shades can hide?
> They pierce my thickets, through my grot they glide,
> By land, by water, they renew the charge,
> They stop the chariot, and they board the barge.   10
> No place is sacred, not the church is free,
> Ev'n Sunday shines no Sabbath-day to me:
> Then from the Mint[2] walks forth the man of rhyme,
> Happy! to catch me, just at dinner-time.
>
>   Is there a parson, much bemused in beer,   15
> A maudlin poetess, a rhyming peer,
> A clerk, foredoom'd his father's soul to cross,
> Who pens a stanza, when he should engross?
> Is there, who, lock'd from ink and paper, scrawls
> With desperate charcoal round his darken'd walls?   20
> All fly to Twit'nam, and in humble strain

---

[1] John Serle, his old and faithful servant.

[2] The Mint in Southwark was a sanctuary for insolvent debtors. It
included several streets and alleys. Nahum Tate, the poet, died in the
Mint in 1716. The privilege was finally suppressed in the reign of George I.

Apply to me, to keep them mad or vain.
Arthur, whose giddy son neglects the laws,[1]
Imputes to me and my damn'd works the cause:
Poor Cornus sees his frantic wife elope,   25
And curses wit, and poetry, and Pope.

    Friend to my life! (which did not you prolong,
The world had wanted many an idle song)
What drop or nostrum can this plague remove?
Or which must end me, a fool's wrath or love?   30
A dire dilemma! either way I'm sped,
If foes, they write, if friends, they read me dead.
Seized and tied down to judge, how wretched I!
Who can't be silent, and who will not lie:
To laugh, were want of goodness and of grace,   35
And to be grave, exceeds all power of face.
I sit with sad civility, I read
With honest anguish, and an aching head;
And drop at last, but in unwilling ears,
This saving counsel,—"Keep your piece nine years."   40

    "Nine years!" cries he, who, high in Drury Lane,
Lull'd by soft zephyrs through the broken pane,
Rhymes ere he wakes, and prints before Term ends,
Obliged by hunger, and request of friends:
"The piece, you think, is incorrect? why take it,   45
I'm all submission; what you'd have it, make it."

    Three things another's modest wishes bound,
My friendship, and a prologue, and ten pound.

    Pitholeon sends to me: "You know his grace,
I want a patron; ask him for a place."   50
Pitholeon libell'd[2] me—"But here's a letter
Informs you, Sir, 'twas when he knew no better.
Dare you refuse him? Curll invites to dine,
He'll write a journal, or he'll turn divine."
Bless me! a packet.[3] "'Tis a stranger sues,   55
A virgin tragedy, an orphan Muse."
If I dislike it, "Furies, death and rage!"
If I approve, "Commend it to the stage."

---

[1] Arthur Moore, father of the poetical James Moore Smythe.
[2] A foolish poet of Rhodes, who pretended much to Greek. *Schol. in Horat.* I. i.
[3] Alludes to a tragedy called *The Virgin Queen*, by Mr. R. Barford (published 1729), who displeased Pope by daring to adopt the fine machinery of his sylphs in an heroi-comical poem called *The Assembly.*— WARTON.

There (thank my stars) my whole commission ends,
The players and I are, luckily, no friends; 60
Fired that the house reject him, "'Sdeath! I'll print it,
And shame the fools—Your interest, Sir, with Lintot."
Lintot, dull rogue! will think your price too much:
"Not, Sir, if you revise it, and retouch."
All my demurs but double his attacks: 65
And last he whispers, "Do; and we go snacks."
Glad of a quarrel, straight I clap the door:
Sir, let me see your works and you no more.
   'Tis sung, when Midas' ears began to spring
(Midas, a sacred person and a king), 70
His very minister who spied them first
(Some say his queen) was forced to speak or burst:[1]
And is not mine, my friend, a sorer case,
When every coxcomb perks them in my face?
   A. Good friend, forbear! you deal in dangerous things, 75
I'd never name queens, ministers, or kings:
Keep close to ears, and those let asses prick,
'Tis nothing—— *P.* Nothing? if they bite and kick?
Out with it, DUNCIAD! let the secret pass,
That secret to each fool, that he's an ass: 80
The truth once told (and wherefore should we lie?)
The Queen of Midas slept, and so may I.
   You think this cruel? Take it for a rule,
No creature smarts so little as a fool.
Let peals of laughter, Codrus! round thee break, 85
Thou unconcerned canst hear the mighty crack:
Pit, box, and gallery in convulsions hurl'd,
Thou stand'st unshook amidst a bursting world.[2]
Who shames a scribbler? break one cobweb through,
He spins the slight, self-pleasing thread anew: 90
Destroy his fib or sophistry, in vain,
The creature's at his dirty work again,

[1] The story is told by some of his barber, but by Chaucer of his Queen.
The poet intends a sarcastic allusion to Queen Caroline and Sir Robert
Walpole.

[2] Alluding to Horace:

> " Si fractus illabatur orbis,
> Impavidum ferient ruinæ."

Or rather to Addison's version:

> " Should the whole frame of Nature round him break,
> In ruin and confusion hurl'd,
> He unconcern'd would hear the mighty crack,
> And stand secure amidst a falling world."

Throned in the centre of his thin designs,
Proud of a vast extent of flimsy lines!
Whom have I hurt? has poet yet, or peer,   95
Lost the arch'd eyebrow, or Parnassian sneer?
And has not Colley still his lord, and whore?
His butchers Henley, his Freemasons Moore?[1]
Does not one table Bavius still admit?
Still to one bishop Philips seem a wit?[2]   100
Still Sappho—— A. Hold! for God's sake—you'll offend:
No names—be calm—learn prudence of a friend.
I too could write, and I am twice as tall;
But foes like these—— P. One flatterer's worse than all.
Of all mad creatures, if the learn'd are right,   105
It is the slaver kills, and not the bite.
A fool quite angry is quite innocent:
Alas! 'tis ten times worse when they repent.
    One dedicates in high heroic prose,
And ridicules beyond a hundred foes: 110
One from all Grub Street will my fame defend,
And, more abusive, calls himself my friend.
This prints my letters, that expects a bribe,
And others roar aloud, "Subscribe, subscribe!"
    There are, who to my person pay their court: 115
I cough like Horace, and, though lean, am short.
Ammon's great son one shoulder had too high—
Such Ovid's nose,—and, "Sir! you have an eye."[3]
Go on, obliging creatures, make me see
All that disgraced my betters met in me.   120
Say, for my comfort, languishing in bed,
"Just so immortal Maro held his head";
And, when I die, be sure you let me know
Great Homer died three thousand years ago."
Why did I write? what sin to me unknown   125
Dipp'd me in ink, my parents', or my own?
As yet a child, nor yet a fool to fame,
I lisp'd in numbers, for the numbers came.
I left no calling for this idle trade,

[1] Orator Henley preached in Newport and Clare Markets. James Moore Smythe was a Freemason and frequently headed processions.
[2] The Bavius of this couplet has not been named. Shadwell used to represent the character, but he had been dead long ere this Epistle was written. Dennis died in January of the same year, 1733–4. The bishop alluded to was Bishop Boulter, Primate of Ireland, to whom Ambrose Philips was for some time secretary.
[3] Warburton mentions that Pope's eye was "fine, sharp, and piercing."

No duty broke, no father disobey'd: 130
The Muse but served to ease some friend, not wife,
To help me through this long disease, my life;
To second, ARBUTHNOT! thy art and care,
And teach the being you preserved to bear.

But why then publish? Granville the polite, 135
And knowing Walsh, would tell me I could write;
Well-natured Garth inflamed with early praise,
And Congreve loved, and Swift endured my lays;
The courtly Talbot, Somers, Sheffield read,
Even mitred Rochester would nod the head,[1] 140
And St. John's self (great Dryden's friend before)
With open arms received one poet more.
Happy my studies, when by these approved!
Happier their author, when by these beloved!
From these the world will judge of men and books, 145
Not from the Burnets, Oldmixons, and Cookes.[2]

Soft were my numbers; who could take offence
While pure description held the place of sense?
Like gentle Fanny's was my flowery theme,
A painted mistress, or a purling stream.[3] 150
Yet then did Gildon draw his venal quill;
I wish'd the man a dinner, and sate still.
Yet then did Dennis rave in furious fret;
I never answer'd—I was not in debt.
If want provoked, or madness made them print, 155
I waged no war with Bedlam or the Mint.

Did some more sober critic come abroad—
If wrong, I smiled; if right, I kiss'd the rod.
Pains, reading, study, are their just pretence,
And all they want is spirit, taste, and sense. 260
Commas and points they set exactly right,
And 'twere a sin to rob them of their mite;
Yet ne'er one sprig of laurel graced these ribalds,
From slashing Bentley down to piddling Tibbalds:
Each wight, who reads not, and but scans and spells, 165
Each word-catcher, that lives on syllables,
Even such small critics, some regard may claim,
Preserved in Milton's or in Shakespeare's name.
Pretty! in amber to observe the forms

[1] All these (except Swift) were patrons or admirers of Dryden.
[2] Authors of secret and scandalous history. They will be found in the *Dunciad*, with Gildon, Dennis, etc., subsequently introduced.
[3] "A painted meadow, or a purling stream," is a verse of Mr. Addison's.

Of hairs, or straws, or dirt, or grubs, or worms!   170
The things, we know, are neither rich nor rare,
But wonder how the devil they got there.
   Were others angry—I excused them too;
Well might they rage, I gave them but their due.
A man's true merit 'tis not hard to find;   175
But each man's secret standard in his mind,
That casting-weight pride adds to emptiness,
This, who can gratify, for who can guess?
The bard whom pilfer'd Pastorals renown,
Who turns a Persian tale for half-a-crown,[1]   180
Just writes to make his barrenness appear,
And strains from hard-bound brains, eight lines a-year;
He, who still wanting, though he lives on theft,
Steals much, spends little, yet has nothing left:
And he, who now to sense, now nonsense leaning,   185
Means not, but blunders round about a meaning:
And he, whose fustian's so sublimely bad,
It is not poetry, but prose run mad:
All these, my modest satire bade translate,
And own'd that nine such poets made a Tate.   190
How did they fume, and stamp, and roar, and chafe!
And swear, not Addison himself was safe.
   Peace to all such! but were there one whose fires
True genius kindles, and fair fame inspires;
Blest with each talent, and each art to please,   195
And born to write, converse, and live with ease;
Should such a man, too fond to rule alone,
Bear, like the Turk, no brother near the throne,
View him with scornful, yet with jealous eyes,
And hate for arts that caused himself to rise;   200
Damn with faint praise, assent with civil leer,
And, without sneering, teach the rest to sneer;
Willing to wound, and yet afraid to strike,
Just hint a fault, and hesitate dislike;
Alike reserved to blame, or to commend,   205
A timorous foe, and a suspicious friend;
Dreading e'en fools, by flatterers besieged,
And so obliging, that he ne'er obliged;
Like Cato, give his little senate laws,
And sit attentive to his own applause;   210
While wits and Templars every sentence raise,

---

[1] Ambrose Philips translated a book called the *Persian Tales*.

And wonder with a foolish face of praise—
Who but must laugh, if such a man there be?
Who would not weep, if Atticus were he?

What though my name stood rubric on the walls, 215
Or plaster'd posts, with claps, in capitals?
Or smoking forth, a hundred hawkers load,
On wings of winds came flying all abroad?[1]
I sought no homage from the race that write;
I kept, like Asian monarchs, from their sight: 220
Poems I heeded (now be-rhym'd so long)
No more than thou, great George! a birthday song.
I ne'er with wits or witlings pass'd my days,
To spread about the itch of verse and praise;
Nor like a puppy, daggled through the town, 225
To fetch and carry, sing-song up and down;
Nor at rehearsals sweat, and mouth'd, and cried,
With handkerchief and orange at my side;
But sick of fops, and poetry, and prate,
To Bufo left the whole Castalian state. 230

Proud as Apollo on his forked hill,
Sate full-blown Bufo, puff'd by every quill;[2]
Fed with soft dedication all day long,
Horace and he went hand in hand in song.
His library (where busts of poets dead 235
And a true Pindar stood without a head)
Received of wits an undistinguish'd race,
Who first his judgment asked, and then a place:
Much they extoll'd his pictures, much his seat,
And flatter'd every day, and some days eat: 240
Till grown more frugal in his riper days,
He paid some bards with port, and some with praise,
To some a dry rehearsal was assign'd,
And others (harder still) he paid in kind.
Dryden alone (what wonder?) came not nigh, 245
Dryden alone escaped this judging eye:
But still the great have kindness in reserve,
He help'd to bury whom he help'd to starve.[3]

May some choice patron bless each grey goose quill!
May every Bavius have his Bufo still! 250
So when a statesman wants a day's defence,

[1] Hopkins in the 104th Psalm.
[2] The Earl of Halifax, partly, and partly Bubb Dodington.
[3] Dryden, after having lived in exigencies, had a magnificent funeral
bestowed upon him by the contribution of several persons of quality.

Or Envy holds a whole week's war with Sense,
Or simple pride for flattery makes demands,
May dunce by dunce be whistled off my hands!
Bless'd be the great! for those they take away,   255
And those they left me—for they left me GAY;
Left me to see neglected Genius bloom,
Neglected die, and tell it on his tomb:
Of all thy blameless life the sole return
My verse, and QUEENSBERRY weeping o'er thy urn! 260
    Oh let me live my own, and die so too!
(To live and die is all I have to do:)
Maintain a poet's dignity and ease,
And see what friends, and read what books I please:
Above a patron, though I condescend   265
Sometimes to call a minister my friend.
I was not born for courts or great affairs:
I pay my debts, believe, and say my prayers;
Can sleep without a poem in my head,
Nor know if Dennis be alive or dead.   270
    Why am I ask'd what next shall see the light?
Heavens! was I born for nothing but to write?
Has life no joys for me? or (to be grave)
Have I no friend to serve, no soul to save?
"I found him close with Swift—Indeed? no doubt 275
(Cries prating Balbus) something will come out."
'Tis all in vain, deny it as I will:
"No, such a genius never can lie still";
And then for mine obligingly mistakes
The first lampoon Sir Will or Bubo makes.[1]   280
Poor guiltless I! and can I choose but smile,
When every coxcomb knows me by my style?
    Cursed be the verse, how well soe'er it flow,
That tends to make one worthy man my foe,
Give Virtue scandal, Innocence a fear,   285
Or from the soft-eyed virgin steal a tear!
But he who hurts a harmless neighbour's peace,
Insults fall'n worth, or beauty in distress,
Who loves a lie, lame slander helps about,

---

[1] Sir William Yonge, Secretary-at-War. Sir Robert Walpole used to say that nothing short of Yonge's talents could have supported his character, and nothing but his character could have kept down his talents. Horace Walpole remarks that he could scarce talk common sense in private on political subjects, on which in public he would be the most animated speaker.

Who writes a libel, or who copies out; 290
That fop, whose pride affects a patron's name,
Yet absent, wounds an author's honest fame;
Who can your merit selfishly approve,
And show the sense of it without the love;
Who has the vanity to call you friend, 295
Yet wants the honour, injured, to defend;
Who tells whate'er you think, whate'er you say,
And if he lie not, must at least betray;
Who to the dean and silver bell can swear,
And sees at Canons what was never there; [1] 300
Who reads, but with a lust to misapply,
Makes satire a lampoon, and fiction lie;
A lash like mine no honest man shall dread,
But all such babbling blockheads in his stead.

    Let Sporus tremble [2]—— *A.* What? that thing of silk, 305
Sporus, that mere white curd of ass's milk?
Satire or sense, alas! can Sporus feel,
Who breaks a butterfly upon a wheel?
    P. Yet let me flap this bug with gilded wings,
This painted child of dirt, that stinks and stings; 310
Whose buzz the witty and the fair annoys,
Yet wit ne'er tastes, and beauty ne'er enjoys:
So well-bred spaniels civilly delight
In mumbling of the game they dare not bite.
Eternal smiles his emptiness betray, 315
As shallow streams run dimpling all the way.
Whether in florid impotence he speaks,
And, as the prompter breathes, the puppet squeaks;
Or at the ear of Eve, familiar toad! [3]
Half froth, half venom, spits himself abroad, 320
In puns, or politics, or tales, or lies,
Or spite, or smut, or rhymes, or blasphemies.
His wit all see-saw, between that and this,
Now high, now low, now master up, now miss,
And he himself one vile antithesis. 325
Amphibious thing! that acting either part,
The trifling head, or the corrupted heart;
Fop at the toilet, flatterer at the board,

[1] Meaning the man who would have persuaded the Duke of Chandos that Mr. P. meant him in those circumstances ridiculed in the *Epistle on Taste*.
[2] Lord Hervey.
[3] See Milton, book iv.

Now trips a lady, and now struts a lord.
Eve's tempter thus the Rabbins have express'd,   330
A cherub's face, a reptile all the rest.
Beauty that shocks you, parts that none will trust,
Wit that can creep, and pride that licks the dust.

   Not Fortune's worshipper, nor Fashion's fool,
Not Lucre's madman, nor Ambition's tool,   335
Not proud, nor servile; be one poet's praise,
That, if he pleased, he pleased by manly ways:
That flattery, even to kings, he held a shame,
And thought a lie in verse or prose the same;
That not in Fancy's maze he wander'd long,   340
But stoop'd to Truth, and moralised his song:
That not for Fame, but Virtue's better end,
He stood the furious foe, the timid friend,
The damning critic, half-approving wit,
The coxcomb hit, or fearing to be hit;   345
Laughed at the loss of friends he never had,
The dull, the proud, the wicked, and the mad;
The distant threats of vengeance on his head,
The blow unfelt, the tear he never shed;[1]
The tale revived, the lie so oft o'erthrown,[2]   350
Th' imputed trash, and dulness not his own;[3]
The morals blacken'd when the writings 'scape,
The libell'd person, and the pictured shape;
Abuse, on all he loved, or loved him, spread,[4]
A friend in exile, or a father dead;   355
The whisper, that to greatness still too near,
Perhaps yet vibrates on his sovereign's ear—
Welcome for thee, fair Virtue! all the past:
For thee, fair Virtue! welcome even the last!
   A. But why insult the poor, affront the great?   360

[1] The " blow unfelt " most probably alludes to the pretended whipping of Pope in Ham Walks, a piece of malicious mirth which was ascribed to Lady Mary Wortley Montagu. See *Life of Pope.*

[2] As that he received subscriptions for Shakespeare, that he set his name to Mr. Broome's verses, etc., which, though publicly disproved, were, nevertheless, shamelessly repeated in the libels, and even in that called the " Nobleman's Epistle."

[3] Such as profane psalms, court-poems, and other scandalous things printed in his name by Curll and others.

[4] Namely, on the Duke of Buckingham, the Earl of Burlington, Lord Bathurst, Lord Bolingbroke, Bishop Atterbury, Dr. Swift, Dr. Arbuthnot, Mr. Gay, his friends, his parents, and his very nurse, aspersed in printed papers by James Moore, G. Duckett, L. Welsted, Tho. Bentley and other obscure persons.

P. A knave's a knave, to me, in every state;
Alike my scorn, if he succeed or fail,
Sporus at court, or Japhet in a jail,[1]
A hireling scribbler, or a hireling peer,
Knight of the post corrupt, or of the shire;   365
If on a pillory, or near a throne,
He gain his prince's ear, or lose his own.

　　Yet soft by nature, more a dupe than wit,
Sappho can tell you how this man was bit:
This dreaded satirist Dennis will confess   370
Foe to his pride, but friend to his distress:
So humble, he has knocked at Tibbald's door,
Has drunk with Cibber, nay has rhymed for Moore.[2]
Full ten years slander'd, did he once reply?
Three thousand suns went down on Welsted's lie;[3]   375
To please a mistress one aspersed his life;
He lash'd him not, but let her be his wife:
Let Budgell charge low Grub Street on his quill,[4]
And write whate'er he pleased, except his will;[5]
Let the two Curlls of town and court abuse   380
His father, mother, body, soul, and Muse.[6]
Yet why? that father held it for a rule,
It was a sin to call our neighbour fool:
That harmless mother thought no wife a whore:
Hear this, and spare his family, James Moore!   385

[1] Japhet Crook, the forger.
[2] See "Testimonies of Authors" prefixed to the *Dunciad.* Pope had given James Moore Smythe some lines, with leave to insert them in his comedy *The Rival Modes.* At the same time he told him they would be known for his (Mr. Pope's), *some copies being got abroad.* The verses now form part of the *Moral Essays,* Ep. II. ver. 243 to 248, the first line being originally:

　　　　"See how the world its pretty slaves rewards!"

[3] This man had the impudence to tell, in print, that Mr. P. had occasioned a lady's death, and to name a person he never heard of. He also published that he libelled the Duke of Chandos; with whom, it was added, that he had lived in familiarity, and received from him a present of five hundred pounds—the falsehood of both which is known to his grace. Mr. P. never received any present, further than the subscriptions for *Homer,* from him, or from any great man whatsoever.
[4] Budgell, in a weekly pamphlet called the *Bee,* bestowed much abuse on him, in the imagination that he writ some things about the last will of Dr. Tindal in the *Grub Street Journal.*
[5] Alluding to Tindal's will, by which, and other indirect practices, Budgell, to the exclusion of the next heir, a nephew, got to himself almost the whole fortune of a man entirely unrelated to him.
[6] In some of Curll's and other pamphlets, Mr. Pope's father was said to be a mechanic, a hatter, a farmer, nay a bankrupt.

Unspotted names, and memorable long!
If there be force in virtue, or in song.

   Of gentle blood (part shed in honour's cause,
While yet in Britain honour had applause)
Each parent sprung— *A.* What fortune, pray?— *P.* Their own,
And better got, than Bestia's from the throne.   391
Born to no pride, inheriting no strife,
Nor marrying discord in a noble wife,[1]
Stranger to civil and religious rage,
The good man walk'd innoxious through his age.   395
No courts he saw, no suits would ever try,
Nor dared an oath, nor hazarded a lie.
Unlearn'd, he knew no schoolman's subtle art,
No language, but the language of the heart.
By nature honest, by experience wise,   400
Healthy by temperance, and by exercise,
His life, though long, to sickness pass'd unknown,
His death was instant, and without a groan.
O grant me thus to live, and thus to die!
Who sprung from kings shall know less joy than I.   405

   O friend! may each domestic bliss be thine!
Be no unpleasing melancholy mine:
Me, let the tender office long engage,
To rock the cradle of reposing age,
With lenient arts extend a mother's breath,   410
Make languor smile, and smooth the bed of death.
Explore the thought, explain the asking eye,
And keep awhile one parent from the sky!
On cares like these if length of days attend,
May Heaven, to bless those days, preserve my friend,   415
Preserve him social, cheerful, and serene,
And just as rich as when he served a queen.[2]

   A. Whether that blessing be denied or given,
Thus far was right, the rest belongs to Heaven.

---

[1] Alluding to Addison's marriage with the Countess of Warwick, and Dryden's with Lady Elizabeth Howard. Neither of these connections is said to have been happy.

[2] On the death of Queen Anne, Arbuthnot, like the attendants at the court, was displaced, and had to leave his apartments at St. James's. He removed to Dover Street, "hoping still," as he said, "to keep a little habitation warm in town," and to afford half a pint of claret to his old friends.

SATIRES AND EPISTLES OF HORACE IMITATED

Ludentis speciem dabit, et torquebitur.—HORACE.

[He seems with freedom, what with pain he proves,
And now a Satyr, now a Cyclops moves.—FRANCIS.]

The occasion of publishing these Imitations was the clamour raised on some of my Epistles. An answer from Horace was both more full, and of more dignity, than any I could have made in my own person; and the example of much greater freedom in so eminent a divine as Dr. Donne seemed a proof with what indignation and contempt a Christian may treat vice or folly, in ever so low or ever so high a station. Both these authors were acceptable to the princes and ministers under whom they lived. The *Satires* of Dr. Donne I versified at the desire of the Earl of Oxford, while he was Lord Treasurer, and of the Duke of Shrewsbury, who had been Secretary of State: neither of whom looked upon a satire on vicious courts as any reflection on those they served in. And indeed there is not in the world a greater error than that which fools are so apt to fall into, and knaves with good reason to encourage, the mistaking a Satirist for a Libeller; whereas to a true Satirist nothing is so odious as a Libeller, for the same reason as to a man truly virtuous nothing is so hateful as a hypocrite.

Uni æquus Virtuti atque ejus Amicis.

SATIRE I

TO MR. FORTESCUE

P. THERE are (I scare can think it, but am told)
There are, to whom my satire seems too bold:
Scarce to wise Peter complaisant enough,
And something said of Chartres much too rough.
The lines are weak, another's pleased to say,   5
Lord Fanny spins a thousand such a day.
Tim'rous by nature, of the rich in awe,
I come to Counsel learned in the law:
You'll give me, like a friend both sage and free,
Advice; and (as you use) without a fee.   10
    F. I'd write no more.
                              P. Not write? but then I think,
And, for my soul, I cannot sleep a wink:
I nod in company, I wake at night,
Fools rush into my head, and so I write.

F. You could not do a worse thing for your life.   15
Why, if the nights seem tedious—take a wife
Or rather truly, if your point be rest,
Lettuce and cowslip wine; *Probatum est.*
But talk with Celsus, Celsus will advise
Hartshorn, or something that shall close your eyes.   20
Or, if you needs must write, write Cæsar's praise,
You'll gain at least a knighthood or the bays.

P. What! like Sir Richard, rumbling, rough, and fierce,
With ARMS and GEORGE and BRUNSWICK crowd the verse,
Rend with tremendous sound your ears asunder,   25
With gun, drum, trumpet, blunderbuss, and thunder?
Or, nobly wild, with Budgell's fire and force,
Paint angels trembling round his falling horse? [1]

F. Then all your Muse's softer art display,
Let Carolina smooth the tuneful lay,   30
Lull with Amelia's liquid name the Nine, [2]
And sweetly flow through all the Royal line.

P. Alas! few verses touch their nicer ear;
They scarce can bear their Laureate twice a year;
And justly Cæsar scorns the poet's lays,—   35
It is to history he trusts for praise.

F. Better be Cibber, I'll maintain it still,
Than ridicule all taste, blaspheme quadrille,
Abuse the City's best good men in metre,
And laugh at peers that put their trust in Peter. [3]   40
E'en those you touch not, hate you.
                              P. What should ail them?

F. A hundred smart in Timon and in Balaam:
The fewer still you name, you wound the more;
Bond is but one, but Harpax is a score.

P. Each mortal has his pleasure: none deny   45
Scarsdale his bottle, Darty his ham-pie; [4]
Ridotta sips and dances, till she see
The doubling lustres dance as fast as she;
F—— loves the senate, Hockley-hole his brother, [5]

---

[1] The horse on which his majesty charged at the battle of Oudenarde; when the Pretender and the princes of the blood of France fled before him.—WARBURTON.
[2] Queen Caroline and the Princess Amelia.
[3] Peter Walter, the scrivener and land-steward. whom Pope so frequently mentions.
[4] Lord Scarsdale and Mr. Dartineuf. See Additional Notes.
[5] The F—— who loved the senate was most likely Stephen Fox.

Like, in all else, as one egg to another.　　　50
I love to pour out all myself, as plain
As downright Shippen, or as old Montaigne:
In them, as certain to be loved as seen,
The soul stood forth, nor kept a thought within;
In me what spots (for spots I have) appear,　　55
Will prove at least the medium must be clear.
In this impartial glass, my Muse intends
Fair to expose myself, my foes, my friends;
Publish the present age; but, where my text
Is vice too high, reserve it for the next:　　60
My foes shall wish my life a longer date,
And every friend the less lament my fate.
My head and heart thus flowing through my quill,
Verse-man or prose-man, term me which you will,[1]
Papist or Protestant, or both between,　　65
Like good Erasmus, in an honest mean,
In moderation placing all my glory,
While Tories call me Whig, and Whigs a Tory.

　　Satire's my weapon, but I'm too discreet
To run a-muck, and tilt at all I meet;　　70
I only wear it in a land of hectors,
Thieves, supercargoes, sharpers, and directors.
Save but our Army! and let Jove incrust
Swords, pikes, and guns, with everlasting rust!
Peace is my dear delight—not Fleury's more:[2]　　75
But touch me, and no minister so sore.
Whoe'er offends, at some unlucky time
Slides into verse, and hitches in a rhyme,
Sacred to ridicule his whole life long,
And the sad burthen of some merry song.　　80
　　Slander or poison dread from Delia's rage,[3]
Hard words or hanging, if your judge be Page.[4]
From furious Sappho scarce a milder fate,[5]
Pox'd by her love, or libell'd by her hate.
Its proper power to hurt each creature feels;　　85
Bulls aim their horns, and asses lift their heels;

---

[1] Lord Bathurst, who, Pope told Spence, used to term Prior his verse-man, and Erasmus Lewis his prose-man.
[2] Cardinal Fleury, Prime Minister of France under Louis XV., born in 1653; died in 1743.
[3] Countess of Deloraine.
[4] Sir Francis Page.
[5] See notes at the end of the Satire.

'Tis a bear's talent not to kick, but hug;
And no man wonders he's not stung by pug.
So drink with Walters, or with Chartres eat,
They'll never poison you, they'll only cheat. 90

   Then, learned sir! (to cut the matter short)
Whate'er my fate, or well or ill at Court;
Whether old age, with faint but cheerful ray,
Attends to gild the evening of my day,
Or death's black wing already be display'd, 95
To wrap me in the universal shade;
Whether the darken'd room to Muse invite,
Or whiten'd wall provoke the skewer to write:
In durance, exile, Bedlam, or the Mint,
Like Lee or Budgell,[1] I will rhyme and print. 100

   F. Alas, young man! your days can ne'er be long,
In flower of age you perish for a song!
Plums and directors, Shylock and his wife,
Will club their testers, now, to take your life!

   P. What! arm'd for Virtue, when I point the pen, 105
Brand the bold front of shameless guilty men;
Dash the proud gamester in his gilded car;
Bare the mean heart that lurks beneath a star;
Can there be wanting, to defend her cause,
Lights of the Church, or guardians of the laws? 110
Could pension'd Boileau lash, in honest strain,
Flatterers and bigots even in Louis' reign?
Could Laureate Dryden pimp and friar engage,
Yet neither Charles nor James be in a rage?
And I not strip the gilding off a knave, 115
Unplaced, unpension'd, no man's heir, or slave?
I will, or perish in the generous cause.
Hear this and tremble! you, who 'scape the laws:
Yes, while I live, no rich or noble knave
Shall walk the world, in credit, to his grave. 120
To VIRTUE ONLY, AND HER FRIENDS, A FRIEND:
The world beside may murmur, or commend.
Know, all the distant din that world can keep,

---

[1] Budgell we have again in the *Dunciad* and *Epistles*. Nathaniel
Lee, the dramatist, had frequent attacks of insanity, and was at one period
of his life four years in Bedlam. He wrote eleven plays, and possessed
genius (as Addison admitted) well adapted for tragedy, though clouded
by occasional rant, obscurity, and bombast. Latterly, this ill-starred poet
depended for subsistence on a small weekly allowance from tne theatre.
He died in 1691 or 1692.

Rolls o'er my grotto, and but soothes my sleep.
There, my retreat the best companions grace,   125
Chiefs out of war, and statesmen out of place.
There St. John mingles with my friendly bowl
The feast of reason and the flow of soul:
And he, whose lightning pierced the Iberian lines,
Now forms my quincunx, and now ranks my vines,   130
Or tames the genius of the stubborn plain,
Almost as quickly as he conquered Spain.[1]
   Envy must own, I live among the great,
No pimp of pleasure, and no spy of state,
With eyes that pry not, tongue that ne'er repeats,   135
Fond to spread friendships, but to cover heats;
To help who want, to forward who excel;—
This, all who know me, know; who love me, tell:
And who unknown defame me, let them be
Scribblers or peers, alike are mob to me.   140
This is my plea, on this I rest my cause—
What saith my counsel, learned in the laws?
   F. Your plea is good; but still I say, beware!
Laws are explain'd by men—so have a care.
It stands on record, that in Richard's times   145
A man was hanged for very honest rhymes;
Consult the statute, *quart.* I think it is,
Edwardi Sext. or *prim. et quint. Eliz.*
See Libels, Satires—here you have it—read.
   P. Libels and Satires! lawless things indeed!   150
But grave epistles, bringing vice to light,
Such as a king might read, a bishop write;
Such as Sir Robert would approve——
                    F. Indeed!
The case is alter'd—you may then proceed;
In such a cause the plaintiff will be hiss'd,   155
My lords the judges laugh, and you're dismiss'd.

---

[1] Charles Mordaunt, Earl of Peterborough, who in the year 1705 took Barcelona, and in the winter following, with only 280 horse and 900 foot, enterprising and accomplishing the conquest of Valencia.

ADDITIONAL NOTES

DARTINEUF

Ver. 46. *Darty his ham-pie.* Charles Dartineuf, or Dartiquenave, was Paymaster of the Board of Works and Surveyor of the Royal Gardens in 1736. He was, as Swift describes him, a " true epicure," and a man " that knows everything and everybody; where a knot of rabble are going on a holiday, and where they were last." His partiality for ham pie has been confirmed by Warburton and Dodsley. Pope, he said, had done justice to his taste; if he had given him *sweet pie* he never could have pardoned him. Lord Lyttelton, in his *Dialogues of the Dead,* has introduced Dartineuf discoursing with Apicius on the subject of good eating, ancient and modern. His favourite dish, ham pie, is there commemorated; but Dartineuf is made to lament his ill-fortune in having lived before turtle-feasts were known in England. Swift, in his *Journal to Stella,* mentions dining with Dartineuf one day at James's. " James," he says, " is Clerk of the Kitchen to the queen, and has a snug little house at St. James's, and we had the queen's wine, *and such fine victuals I could not eat it.*" The masculine tastes of Swift made him reject the epicurism of his friend, as Sir Walter Scott preferred his simple Scotch fare—sheep's head and whisky punch— to French wines and French cookery. Pope and Gay would have had more sympathy with the accomplished epicure. But Dartineuf had higher tastes than those which the Clerk of the Kitchen gratified. He was a well-educated, well-informed man, and a peculiarly agreeable companion. He was a writer in the *Tatler,* though only one of his papers has been ascertained. This is on a congenial subject—the cheerful use of wine, which he considers to be designed for a " loftier indulgence of nature " than merely satisfying thirst. He describes the beneficial effects of wine in the case of one of his friends, and this friend is supposed to have been Addison:

" I have the good fortune," he says, " to be intimate with a gentleman who has an inexhaustible source of wit to entertain the curious, the grave, the humorous, and the frolic. He can transform himself into different shapes, and adapt himself to every company; yet, in a coffee-house, or in the ordinary course of affairs, appears rather dull than sprightly. You can seldom get him to the tavern, but, when once he is arrived to his pint, and begins to look about, and like his company, you admire a thousand things in him which before lay buried. Then you discover the brightness of his mind and the strength of his judgment, accompanied with the most graceful mirth. In a word, by this enlivening aid he is whatever is polite, instructive and diverting. What makes him still more agreeable is that he tells a story, serious or comical, with as much delicacy of humour as Cervantes himself. And for all this, at other times, even after a long knowledge of him, you shall scarce discern in this incomparable person a whit more than what might be expected from one of a common capacity. Doubtless there are men of great parts that are guilty of downright bashfulness that, by a strange hesitation and reluctance to speak, murder the finest and most elegant thoughts, and render the most lively conceptions flat and heavy. In this case a certain quantity of my white or red cordial—which you will—is an easy but an infallible remedy. It awakens the judgment, quickens memory, ripens understanding, disperses melancholy, cheers the heart; in a word, restores the whole man to himself and his friends without the least pain or indisposition to the patient."—*Tatler,* No. 252.

Dartineuf's fine dishes and wines could not have much shortened his life. This paper in the *Tatler* was written in 1710, and he did not die till

1737. In some of the accounts of this gentleman he is said to have been the *élève* of a refugee French family whose name he took; while others represent him as an illegitimate son of Charles II.

WILL SHIPPEN

Ver. 52. *As downright Shippen, or as old Montaigne.* Of the French essayist, Michael de Montaigne, it is useless here to speak. His delightful volumes, whether in the original or in the racy homespun English of Charles Cotton, are as popular and as likely to be lasting as the Poetical Essays of Pope. William Shippen, or " Honest Will Shippen," as he was called, resembled Montaigne only in his plain speaking; and had it not been for this line of Pope, his name would long since have dropped from all but the bye-corners of history. He was, however, a noted Tory and Jacobite leader in the reigns of George I. and George II. He was sent to the Tower for saying in the House of Commons, and refusing to retract the expression, that part of the king's speech (George I.) " seemed rather to be calculated for the meridian of Germany than Great Britain; and that 'twas a great misfortune that the king was a stranger to our language and constitution." Shippen was above thirty years in parliament. He openly avowed his desire to have the Stuarts restored: and when asked how he would vote on certain occasions, he used jocularly to answer, " I cannot tell until I hear from Rome." Notwithstanding his Jacobitism, Shippen had a personal regard for Walpole, and would occasionally remark, " Robin and I are honest men; he is for King George and I for King James; but as for these fellows with the long cravats (Sandys, Rushout and others), they only desire places either under King George or King James." Various efforts were made to silence or to soften Shippen, but he was incorruptible. At this time he had only about £400 a year and, though bred in the law, had no professional practice. He afterwards married the daughter of Sir Richard Stote, of Northumberland, with whom he had a fortune of £70,000. Sheffield, Duke of Buckingham, has also commemorated old Shippen. In his verses on the election of a poet laureate, he says:

> " To Shippen, Apollo was cold with respect,
>   But said in a greater assembly he shined,
>   *As places are things he had ever declined.*"

This was as early as 1719, when Eusden was appointed laureate. Shippen was fully as well qualified for the office, for he had written *Faction Displayed* and some other political verses. Considering the strong Jacobite predilection of this politician, it is surprising that he could take the oaths to the reigning sovereign. Walpole is said on one occasion to have charged him—no doubt as a mere piece of humour—with kissing his thumb instead of the New Testament, upon which the other exclaimed, " Ah, Robin, that's not fair." Shippen's speeches are described as " generally containing some pointed period, which he uttered with great animation; he usually spoke in a low tone of voice, with too great rapidity, and held his glove before his mouth." He died in 1743, aged seventy-one.

COUNTESS OF DELORAINE

Ver. 81. *Slander or poison dread from Delia's rage.* Mary Howard, Countess of Deloraine, bears the " sad burden " of this imputation. She was the young widow of Henry Scott, second son of the Duke of Monmouth and Anne, Duchess of Buccleuch, and who had been created Earl of Deloraine in 1706. Delia was governess—apparently a very unfit one—to the young princesses, daughters of George II., and was a favourite with the king, with whom she generally played cards in the evenings in the princesses' apartments. Sir Robert Walpole considered Lady Deloraine as a dangerous person about the court, for she possessed, according to the shrewd minister, a weak head, a pretty face, a lying tongue and a false heart. Lord Hervey, in his *Court Ballad*, written in 1742, sarcastically styles her " *virtuous*, and *sober*, and *wise* Deloraine "; and in his *Memoirs*, under date of 1735, he describes her as " one of the vainest as well as one of the simplest women that ever lived; but to this wretched head," he adds, " there was certainly joined one of the prettiest faces that ever was formed; which, though she was now five-and-thirty, had a bloom upon it, too, that not one woman in ten thousand has at fifteen." Horace Walpole, the unrivalled court gossip and scandal-monger, gives a ludicrous anecdote illustrating the manners of the court circle. " There has been a great fracas at Kensington (1742). One of the mesdames (the princesses) pulled the chair from under Countess Deloraine at cards, who, being provoked that her monarch was diverted with her disgrace, with the malice of a hobby-horse gave him just such another fall. But, alas! the monarch, like Louis XIV., is mortal in the part that touched the ground, and was so hurt and so angry that the countess is disgraced, and her German rival remains in the sole and quiet possession of her royal master's favour." The story of the poisoning to which Pope alludes was a common rumour at the time, the alleged victim being a Miss Mackenzie, a beauty, who died suddenly, and was said to have been poisoned in a fit of jealousy by Lady Deloraine. It was probably a mere piece of scandal at the expense of a *worthless* though no doubt *envied* court favourite. No proceedings appear to have followed upon the report; it did not affect the countess's position at court; nor did it prevent her getting a second husband in the person of a country squire, W. Wyndham, Esq., of Carsham. She died in 1744, when she could only have been about forty-two years of age.

In a contemporary rhyming Epistle to Pope, in the *Scots Magazine* for April 1740, the poisoning case is alluded to in the following passage, but the writer appears to make Lord Deloraine (who died in 1730) the victim, and to hint at the recovery of Miss Mackenzie:

> " When that of late you lash'd the poisoning dame,
> Did you do right to screen her guilty name?
> D——'s fatal skill who has not heard?
> A h—b—d victim the whole town has scared;
> Escupalius' aid almost too late
> To make M—— void the chocolate.
> How is a secret rival to be fear'd,
> When lust prevails and reason is debarr'd! "

LADY MARY WORTLEY MONTAGU

Ver. 83. *From furious Sappho scarce a milder fate.* Pope denied that this abominable couplet applied to Lady Mary, but it contains the same gross imputation which he had undoubtedly made against her five years before in the *Dunciad* (book ii. v. 136). The town seems also to have entertained the conviction that Lady Mary was aimed at, and Lord Marchmont, the poet's friend, concurred in the general belief. The lady herself (we must think with singular indelicacy) applied to Lord Peterborough on the subject. His Lordship writes to her as follows:

" MADAM,—I was very unwilling to have my name made use of in an affair in which I have no concern, and therefore would not engage myself to speak to Mr. Pope; but he, coming to my house the moment you went away, I gave him as exact an account as I could of our conversation. He said to me what I had taken the liberty to say to you, that he wondered how the town would apply these lines to any but some noted common woman; that he should be yet more surprised if you should take them to yourself. He named to me four remarkable poetesses and scribblers, Mrs. Centlivre, Mrs. Haywood, Mrs. Manly and Mrs. Behn, ladies famous indeed in their generation, and some of them esteemed to have given very unfortunate favours to their friends, assuring me that such only were the objects of his satire. I hope this assurance will prevent your further mistake, and any consequences upon so odd a subject. I have nothing more to add.

> "Your ladyship's most humble and obedient servant,
>
> "Peterborough."

The authoresses here named were, with one exception, all dead, and pretty well forgotten. Mrs. Behn had died forty-four years before; Mrs. Centlivre ten years; and Mrs. Manly nine. Mrs. Haywood still lived; but her latter works were unexceptionable in point of morality, but she had attacked Martha Blount in her *Memoirs of a Certain Island* . . . 1724. That the miserable dead poetasters could inspire either fear or anger, is an idea too ridiculous to be entertained for a moment. The Sappho of Pope must have some resemblance in power to the Delia of the same passage—the courtly, sensual, false, and even murderous Countess Deloraine.

Lady Mary and the town felt this; the cry had gone out against her, and instead of adopting the sensible advice of the gallant Peterborough, the indignant lady prepared for a *furious* poetical war. She gained the willing assistance of her friend, Lord Hervey, who had already smarted under the lash of Pope; and between them was composed that crude, coarse, undignified, but not imbecile satire, entitled *Verses Addressed to the Imitator of the First Satire of the Second Book of Horace*. The opening lines refer to Pope's system of printing the text of Horace on one page and his own imitation on the opposite page:

> "In two large columns on thy motley page,
> Where Roman wit is striped with English rage;
> Where ribaldry to satire makes pretence,
> And modern scandal rolls with ancient sense:
> Whilst on one side we see how Horace thought;
> And on the other how he never wrote:
> Who can believe, who view the bad, the good,
> That the dull copyist better understood
> That spirit he pretends to imitate
> Than heretofore that Greek he did translate?
>
> "Thine is just such an image of *his* pen,
> As thou thyself art of the sons of men:
> Where our own species in burlesque we trace,
> A sign-post likeness of the human race,
> That is at once resemblance and disgrace.
>
> "Horace can laugh, is delicate, is clear,
> You only coarsely rail, or darkly sneer:
> His style is elegant, his diction pure,
> Whilst none thy crabbed numbers can endure;
> *Hard as thy heart, and as thy birth obscure.*"

The proper objects of satire are then defined, and Pope's enormities of course pointed out:

> " Is this the thing to keep mankind in awe,
> *To make those tremble who escape the law?*
> Is this *the ridicule* to live so long,
> The *deathless satire* and *immortal song?*

No: like the self-blown praise, thy scandal flies;
And, as we're told of wasps, it stings and dies.
Then whilst with coward hand you stab a name,
And try, at least, to assassinate our fame,
Like the first bold assassin's be thy lot,
Ne'er be thy guilt forgiven or forgot;
But, as thou hat'st, be hated by mankind,
And with the emblem of thy crooked mind
Mark'd on thy back, like Cain, by God's own hand,
Wander, like him, accursed through the land."

Lady Mary knew well where the dreaded enemy was most vulnerable. The allusions to obscure birth and personal deformity—though utterly disgraceful to the noble writers of the verses—pierced most deeply, and were sure to provoke a reply. Pope, however, paused to collect his strength. He had higher game to fly at than the Dennises, Welsteds and James Moore Smythes, and there was personal danger in attacking too fiercely even a Vice-Chamberlain of the court and a lady who numbered so many lords as friends and relatives in her train. In this portentous calm, Lord Hervey tried a second blow. It does not appear that Lady Mary lent her aid to this new effort, and consequently it is vastly inferior to the first. It is in the form of a *Letter from a Nobleman at Hampton Court to a Doctor of Divinity* (Dr. Sherwin). A few lines will suffice:

" Guiltless of thought, each blockhead may compose
This nothing-meaning verse, as well as prose;
And Pope with justice of such lines may say,
His Lordship ' spins a thousand such a day.'
Such Pope himself might write, who ne'er could think,
He who at crambo plays with pen and ink,
And is called Poet, 'cause in rhyme he wrote
What Dacier construed, and what Homer thought."

Pope was now ready both in prose and verse. The former was a *Letter to a Noble Lord, on occasion of some Libels written and propagated at Court in the Year* 1732-3. The letter was shown to some friends, but not published. The poetical reply was contained in the *Epistle to Dr. Arbuthnot*, and included that most tremendous of all his invectives, the character of Sporus, in which Lord Hervey's appearance, character, tastes and habits are so unmercifully, yet in many points so truly, satirised and delineated.

The year preceding his death, Lord Hervey published a poetical essay— an attempt at ethics—on *The Difference between Verbal and Practical Virtue, exemplified in some Instances, both Ancient and Modern.* Pope is the modern instance, and he is charged with all manner of crimes—as lost to decency and honour, libelling the living and aspersing the dead. The conclusion of this sketch is forcible and poetical:

" Such is th' injustice of his daily theme,
And such the lust that breaks his nightly dream,
That vestal fire of undecaying hate,
Which Time's cold tide itself can ne'er abate."

But was Hervey's resentment less durable or less vindictive?

Lady Mary wisely withdrew from the contest: there were poisoned arrows on both sides, but Pope's were unerring and irresistible. She went abroad in 1739. Spence and Walpole met her next year in Rome. The good-natured Spence reported pretty favourably. " She is one of the most shining characters in the world, but shines like a comet; she is all irregularity, and always wandering; the most wise, most imprudent; loveliest, most disagreeable; best-natured, cruellest woman in the world; ' all things by turns and nothing long '!" Walpole had as strong an aversion to Lady Mary as Pope himself, being from certain family connections biassed from his birth against her. He mentions the wandering lady's eccentricities. " Her dress, her avarice and her impudence must amaze anyone that never heard her name. She wears a foul mob that does not cover her greasy black locks, that hang loose, never combed or curled, an old mazarine blue wrapper, that gapes open and discovers a canvas petticoat. Her face swelled violently on one side, partly covered with a plaster, and partly with white paint, which for cheapness she has bought coarse," etc. A libellous caricature! Lady Mary did not return till she was past seventy—a worn-out wanderer, and a victim to cancer. The scene was soon closed; but she has two imperishable claims on the world's gratitude—her courageous perseverance in introducing the art of inoculation, which she had learned in Turkey, and her *Letters from Abroad*, so full of fine description and novel facts, of intelligence and animation.

THE SECOND SATIRE OF THE SECOND BOOK OF HORACE

TO MR. BETHEL

Hugh Bethel, Esq., to whom this Epistle is addressed, is the same gentleman alluded to by Pope in graceful and complimentary terms in his *Essay on Man*. He possessed landed property in the East Riding of Yorkshire, and appears to have been an amiable and excellent country gentleman. In a letter to Allen, Pope says—" I have known and esteemed him (Mr. Bethel) for every moral virtue these twenty years and more. He has all the charity, without any of the weakness of ——; and, I firmly believe, never said a thing he did not think, nor did a thing he could not tell." One of the last acts of the poet's life seems to have been dictating a letter to him. The poet's friend, "blameless Bethel," was M.P. for Pontefract 1715–22. They were early acquainted, for a copy of the first edition of his poems, 1717, was presented by Pope to Mr. Bethel, with a highly complimentary Latin inscription. The *Gentleman's Magazine* thus announces the death of Mr. Bethel: "Died at Ealing, Middlesex, on January 16th, 1748, Hugh Bethel, Esq. His estate of £2000 per annum goes to his brother, Slingsby Bethel, Esq., M.P. for London."

WHAT, and how great, the virtue and the art
To live on little with a cheerful heart
(A doctrine sage, but truly none of mine);
Let's talk, my friends, but talk before we dine.
Not when a gilt buffet's reflected pride   5
Turns you from sound philosophy aside;
Not when from plate to plate your eyeballs roll,
And the brain dances to the mantling bowl.
 Hear Bethel's sermon, one not versed in schools,
But strong in sense, and wise without the rules.   10

Go, work, hunt, exercise! (he thus began)
Then scorn a homely dinner, if you can.
Your wine lock'd up, your butler stroll'd abroad,
Or fish denied (the river yet unthaw'd),
If then plain bread and milk will do the feat,   15
The pleasure lies in you and not the meat.

Preach as I please, I doubt our curious men
Will choose a pheasant still before a hen;
Yet hens of Guinea full as good I hold,
Except you eat the feathers green and gold.   20
Of carps and mullets why prefer the great
(Though cut in pieces ere my lord can eat),
Yet for small turbots such esteem profess?
Because God made these large, the other less.
Oldfield with more than harpy throat endued,[1]   25
Cries, "Send me, gods! a whole hog barbecued!"[2]
Oh, blast it, south winds! till a stench exhale
Rank as the ripeness of a rabbit's tail.
By what criterion do you eat, d'ye think,
If this is prized for sweetness, that for stink?   30
When the tired glutton labours through a treat,
He finds no relish in the sweetest meat;
He calls for something bitter, something sour,
And the rich feast concludes extremely poor:
Cheap eggs, and herbs, and olives still we see;   35
Thus much is left of old simplicity!
The robin redbreast till of late had rest,
And children sacred held a martin's nest,
Till beccaficos sold so devilish dear
To one that was, or would have been, a peer.   40
Let me extol a cat, on oysters fed,
I'll have a party at the Bedford Head;[3]
Or e'en to crack live crawfish recommend;
I'd never doubt at Court to make a friend.

'Tis yet in vain, I own, to keep a pother   45
About one vice, and fall into the other:
Between excess and famine lies a mean;
Plain, but not sordid; though not splendid, clean.
Avidien, or his wife (no matter which,

---

[1] Warburton says a glutton of the name of Oldfield ran through a fortune of £1500 a year in the simple luxury of good eating.
[2] A West Indian term of gluttony; a hog roasted whole, stuffed with spice, and basted with Madeira wine.
[3] A famous eating-house in Southampton Street, Covent Garden.

For him you'll call a dog, and her a bitch)[1]   50
Sell their presented partridges and fruits,
And humbly live on rabbits and on roots:
One half-pint bottle serves them both to dine,
And is at once their vinegar and wine.
But on some lucky day (as when they found   55
A lost bank-bill, or heard their son was drown'd),
At such a feast, old vinegar to spare,
Is what two souls so generous cannot bear:
Oil, though it stink, they drop by drop impart,
But souse the cabbage with a bounteous heart.   60

   He knows to live, who keeps the middle state,
And neither leans on this side nor on that;
Nor stops, for one bad cork, his butler's pay,
Swears, like Albutius, a good cook away;
Nor lets, like Nævius, every error pass,   65
The musty wine, foul cloth, or greasy glass.

   Now hear what blessings temperance can bring
(Thus said our friend, and what he said I sing):
First health: the stomach (cramm'd from every dish,
A tomb of boil'd and roast, and flesh and fish,   70
Where bile, and wind, and phlegm, and acid jar,
And all the man is one intestine war),
Remembers oft the school-boy's simple fare,
The temperate sleeps, and spirits light as air.

   How pale each worshipful and reverend guest   75
Rise from a clergy, or a city feast!
What life in all that ample body, say?
What heavenly particle inspires the clay?
The soul subsides, and wickedly inclines
To seem but mortal, even in sound divines.   80

   On morning wings how active springs the mind
That leaves the load of yesterday behind!
How easy every labour it pursues!
How coming to the poet every Muse!
Not but we may exceed, some holy time,   85
Or tired in search of truth, or search of rhyme;
Ill-health some just indulgence may engage;
And more the sickness of long life, old age:
For fainting age what cordial drop remains,
If our intemperate youth the vessel drains?   90

[1] Avidien was Edward Wortley Montagu; his wife, the never-forgotten and never-forgiven Lady Mary.

Our fathers praised rank venison. You suppose,
Perhaps, young men! our fathers had no nose.
Not so: a buck was then a week's repast,
And 'twas their point, I ween, to make it last;
More pleased to keep it till their friends could come,   95
Than eat the sweetest by themselves at home.
Why had not I in those good times my birth,
Ere coxcomb-pies or coxcombs were on earth?

    Unworthy he, the voice of fame to hear,
That sweetest music to an honest ear   100
(For 'faith, Lord Fanny! you are in the wrong,
The world's good word is better than a song);
Who has not learn'd fresh sturgeon and ham-pie
Are no rewards for want and infamy!
When luxury has licked up all thy pelf,   105
Cursed by thy neighbours, thy trustees, thyself,
To friends, to fortune, to mankind a shame,
Think how posterity will treat thy name;
And buy a rope, that future times may tell
Thou hast at least bestowed one penny well.   110

    "Right," cries his Lordship, "for a rogue in need
To have a taste is insolence indeed:
In me 'tis noble, suits my birth and state,
My wealth unwieldy, and my heap too great."
Then, like the sun, let bounty spread her ray,   115
And shine that superfluity away.
Oh impudence of wealth! with all thy store,
How darest thou let one worthy man be poor?
Shall half the new-built churches round thee fall?
Make quays, build bridges, or repair Whitehall: 120
Or to thy country let that heap be lent,
As M**o's was, but not at five per cent.[1]

    Who thinks that Fortune cannot change her mind,
Prepares a dreadful jest for all mankind.
And who stands safest? tell me, is it he   125
That spreads and swells in puff'd prosperity;
Or, blest with little, whose preventing care
In peace provides fit arms against a war?

    Thus Bethel spoke, who always speaks his thought,
And always thinks the very thing he ought: 130
His equal mind I copy what I can,
And, as I love, would imitate the man.

[1] The Duchess of Marlborough, who actually reduced her loans to the government from 6 to 4 per cent.

In South Sea days not happier, when surmised
The lord of thousands, than if now excised; [1]
In forest planted by a father's hand,   135
Than in five acres now of rented land.
Content with little, I can piddle here,
On broccoli and mutton round the year;
But ancient friends (though poor, or out of play),
That touch my bell, I cannot turn away.   140
'Tis true, no turbots dignify my boards,
But gudgeons, flounders, what my Thames affords:
To Hounslow Heath I point, and Bansted Down,
Thence comes your mutton, and these chicks my own:
From yon old walnut-tree a shower shall fall;   145
And grapes, long lingering on my only wall,
And figs from standard and espalier join;
The devil is in you if you cannot dine:
Then cheerful healths (your mistress shall have place),
And, what's more rare, a poet shall say grace.   150
    Fortune not much of humbling me can boast:
Though double taxed, how little have I lost! [2]
My life's amusements have been just the same,
Before and after standing armies came.
My lands are sold; my father's house is gone;   155
I'll hire another's; is not that my own,
And yours, my friends? through whose free opening gate
None comes too early, none departs too late;
(For I, who hold sage Homer's rule the best,
Welcome the coming, speed the going guest).   160
"Pray Heaven it last! (cries Swift!) as you go on;
I wish to God this house had been your own:
Pity! to build without a son or wife;
Why, you'll enjoy it only all your life."
Well, if the use be mine, can it concern one,   165
Whether the name belong to Pope or Vernon? [3]

[1] Warburton states that Pope had South Sea stock, which he did not sell out, that was valued at between £20,000 and £30,000 when it fell. This must have been a *nominal*—literally a South Sea valuation. He could not have invested more than two or three thousand pounds, if so much, in the South Sea stock, and its depreciation deprived him of none of the comforts or elegancies of life to which he had been accustomed. For an account of Walpole's Excise Bill, here alluded to, see Lord Hervey's *Memoirs*.

[2] Roman Catholics and Nonjurors had at that time to pay additional taxes.

[3] Mrs. Vernon, from whom he had a lease for life of his house and garden at Twickenham. She died about a year before Pope.

What's property? dear Swift! you see it alter
From you to me, from me to Peter Walter;
Or, in a mortgage, prove a lawyer's share;
Or, in a jointure, vanish from the heir;   170
Or, in pure equity (the case not clear)
The Chancery takes your rents for twenty year:
At best, it falls to some ungracious son,
Who cries, "My father's damn'd, and all's my own."
Shades, that to Bacon could retreat afford,   175
Become the portion of a booby lord;[1]
And Helmsley,[2] once proud Buckingham's delight,
Slides to a scrivener or a city knight:
Let lands and houses have what lords they will,
Let us be fix'd, and our own masters still.   180

ADDITIONAL NOTE

EDWARD WORTLEY MONTAGU AND HIS SON

Ver. 49. *Avidien, or his wife.* Mr. Wortley, the husband of Lady Mary, was the son of the Hon. Sidney Montagu, and by his mother, Mrs. Anne Wortley, he inherited the large Wortley estate in Yorkshire, where most of his latter years were passed. At the date of Pope's satire Mr. Wortley and Lady Mary were living together. She went abroad a second time in 1729, and did not return till after the death of her husband in 1761. They seem to have parted by mutual consent; there was nothing domestic in the witty lady's character; but she kept up a friendly correspondence with her husband to the last. Writing to him from Avignon in 1745, she says, "Since the death of Pope I know nobody that is an enemy to either of us." *She* was never without enemies, or at least quarrels, the natural result of her own caprice, violence and proneness to satire. Mr. Wortley continued quietly in his retreat near Sheffield, hoarding up money, and watching over his health. He amassed an immense fortune, nearly a million of money, exclusive of his estates, and lived to a great age. In 1756, Horace Walpole looked in upon him at Wharncliffe. "Old Wortley Montagu," he says, "lives on the very spot where the dragon of Wantley did, only I believe the latter was much better lodged. You never saw such a wretched hovel; lean, unpainted, and half its nakedness barely shaded with harateen, stretched till it cracks. Here the miser hoards health and money, his only two objects. He has chronicles in behalf of the air, and battens on Tokay, his single indulgence, as he has heard it is particularly salutary. But the savageness of the scene would charm

[1] William, the first Lord Grimston, then occupant of Gorhambury, near St. Albans.
[2] Helmsley, in Yorkshire, which had belonged to Villiers, Duke of Buckingham, was purchased by Sir Charles Duncombe, Knight, Lord Mayor of London in 1709, and M.P. for Downton, Wilts. He changed the name of the place to Duncombe Park: now a girls' school.

your Alpine taste. It is tumbled with fragments of mountains, that look ready for building the world. One scrambles over a huge terrace, on which mountain ashes and various trees spring out of the very rocks; and at the brown is the den, but not spacious enough for such an inmate. However, I am persuaded it furnished Pope with this line, so exactly it answer to the picture:

'On rifted rocks, the dragon's late abodes.'

I wanted to ask if Pope had not visited Lady Mary Wortley here during their intimacy, but could one put that question to Avidien himself? There remains an ancient old inscription here, which has such a whimsical mixture of devotion and romanticness that I must transcribe it, 'Preye for the soul of Sir Thomas Wortley, Knight of the body to the Kings Edward IV., Richard III., Henry VII., Henry VIII., whose faults God pardon. He caused a Lodge to be built on this crag in the midst of Wharn-cliffe to hear the hart's bell, in the year of our Lord 1510.' It was a chace, and what he meant to hear was the noise of the stags."

Pope alludes (ver. 56) to the son of Wortley and Lady Mary. The allusion is harsh and unjust, for there was no want of proper feeling on the part of the parents towards this most extraordinary and profligate youth. This second Edward Wortley was worthy of a niche in Pope's gallery of originals. He ran off on three separate occasions from Westminster School, sailed as a cabin boy to Spain, was discovered and restored to his parents. He next travelled with a tutor on the Continent, returned to England, and sat for two parliaments in the House of Commons. Extravagance brought debt, and debt forced him abroad; in France he cheated a Jew—a mar-vellous instance of his adroitness—and was subjected to a short im-prisonment; in Italy he adopted the Roman Catholic religion; and in Turkey he became a strict Mahommedan. His father deprived him by his will of the succession to the family estate.

"But even this step," says Lord Wharncliffe, "was not taken without a sufficient provision being made for him; and, in the event of his having an heir legitimately born, the estate was to return to that heir, to the exclusion of his sister Lady Bute's children. This provision in Mr. Wortley's will he endeavoured to take advantage of in a manner which is highly characteristic. Mr. Edward Wortley, early in life, was married in a way not then uncommon, namely, a Fleet marriage. With that wife he did not live long, and he had no issue. After his father's death he lived several years in Egypt, and there is supposed to have professed the religion of Mahommed, and indulged in the plurality of wives permitted by that faith. In the year 1776, Mr. E. Wortley, then living at Venice, his wife being dead, through the agency (as is supposed) of his friend Romney the painter, caused an advertisement to be inserted in the *Public Advertiser* of April 16th in that year, in the following words:

"'A gentleman who has filled two successive seats in Parliament, is nearly sixty years of age, lives in great splendour and hospitality, and from whom a considerable estate must pass if he dies without issue, hath no objection to marry a widow or single lady, provided the party be of genteel birth, polite manners, and is five or six months gone in her preg-nancy. Letters directed to —— Brecknock, Esq., at Will's Coffee House, will be honoured with due attention, secrecy and every mark of respect.'

"It has always been believed in the family that this advertisement was successful, and that a woman having the qualifications required by it was actually sent to Paris to meet Mr. E. Wortley, who got as far as Lyons on his way thither. There, however, while eating a beccafico for supper, a bone stuck in his throat, and occasioned his death; thus putting an end to this honest scheme."

The scheme could not have stood an examination in a court of law, but it formed a fitting close to such a life.

THE FIRST EPISTLE OF THE
FIRST BOOK OF HORACE

TO LORD BOLINGBROKE

Written in 1738, when Pope was in his forty-ninth year. Hence
the allusion in the opening lines to the " Sabbath of his days."
Bolingbroke was then sixty, and it is curious to find the younger
friend gently reproach his older philosophical associate for breaking
the sacred calm of his poetic retirement.   The restless peer was
then in France. Unable to procure a restoration to his seat in the
House of Lords, he had for ten years waged a war of pamphlets and
newspaper essays against the Walpole administration, till, tired of
the fruitless contest, and quarrelling with his own party, he again
retired to France, and remained there from 1735 to 1742.

ST. JOHN, whose love indulged my labours past,
Matures my present, and shall bound my last!
Why will you break the Sabbath of my days?
Now sick alike of envy and of praise.
Public too long, ah, let me hide my age!   5
See modest Cibber now has left the stage:
Our generals now, retired to their estates,
Hang their old trophies o'er the garden gates;
In life's cool evening satiate of applause,
Nor fond of bleeding, even in Brunswick's cause.   10
　　A voice there is, that whispers in my ear
('Tis Reason's voice, which sometimes one can hear),
"Friend Pope! be prudent, let your Muse take breath,
And never gallop Pegasus to death;
Lest stiff, and stately, void of fire or force,   15
You limp, like Blackmore on a Lord Mayor's horse." [1]
　　Farewell, then, verse, and love, and every toy,
The rhymes and rattles of the man or boy;
What right, what true, what fit we justly call,
Let this be all my care, for this is all: 20
To lay this harvest up, and hoard with haste,
What every day will want, and most, the last.
　　But ask not, to what doctors I apply?
Sworn to no master, of no sect am I:
As drives the storm, at any door I knock: 25

[1] Sir Richard Blackmore, also conspicuous in the *Dunciad*; a good
man but a heavy, pompous and unreadable poet. He had been nine years
dead when this Epistle was written.

And house with Montaigne now, or now with Locke;
Sometimes a patriot, active in debate,
Mix with the world, and battle for the state,
Free as young Lyttelton,[1] her cause pursue,
Still true to virtue, and as warm as true;   30
Sometimes with Aristippus, or St. Paul,
Indulge my candour, and grow all to all;
Back to my native moderation slide,
And win my way by yielding to the tide.

Long, as to him who works for debt, the day,   35
Long as the night to her whose love's away,
Long as the year's dull circle seems to run,
When the brisk minor pants for twenty-one;
So slow the unprofitable moments roll,
That lock up all the functions of my soul;   40
That keep me from myself; and still delay
Life's instant business to a future day:
That task, which as we follow or despise,
The eldest is a fool, the youngest wise:
Which done, the poorest can no wants endure;   45
And which, not done, the richest must be poor.

Late as it is, I put myself to school,
And feel some comfort not to be a fool.
Weak though I am of limb, and short of sight,
Far from a lynx, and not a giant quite;   50
I'll do what Mead and Cheselden advise,[2]
To keep these limbs, and to preserve these eyes.
Not to go back, is somewhat to advance,
And men must walk at least before they dance.

Say, does thy blood rebel, thy bosom move   55
With wretched avarice, or as wretched love?
Know, there are words, and spells, which can control
Between the fits this fever of the soul:
Know, there are rhymes, which, fresh and fresh applied,

---

[1] George, first Lord Lyttelton, then Secretary to the Prince of Wales, in which capacity he was highly serviceable to Thomson, Mallet and other men of letters. His *Poems*, *Dialogues of the Dead*, *History of Henry II.*, and *Dissertation on the Conversion of St. Paul* have given him a respectable rank in literature. It appears from Lyttelton's *Correspondence*, published in 1845, that he wrote his treatise on St. Paul's conversion chiefly with a view to meet the case of Thomson, who, in that sceptical age, was troubled with sceptical doubts and was virtually a Deist.

[2] Dr. Mead was then physician to the king, and he kept his high position in his profession till his death. Dr. Cheselden was a skilful and popular surgeon and anatomist.

Will cure the arrant'st puppy of his pride.   60
Be furious, envious, slothful, mad or drunk,
Slave to a wife, or vassal to a punk,
A Switz, a High-Dutch, or a Low-Dutch bear;
All that we ask is but a patient ear.

'Tis the first virtue, vices to abhor: 65
And the first wisdom, to be fool no more.
But to the world no bugbear is so great,
As want of figure, and a small estate.
To either India see the merchant fly,
Scared at the spectre of pale poverty!   70
See him, with pains of body, pangs of soul,
Burn through the tropic, freeze beneath the pole!
Wilt thou do nothing for a nobler end,
Nothing, to make philosophy thy friend?
To stop thy foolish views, thy long desires,   75
And ease thy heart of all that it admires?
Here Wisdom calls: "Seek Virtue first, be bold!
As gold to silver, virtue is to gold."
There, London's voice: "Get money, money still!
And then let Virtue follow, if she will."   80
This, this the saving doctrine, preach'd to all,
From low St. James's up to high St. Paul! [1]
From him whose quill stands quiver'd at his ear,
To him who notches sticks at Westminster. [2]

   Barnard in spirit, sense, and truth abounds; [3]   85
"Pray, then, what wants he?" Fourscore thousand pounds;
A pension, or such harness for a slave
As Bug now has, and Dorimant would have. [4]
Barnard, thou art a cit, with all thy worth;
But Bug and D*l, their honours, and so forth.   90

   Yet every child another song will sing,
"Virtue, brave boys! 'tis virtue makes a king."
True, conscious honour is to feel no sin,

---

[1] An allusion to the *Low Church* opinions then prevalent at the court at
St. James's, and strongly patronised by Queen Caroline.
[2] The Exchequer tallies.
[3] Sir John Barnard, whom Chatham styled "the great commoner," was
at this time Lord Mayor of London.
[4] Warton remarks: "It cannot now be discovered to whom these names
belong—so soon does satire become unintelligible. The same may be said
of verse 112." Bug was the nickname of Henry de Grey, Duke of Kent,
"strong in nothing but money and smell," and Dorimant may stand for
that venal but good-humoured politician, Bubb Dodington. The *circum-
stances* and *character* in each case will apply. "D——" was probably
Delaval, the first lord of that name.

He's arm'd without that's innocent within;
Be this thy screen, and this thy wall of brass; 95
Compared to this a minister's an ass.

And say, to which shall our applause belong,
This new Court-jargon, or the good old song?
The modern language of corrupted peers,
Or what was spoke at Cressy or Poitiers? 100
Who counsels best? who whispers, "Be but great,
With praise or infamy leave that to fate;
Get place and wealth—if possible with grace;
If not, by any means get wealth and place."
For what? to have a box where eunuchs sing, 105
And foremost in the circle eye a king.
Or he, who bids thee face with steady view
Proud fortune, and look shallow greatness through:
And, while he bids thee, sets the example too?
If such a doctrine, in St. James's air, 110
Should chance to make the well-dressed rabble stare;
If honest S*z [1] take scandal at a spark,
That less admires the palace than the park:
Faith, I shall give the answer Reynard gave:
"I cannot like, dread sir, your royal cave: 115
Because I see, by all the tracks about,
Full many a beast goes in, but none comes out."
Adieu to Virtue, if you're once a slave:
Send her to Court, you send her to her grave.

Well, if a king's a lion, at the least 120
The people are a many-headed beast:
Can they direct what measures to pursue,
Who know themselves so little what to do?
Alike in nothing but one lust of gold,
Just half the land would buy, and half be sold: 125
Their country's wealth our mightier misers drain,
Or cross, to plunder provinces, the main;
The rest, some farm the poor-box, some the pews;
Some keep assemblies, and would keep the stews;
Some with fat bucks on childless dotards fawn; 130
Some win rich widows by their chine and brawn;
While with the silent growth of ten per cent.,

---

[1] Augustus Schutz, " the elder of two sons of Baron Schutz, a German who came over with George I. and settled his family in England. Augustus had been equerry to George II. when prince, and became Master of the Robes and Privy Purse to the king, with whom he was in great personal favour."—*Note by Mr. Croker in Lord Hervey's "Memoirs."*

In dirt and darkness, hundreds stink content.
   Of all these ways, if each pursues his own,
Satire, be kind, and let the wretch alone: 135
But show me one who has it in his power
To act consistent with himself an hour.
Sir Job sail'd forth, the evening bright and still,
"No place on earth (he cried) like Greenwich hill!"
Up starts a palace, lo, the obedient base   140
Slopes at its foot, the woods its sides embrace,
The silver Thames reflects its marble face.
Now let some whimsy, or that devil within
Which guides all those who know not what they mean,
But give the knight (or give his lady) spleen;   145
"Away, away! take all your scaffolds down,
For snug's the word: My dear! we'll live in town."
   At amorous Flavio is the stocking thrown?
That very night he longs to lie alone.
The fool whose wife elopes some thrice a quarter,   150
For matrimonial solace dies a martyr.
Did ever Proteus, Merlin, any witch,
Transform themselves so strangely as the rich?
Well, but the poor—the poor have the same itch;
They change their weekly barber, weekly news,   155
Prefer a new japanner to their shoes.
Discharge their garrets, move their beds, and run
(They know not whither) in a chaise and one;
They hire their sculler, and, when once aboard,
Grow sick, and damn the climate—like a lord.   160
   You laugh, half beau, half sloven if I stand,
My wig all powder, and all snuff my band;
You laugh, if coat and breeches strangely vary,
White gloves, and linen worthy Lady Mary!
But, when no prelate's lawn with hair-shirt lined   165
Is half so incoherent as my mind;
When (each opinion with the next at strife,
One ebb and flow of follies all my life)
I plant, root up; I build, and then confound;
Turn round to square, and square again to round;   170
You never change one muscle of your face,
You think this madness but a common case,
Nor once to Chancery, nor to Hale apply;[1]

¹ Dr. Hale, of Lincoln's Inn Fields, a physician employed in cases of insanity; he was doctor at Bedlam.

Yet hang your lip, to see a seam awry!
Careless how ill I with myself agree,   175
Kind to my dress, my figure, not to me.
Is this my guide, philosopher, and friend?
This he who loves me, and who ought to mend;
Who ought to make me (what he can, or none),
That man divine whom wisdom calls her own;   180
Great without title, without fortune bless'd;
Rich, e'en when plunder'd, honour'd while oppress'd;
Loved without youth, and follow'd without power;
At home, though exiled—free, though in the Tower;
In short, that reasoning, high, immortal thing,   185
Just less than Jove, and much above a king,
Nay, half in Heaven—except (what's mighty odd)
A fit of vapours clouds this demi-god?

THE SIXTH EPISTLE OF THE
FIRST BOOK OF HORACE

TO MR. MURRAY

The Hon. William Murray, Lord Mansfield. He was the fourth
son of David, Lord Stormont, and was born in 1705. At the date
of this Epistle (1737) Murray had not obtained any Government
appointment, but in 1742 he was made Solicitor-General. In 1754
he succeeded to the office of Attorney-General, which he held till
1756, when he was appointed Chief Justice of the Court of King's
Bench, and was created Baron Murray of Mansfield. He held the
office of Chief Justice (having repeatedly declined that of Lord
Chancellor) till his resignation in 1788. He died in 1793. As a
strenuous supporter of high monarchical principles, Lord Mansfield
was for a time unpopular, and was attacked by Junius with all the
virulence and brilliant invective of that writer. His votes in favour
of Catholic Relief also exposed him to the fury of the mob, and in
the riots of 1780 his town house, with a valuable library and collec-
tion of manuscripts, was burned to the ground. In his legal capacity,
no judge has been more eminent than Mansfield. He possessed a
clear and penetrating judgment, an intellect at once refined, subtle,
and comprehensive, and great powers of eloquence adapted to the
bar and the bench. In Parliament he was not so successful, nor was
he ambitious of shining as a politician. In private life he possessed
those graces and accomplishments which early attracted the admira-
tion of Pope, and which continued to delight his friends after he

had passed his eightieth year. The poet's prediction that he should
be interred " where kings and poets lie " was realised. He was
buried in Westminster Abbey, and a costly monument, one of the
best works of Flaxman, covers his remains.

Not to admire, is all the art I know,
To make men happy, and to keep them so.
(Plain truth, dear Murray, needs no flowers of speech,
So take it in the very words of Creech.) [1]
    This vault of air, this congregated ball,   5
Self-centred sun, and stars that rise and fall.
There are, my friend, whose philosophic eyes
Look through, and trust the Ruler with his skies;
To Him commit the hour, the day, the year,
And view this dreadful All without a fear.   10
    Admire we then what earth's low entrails hold,
Arabian shores, or Indian seas infold;
All the mad trade of fools and slaves for gold?
Or popularity? or stars and strings?
The mob's applauses, or the gifts of kings?   15
Say with what eyes we ought at Courts to gaze,
And pay the great our homage of amaze?
    If weak the pleasure that from these can spring,
The fear to want them is as weak a thing:
Whether we dread, or whether we desire,   20
In either case, believe me, we admire:
Whether we joy or grieve, the same the curse,
Surprised at better, or surprised at worse.
Thus good or bad, to one extreme betray
The unbalanced mind, and snatch the man away: 25
For Virtue's self may too much zeal be had;
The worst of madmen is a saint run mad.
Go then, and, if you can, admire the state
Of beaming diamonds, and reflected plate;
Procure a taste to double the surprise,   30
And gaze on Parian charms with learned eyes:
Be struck with bright brocade, or Tyrian dye,
Our birthday nobles' splendid livery.
If not so pleased, at council-board rejoice,
To see their judgments hang upon thy voice;   35
From morn to night, at senate, rolls, and hall,
Plead much, read more, dine late, or not at all.

[1] From whose translation of Horace the first two lines are taken.

But wherefore all this labour, all this strife?
For fame, for riches, for a noble wife?
Shall one whom Nature, learning, birth conspired   40
To form, not to admire but be admired,
Sigh, while his Chloe, blind to wit and worth,
Weds the rich dulness of some son of earth?
Yet time ennobles, or degrades each line;
It brighten'd Craggs's, and may darken thine:[1]   45
And what is fame? the meanest have their day,
The greatest can but blaze, and pass away.
Graced as thou art, with all the power of words,
So known, so honour'd, at the House of Lords:
Conspicuous scene! another yet is nigh   50
(More silent far), where kings and poets lie;
Where Murray (long enough his country's pride)
Shall be no more than Tully, or than Hyde!

Rack'd with sciatics, martyr'd with the stone,
Will any mortal let himself alone?   55
See Ward by batter'd beaux invited over,
And desperate Misery lays hold on Dover.
The case is easier in the mind's disease;
There all men may be cured, whene'er they please.
Would ye be bless'd? despise low joys, low gains;   60
Disdain whatever Cornbury disdains;[2]
Be virtuous, and be happy for your pains.

But art thou one, whom new opinions sway,
One who believes as Tindal leads the way,
Who virtue and a church alike disowns,   65

[1] From the mention of "Chloe" in this passage, it has been assumed that Murray was rejected by some lady to whom he had paid his addresses. He was married shortly afterwards to Lady Betty Finch, daughter of Daniel, Earl of Nottingham. The elder Craggs was originally a footman to Lady Mordaunt, Duchess of Norfolk. The bulk of his fortune was made as an army contractor, and he was afterwards joint Postmaster-General with Lord Cornwallis. He was deeply involved in the South Sea delusion, and had profited by the public credulity to such an extent that his estate was seized by the House of Commons. He left about a million and a half of money—amassed, it is said, on purpose to give wealth and honours to his son, the friend of Pope, and one of the Secretaries of the Treasury. The son died of the smallpox, and the old man, broken-hearted, died a few weeks afterwards of apoplexy, brought on, as was supposed, partly by grief, and partly by dread of the examination and exposure of his delinquencies in the South Sea case before the House of Commons.

[2] Henry Viscount Cornbury disdained a pension. On his return from travelling abroad, the Earl of Essex, his brother-in-law, said he had got a pension for him. He replied, "How could you tell, my lord, that I was to be sold, or, at least, how came you to know my price so exactly?" He died in 1753, aged forty-three.

Thinks that but words, and this but brick and stones?
Fly then, on all the wings of wild desire,
Admire whate'er the maddest can admire.
Is wealth thy passion? Hence! from pole to pole,
Where winds can carry, or where waves can roll,   70
For Indian spices, for Peruvian gold,
Prevent the greedy, or outbid the bold:
Advance thy golden mountain to the skies;
On the broad base of fifty thousand rise,
Add one round hundred, and (if that's not fair)   75
Add fifty more, and bring it to a square.
For, mark the advantage; just so many score
Will gain a wife with half as many more,
Procure her beauty, make that beauty chaste,
And then such friends—as cannot fail to last.   80
A man of wealth is dubb'd a man of worth,
Venus shall give him form, and Anstis birth.
(Believe me, many a German prince is worse,
Who, proud of pedigree, is poor of purse.)
His wealth brave Timon gloriously confounds;   85
Ask'd for a groat, he gives a hundred pounds;
Or if three ladies like a luckless play,
Takes the whole house upon the poet's day.
Now, in such exigencies not to need,
Upon my word, you must be rich indeed;   90
A noble superfluity it craves,
Not for yourself, but for your fools and knaves:
Something, which for your honour they may cheat,
And which it much becomes you to forget.
If wealth alone then make and keep us bless'd,   95
Still, still be getting, never, never rest.

But if to power and place your passion lie,
If in the pomp of life consist the joy;
Then hire a slave, or (if you will) a lord
To do the honours, and to give the word;   100
Tell at your levée, as the crowds approach,
To whom to nod, whom take into your coach,
Whom honour with your hand: to make remarks,
Who rules in Cornwall, or who rules in Berks:
"This may be troublesome, is near the chair: 105
That makes three members, this can choose a mayor."
Instructed thus, you bow, embrace, protest,
Adopt him son, or cousin at the least,

Then turn about, and laugh at your own jest.
   Or if your life be one continued treat,   110
If to live well 'means nothing but to eat;
Up, up! cries Gluttony, 'tis break of day,
Go drive the deer, and drag the finny-prey;
With hounds and horns go hunt an appetite—
So Russel[1] did, but could not eat at night,   115
Call'd, happy dog! the beggar at his door,
And envied thirst and hunger to the poor.
   Or shall we every decency confound,
Through taverns, stews, and bagnios take our round,
Go dine with Chartres, in each vice outdo   120
K—l's lewd cargo, or Ty—y's crew,[2]
From Latian syrens, French Circæan feasts,
Return well travell'd, and transform'd to beasts;
Or for a titled punk, or foreign flame,
Renounce our country, and degrade our name?   125
   If, after all, we must with Wilmot own,[3]
The cordial drop of life is love alone,
And Swift cry wisely, "Vive la Bagatelle!"
The man that loves and laughs, must sure do well.
   Adieu—if this advice appear the worst,   130
E'en take the counsel which I gave you first:
Or better precepts if you can impart,
Why do, I'll follow them with all my heart.

---

[1] Lord Edward (?) Russell, who ruined his constitution by luxurious living, and though he did not love sport, took out his dogs every day to hunt for an appetite.

[2] Lords Kinnoul and Tyrawley, two ambassadors noted for wild immorality. The latter returned from Lisbon in 1742, and, as Horace Walpole states, brought three wives and fourteen children with him. He lived to the age of eighty-five, dying in 1773.

[3] The Earl of Rochester.

THE FIRST EPISTLE OF THE
SECOND BOOK OF HORACE

Published in 1737. Pope prefixed to it the following

ADVERTISEMENT

" The reflections of Horace, and the judgments passed in his
Epistle to Augustus, seemed so seasonable to the present times,
that I could not help applying them to the use of my own country.
The author thought them considerable enough to address them to
his prince, whom he paints with all the great and good qualities of
a monarch upon whom the Romans depended for the increase of an
absolute empire. But to make the poem entirely English, I was
willing to add one or two of those which contribute to the happiness
of a free people, and are more consistent with the welfare of our
neighbours.

" This Epistle will show the learned world to have fallen into two
mistakes: one, that Augustus was a patron of poets in general,
whereas he not only prohibited all but the best writers to name
him, but recommended that care even to the civil magistrate:
Admonebat Prætores, ne paterentur Nomen suum obsolefieri, etc.
The other, that this piece was only a general discourse of poetry,
whereas it was an apology for the poets, in order to render Augustus
more their patron. Horace here pleads the cause of his contem-
poraries, first, against the taste of the town, whose humour it was
to magnify the authors of the preceding age; secondly, against the
court and nobility, who encouraged only the writers for the theatre;
and lastly, against the emperor himself, who had conceived them of
little use to the government. He shows (by a view of the progress
of learning and the change of taste among the Romans) that the
introduction of the polite arts of Greece had given the writers of
his time great advantages over their predecessors; that their
morals were much improved, and the licence of those ancient poets
restrained: that satire and comedy were become more just and
useful: that whatever extravagances were left on the stage were
owing to the ill-taste of the nobility; that poets, under due regula-
tions, were in many respects useful to the State; and concludes that
it was upon them the emperor himself must depend for his fame
with posterity.

" We may further learn from this Epistle, that Horace made his
court to this great prince by writing with a decent freedom toward
him, with a just contempt of his low flatterers, and with a manly
regard to his own character."

Pope's imitation is a satire on George II.—the British Augustus
—and on the follies and flatteries of the age. He also reviews the
literature of that and preceding reigns; and concludes with an
ironical panegyric on the king, conceived and expressed in his
happiest manner.

TO AUGUSTUS

WHILE you, great patron of mankind! sustain
The balanced world, and open all the main;
Your country, chief, in arms abroad defend,
At home, with morals, arts, and laws amend;
How shall the Muse from such a monarch steal   5
An hour, and not defraud the public weal?
Edward and Henry, now the boast of fame,
And virtuous Alfred, a more sacred name,
After a life of gen'rous toils endured,
The Gaul subdued, or property secured,   10
Ambition humbled, mighty cities storm'd,
Or laws establish'd, and the world reform'd;
Closed their long glories with a sigh, to find
The unwilling gratitude of base mankind!
All human virtue, to its latest breath,   15
Finds envy never conquer'd, but by death.
The great Alcides, every labour pass'd,
Had still this monster to subdue at last.
Sure fate of all, beneath whose rising ray
Each star of meaner merit fades away!   20
Oppress'd we feel the beam directly beat,
Those suns of glory please not till they set.
   To thee, the world its present homage pays,
The harvest early, but mature the praise:
Great friend of liberty! in kings a name   25
Above all Greek, above all Roman fame:
Whose word is truth, as sacred and revered,
As Heaven's own oracles from altars heard.
Wonder of kings! like whom, to mortal eyes
None e'er has risen, and none e'er shall rise.   30
   Just in one instance, be it yet confess'd
Your people, sir, are partial in the rest:
Foes to all living worth except your own,
And advocates for folly dead and gone.
Authors, like coins, grow dear as they grow old;   35
It is the rust we value, not the gold.
Chaucer's worst ribaldry is learn'd by rote,
And beastly Skelton heads of houses quote: [1]
One likes no language but the *Faery Queen*;

[1] Skelton, Poet Laureate to Henry VIII.

A Scot will fight for Christ's Kirk o' the Green:[1]   40
And each true Briton is to Ben so civil,
He swears the Muses met him at the Devil.[2]

    Though justly Greece her eldest sons admires,
Why should not we be wiser than our sires?
In every public virtue we excel;   45
We build, we paint, we sing, we dance as well;
And learned Athens to our art must stoop,
Could she behold us tumbling through a hoop.

    If time improve our wits as well as wine,
Say at what age a poet grows divine?   50
Shall we, or shall we not, account him so,
Who died, perhaps, an hundred years ago?
End all dispute; and fix the year precise
When British bards begin to immortalise?

    "Who lasts a century can have no flaw,   55
I hold that wit a classic, good in law."

    Suppose he wants a year, will you compound?
And shall we deem him ancient, right and sound,
Or damn to all eternity at once,
At ninety-nine, a modern and a dunce?   60

    "We shall not quarrel for a year or two;
By courtesy of England, he may do."

    Then, by the rule that made the horse-tail bare,
I pluck out year by year, as hair by hair,
And melt down ancients like a heap of snow: 65
While you, to measure merits, look in Stowe,
And estimating authors by the year,
Bestow a garland only on a bier.

    Shakespeare (whom you and every play-house bill
Style the divine, the matchless, what you will),   70
For gain, not glory, wing'd his roving flight,
And grew immortal in his own despite.
Ben, old and poor, as little seem'd to heed
The life to come, in every poet's creed.
Who now reads Cowley? if he pleases yet,   75
His moral pleases, not his pointed wit;
Forgot his epic, nay Pindaric art,
But still I love the language of his heart.

    "Yet surely, surely, these were famous men!
What boy but hears the sayings of old Ben?   80

---

[1] A ballad made by a king of Scotland.
[2] The Devil Tavern, where Ben Jonson held his poetical club.

In all debates where critics bear a part,
Not one but nods, and talks of Jonson's art,
Of Shakespeare's nature, and of Cowley's wit;
How Beaumont's judgment check'd what Fletcher writ;
How Shadwell hasty, Wycherley was slow;   85
But, for the passions, Southern sure and Rowe.
These, only these, support the crowded stage,
From eldest Heywood down to Cibber's age."
 All this may be; the people's voice is odd,
It is, and it is not, the voice of God.   90
To *Gammer Gurton* if it give the bays,[1]
And yet deny the *Careless Husband* praise,
Or say our fathers never broke a rule;
Why then, I say, the public is a fool.
But let them own, that greater faults than we   95
They had, and greater virtues, I'll agree.
Spenser himself affects the obsolete,
And Sidney's verse halts ill on Roman feet:
Milton's strong pinion now not Heaven can bound,
Now serpent-like, in prose he sweeps the ground;   100
In quibbles, angel and archangel join,
And God the Father turns a school-divine.
Not that I'd lop the beauties from his book,
Like slashing Bentley with his desperate hook,
Or damn all Shakespeare, like the affected fool   105
At Court, who hates whate'er he read at school.[2]
 But for the wits of either Charles's days,
The mob of gentlemen who wrote with ease;
Sprat, Carew, Sedley, and a hundred more,
(Like twinkling stars the *Miscellanies* o'er)   110
One simile, that solitary shines
In the dry desert of a thousand lines,
Or lengthen'd thought that gleams through many a page,
Has sanctified whole poems for an age.

[1] A piece of very low humour, one of the first printed plays in English, written about the year 1565 by William Stevenson, of Christ's College, Cambridge. The song of "Jolly Good Ale" in this rude drama is the best part of it, and it is still deservedly a favourite.
 The *Careless Husband*, noticed in the next line, is Colley Cibber's best play, produced in 1706.
 [2] An indirect satire on Lord Hervey, who in his *Epistle to a Doctor of Divinity from a Nobleman at Hampton Court* has these lines:

"All I learn'd from Dr. Friend at school
Has quite deserted this poor John Trot head,
And left plain native English in its stead."

I lose my patience, and I own it too,   115
When works are censured, not as bad but new;
While if our elders break all reason's laws,
These fools demand not pardon, but applause.
  On Avon's bank, where flowers eternal blow,
If I but ask, if any weed can grow;   120
One tragic sentence if I dare deride,
Which Betterton's grave action dignified,[1]
Or well-mouth'd Booth with emphasis proclaims
(Though but, perhaps, a muster-roll of names),
How will our fathers rise up in a rage,   125
And swear, all shame is lost in George's age!
You'd think no fools disgraced the former reign,
Did not some grave examples yet remain,
Who scorn a lad should teach his father skill,
And, having once been wrong, will be so still.   130
He, who to seem more deep than you or I,
Extols old bards, or Merlin's prophecy,
Mistake him not; he envies, not admires,
And to debase the sons, exalts the sires.
Had ancient times conspired to disallow   135
What then was new, what had been ancient now?
Or what remain'd, so worthy to be read
By learned critics, of the mighty dead?
In days of ease, when now the weary sword
Was sheath'd, and luxury with Charles restored;   140
  In every taste of foreign courts improved,
"All, by the king's example, lived and loved." [2]
Then peers grew proud in horsemanship to excel,[3]
Newmarket's glory rose, as Britain's fell;
The soldier breathed the gallantries of France,   145
And every flowery courtier writ romance.
Then marble, soften'd into life, grew warm,
And yielding metal flow'd to human form:
Lely on animated canvas stole
The sleepy eye, that spoke the melting soul.   150
No wonder then, when all was love and sport,

[1] Thomas Betterton (born in 1635, died in 1710) was the Roscius of his times. Barton Booth was born in 1681 and died in 1733. He was a splendid declaimer, and the original Cato in Addison's tragedy.
[2] A verse of the Lord Lansdowne.
[3] The Duke of Newcastle's *Book of Horsemanship*; the *Romance of Parthenissa*, by the Earl of Orrery; and most of the French romances translated by persons of quality.

The willing Muses were debauch'd at Court:
On each enervate string they taught the note [1]
To pant, or tremble through an eunuch's throat.
   But Britain, changeful as a child at play,   155
Now calls in princes, and now turns away.
Now Whig, now Tory, what we loved we hate;
Now all for pleasure, now for Church and State;
Now for prerogative, and now for laws;
Effects unhappy! from a noble cause.   160
   Time was, a sober Englishman would knock
His servants up, and rise by five o'clock;
Instruct his family in every rule,
And send his wife to church, his son to school.
To worship like his fathers was his care;   165
To teach their frugal virtues to his heir:
To prove that luxury could never hold;
And place, on good security, his gold.
Now times are changed, and one poetic itch
Has seized the court and city, poor and rich: 170
Sons, sires, and grandsires, all will wear the bays,
Our wives read Milton, and our daughters plays,
To theatres, and to rehearsals throng,
And all our grace at table is a song.
I, who so oft renounce the Muses, lie,   175
Not ——'s self e'er tells more fibs than I;
When sick of Muse, our follies we deplore,
And promise our best friends to rhyme no more;
We wake next morning in a raging fit
And call for pen and ink to show our wit.   180
   He served a 'prenticeship, who sets up shop;
Ward tried on puppies, and the poor, his drop; [2]
E'en Radcliffe's doctors travel first to France,
Nor dare to practise till they've learn'd to dance.
Who builds a bridge that never drove a pile?   185
(Should Ripley venture, all the world would smile)
But those who cannot write, and those who can,
All rhyme, and scrawl, and scribble, to a man.
   Yet, sir, reflect, the mischief is not great;

---

[1] *The Siege of Rhodes*, by Sir William Davenant, the first opera sung in England.

[2] A famous empiric, whose pill and drop had several surprising effects, and were one of the principal subjects of writing and conversation at this time.

These madmen never hurt the Church or State; 190
Sometimes the folly benefits mankind;
And rarely avarice taints the tuneful mind.
Allow him but his plaything of a pen,
He ne'er rebels, or plots, like other men;
Flight of cashiers, or mobs, he'll never mind; [1] 195
And knows no losses while the Muse is kind.
To cheat a friend, or ward, he leaves to Peter;
The good man heaps up nothing but mere metre,
Enjoys his garden and his book in quiet;
And then—a perfect hermit in his diet. 200

Of little use the man you may suppose,
Who says in verse what others say in prose;
Yet let me show a poet's of some weight,
And (though no soldier) useful to the State.
What will a child learn sooner than a song? 205
What better teach a foreigner the tongue?
What's long or short, each accent where to place,
And speak in public with some sort of grace.
I scarce can think him such a worthless thing,
Unless he praise some monster of a king; 210
Or virtue or religion turn to sport,
To please a lewd or unbelieving court.
Unhappy Dryden!—in all Charles's days,
Roscommon only boasts unspotted bays;
And in our own (excuse from courtly stains) 215
No whiter page than Addison remains.
He from the taste obscene reclaims our youth,
And sets the passions on the side of truth,
Forms the soft bosom with the gentlest art,
And pours each human virtue in the heart. 220
Let Ireland tell, how wit upheld her cause,
Her trade supported, and supplied her laws;
And leave on Swift this grateful verse engraved,
"The rights a court attack'd, a poet saved." [2]
Behold the hand that wrought a nation's cure, 225
Stretch'd to relieve the idiot and the poor, [3]

[1] Alluding to the flight of Mr. Knight, the principal cashier of the South
Sea Company. He had fled to save the reputation of the ministry, and was
allowed to return to England, where he lived many years in wealth and
comfort. He died in 1744.

[2] Pope, it is said, was threatened with a prosecution in consequence of
this verse. It refers to "Drapier's Letters."

[3] A foundation for the maintenance of idiots and a fund for assisting
the poor, by lending small sums of money on demand.

Proud vice to brand, or injured worth adorn,
And stretch the ray to ages yet unborn.
Not but there are, who merit other palms;
Hopkins and Sternhold glad the heart with psalms:[1]   230
The boys and girls whom charity maintains,
Implore your help in these pathetic strains:
How could devotion touch the country pews,
Unless the gods bestow'd a proper Muse?
Verse cheers their leisure, verse assists their work,   235
Verse prays for peace, or sings down Pope and Turk.
The silenced preacher yields to potent strain,
And feels that grace his prayer besought in vain;
The blessing thrills through all the labouring throng,
And Heaven is won by violence of song.   240
  Our rural ancestors, with little blest,
Patient of labour when the end was rest,
Indulged the day that housed their annual grain,
With feasts and offerings, and a thankful strain:
The joy their wives, their sons, and servants share,   245
Ease of their toil, and partners of their care:
The laugh, the jest, attendants on the bowl,
Smooth'd every brow, and open'd every soul:
With growing years the pleasing licence grew,
And taunts alternate innocently flew.   250
But times corrupt, and Nature ill-inclined,
Produced the point that left a sting behind;
Till friend with friend, and families at strife,
Triumphant malice raged through private life.
Who felt the wrong, or fear'd it, took the alarm,   255
Appeal'd to law, and justice lent her arm.
At length, by wholesome dread of statutes bound,
The poets learn'd to please, and not to wound:
Most warp'd to flattery's side; but some, more nice,
Preserved the freedom, and forbore the vice.   260
Hence satire rose, that just the medium hit,
And heals with morals, what it hurts with wit.
  We conquer'd France, but felt our captive's charms;
Her arts victorious triumph'd o'er our arms:
Britain to soft refinements less a foe,   265
Wit grew polite, and numbers learn'd to flow.

---

[1] Sternhold, one of the versifiers of the old singing psalms. He was a courtier and Groom of the Robes to Henry VIII., and of the Bedchamber to Edward VI.

Waller was smooth; but Dryden taught to join
The varying verse, the full-resounding line,
The long majestic march and energy divine.[1]
Though still some traces of our rustic vein   270
And splayfoot verse remain'd, and will remain.
Late, very late, correctness grew our care,
When the tired nation breathed from civil war.
Exact Racine, and Corneille's noble fire,
Show'd us that France had something to admire.   275
Not but the tragic spirit was our own,
And full in Shakespeare, fair in Otway shone:
But Otway fail'd to polish or refine,
And fluent Shakespeare scarce effaced a line.
Even copious Dryden wanted, or forgot,   280
The last and greatest art, the art to blot.
Some doubt, if equal pains, or equal fire,
The humbler Muse of comedy require.
       But in known images of life, I guess
The labour greater, as the indulgence less.   285
Observe how seldom even the best succeed:
Tell me if Congreve's fools are fools indeed?
What pert low dialogue has Farquhar writ!
How Van wants grace, who never wanted wit!
The stage how loosely does Astræa tread,[2]   290
Who fairly puts all characters to bed!
And idle Cibber, how he breaks the laws,
To make poor Pinky eat with vast applause!
But fill their purse, our poets' work is done,
Alike to them, by pathos or by pun.   295
       O you! whom Vanity's light bark conveys
On Fame's mad voyage by the wind of praise,
With what a shifting gale your course you ply,
For ever sunk too low, or borne too high!
Who pants for glory finds but short repose,   300
A breath revives him, or a breath o'erthrows.
Farewell the stage! if just as thrives the play,
The silly bard grows fat, or falls away.
       There still remains, to mortify a wit,
The many-headed monster of the pit;   305

[1] Waller about this time, with the Earl of Dorset, Mr. Godolphin, and others, translated the *Pompey* of Corneille; and the more correct French poets began to be in reputation.
[2] A name taken by Mrs. Aphra Behn.

A senseless, worthless, and unhonour'd crowd;
Who, to disturb their betters mighty proud,
Clattering their sticks before ten lines are spoke,
Call for the farce, the bear, or the black-joke.
What dear delight to Britons farce affords!   310
Ever the taste of mobs, but now of lords
(Taste, that eternal wanderer, which flies
From heads to ears, and now from ears to eyes).
The play stands still; damn action and discourse,
Back fly the scenes, and enter foot and horse;   315
Pageants on pageants, in long order drawn,
Peers, heralds, bishops, ermine, gold and lawn;
The champion, too! and to complete the jest,
Old Edward's armour beams on Cibber's breast.[1]
With laughter sure Democritus had died,   320
Had he beheld an audience gape so wide.
Let bear or elephant be e'er so white,
The people, sure, the people are the sight!
Ah, luckless poet! stretch thy lungs and roar,
That bear or elephant shall heed thee more;   325
While all its throats the gallery extends,
And all the thunder of the pit ascends!
Loud as the wolves, on Orcas' stormy steep,[2]
Howl to the roarings of the Northern deep.
Such is the shout, the long-applauding note,   330
At Quin's high plume, or Oldfield's petticoat;
Or when from Court a birthday suit bestow'd,
Sinks the lost actor in the tawdry load.
Booth enters—hark! the universal peal!
"But has he spoken?" Not a syllable.   335
What shook the stage, and made the people stare?
Cato's long wig, flower'd gown, and lacquer'd chair.

  Yet lest you think I rally more than teach,
Or praise malignly arts I cannot reach,
Let me for once presume to instruct the times,   340
To know the poet from the man of rhymes:
'Tis he who gives my breast a thousand pains,
Can make me feel each passion that he feigns;
Enrage, compose, with more than magic art,

---

[1] The coronation of Henry VIII. and Queen Anne Boleyn, in which the playhouses vied with each other to represent all the pomp of a coronation. In this noble contention, the armour of one of the kings of England was borrowed from the Tower to dress the champion.
[2] The furthest northern promontory of Scotland, opposite the Orcades.

With pity, and with terror, tear my heart;   345
And snatch me, o'er the earth, or through the air,
To Thebes, to Athens, when he will, and where.
     But not this part of the poetic state
Alone, deserves the favour of the great:
Think of those authors, sir, who would rely   350
More on a reader's sense, than gazer's eye.
Or who shall wander where the Muses sing?
Who climb their mountain, or who taste their spring?
How shall we fill a library with wit,[1]
When Merlin's cave is half unfurnish'd yet?[2]   355
     My liege! why writers little claim your thought
I guess; and, with their leave, will tell the fault:
We poets are (upon a poet's word)
Of all mankind, the creatures most absurd:
The season, when to come, and when to go,   360
To sing, or cease to sing, we never know;
And if we will recite nine hours in ten,
You lose your patience just like other men.
Then, too, we hurt ourselves, when to defend
A single verse, we quarrel with a friend;   365
Repeat unask'd; lament, the wit's too fine
For vulgar eyes, and point out every line.
But most, when straining with too weak a wing,
We needs will write epistles to the king;
And from the moment we oblige the town,   370
Expect a place, or pension from the Crown;
Or dubb'd historians by express command,
To enrol your triumphs o'er the seas and land,
Be call'd to Court to plan some work divine,
As once for Louis, Boileau and Racine.   375
     Yet think, great sir! (so many virtues shown)
Ah think, what poet best may make them known?
Or choose, at least, some minister of grace,
Fit to bestow the laureate's weighty place.
     Charles, to late times to be transmitted fair,   380
Assign'd his figure to Bernini's care;
And great Nassau to Kneller's hand decreed
To fix him graceful on the bounding steed;

[1] *Munus Apolline dignum.* The Palatine library then building by
Augustus.
[2] A building in the royal gardens of Richmond, where is a small but
choice collection of books.
The collection was made by Queen Caroline.

So well in paint and stone they judged of merit;
But kings in wit may want discerning spirit.   385
The hero William, and the martyr Charles,
One knighted Blackmore, and one pension'd Quarles; [1]
Which made old Ben and surly Dennis swear,
"No Lord's anointed, but a Russian bear."
 Not with such majesty, such bold relief,   390
The forms august of king, or conqu'ring chief,
E'er swell'd on marble, as in verse have shined
(In polish'd verse) the manners and the mind.
Oh! could I mount on the Mæonian wing,
Your arms, your actions, your repose to sing!   395
What seas you traversed, and what fields you fought!
Your country's peace, how oft, how dearly bought!
How barb'rous rage subsided at your word,
And nations wonder'd, while they dropp'd the sword!
How, when you nodded, o'er the land and deep,   400
Peace stole her wing, and wrapp'd the world in sleep;
Till earth's extremes your mediation own,
And Asia's tyrants tremble at your throne.
But verse, alas! your Majesty disdains;
And I'm not used to panegyric strains: 405
The zeal of fools offends at any time,
But most of all the zeal of fools in rhyme.
Besides, a fate attends on all I write,
That when I aim at praise, they say I bite.
A vile encomium doubly ridicules: 410
There's nothing blackens like the ink of fools.
If true, a woeful likeness; and if lies,
"Praise undeserved is scandal in disguise":
Well may he blush who gives it, or receives;
And when I flatter, let my dirty leaves   415
(Like journals, odes, and such forgotten things
As Eusden, Philips, Settle, writ of kings)
Clothe spice, line trunks, or flutt'ring in a row,
Befringe the rails of Bedlam and Soho.

---

[1] Quarles held a small sinecure place in the court of James I., but there is no record of his being pensioned by Charles, in support of whose cause he lost his property, books, etc., by which his death (1644) was supposed to be hastened.

THE SECOND EPISTLE OF THE
SECOND BOOK OF HORACE

This Second Epistle was also published in 1737. Colonel Cotterell, to whom it is addressed, was son of Sir Charles Ludowick Cotterell, who succeeded his father in 1686 as Master of the Ceremonies, and in 1697 was appointed one of the Commissioners of the Privy Seal. The family had been long established at their seat of Rousham Hall, near Oxford, and Pope's friend was the founder of the Cotterells of Hadley, in Middlesex. Sir William Trumbull, the poet's early patron and friend in " the Forest," was married into this family. Colonel Cotterell died at Bath, 13th October, 1746.

DEAR Colonel, Cobham's and your country's friend!
You love a verse, take such as I can send.
A Frenchman comes, presents you with his boy,
Bows and begins:—"This lad, sir, is of Blois: [1]
Observe his shape how clean! his locks how curl'd!   5
My only son;—I'd have him see the world:
His French is pure; his voice too—you shall hear.
Sir, he's your slave, for twenty pound a year.
Mere wax as yet, you fashion him with ease,
Your barber, cook, upholsterer, what you please: 10
A perfect genius at an opera song—
To say too much, might do my honour wrong.
Take him, with all his virtues, on my word;
His whole ambition was to serve a lord:
But, sir, to you, with what would I not part?   15
Though faith, I fear, 'twill break his mother's heart.
Once (and but once) I caught him in a lie,
And then, unwhipp'd, he had the grace to cry:
The fault he has I fairly shall reveal,
(Could you o'erlook but that) it is, to steal."   20
    If, after this, you took the graceless lad,
Could you complain, my friend, he proved so bad?
Faith, in such case, if you should prosecute,
I think Sir Godfrey should decide the suit; [2]
Who sent the thief that stole the cash away,   25
And punish'd him that put it in his way.

---

[1] A town in Beauce, where the French tongue is spoke in great purity.
[2] Sir Godfrey Kneller.   An eminent Justice of Peace, who decided much in the manner of Sancho Pança.

Consider then, and judge me in this light;
I told you when I went, I could not write;
You said the same; and are you discontent
With laws, to which you gave your own assent?   30
Nay, worse, to ask for verse at such a time!
D'ye think me good for nothing but to rhyme?

In Anna's wars, a soldier, poor and old,
Had dearly earn'd a little purse of gold:
Tired with a tedious march, one luckless night,   35
He slept, poor dog! and lost it, to a doit.
This put the man in such a desperate mind,
Between revenge, and grief, and hunger join'd,
Against the foe, himself, and all mankind,
He leap'd the trenches, scaled a castle wall,   40
Tore down a standard, took the fort and all.
"Prodigious well!" his great commander cried,
Gave him much praise, and some reward beside.
Next pleased his excellence a town to batter
(Its name I know not, and 'tis no great matter);   45
"Go on, my friend (he cried), see yonder walls!
Advance and conquer! go where glory calls!
More honours, more rewards, attend the brave."
Don't you remember what reply he gave?
"D'ye think me, noble general, such a sot?   50
Let him take castles who has ne'er a groat."
    Bred up at home, full early I begun
To read in Greek the wrath of Peleus' son.
Besides, my father taught me, from a lad,
The better art to know the good from bad: 55
(And little sure imported to remove,
To hunt for Truth in Maudlin's learned grove.)
But knottier points we knew not half so well,
Deprived us soon of our paternal cell;
And certain laws, by sufferers thought unjust,   60
Denied all posts of profit or of trust:
Hopes after hopes of pious Papists fail'd,
While mighty William's thundering arm prevail'd.
For right hereditary tax'd and fined,
He stuck to poverty with peace of mind;   65
And me, the Muses help'd to undergo it;
Convict a Papist he, and I a poet.
But (thanks to Homer) since I live and thrive
Indebted to no prince or peer alive,

Sure I should want the care of ten Monroes,[1]   70
If I would scribble, rather than repose.
    Years following years, steal something every day,
At last they steal us from ourselves away;
In one our frolics, one amusements end,
In one a mistress drops, in one a friend: 75
This subtle thief of life, this paltry time,
What will it leave me, if it snatch my rhyme?
If every wheel of that unwearied mill,
That turn'd ten thousand verses, now stands still?
    But, after all, what would you have me do?   80
When out of twenty I can please not two;
When this Heroics only deigns to praise,
Sharp Satire that, and that Pindaric lays?
One likes the pheasant's wing, and one the leg;
The vulgar boil, the learned roast an egg.   85
Hard task! to hit the palate of such guests,
When Oldfield loves what Dartineuf detests.
    But grant I may relapse, for want of grace,
Again to rhyme: can London be the place?
Who there his Muse, or self, or soul attends,   90
In crowds and courts, law, business, feasts, and friends?
My counsel sends to execute a deed:
A poet begs me I will hear him read:
In Palace Yard at nine you'll find me there—
At ten for certain, sir, in Bloomsbury Square—   95
Before the Lords at twelve my cause comes on—
There's a rehearsal, sir, exact at one,—
"Oh, but a wit can study in the streets,
"And raise his mind above the mob he meets."
Not quite so well, however, as one ought;   100
A hackney-coach may chance to spoil a thought;
And then a nodding beam, or pig of lead,
God knows, may hurt the very ablest head.
Have you not seen, at Guildhall's narrow pass,
Two aldermen dispute it with an ass?   105
And peers give away, exalted as they are,
Even to their own S-r-v--nce in a car?
    Go, lofty poet! and, in such a crowd,
Sing thy sonorous verse—but not aloud.
Alas! to grottoes and to groves we run,   110
To ease and silence, every Muse's son:

[1] Dr. Monroe, physician to Bedlam Hospital.

Blackmore himself, for any grand effort,
Would drink and doze at Tooting or Earl's Court.[1]
How shall I rhyme in this eternal roar?
How match the bards whom none e'er match'd before? 115
 The man, who, stretch'd in Isis' calm retreat,
To books and study gives seven years complete,
See! strow'd with learned dust, his nightcap on,
He walks, an object new beneath the sun!
The boys flock round him, and the people stare: 120
So stiff, so mute! some statue you would swear,
Stepp'd from its pedestal to take the air!
And here, while town, and court, and city roars,
With mobs, and duns, and soldiers, at their doors!
Shall I, in London, act this idle part?
Composing songs, for fools to get by heart? 125
 The Temple late two brother serjeants saw,
Who deem'd each other oracles of law;
With equal talents, these congenials souls,
One lull'd the Exchequer, and one stunn'd the Rolls; 130
Each had a gravity would make you split,
And shook his head at Murray, as a wit.
'Twas, "Sir, your law"—and "Sir, your eloquence,"
"Yours, Cowper's manner—and yours Talbot's sense."
 Thus we dispose of all poetic merit, 135
Yours Milton's genius, and mine Homer's spirit.
Call Tibbald Shakespeare, and he'll swear the Nine,
Dear Cibber! never match'd one ode of thine.
Lord! how we strut through Merlin's Cave, to see
No poets there, but, Stephen, you and me. 140
Walk with respect behind, while we at ease
Weave laurel crowns, and take what names we please.
"My dear Tibullus!" if that will not do,
"Let me be Horace, and be Ovid you:
Or, I'm content, allow me Dryden's strains, 145
And you shall rise up Otway for your pains."
Much do I suffer, much, to keep in peace
This jealous, waspish, wrong-head, rhyming race;
And much must flatter, if the whim should bite
To court applause by printing what I write: 150
But let the fit pass o'er, I'm wise enough
To stop my ears to their confounded stuff.
 In vain bad rhymers all mankind reject,

---

[1] Then rural resorts.

They treat themselves with most profound respect;
'Tis to small purpose that you hold your tongue,					155
Each, praised within, is happy all day long:
But how severely with themselves proceed
The men, who write such verse as we can read!
Their own strict judges, not a word they spare,
That wants or force, or light, or weight, or care,					160
Howe'er unwillingly it quits its place,
Nay though at Court (perhaps) it may find grace:
Such they'll degrade; and sometimes, in its stead,
In downright charity revive the dead;
Mark where a bold expressive phrase appears,					165
Bright through the rubbish of some hundred years;
Command old words, that long have slept, to wake,
Words that wise Bacon or brave Raleigh spake;
Or bid the new be English, ages hence
(For use will father what's begot by sense),					170
Pour the full tide of eloquence along,
Serenely pure, and yet divinely strong,
Rich with the treasures of each foreign tongue;
Prune the luxuriant, the uncouth refine,
But show no mercy to an empty line;					175
Then polish all, with so much life and ease,
You think 'tis Nature, and a knack to please:
"But ease in writing flows from art, not chance;
As those move easiest who have learn'd to dance." [1]
	If such the plague and pains to write by rule,					180
Better (say I) be pleased, and play the fool;
Call, if you will, bad rhyming a disease,
It gives men happiness, or leaves them ease.
There lived *in primo Georgii* (they record)
A worthy member, no small fool, a lord;					185
Who, though the House was up, delighted sate,
Heard, noted, answer'd, as in full debate:
In all but this, a man of sober life,
Fond of his friend, and civil to his wife;
Not quite a madman, though a pasty fell,					190
And much too wise to walk into a well.
Him, the damn'd doctors and his friends immured,
They bled, they cupp'd, they purged; in short, they cured:
Whereat the gentleman began to stare—
"My friends!" he cried, "pox take you for your care!					195

	[1] Lines 362-3 in the *Essay on Criticism*, slightly altered.

That, from a patriot of distinguish'd note,
Have bled and purged me to a simple vote."
　Well, on the whole, plain prose must be my fate:
Wisdom (curse on it!) will come soon or late.
There is a time when poets will grow dull: 200
I'll e'en leave verses to the boys at school:
To rules of poetry no more confined,
I'll learn to smooth and harmonise my mind,
Teach every thought within its bounds to roll,
And keep the equal measure of the soul. 205
　Soon as I enter at my country door,
My mind resumes the thread it dropp'd before·
Thoughts, which at Hyde Park Corner I forgot,
Meet, and rejoin me, in the pensive grot.
There all alone, and compliments apart, 210
I ask these sober questions of my heart:
　If, when the more you drink, the more you crave,
You tell the doctor; when the more you have,
The more you want, why not with equal ease
Confess as well your folly, as disease? 215
The heart resolves this matter in a trice,
"Men only feel the smart, but not the vice."
　When golden angels cease to cure the evil:
You give all royal witchcraft to the devil:
When servile chaplains [1] cry, that birth and place 220
Endue a peer with honour, truth, and grace,
Look in that breast, most dirty D——! be fair,[2]
Say, can you find out one such lodger there?
Yet still, not heeding what your art can teach,
You go to church to hear these flatterers preach. 225
　Indeed, could wealth bestow or wit or merit,
A grain of courage, or a spark of spirit,
The wisest man might blush, I must agree,
If D—— loved sixpence more than he.[3]

[1] Dr. White Kennet had made a fulsome dedication of one of his works to the Duke of Devonshire, through whose influence he was made Dean of Peterborough. In 1718 he was promoted to the bishopric of Peterborough, which he held till his death in 1728. He had written against Atterbury on the subject of the Convocation, and he had seceded from the Tory party to join the Whigs. Dr. Walton, the rector of Whitechapel, put up a painting of the Last Supper as an altar-piece in his church, and Dr. Kennet was represented in the character of Judas!

[2] The "dirty D——" was the Duke of Devonshire—William, the third duke, a staunch Whig, of whom Horace Walpole said, "the Duke's outside was unpolished, his inside unpolishable."

[3] Devonshire, the duke previously alluded to.

If there be truth in law, and use can give 230
A property, that's yours on which you live.
Delightful Abbs Court,[1] if its fields afford
Their fruits to you, confesses you its lord:
All Worldly's hens, nay, partridge, sold to town,
His venison too, a guinea makes your own: 235
He bought at thousands, what with better wit
You purchase as you want, and bit by bit;
Now, or long since, what difference will be found?
You pay a penny, and he paid a pound.

    Heathcote himself, and such large-acred men,[2] 240
Lords of fat E'sham, or of Lincoln Fen,
Buy every stick of wood that finds them heat;
Buy every pullet they afford to eat;
Yet these are wights who fondly call their own
Half that the devil o'erlooks from Lincoln town. 245
The laws of God, as well as of the land,
Abhor a perpetuity should stand:
Estates have wings, and hang in Fortune's power
Loose on the point of every wavering hour:
Ready, by force, or of your own accord, 250
By sale, at least by death, to change their lord.
Man? and for ever? wretch! what wouldst thou have?
Heir urges heir, like wave impelling wave.
All vast possessions (just the same the case
Whether you call them villa, park, or chase), 255
Alas, my Bathurst! what will they avail?
Join Cotswood hills to Saperton's fair dale,
Let rising granaries and temples here,
There mingled farms and pyramids appear,
Link towns to towns with avenues of oak, 260
Enclose whole downs in walls,—'tis all a joke!
Inexorable Death shall level all,
And trees, and stones, and farms, and farmer fall.

    Gold, silver, ivory, vases sculptured high,
Paint, marble, gems, and robes of Persian dye, 265
There are who have not—and thank Heaven there are,
Who, if they have not, think not worth their care.
    Talk what you will of taste, my friend, you'll find
Two of a face, as soon as of a mind.

---

[1] Abbs Court, near Hampton Court. The "Worldly" mentioned in the next couplet was probably Edward Wortley Montagu.
[2] Sir Gilbert Heathcote.

Why, of two brothers, rich and restless one   270
Ploughs, burns, manures, and toils from sun to sun;
The other slights, for women, sports, and wines,
All Townshend's turnips,[1] and all Grosvenor's mines:
Why one like Bu—— with pay and scorn content,[2]
Bows and votes on, in Court and Parliament;   275
One, driven by strong benevolence of soul,
Shall fly, like Oglethorpe, from pole to pole:[3]
Is known alone to that Directing Power
Who forms the genius in the natal hour;
That God of Nature, who, within us still,   280
Inclines our action, not constrains our will;
Various of temper, as of face or frame,
Each individual: his great end the same.

    Yes, sir, how small soever be my heap,
A part I will enjoy, as well as keep;   285
My heir may sigh, and think it want of grace
A man so poor would live without a place:
But sure no statute in his favour says,
How free, or frugal, I shall pass my days:[4]
I, who at sometimes spend, at others spare,   290
Divided between carelessness and care.
'Tis one thing madly to disperse my store;
Another, not to heed to treasure more;

[1] Charles, second Viscount Townshend, Secretary of State to George the First and Second, who, when he retired from business, amused himself in husbandry, and was particularly fond of that kind of rural improvement which arises from turnips; it was the favourite subject of his conversation.
[2] " Bu——," Bubb Dodington, afterwards Lord Melcombe.
[3] Employed in settling the colony of Georgia.
    General Oglethorpe was a remarkable man. He had served under Prince Eugene, and in 1733 he entered upon those services for founding the colony of Georgia which the poet has so finely commemorated. The two eminent brothers, John and Samuel Wesley, accompanied him to Georgia. He returned in 1734, bringing some Indian chiefs with him; and two years afterwards he repaired again to Georgia, accompanied by a second body of emigrants. The war with Spain threatened the destruction of the colony, but Oglethorpe repelled the Spaniards, though he was unsuccessful in an expedition he made against St. Augustin. On his return to England he was employed against the followers of Charles Edward in Scotland, in 1745. He could not come up with them, and was tried for neglect of duty, but acquitted. The circumstance that Oglethorpe was a decided Jacobite perhaps led to this slur on his military character, as it led to subsequent neglect on the part of the court and ministry. The general, however, was repaid by the praises of Pope, Thomson and Dr. Johnson, and by the regard which his amiable character and intelligence inspired. He died in 1785.
    Alluding to the statutes made in England and Ireland to regulate the succession of Papists, etc.

Glad, like a boy, to snatch the first good day,
And pleased, if sordid want be far away.   295
   What is't to me (a passenger, God wot),
Whether my vessel be first-rate or not?
The ship itself may make a better figure,
But I that sail am neither less nor bigger;
I neither strut with every favouring breath,   300
Nor strive with all the tempest in my teeth.
In power, wit, figure, virtue, fortune, placed
Behind the foremost, and before the last.
   "But why all this of avarice? I have none."
I wish you joy, sir, of a tyrant gone;   305
But does no other lord it at this hour,
As wild and mad? the avarice of power?
Does neither rage inflame, nor fear appal?
Not the black fear of death, that saddens all?
With terrors round, can reason hold her throne,   310
Despise the known, nor tremble at the unknown?
Survey both worlds, intrepid and entire,
In spite of witches, devils, dreams, and fire?
Pleased to look forward, pleased to look behind,
And count each birthday with a grateful mind?   315
Has life no sourness, drawn so near its end?
Canst thou endure a foe, forgive a friend?
Has age but melted the rough parts away,
As winter fruits grow mild ere they decay?
Or will you think, my friend, your business done,   320
When, of a hundred thorns, you pull out one?
   Learn to live well, or fairly make your will;
You've play'd, and loved, and eat, and drunk your fill:
Walk sober off, before a sprightlier age
Comes tittering on, and shoves you from the stage: 325
Leave such to trifle, with more grace and ease,
Whom folly pleases, and whose follies please.

THE SATIRES OF DR. JOHN DONNE, DEAN OF ST. PAUL'S, VERSIFIED

> Quid vetat et nosmet Lucili scripta legentes
> Quærere, num illius, num rerum dura negârit
> Versiculos natura magis factos, et euntes
> Mollius?—HORACE.

> [What then forbids our equal right to know
> Why his own verses inharmonious flow?
> Or whether in his subject lies the fault,
> Or in himself, that they're not higher wrought.
>
> FRANCIS.]

The recent revival of interest in the metaphysical poets makes unnecessary any note on Dr. John Donne. In the Augustan age, the notion that satire should be rough, was replaced by the notion that it should be as scrupulously written as any other kind of poetry. Dryden had asked: "Would not Donne's *Satires*, which abound with so much wit, appear more charming, if he had taken care of his words, and of his numbers?" Pope puts the suggestion to the test.

Sir, though (I thank God for it) I do hate
Perfectly all this town; yet there's one state
In all things so excellently best,
That hate towards them breeds pity towards the rest.
Though poetry, indeed, be such a sin,
As I think, that brings dearth and Spaniards in:
Though, like the pestilence and old-fashioned love,
Ridlingly it catch men, and doth remove
Never, till it be starved out; yet their state
Is poor, disarm'd, like Papists, not worth hate.
One (like a wretch, which at barre judged as dead,
Yet prompts him which stands next, and cannot read,
And saves his life) gives idiot-actors means
(Starving himself) to live by 's laboured scenes:
As in some organs puppets dance above,
And bellows pant below which them do move,
One would move love by rhymes; but witchcraft's charms
Bring not now their old fears, nor their old harms;
Rams and slings now are silly battery,
Pistolets are the best artillery;
And they who write to lords, rewards to get,
Are they not like singers at doors for meat?
And they who write, because all write, have still
That 'scuse for writing, and writing ill.

SATIRE II

YES, thank my stars! as early as I knew
This town, I had the sense to hate it too:
Yet here, as e'en in Hell, there must be still
One giant-vice, so excellently ill,

That all beside, one pities, not abhors;   5
As who knows Sappho, smiles at other whores.
   I grant that poetry's a crying sin;
It brought (no doubt) the Excise and Army in:
Catch'd like the plague, or love, the Lord knows how,
But that the cure is starving, all allow.   10
Yet like the Papist's is the poet's state,
Poor and disarm'd, and hardly worth your hate.
   Here a lean bard, whose wit could never give
Himself a dinner, makes an actor live:
The thief condemn'd, in law already dead,   15
So prompts, and saves a rogue who cannot read.
Thus as the pipes of some carved organ move,
The gilded puppets dance and mount above.
Heaved by the breath the inspiring bellows blow:
The inspiring bellows lie and pant below.   20
   One sings the fair: but songs no longer move;
No rat is rhymed to death, nor maid to love:
In love's, in Nature's spite, the siege they hold,
And scorn the flesh, the devil, and all—but gold.
   These write to lords, some mean reward to get,   25
As needy beggars sing at doors for meat.
Those write because all write, and so have still
Excuse for writing, and for writing ill.
   Wretched indeed! but far more wretched yet
Is he who makes his meal on others' wit: 30
'Tis changed, no doubt, from what it was before;
His rank digestion makes it wit no more:
Sense, pass'd through him, no longer is the same;
For food digested takes another name.
   I pass o'er all those confessors and martyrs,   35
Who live like S—tt—n,[1] or who die like Chartres,
Out-cant old Esdras, or out-drink his heir,
Out-usure Jews, or Irishmen out-swear;
Wicked as pages, who in early years
Act sins which Prisca's confessor scarce hears.   40
E'en those I pardon, for whose sinful sake
Schoolmen new tenements in Hell must make;
Of whose strange crimes no canonist can tell
In what commandment's large contents they dwell.

---

[1] General Sir Richard Sutton. Though he had once supported Boling-
broke, he later followed Walpole. He was known as "Satan, Governor of
Hell," and was, Egmont says, "an atheistical, debauched man."

One, one man only, breeds my just offence; 45
Whom crimes gave wealth, and wealth gave impudence:
Time, that at last matures a clap to pox,
Whose gentle progress makes a calf an ox,
And brings all natural events to pass,
Hath made him an attorney of an ass. 50
No young divine, new-beneficed, can be
More pert, more proud, more positive than he.
What further could I wish the fop to do,
But turn a wit, and scribble verses too?
Pierce the soft labyrinth of a lady's ear 55
With rhymes of this per cent. and that per year?
Or court a wife, spread out his wily parts,
Like nets or lime-twigs, for rich widows' hearts;
Call himself barrister to every wench,
And woo in language of the Pleas and Bench? 60
Language which Boreas might to Auster hold,
More rough than forty Germans when they scold.
    Cursed be the wretch, so venal and so vain:
Paltry and proud, as drabs in Drury Lane.
'Tis such a bounty as was never known, 65
If Peter deigns to help you to your own:[1]
What thanks, what praise, if Peter but supplies!
And what a solemn face, if he denies!
Grave, as when prisoners shake the head and swear
'Twas only suretyship that brought 'em there. 70
His office keeps your parchment fates entire,
He starves with cold to save them from the fire;
For you he walks the streets through rain or dust,
For not in chariots Peter puts his trust;
For you he sweats and labours at the laws, 75
Takes God to witness he affects your cause,
And lies to every lord in every thing,
Like a king's favourite, or like a king.
These are the talents that adorn them all,
From wicked Waters e'en to godly * *.[2] 80
Not more of simony beneath black gowns,
Not more of bastardy in heirs to crowns.
In shillings and in pence at first they deal;
And steal so little, few perceive they steal;

[1] Peter Walter, whose name occurs so often in Pope's satires.
[2] Paul Foley, whom Macaulay describes as a lawyer "of spotless integrity and munificent charity."

Till, like the sea, they compass all the land,　　　　85
From Scots to Wight, from Mount to Dover strand:
And when rank widows purchase luscious nights,
Or when a duke to Jansen punts at White's,
Or city heir in mortgage melts away;
Satan himself feels far less joy than they.　　　　90
Piecemeal they win this acre first, then that,
Glean on, and gather up the whole estate.
Then, strongly fencing ill-got wealth by law,
Indentures, covenants, articles they draw,
Large as the fields themselves, and larger far　　　　95
Than civil codes, with all their glosses, are;
So vast, our new divines, we must confess,
Are fathers of the Church for writing less.
But let them write for you, each rogue impairs
The deeds, and dexterously omits, *ses heires*:　　　　100
No commentator can more slily pass
O'er a learn'd, unintelligible place:
Or, in quotation, shrewd divines leave out
Those words that would against them clear the doubt.

So Luther thought the Paternoster long,　　　　105
When doom'd to say his beads and even-song;
But, having cast his cowl, and left those laws,
Adds to Christ's prayer, the power and glory clause.[1]

The lands are bought; but where are to be found
Those ancient woods, that shaded all the ground?　　　　110
We see no new-built palaces aspire,
No kitchens emulate the vestal fire.
Where are those troops of poor, that throng'd of yore
The good old landlord's hospitable door?
Well, I could wish, that still in lordly domes　　　　115
Some beasts were kill'd, though not whole hecatombs;
That both extremes were banish'd from their walls,
Carthusian fasts, and fulsome Bacchanals;
And all mankind might that just mean observe,
In which none e'er could surfeit, none could starve.　　　　120
These, as good works, 'tis true we all allow,
But oh! these works are not in fashion now:
Like rich old wardrobes, things extremely rare,
Extremely fine, but what no man will wear.

Thus much I've said, I trust, without offence;　　　　125

[1] The doxology to the Lord's Prayer, Matthew vi. 13, has been pronounced spurious by biblical critics.

Let no Court sycophant pervert my sense,
Nor sly informer watch these words to draw
Within the reach of treason, or the law.

SATIRE IV

WELL, if it be my time to quit the stage,
Adieu to all the follies of the age!
I die in charity with fool and knave,
Secure of peace at least beyond the grave.
I've had my purgatory here betimes,   5
And paid for all my satires, all my rhymes.
The poet's Hell, its tortures, fiends, and flames,
To this were trifles, toys and empty names.
  With foolish pride my heart was never fired,
Nor the vain itch to admire, or be admired;   10
I hoped for no commission from his grace;
I bought no benefice, I begg'd no place:
Had no new verses, nor new suit to show;
Yet went to Court! the devil would have it so.
But, as the fool that in reforming days   15
Would go to Mass in jest (as story says)
Could not but think, to pay his fine was odd,
Since 'twas no form'd design of serving God;
So was I punish'd, as if full as proud,
As prone to ill, as negligent of good,   20
As deep in debt, without a thought to pay,
As vain, as idle, and as false, as they
Who live at Court, for going once that way!
Scarce was I enter'd, when, behold! there came
A thing which Adam had been posed to name;   25
Noah had refused it lodging in his ark,
Where all the race of reptiles might embark:
A verier monster than on Afric's shore
The sun e'er got, or slimy Nilus bore,
Or Sloane or Woodward's wondrous shelves contain,   30
Nay, all that lying travellers can feign.
The watch would hardly let him pass at noon;
At night would swear him dropp'd out of the moon.
One, whom the mob, when next we find or make
A Popish plot, shall for a Jesuit take,   35

And the wise justice starting from his chair
Cry, " By your priesthood tell me what you are? "
　　Such was the wight: The apparel on his back,
Though coarse, was reverend, and though bare, was black:
The suit, if by the fashion one might guess,　　　　　40
Was velvet in the youth of good Queen Bess,
But mere tuff-taffety what now remain'd;
So time, that changes all things, had ordain'd!
Our sons shall see it leisurely decay,
First turn plain rash, then vanish quite away.　　　　45
　　This thing has travell'd, speaks each language too,
And knows what's fit for every state to do;
Of whose best phrase and courtly accent join'd,
He forms one tongue, exotic and refined.
Talkers I've learn'd to bear; Motteux I knew,　　　　50
Henley himself I've heard, and Budgell too.
The Doctor's wormwood style, the hash of tongues
A pedant makes, the storm of Gonson's lungs,
The whole artillery of the terms of war,
And (all those plagues in one) the bawling Bar;　　　55
These I could bear; but not a rogue so civil,
Whose tongue will compliment you to the devil.
A tongue that can cheat widows, cancel scores,
Make Scots speak treason, cozen subtlest whores,
With royal favourites in flattery vie,　　　　　　　60
And Oldmixon and Burnet both outlie.
　　He spies me out; I whisper, Gracious God!
What sin of mine could merit such a rod?
That all the shot of dulness now must be
From this thy blunderbuss discharged on me!　　　65
Permit (he cries) no stranger to your fame
To crave your sentiment, if ——'s your name.
What speech esteem you most? "The King's," said I.
But the best words? "O, sir, the Dictionary."
You miss my aim; I mean the most acute　　　　　70
And perfect speaker? "Onslow, past dispute."
But, sir, of writers? "Swift, for closer style;
But Ho * * y for a period of a mile." [1]
Why yes, 'tis granted, these indeed may pass:
Good common linguists, and so Panurge was;　　　75
Nay troth, the Apostles (though perhaps too rough)
Had once a pretty gift of tongues enough:

[1] Bishop Hoadley.

Yet these were all poor gentlemen! I dare
Affirm, 'twas travel made them what they were.
    Thus others' talents having nicely shown,   80
He came, by sure transition, to his own:
Till I cried out, " You prove yourself so able,
Pity you was not druggerman at Babel;
For had they found a linguist half so good,
I make no question but the tower had stood."   85
    "Obliging sir! for Courts you sure were made:
Why then for ever buried in the shade?
Spirits like you should see and should be seen,
The king would smile on you—at least the queen."
Ah, gentle sir! you courtiers so cajole us—   90
But Tully has it, *Nunquam minus solus*:
And as for Courts, forgive me, if I say
No lessons now are taught the Spartan way:
Though in his pictures lust be full display'd,
Few are the converts Aretine has made;   95
And though the Court show vice exceeding clear,
None should, by my advice, learn virtue there.
    At this, entranced, he lifts his hands and eyes,
Squeaks, like a high-stretch'd lute-string, and replies:
"Oh, 'tis the sweetest of all earthly things   100
To gaze on princes, and to talk of kings!"
Then, happy man, who shows the tombs! said I,
He dwells amidst the royal family;
He every day from king to king can walk,
Of all our Harries, all our Edwards talk.   105
And get, by speaking truth of monarchs dead,
What few can of the living, ease and bread.
"Lord, sir, a mere mechanic! strangely low,
And coarse of phrase,—your English all are so.
How elegant your Frenchmen!" Mine, d'ye mean?   110
I have but one, I hope the fellow's clean.
"Oh, sir, politely so! nay, let me die:
Your only wearing is your paduasoy."
Not, sir, my only, I have better still,
And this, you see, is but my dishabille.—   115
Wild to get loose, his patience I provoke,
Mistake, confound, object at all he spoke.
But as coarse iron, sharpen'd, mangles more,
And itch most hurts when anger'd to a sore:
So when you plague a fool, 'tis still the curse,   120

You only make the matter worse and worse.
　He pass'd it o'er; affects an easy smile
At all my peevishness, and turns his style.
He asks, "What news?" I tell him of new plays,
New eunuchs, harlequins, and operas.　　　　125
He hears, and as a still with simples in it,
Between each drop it gives, stays half a minute,
Loth to enrich me with too quick replies,
By little, and by little, drops his lies.
Mere household trash! of birthnights, balls, and shows, 130
More than ten Hollinsheds, or Halls, or Stowes.
When the queen frown'd, or smiled, he knows; and what
A subtle minister may make of that:
Who sins with whom: who got his pension rug,
Or quicken'd a reversion by a drug:　　　　135
Whose place is quarter'd out, three parts in four,
And whether to a bishop, or a whore:
Who, having lost his credit, pawn'd his rent,
Is therefore fit to have a government:
Who, in the secret, deals in stocks secure,　　　140
And cheats the unknowing widow and the poor:
Who makes a trust or charity a job,
And gets an Act of Parliament to rob:
Why turnpikes rise, and now no cit nor clown
Can gratis see the country or the town:　　　145
Shortly no lad shall chuck, or lady vole,
But some excising courtier will have toll.
He tells what strumpet places sells for life,
What 'squire his lands, what citizen his wife:
At last (which proves him wiser still than all)　　150
What lady's face is not a whited wall.
　As one of Woodward's patients, sick and sore,
I puke, I nauseate,—yet he thrusts in more:
Trims Europe's balance, tops the statesman's part,
And talks Gazettes and Postboys o'er by heart.　155
Like a big wife at sight of loathsome meat
Ready to cast, I yawn, I sigh, and sweat.
Then, as a licensed spy, whom nothing can
Silence or hurt, he libels the great man;
Swears every place entail'd for years to come,　　160
In sure succession, to the day of doom:
He names the price for every office paid,
And says our wars thrive ill, because delay'd:

Nay hints, 'tis by connivance of the Court,
That Spain robs on, and Dunkirk's still a port.   165
Not more amazement seized on Circe's guests,
To see themselves fall endlong into beasts,
Than mine to find a subject, staid and wise,
Already half turn'd traitor by surprise.
I felt the infection slide from him to me,   170
As in the pox some give it to get free;
And quick to swallow me, methought I saw
One of our giant statues ope its jaw.

In that nice moment, as another lie
Stood just a-tilt, the minister came by.   175
To him he flies, and bows, and bows again,
Then, close as Umbra, joins the dirty train
Not Fannius' self more impudently near,
When half his nose is in his prince's ear.[1]
I quaked at heart; and still afraid, to see   180
All the Court fill'd with stranger things than he,
Ran out as fast as one that pays his bail,
And dreads more actions, hurries from a jail.

Bear me, some god! oh quickly bear me hence
To wholesome solitude, the nurse of sense: 185
Where Contemplation prunes her ruffled wings,[2]
And the free soul looks down to pity kings!
There sober thought pursued the amusing theme,
Till fancy colour'd it, and form'd a dream.
A vision hermits can to Hell transport,   190
And forced e'en me to see the damn'd at Court.
Not Dante dreaming all the infernal state,
Beheld such scenes of envy, sin, and hate.
Base fear becomes the guilty, not the free;
Suits tyrants, plunderers, but suits not me: 195
Shall I, the terror of this sinful town,
Care if a liveried lord or smile or frown?
Who cannot flatter, and detest who can,
Tremble before a noble serving-man?
O my fair mistress, Truth! shall I quit thee   200
For huffing, braggart, puff'd nobility?
Thou, who since yesterday, hast roll'd o'er all
The busy, idle blockheads of the ball,
Hast thou, oh Sun! beheld an emptier sort,

[1] Lord *Fanny*, or Hervey, whispering gossip or scandal at court.
[2] From Milton's *Comus*.

Than such as swell this bladder of a Court?   205
Now pox on those who show a Court in wax![1]
It ought to bring all courtiers on their backs:
Such painted puppets! such a varnish'd race
Of hollow gewgaws, only dress and face!
Such waxen noses, stately, staring things—   210
No wonder some folks bow, and think them kings.

See! where the British youth, engaged no more
At Fig's, at White's, with felons, or a whore,[2]
Pay their last duty to the Court, and come
All fresh and fragrant to the drawing-room;   215
In hues as gay, and odours as divine,
As the fair fields they sold to look so fine.
"That's velvet for a king!" the flatterer swears;
'Tis true, for ten days hence 'twill be King Lear's.
Our Court may justly to our stage give rules,   220
That helps it both to fools' coats and to fools,
And why not players strut in courtiers' clothes?
For these are actors, too, as well as those:
Wants reach all states; they beg, but better dress'd,
And all is splendid poverty at best.   225

Painted for sight, and essenced for the smell,
Like frigates fraught with spice and cochineal,
Sail in the ladies: how each pirate eyes
So weak a vessel, and so rich a prize!
Top-gallant he, and she in all her trim,   230
He boarding her, she striking sail to him:
"Dear Countess! you have charms all hearts to hit!"
And "Sweet Sir Fopling! you have so much wit!"
Such wits and beauties are not praised for nought,
For both the beauty and the wit are bought.   235
'Twould burst e'en Heraclitus with the spleen,
To see those antics, Fopling and Courtin:
The presence seems, with things so richly odd,
The mosque of Mahound, or some queer pagod.
See them survey their limbs by Dürer's rules,[3]   240
Of all beau-kind the best proportion'd fools!
Adjust their clothes, and to confession draw

---

[1] A famous show of the court of France in waxwork.
[2] White's was a noted gaming-house: Fig's, a prize-fighter's academy, where the young nobility received instruction in those days: it was also customary for the nobility and gentry to visit the condemned criminals in Newgate.
[3] Albrecht Dürer.

Those venial sins, an atom, or a straw;
But oh! what terrors must distract the soul,
Convicted of that mortal crime, a hole;   245
Or should one pound of powder less bespread
Those monkey-tails that wag behind their head,
Thus finish'd, and corrected to a hair,
They march, to prate their hour before the fair,
So first to preach a white-gloved chaplain goes,   250
With band of lily, and with cheek of rose,
Sweeter than Sharon, in immaculate trim,
Neatness itself impertinent in him.
Let but the ladies smile, and they are blest:
Prodigious! how the things protest, protest: 255
Peace, fools, or Gonson will for Papists seize you,
If once he catch you at your Jesu! Jesu!
   Nature made every fop to plague his brother,
Just as one beauty mortifies another.
But here's the captain, that will plague them both,   260
Whose air cries, " Arm!" whose very look's an oath:
The captain's honest, sirs, and that's enough,
Though his soul's bullet, and his body buff.
He spits fore-right; his haughty chest before,
Like battering rams, beats open every door: 265
And with a face as red, and as awry,
As Herod's hangdogs in old tapestry,
Scarecrow to boys, the breeding woman's curse,
Has yet a strange ambition to look worse:
Confounds the civil; keeps the rude in awe;   270
Jests like a licensed fool, commands like law,
   Frighted, I quit the room; but leave it so
As men from jails to execution go;
For, hung with deadly sins, I see the wall,[1]
And lined with giants deadlier than 'em all;   275
Each man an Askapart,[2] of strength to toss
For quoits, both Temple Bar and Charing Cross,
Scared at the grisly forms. I sweat, I fly,
And shake all o'er like a discovered spy.
   Courts are too much for wits so weak as mine: 280
Charge them with Heaven's artillery, bold divine!
From such alone the great rebukes endure,
Whose satire's sacred, and whose rage secure:

---

[1] The room hung with old tapestry representing the seven deadly sins.
[2] A giant famous in romances.

'Tis mine to wash a few light stains, but theirs
To deluge sin, and drown a Court in tears.   285
Howe'er, what's now Apocrypha, my wit,
In time to come, may pass for Holy Writ.

EPILOGUE TO THE SATIRES

IN TWO DIALOGUES

WRITTEN IN MDCCXXXVIII

And published separately the same year, the first under the title
of " One Thousand Seven Hundred and Thirty-eight; a Dialogue
something like Horace."

DIALOGUE I

Fr. NOT twice a twelvemonth you appear in print,[1]
And when it comes, the Court see nothing in 't.
You grow correct, that once with rapture writ,
And are, besides, too moral for a wit.
Decay of parts, alas! we all must feel!   5
Why now, this moment, don't I see you steal?
'Tis all from Horace; Horace long before ye
Said, "Tories call'd him Whig, and Whigs a Tory";
And taught his Romans, in much better metre,
"To laugh at fools who put their trust in Peter."   10
  But Horace, sir, was delicate, was nice;
Bubo observes, he lash'd no sort of vice:[2]
Horace would say, Sir Billy served the Crown,
Blunt could do business, H–ggins knew the town;[3]
In Sappho touch the failings of the sex,   15
In reverend bishops note some small neglects,
And own the Spaniard did a waggish thing,
Who cropp'd our ears, and sent them to the king.[4]

[1] These two lines are from Horace: and the only lines that are so in the whole poem; being meant to give a handle to that which follows in the character of an impertinent censurer: " 'Tis all from Horace," etc.

[2] Some guilty persons very fond, like Bubb Dodington, of making such observations.

[3] Huggins was warden of the Fleet Prison, who let the jail to the notorious jailer Thomas Baimbridge, whose gross abuse of his office at length led to inquiry, and who was subsequently expelled and committed to Newgate. Huggins was also deprived of his patent.

[4] Said to be executed by the captain of a Spanish ship on one Jenkins, a captain of an English one.

His sly, polite, insinuating style
Could please at Court, and make Augustus smile: 20
An artful manager, that crept between
His friend and shame, and was a kind of screen.
But 'faith your very friends will soon be sore;
Patriots there are, who wish you'd jest no more—¹
And where's the glory? 'twill be only thought   25
The great man ² never offer'd you a groat.
Go see Sir ROBERT!—³
        P. See Sir ROBERT!—hum—
And never laugh—for all my life to come?
Seen him I have, but in his happier hour
Of social pleasure, ill-exchanged for power;   30
Seen him, uncumber'd with a venal tribe,
Smile without art, and win without a bribe.
Would he oblige me? let me only find,
He does not think me what he thinks mankind.
Come, come, at all I laugh he laughs, no doubt;   35
The only difference is, I dare laugh out.
    F. Why, yes: with Scripture still you may be free;
A horse-laugh, if you please, at Honesty;
A joke on Jekyl,⁴ or some odd old Whig
Who never changed his principle or wig;   40
A patriot is a fool in every age,
Whom all Lord Chamberlains allow the stage:
These nothing hurts; they keep their fashion still,
And wear their strange old virtue, as they will.
    If any ask you, "Who's the man, so near   45
His prince, that writes in verse, and has his ear?"
Why answer, Lyttelton,⁵ and I'll engage
The worthy youth shall ne'er be in a rage:
But were his verses vile, his whisper base,
You'd quickly find him in Lord Fanny's case.⁶   50

¹ This appellation was generally given to those in opposition to the court. Opposite the word "patriots," Lord Marchmont, Pope's friend and executor, wrote "Carteret and Pulteney." See *Marchmont Papers.*
² A phrase, by common use, appropriated to the first minister.
³ Sir Robert Walpole. He was created Earl of Orford in 1742, and died 18th March, 1745, aged sixty-nine.
⁴ Sir Joseph Jekyll, Master of the Rolls. Died a few months after the publication of this poem.
⁵ George Lyttelton, Secretary to the Prince of Wales.
⁶ Lord *Fanny*—Lord Hervey—was then Vice-Chamberlain to the king.

Sejanus, Wolsey,[1] hurt not honest Fleury,[2]
But well may put some statesmen in a fury.
    Laugh then at any, but at fools or foes;
These you but anger, and you mend not those.
Laugh at your friends, and, if your friends are sore,   55
So much the better, you may laugh the more.
To vice and folly to confine the jest,
Sets half the world, God knows, against the rest;
Did not the sneer of more impartial men
At sense and virtue balance all again.   60
Judicious wits spread wide the ridicule,
And charitably comfort knave and fool.
    P. Dear sir, forgive the prejudice of youth:
Adieu distinction, satire, warmth, and truth!
Come, harmless characters, that no one hit;   65
Come, Henley's oratory, Osborne's wit![3]
The honey dropping from Favonio's tongue,
The flowers of Bubo, and the flow of Y—ng![4]
The gracious dew of pulpit eloquence,
And all the well-whipt cream of courtly sense,   70
That first was H—vy's, F—'s next, and then
The S—te's, and then H—vy's once again.[5]
O come, that easy, Ciceronian style,
So Latin, yet so English all the while,
As, though the pride of Middleton and Bland,   75
All boys may read, and girls may understand!
Then might I sing, without the least offence,
And all I sung should be the nation's sense;
Or teach the melancholy Muse to mourn,
Hang the sad verse on Carolina's urn,   80

[1] The one the wicked minister of Tiberius, the other of Henry VIII. The writers against the court usually bestowed these and other odious names on the minister.

[2] Cardinal, and Minister to Louis XV. It was a patriot-fashion, at that time, to cry up his wisdom and honesty.

[3] See them in their places in the *Dunciad*.

[4] In the small edition of 1739 (*Works*, vol. ii.) the last name is given " Y——nge," showing that Sir William Yonge, not Dr. Young, the poet and friend of " Bubo," or Dodington, was meant.

[5] Lord Hervey wrote an epitaph, or *éloge*, on Queen Caroline; Mr. H. Fox moved for and drew up the address of the House of Commons to his majesty on their first meeting after the queen's death; Dr. Alured Clarke wrote an essay on the queen's character; and Bishop Gilbert preached at court on the occasion, and was said to cry in his sermon. The caution and prudence of Pope, in the midst of all his satirical allusions, is shown by his not printing even the name of the senate at length.

And hail her passage to the realms of rest,[1]
All parts perform'd, and all her children bless'd!
So—Satire is no more—I feel it die—
No gazetteer more innocent than I—
And let, a-God's name, every fool and knave   85
Be graced through life, and flatter'd in his grave.
   F. Why so? if Satire knows its time and place,
You still may lash the greatest—in disgrace:
For merit will by turns forsake them all;
Would you know when? exactly when they fall.   90
But let all satire in all changes spare
Immortal S—k, and grave De—re.[2]
Silent and soft, as saints removed to Heaven,
All ties dissolved, and every sin forgiven,
These may some gentle ministerial wing   95
Receive, and place for ever near a king!
There, where no passion, pride, or shame transport,
Lull'd with the sweet Nepenthe of a Court,
There, where no father's, brother's, friend's disgrace
Once break their rest, or stir them from their place: 100
But past the sense of human miseries,
All tears are wiped for ever from all eyes;
No cheek is known to blush, no heart to throb,
Save when they lose a question, or a job.
   P. Good Heaven forbid that I should blast their glory,
Who know how like Whig ministers to Tory,   106
And when three sovereigns died, could scarce be vex'd,
Considering what a gracious prince was next.
Have I, in silent wonder, seen such things
As pride in slaves, and avarice in kings;   110
And at a peer, or peeress, shall I fret,
Who starves a sister, or forswears a debt?[3]
Virtue, I grant you, is an empty boast;
But shall the dignity of Vice be lost?
Ye gods! shall Cibber's son, without rebuke,[4]   115
Swear like a lord, or Rich outwhore a duke?

[1] Queen Consort of King George II. Died 1737. Her death gave occasion, as is observed above, to many indiscreet and mean performances unworthy of her memory.

[2] Charles, Earl of Selkirk, died in March 1739; and Lord De La Warr.

[3] Lady Mary Wortley Montagu had £500 a year for supporting her sister, the Countess of Mar, when suffering from mental alienation, and is said to have treated the countess harshly. The "debt" is an allusion to the affair of M. Ruremonde. See *Dunciad* and *Life of Pope*.

[4] See page 153, note 1, and page 157, note 2.

A favourite's porter with his master vie,
Be bribed as often, and as often lie?
Shall Ward draw contracts with a statesman's skill?
Or Japhet pocket, like his grace, a will? [1]   120
Is it for Bond, or Peter (paltry things),
To pay their debts, or keep their faith, like kings?
If Blount dispatch'd himself, he play'd the man, [2]
And so may'st thou, illustrious Passeran! [3]
But shall a printer, weary of his life, [4]   125
Learn, from their books, to hang himself and wife?
This, this, my friend, I cannot, must not bear;
Vice thus abused, demands a nation's care;
This calls the Church to deprecate our sin,
And hurls the thunder of the laws on gin. [5]   130

   Let modest Foster, if he will, excel
Ten Metropolitans in preaching well; [6]
A simple Quaker, or a Quaker's wife, [7]
Outdo Landaff in doctrine,—yea, in life: [8]
Let humble Allen, [9] with an awkward shame,   135
Do good by stealth, and blush to find it fame.
Virtue may choose the high or low degree,
'Tis just alike to virtue, and to me;
Dwell in a monk, or light upon a king,
She's still the same beloved, contented thing.   140
Vice is undone, if she forgets her birth,
And stoops from angels to the dregs of earth:
But 'tis the fall degrades her to a whore;
Let greatness own her, and she's mean no more,

[1] The Archbishop of Canterbury, Dr. Wake, was said to have secreted the will of King George I, for reasons which proved valid.
[2] Author of *The Oracles of Reason*, who shot himself.
[3] Author of another book of the same stamp, called *A Philosophical Discourse on Death*, being a defence of suicide. He was a nobleman of Piedmont, banished from his country.
[4] A fact that happened in London a few years past. The unhappy man left behind him a paper justifying his actions by the reasonings of some of these authors. This case is reported in the *Gentleman's Magazine* for April, 1732.
[5] The exorbitant use of which had almost destroyed the lowest rank of the people, till it was restrained by an Act of Parliament in 1736.
[6] Dr. James Foster, a minister of the Independents, and afterwards a Baptist. He was long a popular preacher in London.
[7] The Quaker's wife was Mrs. Drummond, one of the notabilities of her day. She was actually sister of George Drummond.
[8] A poor bishopric in Wales, as poorly supplied, says Pope. It was then supplied by Dr. John Harris.
[9] Mr. Allen was a man of fortune, and Mayor of Bath. See Pope's Letter to Allen, 28th April, 1738.

Her birth, her beauty, crowds and courts confess,   145
Chaste matrons praise her, and grave bishops bless;
In golden chains the willing world she draws,
And hers the gospel is, and hers the laws,
Mounts the tribunal, lifts her scarlet head,
And sees pale Virtue carted in her stead.   150
Lo! at the wheels of her triumphal car,
Old England's genius, rough with many a scar,
Dragg'd in the dust! his arms hang idly round,
His flag inverted trails along the ground!
Our youth, all liveried o'er with foreign gold,   155
Before her dance: behind her, crawl the old!
See thronging millions to the pagod run,
And offer country, parent, wife, or son!
Hear her black trumpet through the land proclaim,
That NOT TO BE CORRUPTED IS THE SHAME!   160
In soldier, churchman, patriot, man in power,
'Tis avarice all, ambition is no more!
See, all our nobles begging to be slaves!
See, all our fools aspiring to be knaves!
The wit of cheats, the courage of a whore,   165
Are what ten thousand envy and adore:
All, all look up, with reverential awe,
At crimes that 'scape, or triumph o'er the law:
While truth, worth, wisdom, daily they decry—
"Nothing is sacred now but villainy."   170
   Yet may this verse (if such a verse remain)
Show there was one who held it in disdain.

DIALOGUE II

Fr. 'TIS all a libel—Paxton (sir) will say.[1]
   P. Not yet, my friend! to-morrow, 'faith, it may;
And for that very cause I print to-day.
How should I fret to mangle every line,
In reverence to the sins of thirty-nine!
Vice with such giant strides comes on amain,   5

[1] Nicholas Paxton, Solicitor to the Treasury, who died in 1744. Two years before this, Paxton was examined by the Secret Committee appointed to inquire into the conduct of Walpole, then Lord Orford. In eleven years, according to the Committee's Report, Mr. Paxton received £94,000 *unaccounted for*. He refused to answer inquiries respecting a sum of £500 given at Lord Limerick's election, and was committed to Newgate, where he remained from April to July.

Invention strives to be before in vain;
Feign what I will, and paint it e'er so strong,
Some rising genius sins up to my song.

    F. Yet none but you by name the guilty lash;   10
E'en Guthrie [1] saves half Newgate by a dash.
Spare then the person, and expose the vice.

    P. How, sir! not damn the sharper, but the dice?
Come on, then, Satire! general, unconfined,
Spread thy broad wing, and souse on all the kind.   15
Ye statesmen, priests, of one religion all!
Ye tradesmen vile, in army, court, or hall!
Ye reverend atheists.   *F*. Scandal! name them, who?

    P. Why that's the thing you bid me not to do.
Who starved a sister, who forswore a debt,   20
I never named; the town's inquiring yet.
The poisoning dame— *F*. You mean— *P*. I don't— *F*. You do.

    P. See, now I keep the secret, and not you!
The bribing statesman— *F*. Hold, too high you go.

    P. The bribed elector— *F*. There you stoop too low.   25

    P. I fain would please you, if I knew with what;
Tell me, which knave is lawful game, which not?
Must great offenders, once escaped the Crown,
Like royal harts, be never more run down?
Admit your law to spare the knight requires?   30
As beasts of Nature may we hunt the squires?
Suppose I censure—you know what I mean—
To save a bishop, may I name a dean?

    F. A dean, sir? no; his fortune is not made,
You hurt a man that's rising in the trade.   35

    P. If not the tradesman who set up to-day,
Much less the 'prentice who to-morrow may.
Down, down, proud Satire! though a realm be spoil'd,
Arraign no mightier thief than wretched Wild; [2]
Or, if a court or country's made a job,   40
Go drench a pickpocket, and join the mob.

    But, sir, I beg you (for the love of vice!),
The matter's weighty, pray consider twice;
Have you less pity for the needy cheat,
The poor and friendless villain, than the great?   45
Alas! the small discredit of a bribe

[1] The ordinary of Newgate, who published the *Memoirs of the Malefactors*, and was often prevailed upon to be so tender of their reputation as to set down no more than the initials.

[2] Jonathan Wild, a thief and thief-impeacher. Hanged 1725.

Scarce hurts the lawyer, but undoes the scribe,
Then better sure it charity becomes
To tax directors, who (thank God) have plums;
Still better, ministers; or, if the thing   50
May pinch e'en there—why lay it on a king.
    F. Stop! stop!

                P. Must Satire, then, nor rise nor fall?
Speak out, and bid me blame no rogues at all.
    F. Yes, strike that Wild, I'll justify the blow.
    P. Strike? why the man was hang'd ten years ago: 55
Who now that obsolete example fears?
E'en Peter trembles only for his ears.[1]
    F. What, always Peter? Peter thinks you mad,
You make men desperate, if they once are bad:
Else might he take to virtue some years hence—   60
    P. As S——k, if he lives, will love the Prince,
    F. Strange spleen to S——k!

                P. Do I wrong the man?
God knows, I praise a courtier where I can.
When I confess there is who feels for fame,
And melts to goodness, need I Scarborough name?[2]   65
Pleased, let me own, in Esher's peaceful grove[3]
(Where Kent and Nature vie for Pelham's love),
The scene, the master, opening to my view;
I sit and dream I see my Craggs anew!
    E'en in a bishop I can spy desert;   70
Secker is decent, Rundle has a heart,
Manners with candour are to Benson given,
To Berkeley, every virtue under Heaven.[4]
    But does the Court a worthy man remove?

[1] Peter had the year before this narrowly escaped the pillory for forgery, and got off with only a severe rebuke from the bench.
[2] Richard Lumley, second Earl of Scarborough, resigned his post of Master of the Horse in 1733-4. On 4th February, 1740, he committed suicide by shooting himself.
[3] The house and gardens of Esher, in Surrey, belonging to the Honourable Mr. Pelham, brother to the Duke of Newcastle. Died 6th March, 1754, when he was barely sixty-one years of age. Pelham's place was embellished under the direction of Kent, whom Pope had instructed in landscape gardening.
[4] Dr Thomas Secker (born 1693, died 1768) rose to be Archbishop of Canterbury, and placed the crown upon the head of George III. Dr. Thomas Rundle (born 1686, died 1743) was finally made Bishop of Derry.
The Benson alluded to is perhaps Dr. George Benson, a learned Nonconformist divine who officiated many years in London. Died 1762, aged sixty-three. Dr. George Berkeley, Bishop of Cloyne (born 1684, died 1753), was the famous philosopher.

That instant, I declare, he has my love: 75
I shun his zenith, court his mild decline;
Thus Somers [1] once, and Halifax,[2] were mine.
Oft, in the clear, still mirror of retreat,
I studied Shrewsbury,[3] the wise and great:
Carleton's [4] calm sense, and Stanhope's [5] noble flame, 80
Compared, and knew their generous end the same:
How pleasing Atterbury's softer hour![6]
How shined the soul, unconquer'd in the Tower!
How can I Pulteney,[7] Chesterfield,[8] forget
While Roman spirit charms, and Attic wit? 85
Argyll,[9] the State's whole thunder born to wield,
And shake alike the senate and the field?
Or Wyndham,[10] just to freedom and the throne,
The master of our passions, and his own?
Names, which I long have loved, nor loved in vain, 90
Rank'd with their friends, not number'd with their train;
And, if yet higher the proud list should end,
Still let me say,—No follower, but a friend.[11]

    Yet think not, Friendship only prompts my lays;—
I follow Virtue; where she shines, I praise: 95
Point she to priest or elder, Whig or Tory,
Or round a Quaker's beaver cast a glory.
I never (to my sorrow I declare)
Dined with the Man of Ross, or my Lord Mayor.

[1] John, Lord Somers, died 1716. He had been Lord Keeper in the reign of William III., who took from him the seals in 1700.

[2] Disgraced in 1710, on the change of Queen Anne's ministry.

[3] Charles Talbot, Duke of Shrewsbury, had been Secretary of State, Ambassador in France, Lord-Lieutenant of Ireland, Lord Chamberlain, and Lord Treasurer. He several times quitted his employments, and was often recalled. Died 1718.

[4] Hen. Boyle, Lord Carleton (nephew of the famous Robert Boyle), who was Secretary of State under William III., and President of the Council under Queen Anne. Dismissed 1710. Died 1725.

[5] James, Earl Stanhope. General in Spain, and Secretary of State. After many victories, was defeated and made prisoner. Died 1721.

[6] Of all the parties here named, Atterbury only was the friend of Pope. The remarkable history of this prelate will be found in Pope's *Life*. His turbulence and ambition were strangely contrasted with the gentle, affectionate tone of his letters. He was exiled in 1723.

[7] William Pulteney, Earl of Bath, the successful antagonist of Walpole. Dismissed office 1725. Died 1764.

[8] The witty Lord Chesterfield, Philip Dormer Stanhope. Author of the celebrated *Letters*. Dismissed office 1733. Died 1773, aged seventy-nine.

[9] John, the second and *great* Duke of Argyll, born in 1678. Dismissed 1716. Died September, 1743.

[10] Sir William Wyndham, Chancellor of the Exchequer under Queen Anne. Dismissed 1714 and impeached. Died 1740.

[11] An allusion by Pope to his intimacy with the Prince of Wales.

Some, in their choice of friends (nay, look not grave),   100
Have still a secret bias to a knave:
To find an honest man I beat about,
And love him, court him, praise him, in or out.
   F. Then why so few commended?

                            P. Not so fierce;
Find you the virtue, and I'll find the verse.   105
But random praise—the task can ne'er be done:
Each mother asks it for her booby son,
Each widow asks it for "the best of men,"
For him she weeps, for him she weds again.
Praise cannot stoop, like satire, to the ground: 110
The number may be hang'd, but not be crown'd.
Enough for half the greatest of these days,
To 'scape my censure, not expect my praise.
Are they not rich? what more can they pretend?
Dare they to hope a poet for their friend?   115
What Richelieu wanted, Louis scarce could gain,
And what young Ammon wish'd, but wish'd in vain.
No power the Muse's friendship can command;
No power, when Virtue claims it, can withstand:
To Cato, Virgil paid one honest line;   120
O let my country's friends illumine mine!
—What are you thinking?

                   F. Faith, the thought's no sin:
I think your friends are out, and would be in.
   P. If merely to come in, sir, they go out,
The way they take is strangely round about.   125
   F. They, too, may be corrupted, you'll allow?
   P. I only call those knaves who are so now.
Is that too little? Come then, I'll comply—
Spirit of Arnall![1] aid me while I lie.
Cobham's a coward, Polwarth[2] is a slave,   130
And Lyttelton a dark designing knave;
St. John has ever been a wealthy fool—
But, let me add, Sir Robert's mighty dull;
Has never made a friend in private life,
And was, besides, a tyrant to his wife.[3]   135
   But pray, when others praise him, do I blame?

---

[1] Look for him in his place, *Dunciad*, book ii. verse 315.
[2] The Hon. Hugh Hume, son of Alexander, Earl of Marchmont, grandson of Patrick, Earl of Marchmont. Died January 1794, aged eighty-six.
[3] An ironical allusion to Walpole's carelessness and unconcern as a husband. His maxim was "to go his own way, and let madam go hers."

Call Verres, Wolsey, any odious name?
Why rail they then, if but a wreath of mine,
Oh all-accomplished St. John! deck thy shrine?
    What! shall each spur-galled hackney of the day,   140
When Paxton gives him double pots and pay,
Or each new-pension'd sycophant, pretend
To break my windows if I treat a friend;[1]
Then wisely plead, to me they meant no hurt,
But 'twas my guest at whom they threw the dirt?   145
Sure, if I spare the minister, no rules
Of honour bind me, not to maul his tools;
Sure, if they cannot cut, it may be said
His saws are toothless, and his hatchets lead.
    It anger'd Turenne, once upon a day,   150
To see a footman kick'd that took his pay;
But when he heard the affront the fellow gave,
Knew one a man of honour, one a knave;
The prudent general turn'd it to a jest,
And begg'd he'd take the pains to kick the rest: 155
Which not at present having time to do—
    F. Hold, sir! for God's sake, where's the affront to you?
Against your worship when had S——k writ?
Or P—ge pour'd forth the torrent of his wit?[2]
Or grant the bard whose distich all commend   160
("In power a servant, out of power a friend")[3]
To W——le guilty of some venial sin;
What's that to you who ne'er was out nor in?
    The priest whose flattery bedropp'd the Crown,[4]
How hurt he you? he only stain'd the gown.   165
And how did, pray, the florid youth offend,
Whose speech you took, and gave it to a friend?
    P. Faith, it imports not much from whom it came;
Whoever borrow'd, could not be to blame,
Since the whole House did afterwards the same.   170
Let courtly wits to wits afford supply,
As hog to hog in huts of Westphaly:

[1] The poet's windows were actually broken one day when he had Boling-
broke and Bathurst at dinner with him.
[2] Lord Selkirk and Judge Page. The latter was an orator in the style of
Judge Jeffreys.
[3] A verse taken out of a poem to Walpole, written by Bubb Dodington,
Lord Melcombe. Having done duty to one Premier, it was afterwards
addressed to another, Lord Bute.
[4] Glancing at Dr. Alured Clarke's panegyric on Queen Caroline, as the
" florid youth " means Lord Hervey.

If one, through Nature's bounty or his Lord's,
Has what the frugal, dirty soil affords,
From him the next receives it, thick or thin,   175
As pure a mess almost as it came in;
The blessed benefit, not there confined,
Drops to the third, who nuzzles close behind:
From tail to mouth, they feed and they carouse:
The last full fairly gives it to the House.   180
   F. This filthy simile, this beastly line,
Quite turns my stomach—— *P.* So does flattery mine:
And all your courtly civet-cats can vent,
Perfume to you, to me is excrement.
But hear me further:——Japhet, 'tis agreed,   185
Writ not, and Chartres scarce could write or read,
In all the courts of Pindus guiltless quite;
But pens can forge, my friend, that cannot write:
And must no egg in Japhet's face be thrown,
Because the deed he forged was not my own?   190
Must never patriot then declaim at gin,
Unless, good man! he has been fairly in?
No zealous pastor blame a failing spouse,
Without a staring reason on his brows?
And each blasphemer quite escape the rod,   195
Because the insult's not on man, but God?
   Ask you what provocation I have had?
The strong antipathy of good to bad.
When truth or virtue an affront endures,
The affront is mine, my friend, and should be yours.   200
Mine, as a foe profess'd to false pretence,
Who think a coxcomb's honour like his sense;
Mine, as a friend to every worthy mind;
And mine as man, who feel for all mankind.[1]
   F. You're strangely proud.

                   P. So proud, I am no slave: 205
So impudent, I own myself no knave:
So odd, my country's ruin makes me grave.
Yes, I am proud; I must be proud to see
Men not afraid of God, afraid of me:
Safe from the bar, the pulpit, and the throne,   210
Yet touch'd and shamed by ridicule alone.
   O sacred weapon! left for Truth's defence,
Sole dread of folly, vice, and insolence!

   [1] From Terence: " Homo sum: humani nihil a me alienum puto."

To all but Heaven-directed hands denied,
The Muse may give thee, but the gods must guide: 215
Reverent I touch thee! but with honest zeal;
To rouse the watchmen of the public weal,
To virtue's work provoke the tardy Hall,
And goad the prelate slumbering in his stall.
Ye tinsel insects! whom a Court maintains,   220
That counts your beauties only by your stains,
Spin all your cobwebs o'er the eye of day!
The Muse's wing shall brush you all away:
All his grace preaches, all his lordship sings,
All that makes saints of queens, and gods of kings,—   225
All, all but truth, drops dead-born from the press,
Like the last Gazette, or the last address.[1]

When black ambition stains a public cause,[2]
A monarch's sword when mad Vain-glory draws,
Not Waller's wreath can hide the nation's scar,[3]   230
Not Boileau turn the feather to a star.[4]

Not so, when diadem'd with rays divine,
Touch'd with the flame that breaks from Virtue's shrine,
Her priestess Muse forbids the good to die,
And opes the temple of Eternity: 235
There, other trophies deck the truly brave,
Than such an Anstis casts into the grave;[5]
Far other stars than * and * * wear,[6]
And may descend to Mordington[7] from Stair;[8]

[1] Formal replies to the King's speech at openings of Parliament.

[2] The case of Cromwell in the civil war of England; and (ver. 229) of
Louis XIV. in his conquest of the Low Countries.

[3] Waller's poem, *Upon the late Storme*, is here referred to. He is said to
have apologised to Charles II. for his praises of Cromwell, by saying that
poets dealt better with fiction than with truth.

[4] See his *Ode on Namur*; where (to use his own words) "il a fait un
astre de la plume blanche que le Roy porte ordinairement à son chapeau,
et qui est en effet une espèce de comete, fatale à nos ennemis."

[5] It is the custom, at the funeral of great peers, to cast into the grave
the broken staves and ensigns of honour. John Anstis, the principal
Garter King-at-Arms, died 1744.

[6] Lord Marchmont put opposite these blanks the names of "George"
and "Frederick," meaning the king and Prince of Wales. Warton con-
jectured that the Dukes of Kent and Grafton were the persons satirised;
but Lord Marchmont's intimacy with Pope gives authority to his
emendation.

[7] Lord Mordington, a Scotch nobleman, who is said to have sunk so low
from the blood of the Douglases as to have married a wife who kept a
gaming house in Covent Garden! Died 10th June, 1741.

[8] John Dalrymple, Earl of Stair, Knight of the Thistle, served in all the
wars under the Duke of Marlborough, and afterwards as Ambassador in
France.

(Such as on Hough's unsullied mitre shine,   240
Or beam, good Digby, from a heart like thine): [1]
Let Envy howl, while Heaven's whole chorus sings,
And bark at honour not conferr'd by kings;
Let Flattery sickening see the incense rise,
Sweet to the world, and grateful to the skies: 245
Truth guards the poet, sanctifies the line,
And makes immortal verse as mean as mine.

Yes, the last pen for Freedom let me draw,
When Truth stands trembling on the edge of law;
Here, last of Britons! let your names be read;   250
Are none, none living? let me praise the dead,
And for that cause which made your father shine,
Fall by the votes of their degenerate line.

F. Alas! alas! pray end what you began,
And write next winter more Essays on Man.

ADDITIONAL NOTE

DEATH OF QUEEN CAROLINE

Dial. i. v. 82. All parts perform'd, and all her children bless'd. **A** double sarcasm is conveyed in this line: the queen did not take the sacrament in her last illness, and she did not send her blessing to her son, the Prince of Wales. Both circumstances were much canvassed at the time, and the most contradictory reports prevailed. Coxe, in his *Memoirs of Walpole,* states that the queen sent her blessing to her son, with a message of forgiveness; but the minute details of Lord Hervey, an eye-witness, disprove the assertion; and Pope, who had access to correct information, at the courts both of the king and the prince, seems to have known the actual facts of the case. The queen was taken ill on the 9th November, 1737, and continued getting worse. On the 11th the prince sent to request that he might see her, but the king said this was like one of the *scoundrel's* tricks, and he forbade the prince to send messages or approach St. James's. The queen herself was no less decided. In fact, the family feud was of the bitterest description, and of many years' standing. Its cause has never been satisfactorily explained, but in the rival courts there were never wanting occasions for fresh enmity and exasperation. The king, it appears, relaxed so far as to say to her majesty that, if she had the least mind to see her son, he had no objection to it. " I am so far," said the queen, " from desiring to see him, that nothing but your absolute commands should ever make me consent to it. For what should I see him? For him to tell me a hundred lies, and to give myself at this time a great deal of trouble to no purpose. If anything I could say to him would alter his behaviour I

---

[1] Dr. John Hough, Bishop of Worcester, and the Lord Digby. The one an asserter of the Church of England, in opposition to the false measures of King James II.; the other as firmly attached to the cause of that king,

would see him with all my heart; but I know that is impossible. Whatever advice I gave him he would thank me for, *pleureoit comme un veau* all the while I was speaking, and swear to follow my directions, and would laugh at me the moment he was out of the room, and do just the contrary of all I bid him the moment I was dead. And, therefore, if I should grow worse, and be weak enough to talk of seeing him, I beg you, sir, to conclude that I doat or rave." The speech was characteristic of Caroline—a strong-minded, resolute, ambitious woman, with little tenderness or religion. She was then dying of the effects of a rupture, which she had courageously concealed for fourteen years, and she would have died without declaring it, had not the king communicated the fact to her attendants. This delicacy was not (as Lord Harvey says) merely an ill-timed coquetry at fifty-four that would hardly have been excusable at twenty-five. She feared to lose the power over the king, which she had held firmly in spite of all his mistresses, and was in constant apprehension of making her person distasteful to her husband. The prince continued to send messages to the dying queen, and the messengers got into the palace, but the queen wished to have the *ravens* (who, she said, were only there to watch her death, and would gladly tear her to pieces whilst she was alive) turned out of the house, and the old king was inexorable. About the seventh day of the queen's illness, the Archbishop of Canterbury, Dr. Potter, was sent for. He continued to attend every morning and evening, but her majesty did not receive the sacrament. Some of Lord Hervey's revelations are curious enough. Her majesty, it appears advised the king, in case she died, to marry again. George sobbed and shed tears: "whilst in the midst of this passion, wiping his eyes and sobbing between every word, with much ado he got out this answer: 'Non, j'aurai des maîtresses'; to which the queen made no other reply than "Ah! mon Dieu! cela n'empêche pas.'"

When she had finished all she had to say on these subjects, she said she fancied she could sleep. The king said many things to her, and kissed her face and her hands a hundred times; but even at this time, on her asking for her watch, which hung by the chimney, in order to give it to him to take care of her seal, the natural *brusquerie* of his temper, even in these moments, broke out, which showed how addicted he.was to snapping without being angry, and that he was often capable of using those worst whom he loved best; for, on this proposal of giving him the watch to take care of the seal with the queen's arms, in the midst of sobs and tears, he raised and quickened his voice, and said, "Ah, my God! let it alone: the queen has always such strange fancies. Who should meddle with your seal? It is not as safe there as in my pocket?"

During their night-watches, the king and Lord Hervey had many conversations, all which the Court-Boswell reports fully. George wished to impress upon the Privy Seal that the queen's affectionate behaviour was the natural effect of an amorous attacthment to his person, and an adoration of his great genius! He narrated instances of his own intrepidity, during a severe illness and in a great storm; and one night while he was discoursing in this strain the Princess Emily, who lay upon a couch in the room, pretended to fall asleep. Soon after his majesty went into the queen's room.

"As soon as his back was turned Princess Emily started up, and said, 'Is he gone? How tiresome he is!' Lord Hervey replied only, 'I thought your royal highness had been asleep.' 'No,' said the Princess Emily; 'I only shut my eyes that I might not join in the *ennuyant* conversation, and wish I could have shut my ears too. In the first place, I am sick to death of hearing of his great courage every day of my life; in the next place, one thinks now of mamma, and not of him. Who cares for his old storm? I believe, too, it is a great lie, and that he was as much afraid as I should have been, for all what he says now.'"

Other glimpses of the interior of this strange court at this time are furnished by Lord Hervey. Walpole appears in no better light than the coarse, boasting sovereign. But at length the last scene came. There had been about eleven days of suffering:

"On Sunday, the 20th November, in the evening, she asked Dr. Tesier —with no seeming impatience under any article of her present circumstances but their duration—how long he thought it was possible for all this to last? to which he answered, 'Je crois que votre majesté sera bientôt soulagée.' And she calmly replied, 'Tant mieux.' About ten o'clock on Sunday night, the king being in bed and asleep, on the floor at the foot of the queen's bed, and the Princess Emily in a couch-bed in a corner of the room, the queen began to rattle in the throat; and Mrs. Purcel giving the alarm that she was expiring, all in the room started up. Princess Caroline was sent for, and Lord Hervey, but before the last arrived the queen was just dead. All she said before she died was, 'I have now got an asthma; open the window.' Then she said, 'Pray,' upon which the Princess Emily began to read some prayers, of which she scarce repeated ten words before the queen expired. The Princess Caroline held a looking-glass to her lips, and finding there was not the least damp upon it, cried, ''Tis over.'"

George did not marry again, but contented himself with "des maîtresses." He survived nearly twenty-three years, dying suddenly on the 25th October, 1760. He directed that 'his remains and those of the queen should be *mingled together*, and accordingly one side of each of the wooden coffins was withdrawn and the two bodies placed together in a stone sarcophagus.

IMITATIONS OF HORACE

BOOK I. EPISTLE VII

IMITATED IN THE MANNER OF DR. SWIFT

'Tis true, my Lord, I gave my word
I would be with you, June the third;
Changed it to August, and (in short)
Have kept it—as you do at court.
You humour me when I am sick,   5
Why not when I am splenetic?
In town, what objects could I meet?
The shops shut up in every street,
And funerals black'ning all the doors,
And yet more melancholy whores: 10
And what a dust in every place!
And a thin court that wants your face,
And fevers raging up and down,
And W* and H** both in town! [1]

    "The dog-days are no more the case."   15
'Tis true, but winter comes apace:

[1] Possibly Ward and Henley, representative quacks.

Then southward let your bard retire,
Hold out some months 'twixt sun and fire,
And you shall see, the first warm weather,
Me and the butterflies together.   20
My Lord, your favours well I know;
'Tis with distinction you bestow;
And not to everyone that comes,
Just as a Scotchman does his plums.
"Pray take them, sir,—enough's a feast: 25
Eat some, and pocket up the rest."—
What, rob your boys? those pretty rogues!
"No, sir, you'll leave them to the hogs."
Thus fools with compliments besiege ye,
Contriving never to oblige ye.   30
Scatter your favours on a fop,
Ingratitude's the certain crop;
And 'tis but just, I'll tell ye wherefore,
You give the things you never care for.
A wise man always is, or should,   35
Be mighty ready to do good;
But makes a difference in his thought
Betwixt a guinea and a groat.
    Now this I'll say, you'll find in me
A safe companion and a free;   40
But if you'd have me always near—
A word, pray, in your honour's ear.
I hope it is your resolution
To give me back my constitution
The sprightly wit, the lively eye,   45
The engaging smile, the gaiety,
That laugh'd down many a summer sun,
And kept you up so oft till one:
And all that voluntary vein,
As when Belinda raised my strain.[1]   50
    A weasel once made shift to slink
In at a corn-loft through a chink;
But having amply stuff'd his skin,
Could not get out as he got in:
Which one belonging to the house   55
('Twas not a man, it was a mouse)

[1] In *The Rape of the Lock* we see the first playful effort of satire without ill-nature, at once gay, elegant and delightful:

"Belinda smiles, and all the world is gay."

Observing, cried, "You 'scape not so,
Lean as you came, sir, you must go."
　　Sir, you may spare your application,
I'm no such beast, nor his relation; 60
Nor one that temperance advance,
Cramm'd to the throat with ortolans:
Extremely ready to resign
All that may make me none of mine.
South Sea subscriptions take who please, 65
Leave me but liberty and ease.
'Twas what I said to Craggs and Child,[1]
Who praised my modesty, and smiled.
Give me, I cried (enough for me),
My bread, and independency! 70
So bought an annual rent or two,
And lived—just as you see I do;
Near fifty, and without a wife,
I trust that sinking fund, my life.
Can I retrench? Yes, mighty well, 75
Shrink back to my paternal cell,
A little house, with trees a-row,
And, like its master, very low.
There died my father, no man's debtor,
And there I'll die, nor worse, nor better. 80
　　To set this matter full before ye,
Our old friend Swift will tell his story.
　　"Harley, the nation's great support,"—
But you may read it, I stop short.

BOOK II.　SATIRE VI

THE FIRST PART IMITATED IN THE YEAR 1714, BY DR. SWIFT;
THE LATTER PART ADDED AFTERWARDS

I'VE often wish'd that I had clear,
For life, six hundred pounds a-year,
A handsome house to lodge a friend;
A river at my garden's end;
A terrace-walk, and half a rood
Of land, set out to plant a wood. 5

---

[1] Craggs the younger, and Sir Francis Child, the eminent banker and M.P. for Middlesex, who died in 1740.

Well, now I have all this and more,
I ask not to increase my store;
But here a grievance seems to lie,
All this is mine but till I die,   10
I can't but think 'twould sound more clever,
To me and to my heirs for ever.

If I ne'er got or lost a groat,
By any trick, or any fault;
And if I pray by reason's rules,   15
And not like forty other fools:
As thus, "Vouchsafe, O gracious Maker!
To grant me this and t'other acre:
Or, if it be Thy will and pleasure,
Direct my plough to find a treasure":   20
But only what my station fits,
And to be kept in my right wits.
Preserve, Almighty Providence!
Just what You gave me, competence:
And let me in these shades compose   25
Something in verse as true as prose:
Removed from all the ambitious scene,
Nor puff'd by pride, nor sunk by spleen.

In short, I'm perfectly content,
Let me but live on this side Trent;[1]   30
Nor cross the Channel twice a year,
To spend six months with statesmen here.

I must, by all means, come to town,
'Tis for the service of the crown.
"Lewis, the dean will be of use,   35
Send for him up; take no excuse."
The toil, the danger of the seas;
Great ministers ne'er think of these;
Or let it cost five hundred pound,
No matter where the money's found: 40
It is but so much more in debt,
And that they ne'er considered yet.

"Good Mr. Dean, go change your gown,
Let my lord know you're come to town."
I hurry me in haste away,   45
Not thinking it is levee-day;
And find his honour in a pound,

[1] Swift always considered his preferment to the Deanery of St. Patrick's
as a banishment.

Hemm'd by a triple circle round.
Chequered with ribands blue and green:
How should I thrust myself between?   50
Some wag observes me thus perplex'd,
And smiling, whispers to the next,
"I thought the Dean had been too proud
To justle here among a crowd."
Another, in a surly fit,   55
Tells me I have more zeal than wit:
"So eager to express your love,
You ne'er consider whom you shove;
But rudely press before a duke."
I own I'm pleased with this rebuke,   60
And take it kindly meant to show
What I desire the world should know.
   I get a whisper, and withdraw;
When twenty fools I never saw
Come, with petitions fairly penn'd,   65
Desiring I would stand their friend.
   This humbly offers me his case—
That begs my interest for a place—
A hundred other men's affairs,
Like bees, are humming in my ears.   70
"To-morrow my appeal comes on,
Without your help the cause is gone":
The duke expects my lord and you,
About some great affair, at two—
"Put my Lord Bolingbroke in mind,   75
To get my warrant quickly sign'd:
Consider, 'tis my first request."
Be satisfied, I'll do my best:
Then presently he falls to tease,
"You may for certain, if you please;   80
I doubt not, if his lordship knew—
And, Mr. Dean, one word from you"—
   'Tis (let me see) three years and more
(October next it will be four)
Since Harley bid me first attend,   85
And chose me for an humble friend;
Would take me in his coach to chat,
And question me of this and that;
As "What's o'clock?" and "How's the wind?"
"Whose chariot's that we left behind?"   90

Or gravely try to read the lines
Writ underneath the country signs;
Or "Have you nothing new to-day
From Pope, from Parnell, or from Gay?"
Such tattle often entertains   95
My lord and me as far as Staines,
As once a week we travel down
To Windsor, and again to town,
Where all that passes, *inter nos*,
Might be proclaimed at Charing Cross,   100
    Yet some I know with envy swell
Because they see me used so well:
"How think you of our friend the dean?
I wonder what some people mean;
My lord and he are grown so great,   105
Always together *tête-à-tête*.
What, they admire him for his jokes—
See but the fortune of some folks!"
There flies about a strange report
Of some express arrived at court;   110
I'm stopp'd by all the fools I meet,
And catechised in every street.
"You, Mr. Dean, frequent the great;
Inform us, will the Emperor treat,
Or do the prints and papers lie?"   115
'Faith, sir, you know as much as I.
"Ah, doctor, how you love to jest.
'Tis now no secret."—I protest
'Tis one to me—"Then tell us, pray,
When are the troops to have their pay?"   120
And, though I solemnly declare
I know no more than my Lord Mayor,
They stand amazed, and think me grown
The closest mortal ever known.
    Thus in a sea of folly toss'd,   125
My choicest hours of life are lost;
Yet always wishing to retreat,
Oh, could I see my country-seat!
There, leaning near a gentle brook,
Sleep, or peruse some ancient book,   130
And there in sweet oblivion drown
Those cares that haunt the court and town,
O charming noons! and nights divine!

Or when I sup, or when I dine;
My friends above, my folks below,   135
Chatting and laughing all a-row:
The beans and bacon set before 'em,
The grace-cup served with all decorum:
Each willing to be pleased and please,
And e'en the very dogs at ease!   140
Here no man prates of idle things,
How this or that Italian sings,
A neighbour's madness, or his spouse's,
Or what's in either of the Houses:
But something much more our concern,   145
And quite a scandal not to learn:
Which is the happier, or the wiser,
A man of merit or a miser?
Whether we ought to choose our friends
For their own worth or our own ends?   150
What good, or better, we may call,
And what the very best of all?
     Our friend Dan Prior told (you know)
A tale extremely à propos:[1]
Name a town-life, and in a trice   155
He had a story of two mice.
Once on a time (so runs the fable)
A country mouse, right hospitable,
Received a town mouse at his board,
Just as a farmer might a lord.   160
A frugal mouse upon the whole,
Yet loved his friend, and had a soul,
Knew what was handsome, and would do 't,
On just occasion, coûte qui coûte,
He brought him bacon (nothing lean),   165
Pudding that might have pleased a dean;
Cheese such as men in Suffolk make,
But wish'd it Stilton for his sake;
Yet to his guest though no way sparing,
He ate himself the rind and paring.   170
Our courtier scarce would touch a bit,
But show'd his breeding and his wit;
He did his best to seem to eat,

---

[1] Prior has several little apologues on mice. His first work was *The City and Country Mouse*, a parody on Dryden's *Hind and Panther*, by Prior and Montagu (afterwards Lord Halifax).

And cried, "I vow you're mighty neat.
But Lord! my friend, this savage scene!   175
For God's sake come and live with men:
Consider mice, like men, must die,
Both small and great, both you and I:
Then spend your life in joy and sport
(This doctrine, friend, I learn'd at court)."   180
    The veriest hermit in the nation
May yield, God knows, to strong temptation.
Away they come, through thick and thin,
To a tall house near Lincoln's Inn;
('Twas on the night of a debate   185
When all their Lordships had sat late.)
    Behold the place where if a poet
Shined in description he might show it;
Tell how the moonbeam trembling falls,
And tips with silver all the walls;   190
Palladian walls, Venetian doors,
Grotesco roofs, and stucco floors:
But let it (in a word) be said
The moon was up and men a-bed,
The napkins white, the carpet red: 195
The guests withdrawn had left the treat,
And down the mice sat *tête-à-tête*.
    Our courtier walks from dish to dish,
Tastes for his friend of fowl and fish;
Tells all their names, lays down the law,   200
"*Que ça est bon ! Ah goutez ça !*
That jelly's rich, this malmsey healing,
Pray dip your whiskers and your tail in."
Was ever such a happy swain?
He stuffs, and swills, and stuffs again.   205
"I'm quite ashamed—'tis mighty rude
To eat so much—but all's so good.
I have a thousand thanks to give—
My lord alone knows how to live."
No sooner said, but from the hall   210
Rush chaplain, butler, dogs, and all:
"A rat, a rat! clap to the door"—
The cat comes bouncing on the floor.
O for the heart of Homer's mice,
Or gods to save them in a trice!   215
(It was by Providence they think,

For your damn'd stucco has no chink.)
"An't please your honour," quoth the peasant,
"This same dessert is not so pleasant:
Give me again my hollow tree,   220
A crust of bread, and liberty!"

BOOK IV. ODE I

TO VENUS

AGAIN? new tumults in my breast?
Ah spare me, Venus! let me, let me rest!
I am not now, alas! the man
As in the gentle reign of my Queen Anne.
Ah, sound no more thy soft alarms,   5
Nor circle sober fifty with thy charms.
Mother too fierce of dear desires!
Turn, turn to willing hearts your wanton fires.
To Number Five direct your doves,
There spread round Murray all your blooming loves;[1]
Noble and young, who strikes the heart   11
With every sprightly, every decent part;
Equal the injured to defend,
To charm the mistress, or to fix the friend.
He, with a hundred arts refined,   15
Shall stretch thy conquests over half the kind:
To him each rival shall submit,
Make but his riches equal to his wit.
Then shall thy form the marble grace
(Thy Grecian form), and Chloe lend the face: 20
His house, embosom'd in the grove,
Sacred to social life and social love,
Shall glitter o'er the pendant green,
Where Thames reflects the visionary scene:
Thither the silver-sounding lyres   25
Shall call the smiling loves and young desires;
There every Grace and Muse shall throng,
Exalt the dance, or animate the song;
There youths and nymphs, in consort gay,
Shall hail the rising, close the parting day.   30
With me, alas! those joys are o'er;

[1] Murray's chambers were at this time in King's Bench Walk, No. 5.

For me the vernal garlands bloom no more.
Adieu! fond hope of mutual fire,
The still-believing, still-renew'd desire;
Adieu! the heart-expanding bowl,   35
And all the kind deceivers of the soul!
But why? ah tell me, ah too dear!
Steals down my cheek the involuntary tear?
Why words so flowing, thoughts so free,
Stop, or turn nonsense, at one glance of thee?   40
Thee, dress'd in Fancy's airy beam,
Absent I follow through the extended dream;
Now, now I seize, I clasp thy charms,
And now you burst (ah cruel!) from my arms,
And swiftly shoot along the Mall,   45
Or softly glide by the canal,
Now shown by Cynthia's silver ray,
And now on rolling waters snatch'd away.

PART OF THE NINTH ODE OF THE
FOURTH BOOK

Lest you should think that verse shall die
    Which sounds the silver Thames along,
Taught on the wings of Truth to fly
    Above the reach of vulgar song;

Though daring Milton sits sublime,   5
    In Spenser native muses play;
Nor yet shall Waller yield to time,
    Nor pensive Cowley's moral lay.

Sages and chiefs long since had birth
    Ere Cæsar was, or Newton named;   10
These raised new empires o'er the earth,
    And those new heavens and systems framed.

Vain was the chief's, the sage's pride!
They had no poet, and they died.
In vain they schemed, in vain they bled!   15
They had no poet, and are dead.

ON RECEIVING FROM THE RIGHT HON. THE LADY FRANCES SHIRLEY A STANDISH AND TWO PENS

Warburton states that the poet was threatened with a prosecution in the House of Lords for the *Epilogue to the Satires*. In great resentment, he began a Third Dialogue, more severe and sublime than the First and Second, which, becoming known, led to a compromise. The prosecution was dropped, and the poet agreed to leave the Third Dialogue unfinished and suppressed. "This affair," adds Warburton, "occasioned this little beautiful poem, to which it alludes throughout, but more especially in the four last stanzas." Lady Frances Shirley was a daughter of Earl Ferrers, who had at that time a house at Twickenham. She died unmarried in 1762.

YES, I beheld the Athenian queen
    Descend in all her sober charms;
"And take," she said, and smiled serene,
    "Take at this hand celestial arms:

Secure the radiant weapons wield; 5
    This golden lance shall guard desert,
And if a vice dares keep the field,
    This steel shall stab it to the heart."

Awed, on my bended knees I fell,
    Received the weapons of the sky; 10
And dipp'd them in the sable well,
    The fount of fame or infamy.

"What well? what weapon?" Flavia cries,
    "A standish, steel and golden pen!
It came from Bertrand's,[1] not the skies; 15
    I gave it you to write again.

But, friend, take heed whom you attack;
    You'll bring a house (I mean of peers),
Red, blue and green, nay white and black,
    L—— and all about your ears.[2] 20

[1] Bertrand's was a toy-shop at Bath.
[2] Lambeth would seem to be here meant. In the *Epilogue to the Satires*, Dial I., ver. 120, Pope had hazarded an allusion to a scandal that the Archbishop of Canterbury had "pocketed" the will of George I. Walpole, however, states that the archbishop produced the will, and that George II. carried it off. To implement it would have been disastrous.

You'd write as smooth again on glass,
    And run, on ivory, so glib,
As not to stick at fool or ass,
    Nor stop at flattery or fib.

Athenian queen! and sober charms!   25
    I tell ye, fool, there's nothing in't:
'Tis Venus, Venus, gives these arms;
    In Dryden's Virgil see the print.

Come, if you'll be a quiet soul,
    That dares tell neither truth nor lies,   30
I'll list you in the harmless roll
    Of those that sing of these poor eyes."

1740

A FRAGMENT OF A POEM

This fragment was first published by Warton, who received it
from Dr. Wilson, Fellow and Librarian of Trinity College, Dublin.
Dr. Wilson informed Warton that he transcribed it from a rough
draft *in Pope's own hand*, obtained from a grandson of Lord Chet-
wynd, the friend of Bolingbroke. Mr. Bowles concluded that this
poem was the beginning of the satire alluded to by Warburton—
the unfinished and suppressed Third Dialogue. The piece has
certainly no marks of the *sublimity* which Warburton mentions, and
possesses only one good line, that supposed to allude to Pulteney—

He foams a patriot to subside a peer.

And Pulteney, it should be recollected, was not created a peer until
two years after the date prefixed to this poem. The " patriot race "
were much divided in 1740, and Pope, in his letters, appears to have
been very desponding as to the future prospects of his country.
Marchmont and Bolingbroke indulged in the same exaggerated
strain; yet we cannot believe that the poet would have satirised
the friends with whom he was in constant intercourse, or that even
the first draft of any of his satires would have been so bald and
disjointed as this fragment.

O WRETCHED B——!¹ jealous now of all,
What God, what mortal, shall prevent thy fall?
Turn, turn thy eyes from wicked men in place,
And see what succour from the patriot race.

¹ Britain. In the case of many of the explanatory names here subjoined
no certainty can be attained.

C——,[1] his own proud dupe, thinks monarchs things   5
Made just for him, as other fools for kings;
Controls, decides, insults thee every hour,
And antedates the hatred due to power.

   Through clouds of passion P——'s[2] views are clear,
He foams a patriot to subside a peer;   10
Impatient sees his country bought and sold,
And damns the market where he takes no gold.

   Grave, righteous S——[3] jogs on till, past belief,
He finds himself companion with a thief.

   To purge and let thee blood, with fire and sword,   15
Is all the help stern S——[4] would afford.

   That those who bind and rob thee, would not kill,
Good C——[5] hopes and candidly sits still.

   Of Ch—s W——[6] who speaks at all,
No more than of Sir Harry[7] or Sir P——?[8]   20
Whose names once up, they thought it was not wrong
To lie in bed, but sure they lay too long.

   G——r,[9] C——m,[10] B——t,[11] pay thee due regards,
Unless the ladies bid them mind their cards.

   And C——d,[12] who speaks so well and writes,   25
Whom (saving W.) every S. harper bites.
Whose wit and . . . equally provoke one,
Finds thee, at best, the butt to crack his joke on.

   As for the rest, each winter up they run,
And all are clear that something must be done.   30

[1] Unsatisfactory suggestions have been made to fill in this name: Cobham, Campbell (Argyll), Cholmondeley. Professor Butt puts forward Carteret, trying to displace Walpole in the King's favour, and, according to A. S. Turberville, a man of "overweening self-confidence" and "arrogant and overbearing manner."

[2] Pulteney, created Earl of Bath in June 1742.

[3] Sandys. Afterwards Lord Sandys, and Speaker of the House of Lords.

[4] Shippen. "Honest Will Shippen," the Jacobite member of the House of Commons.

[5] Cornbury. Viscount Cornbury, son of the second Lord Clarendon.

[6] Sir Charles Hanbury Williams, the lively political rhymester and diplomatist, who was then M.P. for Monmouth, is supposed by Mr. Bowles to be here meant; but Williams was a friend of Walpole, and was selected by Sir Robert as Envoy to Naples in 1737. For this reason, and as the line with Williams' name is defective, perhaps two names were intended—as *Chandos* and *Winchelsea*. Errors may have been made in copying the rough draft of the poem.

[7] [8] Sir Henry Oxenden and Sir Paul Methuen. Sir Paul had been Treasurer of the Household, which office he resigned in disgust at not being made one of the Secretaries of State, in 1729.

[9] [10] [11] Lords Gower, Cobham and Bathurst.

[12] Philip, Lord Chesterfield. The "W." in the next line is perhaps intended for *Walter*, the notorious Peter Walter.

Then, urged by C——t,[1] or by C——t stopp'd,
Inflamed by P——,[2] and by P—— dropp'd;
They follow reverently each wondrous wight,
Amazed that one can read, that one can write:
So geese to gander prone obedience keep,   35
Hiss, if he hiss, and if he slumber, sleep.
Till having done whate'er was fit or fine,
Utter'd a speech, and ask'd their friends to dine;
Each hurries back to his paternal ground,
Content but for five shillings in the pound;   40
Yearly defeated, yearly hopes they give,
And all agree Sir Robert cannot live.

   Rise, rise, great W——,[3] fated to appear,
Spite of thyself, a glorious minister!
Speak the loud language princes   45
And treat with half the . . . .
At length to B——[4] kind, as to thy . . . .
Espouse the nation, you . . . .
   What can thy H——[5] . . . .
Dress in Dutch   50
Though still he travels on no bad pretence,
To show . . . .
   Of those foul copies of thy face and tongue,
Veracious W——,[6] and frontless Young;[7]
Sagacious Bub,[8] so late a friend, and there   55
So late a foe, yet more sagacious H——?[9]
Hervey and Hervey's school, F—, H——y, H——n,[10]
Yea, moral Ebor, or religious Winton.[11]
How! what can O——w,[12] what can D——,[13]
The wisdom of the one and other chair,   60

---

[1] Carteret, afterwards Earl Granville. At this time Lord Carteret and Pulteney were much distrusted by the other "patriots."
[2] Pulteney.
[3] Sir Robert Walpole.
[4] Britain.
[5] Horace Walpole, the brother of Sir Robert.
[6] Winnington. He was successively Lord of the Admiralty, Lord of the Treasury, and Paymaster of the Forces.
[7] Sir William Yonge (for so he spelt the name), Secretary at War.
[8] Bubb Dodington, Lord Melcombe.
[9] Francis Hare, Bishop of Chichester, who died in the year assigned to this fragment, 1740.
[10] Fox, Henley, Hinton.
[11] The Archbishop of York and Bishop of Winchester: Blackburn and Hoadley.
[12] [13] Arthur Onslow, Speaker of the House of Commons, and Lord De La Warr, Chairman of Committees in the House of Lords.

N——— [1] laugh, or D——'s [2] sager [sneer?]
Or thy dread truncheon, M—'s mighty peer? [3]
What help from J——'s [4] opiates canst thou draw,
Or H——k's quibbles voted into law? [5]
   C—, that Roman in his nose alone, [6]   65
Who hears all causes, B———, [7] but thy own,
Or those proud fools who nature, rank and fate
Made fit companions for the sword of state.
   Can the light packhorse or the heavy steer,
The sowsing prelate or the sweating peer,   70
Drag out, with all its dirt and all its weight,
The lumbering carriage of thy broken state?
Alas! the people curse, the carman swears,
The drivers quarrel, and the master stares.
   The plague is on thee, Britain, and who tries   75
To save thee, in the infectious office, dies.
The first firm P——y [8] soon resign'd his breath.
Brave S——w [9] loved thee, and was lied to death.
Good M—m—t's fate tore P——th from thy side, [10]
And thy last sigh was heard when W——m died. [11] 80
   Thy nobles sl—s, thy se—s bought with gold, [12]
Thy clergy perjured, thy whole people sold.
An atheist ᴗ a ⊕''''s ad ......
Blotch thee all o'er, and sink ....
   Alas! on one alone our all relies, [13]   85

[1] Duke of Newcastle.
[2] Lionel, first Duke of Dorset.
[3] Duke of Marlborough. A sarcastic allusion to the second duke, formerly Lord Sunderland.
[4] Probably Sir Joseph Jekyll, though Jekyll died in 1738.
[5] Lord Chancellor Hardwicke.
[6] Sir John Cummins, Chief Justice of the Common Pleas; or Compton, Lord Wilmington, President of the Council.
[7] Britain.   [8] Daniel Pulteney, William Pulteney's cousin.
[9] Lord Scarborough. Pope generally spelt Scarborough and Peterborough with a *w*, instead of *ugh*.
[10] The Earl of Marchmont, who died in January 1740, and Polwarth, his son.
[11] Sir William Wyndham died in June 1740.
[12] Thy nobles slaves, thy senates bought, etc.
[13] The one on whom all relied was probably Frederick, Prince of Wales, with whom Pope was then on terms of intimacy. If the poem is of Jacobite origin, the Chevalier St. George, the Pretender, must have been meant. Mr. Bowles restores the passage as follows:

> "Alas! on one alone our all relies,
> Let him be honest, and he must be wise;
> Let him, no trifler from his father's school,
> Nor like his father's father still a fool,
> Be but a man! unminister'd, alone,
> And free at once the senate and the throne."

Let him be honest, and he must be wise;
Let him no trifler from his   school,
Nor like his .... still a ....
Be but a man! unminister'd, alone,
And free at once the senate and the throne;   90
Esteem the public love his best supply,
A ⊙'s true glory his integrity;
Rich with his .... in his ... strong,
Affect no conquest, but endure no wrong,
Whatever his religion or his blood,   95
His public virtue makes his title good.
Europe's just balance and our own may stand,
And one man's honesty redeem the land.

MISCELLANIES

ARGUS

When wise Ulysses, from his native coast
Long kept by wars, and long by tempests toss'd,
Arrived at last, poor, old, disguised, alone,
To all his friends and even his queen unknown;
Changed as he was with age, and toils, and cares,   5
Furrow'd his reverend face, and white his hairs,
In his own palace forced to ask his bread,
Scorn'd by those slaves his former bounty fed,
Forgot of all his own domestic crew;
The faithful dog alone his rightful master knew!   10
Unfed, unhoused, neglected, on the clay,
Like an old servant, now cashier'd, he lay;
Touch'd with resentment of ungrateful man,
And longing to behold his ancient lord again.
Him when he saw he rose and crawl'd to meet   15
('Twas all he could), and fawn'd, and kiss'd his feet,
Seized with dumb joy—then falling by his side,
Own'd his returning lord, look'd up, and died!

The above was sent by Pope to H. Cromwell, in a letter dated
10th October, 1709, containing a very interesting panegyric upon
dogs.

IMPROMPTU TO LADY WINCHELSEA

OCCASIONED BY FOUR SATIRICAL VERSES ON WOMEN WITS IN "THE RAPE OF THE LOCK"

In vain you boast poetic names of yore,
And cite those Sapphos we admire no more:
Fate doom'd the fall of every female wit;
But doom'd it then, when first Ardelia writ,[1]
Of all examples by the world confess'd,   5
I knew Ardelia could not quote the best;
Who like her mistress on Britannia's throne
Fights and subdues in quarrels not her own.
To write their praise you but in vain essay;
E'en while you write you take that praise away: 10
Light to the stars the sun does thus restore,
But shines himself till they are seen no more.

EPILOGUE TO MR. ROWE'S "JANE SHORE"

DESIGNED FOR MRS. OLDFIELD

Prodigious this! the frail one of our play
From her own sex should mercy find to-day!
You might have held the pretty head aside,
Peep'd in your fans, been serious thus, and cried,
The play may pass—but that strange creature Shore,   5
I can't—indeed now—I so hate a whore—
Just as a blockhead rubs his thoughtless skull
And thanks his stars he was not born a fool;
So from a sister-sinner you shall hear,
"How strangely you expose yourself, my dear!"   10
But let me die, all raillery apart,
Our sex are still forgiving at their heart;
And, did not wicked customs so contrive,
We'd be the best good-natured things alive.
  There are, 'tis true, who téll another tale,   15
That virtuous ladies envy while they rail;
Such rage without betrays the fire within;
In some close corner of the soul they sin;
Still hoarding up, most scandalously nice,
Amidst their virtues, a reserve of vice.   20

_____

[1] Lady Winchelsea's coterie name was Ardelia.

The godly dame, who fleshly failings damns,
Scolds with her maids, or with her chaplain crams.
Would you enjoy soft nights and solid dinners?
'Faith, gallants, board with saints and bed with sinners.
   Well, if our author in the wife offends,   25
He has a husband that will make amends:
He draws him gentle, tender, and forgiving;
And sure such kind good creatures may be living.
In days of old they pardon'd breach of vows,
Stern Cato's self was no relentless spouse: 30
Plu—Plutarch, what's his name that writes his life?
Tells us that Cato dearly loved his wife:
Yet, if a friend a night or so should need her,
He'd recommend her as a special breeder.
To lend a wife, few here would scruple make;   35
But, pray, which of you all would take her back?
Though with the Stoic chief our stage may ring,
The Stoic husband was the glorious thing.
The man had courage, was a sage, 'tis true,
And loved his country—but what's that to you?   40
Those strange examples ne'er were made to fit ye,
But the kind cuckold might instruct the city:
There many an honest man may copy Cato
Who ne'er saw naked sword or look'd in Plato.
   If, after all, you think it a disgrace   45
That Edward's miss thus perks it in your face;
To see a piece of failing flesh and blood,
In all the rest so impudently good;
'Faith, let the modest matrons of the town
Come here in crowds, and stare the strumpet down.   50

PROLOGUE TO "THREE HOURS AFTER MARRIAGE"

Brought on the stage and condemned the first night, 1716.

AUTHORS are judged by strange capricious rules;
The great ones are thought mad, the small ones fools:
Yet sure the best are most severely fated,
For fools are only laugh'd at, wits are hated.
Blockheads with reason men of sense abhor;   5
But fool 'gainst fool is barbarous civil war.

Why on all authors then should critics fall?
Since some have writ, and shown no wit at all.
Condemn a play of theirs, and they evade it,
Cry, "Damn not us, but damn the French who made it."
By running goods, these graceless owlers gain;   11
These are the rules of France, the plots of Spain:
But wit, like wine, from happier climates brought,
Dash'd by these rogues, turns English common draught.
They pall Molière's and Lopez' sprightly strain,   15
And teach dull harlequins to grin in vain.

How shall our author hope a gentler fate,
Who dares most impudently not translate?
It had been civil in these ticklish times,
To fetch his fools and knaves from foreign climes,   20
Spaniards and French abuse to the world's end,
But spare old England, lest you hurt a friend.
If any fool is by our satire bit,
Let him hiss loud, to show you all he's hit.
Poets make characters, as salesmen clothes,   25
We take no measure of your fops and beaus,
But here all sizes and all shapes you meet,
And fit yourselves, like chaps in Monmouth-street.

Gallants! look here, this fool's cap [1] has an air,
Goodly and smart, with ears of Issachar.   30
Let no one fool engross it, or confine,
A common blessing! now 'tis yours, now mine.
But poets in all ages had the care
To keep this cap for such as will to wear.
Our author has it now (for every wit   35
Of course resign'd it to the next that writ):
And thus upon the stage 'tis fairly [2] thrown;
Let him that takes it wear it as his own.

PROLOGUE DESIGNED FOR MR. D'URFEY'S LAST PLAY [3]

Grown old in rhyme, 'twere barbarous to discard
Your persevering, unexhausted bard:
Damnation follows death in other men,
But your damn'd poet lives and writes again.

---

[1] Shows a cap with ears.   [2] Flings down the cap, and exit.
[3] Tom D'Urfey died in 1723.

The adventurous lover is successful still, 5
Who strives to please the fair against her will:
Be kind and make him in his wishes easy,
Who in your own despite has strove to please ye.
He scorn'd to borrow from the wits of yore;
But ever writ as none e'er writ before. 10
You modern wits, should each man bring his claim,
Have desperate debentures on your fame;
And little would be left you, I'm afraid,
If all your debts to Greece and Rome were paid.
From his deep fund our Author largely draws, 15
Nor sinks his credit lower than it was.
Though plays for honour in old time he made,
'Tis now for better reasons—to be paid.
Believe him, he has known the world too long,
And seen the death of much immortal song. 20
He says poor poets lost while players won,
As pimps grow rich while gallants are undone.
Though Tom the poet writ with ease and pleasure,
The comic Tom abounds in other treasure.
Fame is at best an unperforming cheat; 25
But 'tis substantial happiness to eat.
Let ease, his last request, be of your giving,
Nor force him to be damn'd to get his living.

PROLOGUE TO THOMSON'S "SOPHONISBA"[1]

WHEN learning, after the long Gothic night,
Fair o'er the western world, renew'd its light,
With arts arising Sophonisba rose;
The Tragic Muse, returning wept her woes.
With her the Italian scene first learn'd to glow, 5
And the first tears for her were taught to flow:
Her charms the Gallic Muses next inspired;
Corneille himself saw, wonder'd, and was fired.
     What foreign theatres with pride have shown,
Britain, by juster title, makes her own. 10
When freedom is the cause, 'tis hers to fight,
And hers, when freedom is the theme, to write.

[1] Dr. Johnson, in his *Life of Pope*, says, " I have been told by Savage that of the ' Prologue to *Sophonisba* ' the first part was written by Pope, who could not be persuaded to finish it, and that the concluding lines were added by Mallet."

For this a British author bids again
The heroine rise to grace the British scene:
Here, as in life, she breathes her genuine flame;   15
She asks what bosom has not felt the same,
Asks of the British youth—is silence there?
She dares to ask it of the British fair.
To-night our homespun author would be true
At once to nature, history, and you.   20
Well pleased to give our neighbours due applause,
He owns their learning but disdains their laws;
Not to his patient touch, or happy flame,
'Tis to his British heart he trusts for fame.
If France excel him in one freeborn thought,   25
The man, as well as poet, is in fault.
Nature! informer of the poet's art,
Whose force alone can raise or melt the heart,
Thou art his guide; each passion, every line,
Whate'er he draws to please, must all be thine,   30
Be thou his judge: in every candid breast
Thy silent whisper is the sacred test.

OCCASIONED BY SOME VERSES OF HIS GRACE THE DUKE OF BUCKINGHAM

MUSE, 'tis enough: at length thy labour ends,
And thou shalt live, for Buckingham commends.
Let crowds of critics now my verse assail,
Let Dennis write, and nameless numbers rail:
This more than pays whole years of thankless pain,   5
Time, health, and fortune are not lost in vain.
Sheffield approves, consenting Phœbus bends,
And I and Malice from this hour are friends.

The lines by Buckingham compliment Pope on his *Iliad*, and also on his worth as a companion and friend. For a notice of Sheffield, Duke of Buckingham, see Pope, *Essay on Criticism*.

MACER: A CHARACTER

WHEN simple Macer, now of high renown,
First sought a poet's fortune in the town,
'Twas all the ambition his high soul could feel
To wear red stockings and to dine with Steele.

Some ends of verse his betters might afford, 5
And gave the harmless fellow a good word.
Set up with these, he ventured on the town,
And with a borrow'd play outdid poor Crowne;
There he stopp'd short, nor since has writ a tittle,
But has the wit to make the most of little: 10
Like stunted hide-bound trees, that just have got
Sufficient sap at once to bear and rot.
Now he begs verse, and what he gets commends,
Not of the wits his foes, but fools his friends.

So some coarse country wench, almost decay'd, 15
Trudges to town, and first turns chambermaid;
Awkward and supple, each devoir to pay;
She flatters her good lady twice a day;
Thought wondrous honest, though of mean degree,
And strangely liked for her simplicity: 20
In a translated suit, then tries the town,
With borrow'd pins, and patches not her own:
But just endured the winter she began,
And in four months a batter'd harridan.
Now nothing left, but wither'd, pale, and shrunk, 25
To bawd for others, and go shares with Punk.

Ambrose Philips seems to be the person satirised. On the acces-
sion of George I., when the Whigs obtained power, Philips was put
into the commission of the peace, and appointed a Commissioner of
the Lottery. The "borrowed play" was the *Distrest Mother*, from
Racine, which was highly successful. The allusion to "simplicity"
is no doubt intended to refer to Philips' *Pastorals*, and that to the
"translated suit" to his *Persian Tales*, translated for Tonson. The
next piece, "Umbra," refers probably to Walter Carey (see footnote
3, on page 220), who liked writers but whom he bored. Philips and
Budgell, also suggested, were too much in Addison's favour to be
treated as described; James Moore Smythe, also suggested, was only
fifteen when the poem was written.

UMBRA

CLOSE to the best-known author Umbra sits,
The constant index to old Button's wits.
"Who's here?" cries Umbra: "only Johnson."—"O!
Your slave," and exit; but returns with Rowe:
"Dear Rowe, let's sit and talk of tragedies": 5
Ere long Pope enters, and to Pope he flies.

Then up comes Steele: he turns upon his heel,
And in a moment fastens upon Steele;
But cries as soon, "Dear Dick, I must be gone,
For, if I know his tread, here's Addison."   10
Says Addison to Steele, " 'Tis time to go";
Pope to the closet steps aside with Rowe.
Poor Umbra, left in this abandon'd pickle,
E'en sits him down and writes to honest Tickell,
Fool! 'tis in vain from wit to wit to roam;   15
Know sense, like charity, begins at home.

SANDYS' GHOST[1]

OR A PROPER NEW BALLAD ON THE NEW OVID'S "METAMOR-
PHOSES," AS IT WAS INTENDED TO BE TRANSLATED BY
PERSONS OF QUALITY

YE Lords and Commons, men of wit
    And pleasure about town;
Read this ere you translate one bit
    Of books of high renown.

Beware of Latin authors all!   5
    Nor think your verses sterling,
Though with a golden pen you scrawl,
    And scribble in a berlin:

For not the desk with silver nails,
    Nor bureau of expense,
Nor standish well japann'd, avails   10
    To writing of good sense.

Hear how a ghost in dead of night,
    With saucer eyes of fire,
In woeful wise did sore affright   15
    A wit and courtly 'squire.

[1] The last literary labour of Sir Samuel Garth, before his death in 1718, was engaging several "ingenious gentlemen," to undertake a translation of Ovid's *Metamorphoses*. Among these were Mainwaring, Croxall, Ozell, Vernon, Harvey, Leonard Welsted and Pope. Garth himself translated the fourteenth book and part of the fifteenth, besides contributing a preface. In the event the contributors did not turn out quite as foreseen in those verses.

Rare imp of Phœbus, hopeful youth!
　　Like puppy tame that uses
To fetch and carry, in his mouth,
　　The works of all the Muses.　　　　　　　　20

Ah! why did he write poetry,
　　That hereto was so civil;
And sell his soul for vanity,
　　To rhyming and the devil?

A desk he had of curious work,　　　　　　　25
　　With glittering studs about;
Within the same did Sandys lurk,[1]
　　Though Ovid lay without.

Now as he scratch'd to fetch up thought,
　　Forth popp'd the sprite so thin;　　　　　　30
And from the keyhole bolted out,
　　All upright as a pin.

With whiskers, band, and pantaloon,
　　And ruff composed most duly;
This 'squire he dropp'd his pen full soon,[2]　　35
　　While as the light burnt bluely.

"Ho, Master Sam," quoth Sandys' sprite,
　　Write on, nor let me scare ye;
Forsooth, if rhymes fall in not right,
　　To Budgell seek, or Carey.　　　　　　　　40

I hear the beat of Jacob's drums,[3]
　　Poor Ovid finds no quarter!
See first the merry P—— comes[4]
　　In haste without his garter.

Then lords and lordlings, 'squires and knights,　45
　　Wits, witlings, prigs, and peers;
Garth at St. James's, and at White's,
　　Beat up for volunteers.

---

[1] Sandys published his translation of Ovid in 1627.
[2] Samuel Molyneux, as in line 37.
[3] Jacob Tonson, the publisher.　　[4] Pelham, Thomas, Duke of Newcastle.

What Fenton will not do, nor Gay,
    Nor Congreve, Rowe, nor Stanyan,   50
Tom B——t [1] or Tom D'Urfey may,
    John Dunton, Steele, or any one.

If Justice Philips' costive head
    Some frigid rhymes disburses;
They shall like Persian tales be read,   55
    And glad both babes and nurses.

Let W—rw—k's muse with Ash—t join, [2]
    And Ozell's with Lord Hervey's:
Tickell and Addison combine,
    And P—pe [3] translate with Jervas.   60

L—— himself, that lively lord, [4]
    Who bows to every lady,
Shall join with F—— [5] in one accord,
    And be like Tate and Brady. [6]

Ye ladies too draw forth your pen,   65
    I pray where can the hurt lie?
Since you have brains as well as men,
    As witness Lady W—l—y. [7]

Now, Tonson, list thy forces all,
    Review them, and tell noses;   70
For to poor Ovid shall befall
    A strange metamorphosis.

A metamorphosis more strange
    Than all his books can vapour "——
"To what," quoth 'squire, "shall Ovid change?" 75
    Quoth Sandys: "To waste paper."

---

[1] Tom Burnet.
[2] Lord Warwick and Dr. Ashurst.   [3] Pope.
[4] Lord Lansdowne, or Lord Lumley, second Earl of Scarborough.
[5] Philip Frowde, a dramatic writer and fine scholar, a friend of Addison's.
[6] Who produced a rather dull versification of the Psalms.
[7] Lady Mary Wortley Montagu. Some of Lady Mary's *Town Eclogues*
were published in 1716.

THE TRANSLATOR [1]

OZELL, at Sanger's call, invoked his Muse—
For who to sing for Sanger could refuse?
His numbers such as Sanger's self might use.
Reviving Perrault, murdering Boileau, he
Slander'd the ancients first, then Wycherley;   5
Which yet not much that old bard's anger raised,
Since those were slander'd most whom Ozell praised.
Nor had the gentle satire caused complaining,
Had not sage Rowe pronounced it entertaining:
How great must be the judgment of that writer   10
Who the *Plain Dealer* damns, and prints the *Biter* !

THE THREE GENTLE SHEPHERDS [2]

OF gentle Philips will I ever sing,
With gentle Philips shall the valleys ring;
My numbers too for ever will I vary,
With gentle Budgell and with gentle Carey.
Or if in ranging of the names I judge ill,   5
With gentle Carey and with gentle Budgell:
Oh! may all gentle bards together place ye,
Men of good hearts, and men of delicacy.
May satire ne'er befool ye, or beknave ye,
And from all wits that have a knack, God save ye.   10

[1] Sanger was a bookseller who published Ozell's translation of Boileau's *Lutrin*, which Rowe considered entertaining. *The Plain Dealer* is Wycherley's best comedy; *The Biter*, a very indifferent one, by Rowe. As to Ozell, he will be found in the *Dunciad*.

[2] The three shepherds—two of whom Pope never tired of satirising—were Ambrose Philips, Eustace Budgell and Henry Carey. What poor Carey had done to irritate the poet does not appear. He, too, had ridiculed Philips's namby-pamby verses; and his song of *Sally in our Alley* should have formed a passport to favour. Addison, however, had praised it in the *Spectator*, and to this probably Çarey owed his being ranked with the Whig poets. It might be Walter Carey. In the last line Pope alludes to Curll's boast that in prose he was equal to Pope, but in poetry *Pope had a particular knack*! "Mr. Pope," he said, "is no more a gentleman than Mr. Curll, nor more eminent as a poet than he as a bookseller."

THE CHALLENGE

A COURT BALLAD [1716]

To the tune of " To all you Ladies now at Land," etc.

I

To one fair lady out of Court,
　　And two fair ladies in,
Who think the Turk and Pope a sport,
　　And wit and love no sin!
Come, these soft lines, with nothing stiff in,　　5
To Bellenden, Lepell, and Griffin.[1]
　　　　With a fa, la, la.

II

What passes in the dark third row,
　　And what behind the scene,
Couches and crippled chairs I know,　　10
　　And garrets hung with green;
I know the swing of sinful hack,
Where many damsels cry alack.
　　　　With a fa, la, la.

III

Then why to Courts should I repair,　　15
　　Where's such ado with Townshend?[2]
To hear each mortal stamp and swear,
　　And every speech with "zounds" end;
To hear 'em rail at honest Sunderland,[3]
And rashly blame the realm of Blunderland.　　20
　　　　With a fa, la, la.

[1] Ladies of the court of the Princess Caroline. Mary Bellenden became the wife of Colonel Campbell (afterwards Duke of Argyll), and Mary Lepell married Lord Hervey. Both marriages took place in October 1720.

[2] Lord Townshend, a rough but popular minister, had had a rupture with his colleagues Stanhope and Sunderland which ended in his being dismissed the Secretaryship of State and relegated to Ireland as Lord Lieutenant.

[3] The Earl of Sunderland, previously Lord-Lieutenant of Ireland, had been charged with encouraging the native Irish. Hence the talk concerning "Blunderland." Died 1722.

IV

Alas! like Schutz I cannot pun,[1]
  Like Grafton court the Germans;
Tell Pickenbourg how slim she's grown,
  Like Meadows run to sermons;   **25**
To Court ambitious men may roam,
But I and Marlborough stay at home.
      With a fa, la, la.

V

In truth, by what I can discern
  Of courtiers, 'twixt you three,   **30**
Some wit you have, and more may learn
  From Court, than Gay or me:
Perhaps, in time, you'll leave high diet,
To sup with us on milk and quiet.
      With a fa, la, la.   **35**

VI

At Leicester Fields, a house full high,
  With door all painted green,
Where ribbons wave upon the tie,
  (A milliner, I mean;)
There may you meet us three to three,   **40**
For Gay can well make two of me.
      With a fa, la, la.

VII

But should you catch the prudish itch,
  And each become a coward,
Bring sometimes with you Lady Rich,[2]   **45**
  And sometimes Mistress Howard;
For virgins, to keep chaste, must go
Abroad with such as are not so.
      With a fa, la, la.

[1] Augustus Schutz, Equerry to Prince George. The "Grafton" mentioned in the next line was the Duke of Grafton, the second duke, who was one of the Lords of the Bedchamber in 1714, and next year of the Privy Council. "Pickenbourg" and "Meadows" were maids of honour, the latter a sister of Sir Sidney Meadows.

[2] Lady Rich, one of the correspondents of Lady Mary Wortley Montagu, was the wife of Sir Robert Rich, Bart. She was a daughter of Colonel Griffin and sister of Miss Griffin, of the princess's establishment, alluded to in the first stanza. "Mistress Howard," afterwards Countess of Suffolk, is the person alluded to in the next line.

VIII

And thus, fair maids, my ballad ends: 50
  God send the king safe landing;
And make all honest ladies friends
  To armies that are standing;
Preserve the limits of those nations,
And take off ladies' limitations.   55
    With a fa, la, la.

ON BURNET AND DUCKET [1]

Burnet and Ducket, friends in spite,
  Came hissing forth in verse;
Both were so forward, each would write,
  So dull, each hung an A ——
Thus *Amphisbœna* (I have read)
  At either end assails;
None knows which leads, or which is led,
  For both heads are but tails.

ON SHAKESPEARE RESTORED [2]

'Tis generous, Tibald! in thee and thy brothers,
To help us thus to read the works of others:
Never for this can just returns be shown;
For who will help us e'er to read thy own?

ANSWER TO MRS. HOWE [3]

WHAT IS PRUDERY?
                              'Tis a beldam,
  Seen with wit and beauty seldom
'Tis a fear that starts at shadows;
'Tis (no 'tisn't) like Miss Meadows. [4]   5

[1] Thomas Burnet and George Duckett had derided Pope's *Homer* in their
Homerides.
[2] Theobald criticised Pope's edition of Shakespeare in *Shakespeare
Restored*.
[3] "Mrs. Lepell and Mrs. Howe asked Mr. Pope what *Prudery* is."
[4] Also a Maid of Honour: sister to Sir Sidney Meadows.

'Tis a virgin hard of feature,
Old, and void of all good-nature;
Lean and fretful, would seem wise;
Yet plays the fool before she dies.
'Tis an ugly envious shrew,   10
That rails at dear Lepell, and you.

[Miss Sophia Howe was one of the Maids of Honour to the
Princess Caroline. She was a daughter of General Howe, brother
of the first viscount of that name.
  She died 1726.]

ON A CERTAIN LADY AT COURT[1]

I KNOW the thing that's most uncommon;
  (Envy be silent and attend!)
I know a reasonable woman,
  Handsome and witty, yet a friend.

Not warp'd by passion, awed by rumour,   5
  Nor grave through pride, or gay through folly;
An equal mixture of good humour
  And sensible soft melancholy.

"Has she no faults, then (Envy says), sir?"
  Yes, she has one, I must aver: 10
When all the world conspires to praise her,
  The woman's deaf, and does not hear.

A FAREWELL TO LONDON

IN THE YEAR 1715

DEAR, damn'd, distracting town, farewell!
  Thy fools no more I'll tease:
This year in peace, ye critics, dwell,
  Ye harlots, sleep at ease!

Soft B——s and rough C——s, adieu,[2]   5
  Earl Warwick, make your moan,
The lively H——k and you
  May knock up whores alone.

[1] Mrs. Howard, Countess of Suffolk.
[2] There was one Brocas—" Beau Brocas "—whom Pope mentions in an
epistle to H. Cromwell. Ayre also mentions a Mr. Fettiplace Bellers, of
Crown Allins, Gloucestershire, " an intimate acquaintance of Mr. Pope's,
and much esteemed by him."

To drink and droll be Rowe allow'd
  Till the third watchman's toll;   10
Let Jervas gratis paint, and Frowde [1]
  Save threepence and his soul.

Farewell, Arbuthnot's raillery
  On every learned sot;
And Garth, the best good Christian he,   15
  Although he knows it not.

Lintot, farewell! thy bard must go; [2]
  Farewell, unhappy Tonson!
Heaven gives thee for thy loss of Rowe, [3]
  Lean Philips and fat Johnson. [4]   20

Why should I stay? Both parties rage;
  My vixen mistress squalls;
The wits in envious feuds engage:
  And Homer (damn him!) calls.

The love of arts lies cold and dead   25
  In Halifax's urn;
And not one Muse of all he fed
  Has yet the grace to mourn. [5]

My friends, by turns, my friends confound,
  Betray, and are betrayed: 30
Poor Y——r's sold for fifty pounds
  And B——ll is a jade. [6]

Why make I friendships with the great,
  When I no favour seek?
Or follow girls, seven hours in eight,   35
  I need but once a week?

[1] See poem, "Sandys' Ghost," in which Frowde is alluded to.
[2] The publisher of Pope's *Iliad*.
[3] Rowe had the year before, on the accession of George I., been made Poet Laureate, one of the land surveyors of the Port of London, Clerk of the Closet to the Prince of Wales, and Secretary of Presentations under the Lord Chancellor. Such an accumulation of offices might well suspend for a season the poetical and publishing pursuits of Rowe.
[4] The "Johnson" coupled with Ambrose Philips was Charles Johnson, the dramatist, who died in 1748.
[5] The date of Halifax's death was 19th May, 1715.
[6] Mrs. Elizabeth Younger and her sister, Mrs. M. Bicknell, both of whom had acted in *The What d'ye call it*, the latter in *Three Hours after Marriage*.

Still idle, with a busy air,
  Deep whimsies to contrive;
The gayest valetudinaire,
  Most thinking rake, alive.   40

Solicitous for other ends,
  Though fond of dear repose;
Careless or drowsy with my friends,
  And frolic with my foes.

Luxurious lobster-nights, farewell,   45
  For sober, studious days;
And Burlington's delicious meal,
  For salads, tarts, and pease!

Adieu to all, but Gay alone,
  Whose soul, sincere and free,   50
Loves all mankind, but flatters none,
  And so may starve with me.

TO BELINDA [1]

ON THE RAPE OF THE LOCK

PLEASED in these lines, Belinda, you may view
How things are prized, which once belonged to you:
If on some meaner head this Lock had grown,
The nymph despised, the Rape had been unknown.
But what concerns the valiant and the fair,   5
The Muse asserts as her peculiar care.
Thus Helen's rape and Menelaus' wrong
Became the subject of great Homer's song;
And, lost in ancient times, the golden fleece
Was raised to fame by all the wits of Greece.   10
   Had fate decreed, propitious to your prayers,
To give their utmost date to all your hairs;
This lock, of which late ages now shall tell,
Had dropt like fruit, neglected, when it fell.

[1] This is probably the alternative Preface Pope offered Miss Fermor with the Dedication (see page 76).

Nature to your undoing arms mankind 15
With strength of body, artifice of mind;
But gives your feeble sex, made up of fears,
No guard but virtue, no redress but tears.
Yet custom (seldom to your favour gained)
Absolves the virgin when by force constrained. 20
Thus Lucrece lives unblemished in her fame,
A bright example of young Tarquin's shame.
Such praise is yours—and such shall you possess,
Your virtue equal, though your loss be less.
Then smile Belinda at reproachful tongues, 25
Still warm our hearts, and still inspire our songs.
But would your charms to distant times extend,
Let Jervas paint them, and let Pope commend.
Who censured most, more precious hairs would lose,
To have the Rape recorded by his muse. 30

EXTEMPORANEOUS LINES

ON THE PICTURE OF LADY MARY W. MONTAGU, BY KNELLER

THE playful smiles around the dimpled mouth,
That happy air of majesty and truth;
So would I draw (but oh! 'tis vain to try,
My narrow genius does the power deny);
The equal lustre of the heavenly mind, 5
Where every grace with every virtue's join'd;
Learning not vain, and wisdom not severe,
With greatness easy, and with wit sincere;
With just description show the work divine,
And the whole princess in my work should shine. 10

TO MR. GAY

WHO CONGRATULATED HIM ON FINISHING HIS HOUSE
AND GARDENS

AH, friend! 'tis true—this truth you lovers know—
In vain my structures rise, my gardens grow;
In vain fair Thames reflects the double scenes

Of hanging mountains and of sloping greens:
Joy lives not here,—to happier seats it flies,   5
And only dwells where Wortley casts her eyes.
What are the gay parterre, the chequer'd shade,
The morning bower, the evening colonnade,
But soft recesses of uneasy minds,
To sigh unheard in, to the passing winds?   10
So the struck deer in some sequester'd part
Lies down to die, the arrow at his heart;
He, stretch'd unseen in coverts hid from day,
Bleeds drop by drop, and pants his life away.

LINES WRITTEN IN WINDSOR FOREST

" I arrived in the forest by Tuesday noon. I passed the rest of
the day in those woods, where I have so often enjoyed a book and
a friend; I made a hymn as I passed through, which ended with a
sigh that I will not tell you the meaning of."—*Pope to Martha
Blount.*

ALL hail, once pleasing, once inspiring shade!
    Scene of my youthful loves and happier hours!
Where the kind Muses met me as I stray'd,
    And gently press'd my hand, and said, "Be ours!—
Take all thou e'er shalt have, a constant Muse: 5
    At Court thou may'st be liked, but nothing gain:
Stock thou may'st buy and sell, but always lose,
    And love the brightest eyes, but love in vain."

ERINNA

THOUGH sprightly Sappho force our love and praise,
A softer wonder my pleased soul surveys,
The mild Erinna blushing in her bays.
So while the sun's broad beam yet strikes the sight,
All mild appears the moon's more sober light;   5
Serene in virgin majesty she shines,
And unobserved the glaring orb declines.[1]

[1] This simile the poet afterwards inserted in his *Moral Essays*, Ep II.

ON HIS GROTTO AT TWICKENHAM

COMPOSED OF MARBLES, SPARS, GEMS, ORES, AND MINERALS

THOU who shalt stop where Thames' translucent wave
Shines a broad mirror through the shadowy cave;
Where lingering drops from mineral roofs distil,
And pointed crystals break the sparkling rill,
Unpolish'd gems no ray on pride bestow, 5
And latent metals innocently glow:
Approach. Great Nature studiously behold!
And eye the mine without a wish for gold.
Approach: but awful! lo! the Ægerian grot,
Where, nobly pensive, St. John sat and thought; 10
Where British sighs from dying Wyndham stole,
And the bright flame was shot through Marchmont's soul.
Let such, such only, tread this sacred floor,
Who dare to love their country, and be poor!

ON THE COUNTESS OF BURLINGTON CUTTING PAPER

PALLAS grew vapourish once, and odd,
 She would not do the least right thing,
Either for goddess, or for god,
 Nor work, nor play, nor paint, nor sing.

Jove frown'd, and, "Use," he cried, "those eyes 5
 So skilful, and those hands so taper;
Do something exquisite and wise—"
 She bow'd, obey'd him,—and cut paper.

This vexing him who gave her birth,
 Thought by all heaven a burning shame; 10
What does she next, but bids, on earth,
 Her Burlington do just the same.

Pallas, you give yourself strange airs;
 But sure you'll find it hard to spoil
The sense and taste of one that bears 15
 The name of Saville and of Boyle.

Alas! one bad example shown;
    How quickly all the sex pursue!
See, madam, see the arts o'erthrown,
    Between John Overton and you!   20

OF A LADY'S SICKNESS [1]

AH Serenissa, from our arms
Did you for death's preserve your charms;
From us that served so long in vain,
Shall heaven so soon the prize obtain?
Sickness, its courtship, makes the fair   5
As pale as her own lovers are.
    Sure you, the goddess we adore,
Who all celestial seemed before,
While vows and service nothing gained,
Which, were you woman, had obtained;   10
At last in pity, for our sake,
Descend in human form to take,
And by this sickness choose to tell
You are not now invincible.

LINES ON A GROTTO AT CRUX-EASTON, HANTS

Warton says this grotto was adorned with shell-work, and was
constructed by the Misses Lisle, sisters of Dr. Lisle, Chaplain to the
Factory at Smyrna.

HERE, shunning idleness at once and praise,
This radiant pile nine rural sisters raise;
The glittering emblem of each spotless dame,
Clear as her soul and shining as her frame;
Beauty which Nature only can impart,   5
And such a polish as disgraces art;
But Fate disposed them in this humble sort,
And hid in deserts what would charm a Court.

[1] This is No. III of five "Verses in imitation of Waller. By a Youth of
thirteen." Of a Lady singing to her Lute (see page 5) was originally one of
these, and alone was reprinted by him.

VERSES LEFT BY MR. POPE

ON HIS LYING IN THE SAME BED WHICH WILMOT, THE CELEBRATED
EARL OF ROCHESTER, SLEPT IN AT ADDERBURY, THEN
BELONGING TO THE DUKE OF ARGYLL, JULY 9, 1739

WITH no poetic ardours fired
    I press the bed where Wilmot lay;
That here he loved, or here expired,
    Begets no numbers, grave or gay.

Beneath thy roof, Argyll, are bred   5
    Such thoughts as prompt the brave to lie
Stretch'd out in honour's nobler bed,
    Beneath a nobler roof—the sky.

Such flames as high in patriots burn
    Yet stoop to bless a child or wife;   10
And such as wicked kings may mourn,
    When freedom is more dear than life.

A PROLOGUE

TO A PLAY FOR MR. DENNIS'S BENEFIT IN 1733, WHEN HE WAS
OLD, BLIND, AND IN GREAT DISTRESS, A LITTLE BEFORE
HIS DEATH

As when that hero, who in each campaign
Had braved the Goth, and many a Vandal slain,
Lay fortune-struck, a spectacle of woe!
Wept by each friend, forgiven by every foe;
Was there a generous, a reflecting mind,   5
But pitied Belisarius old and blind?
Was there a chief but melted at the sight?
A common soldier but who clubb'd his mite?
Such, such emotions should in Britons rise,
When press'd by want and weakness DENNIS lies;   10
Dennis, who long had warr'd with modern Huns,
Their quibbles routed, and defied their puns:
A desperate bulwark, sturdy, firm, and fierce,
Against the Gothic sons of frozen verse:

How changed from him who made the boxes groan,   15
And shook the stage with thunders all his own!
Stood up to dash each vain pretender's hope,
Maul the French tyrant, or pull down the Pope!
If there's a Briton then, true bred and born,
Who holds dragoons and wooden shoes in scorn;   20
If there's a critic of distinguish'd rage;
If there's a senior, who contemns this age:
Let him to-night his just assistance lend,
And be the critic's, Briton's, old man's friend.

TO MR. LEMUEL GULLIVER

THE GRATEFUL ADDRESS OF THE UNHAPPY HOUYHNHNMS, NOW IN SLAVERY AND BONDAGE IN ENGLAND.[1]

To thee, we wretches of the Houyhnhnm band,
Condemned to labour in a barb'rous land,
Return our thanks. Accept our humble lays,
And let each grateful Houyhnhnm neigh thy praise.

O happy Yahoo, purged from human crimes,   5
By thy sweet sojourn in those virtuous climes,
Where reign our sires! There, to thy country's shame,
Reason, you found, and virtue were the same.
Their precepts razed the prejudice of youth,
And even a Yahoo learned the love of truth.   10

Art thou the first who did the coast explore;
Did never Yahoo tread that ground before?
Yes, thousands. But in pity to their kind,
Or swayed by envy, or through pride of mind,
They hid their knowledge of a nobler race,   15
Which owned, would all their sires and sons disgrace.

[1] Pope, in a letter to Swift, 8th March, 1726-7, writes, "You received, I hope, some commendatory verses from a horse and a Lilliputian to Gulliver and an heroic epistle to Mrs. Gulliver. The bookseller would fain have printed them before the second edition of the book, but I would not permit it without your approbation; nor do I much like them."

You, like the Samian, visit lands unknown,
And by their wiser morals mend your own.
Thus Orpheus travelled to reform his kind,
Came back, and tamed the brutes he left behind.　　　20

You went, you saw, you heard: with virtue fraught,
Then spread those morals which the Houyhnhnms taught.
Our labours here must touch thy gen'rous heart,
To see us strain before the coach and cart;
Compelled to run each knavish jockey's heat!　　　25
Subservient to New-market's annual cheat!
With what reluctance do we lawyers bear,
To fleece their country clients twice a year?
Or managed in your schools, for fops to ride,
How foam, how fret beneath a load of pride!　　　30
Yes, we are slaves—but yet, by reason's force,
Have learnt to bear misfortune, like a horse.

O would the stars, to ease my bonds, ordain,
That gentle Gulliver might guide my rein!
Safe would I bear him to his journey's end,　　　35
For 'tis a pleasure to support a friend.
But if my life be doomed to serve the bad,
O! may'st thou never want an easy pad!

　　　　　　　　　　　　　　　Houyhnhnm.

THE LAMENTATION OF GLUMDALCLITCH FOR THE LOSS OF GRILDRIG

A PASTORAL

Soon as Glumdalclitch miss'd her pleasing care,
She wept, she blubber'd, and she tore her hair.
No British miss sincerer grief has known,
Her squirrel missing, or her sparrow flown.
She furl'd her sampler, and haul'd in her thread,　　　5
And stuck her needle into Grildrig's bed;
Then spread her hands, and with a bounce let fall
Her baby, like the giant in Guildhall.
In peals of thunder now she roars, and now
She gently whimpers like a lowing cow:　　　10
Yet lovely in her sorrow still appears,
Her locks dishevell'd, and her flood of tears.

Seem like the lofty barn of some rich swain,
When from the thatch drips fast a shower of rain.
   In vain she search'd each cranny of the house,   15
Each gaping chink impervious to a mouse.
"Was it for this (she cried) with daily care
Within thy reach I set the vinegar,
And fill'd the cruet with the acid tide,
While pepper-water worms thy bait supplied;   20
Where twined the silver eel around thy hook,
And all the little monsters of the brook?
Sure in that lake he dropp'd; my Grilly's drown'd."
She dragg'd the cruet, but no Grildrig found.
   "Vain is thy courage, Grilly, vain thy boast;   25
But little creatures enterprise the most.
Trembling, I've seen thee dare the kitten's paw,
Nay, mix with children as they play'd at taw,
Nor fear the marbles, as they bounding flew;
Marbles to them, but rolling rocks to you.   30
   "Why did I trust you with that giddy youth?
Who from a page can ever learn the truth?
Versed in Court tricks, that money-loving boy
To some lord's daughter sold the living toy;
Or rent him limb from limb in cruel play,   35
As children tear the wings of flies away.
From place to place o'er Brobdignag I'll roam,
And never will return or bring thee home.
But who has eyes to trace the passing wind?
How then thy fairy footsteps can I find?   40
Dost thou bewilder'd wander all alone,
In the green thicket of a mossy stone;
Or tumbled from the toadstool's slippery round,
Perhaps all maim'd, lie grovelling on the ground?
Dost thou, embosom'd in the lovely rose,   45
Or sunk within the peach's down, repose?
Within the king-cup if thy limbs are spread,
Or in the golden cowslip's velvet head:
O show me, Flora, 'midst those sweets, the flower
Where sleeps my Grildrig in his fragrant bower!   50
   " But ah! I fear thy little fancy roves
On little females, and on little loves;
The pigmy children, and thy tiny spouse,
Thy baby playthings that adorn thy house,
Doors, windows, chimneys, and the spacious rooms,   55

Equal in size to cells of honeycombs,
Hast thou for these now ventured from the shore,
Thy bark a bean-shell, and a straw thy oar?
Or in thy box, now bounding on the main,
Shall I ne'er bear thy self and house again? 60
And shall I set thee on my hand no more,
To see thee leap the lines, and traverse o'er
My spacious palm? Of stature scarce a span,
Mimic the actions of a real man?
No more behold thee turn my watch's key, 65
As seamen at a capstan anchors weigh?
How wert thou wont to walk with cautious tread,
A dish of tea like milk-pail on thy head?
How chase the mite that bore thy cheese away,
And keep the rolling maggot at a bay?" 70
    She said, but broken accents stopp'd her voice,
Soft as the speaking-trumpet's mellow noise:
She sobb'd a storm, and wiped her flowing eyes,
Which seem'd like two broad suns in misty skies!
O squander not thy grief; those tears command 75
To weep upon our cod in Newfoundland:
The plenteous pickle shall preserve the fish,
And Europe taste thy sorrows in a dish.

MARY GULLIVER TO CAPTAIN LEMUEL GULLIVER

ARGUMENT

The captain, some time after his return, being retired to Mr.
Sympson's in the country, Mrs. Gulliver, apprehending from his
late behaviour some estrangement of his affections, writes him the
following expostulating, soothing, and tenderly-complaining epistle.

WELCOME, thrice welcome, to thy native place!
—What, touch me not? what, shun a wife's embrace?
Have I for this thy tedious absence borne,
And waked, and wish'd whole nights for thy return?
In five long years I took no second spouse; 5
What Redriff wife so long hath kept her vows?
Your eyes, your nose, inconstancy betray;
Your nose you stop, your eyes you turn away.
'Tis said that thou should'st cleave unto thy wife;
Once thou didst cleave, and I could cleave for life. 10

Hear, and relent! hark how thy children moan;
Be kind at least to these, they are thy own:
Be bold, and count them all; secure to find
The honest number that you left behind.
See how they pat thee with their pretty paws: 15
Why start you? are they snakes? or have they claws?
Thy Christian seed, our mutual flesh and bone:
Be kind at least to these, they are thy own.

Biddell, like thee, might farthest India rove;
He changed his country, but retain'd his love.   20
There's Captain Pennell,[1] absent half his life,
Comes back, and is the kinder to his wife.
Yet Pennell's wife is brown, compared to me;
And Mrs. Biddell sure is fifty-three.

Not touch me! never neighbour call'd me slut: 25
Was Flimnap's dame more sweet in Lilliput?
I've no red hair to breathe an odious fume;
At least thy consort's cleaner than thy groom.
Why then that dirty stable-boy thy care?
What mean those visits to the sorrel mare?   30
Say by what witchcraft, or what demon led,—
Preferr'st thou litter to the marriage bed!

Some say the devil himself is in that mare:
If so, our dean shall drive him forth by prayer.
Some think you mad, some think you are possess'd;   35
That Bedlam and clean straw will suit you best.
Vain means, alas! this frenzy to appease,
That straw, that straw, would heighten the disease.

My bed (the scene of all our former joys,
Witness two lovely girls, two lovely boys,)   40
Alone I press; in dreams I call my dear,
I stretch my hand, no Gulliver is there!
I wake, I rise, and, shivering with the frost,
Search all the house,—my Gulliver is lost!
Forth in the street I rush with frantic cries;   45
The windows open, all the neighbours rise;
"Where sleeps my Gulliver? O tell me where!"
The neighbours answer, "With the sorrel mare."

At early morn I to the market haste
(Studious in everything to please thy taste);   50
A curious fowl and sparagrass I chose
(For I remember you were fond of those);

[1] Names of the sea captains mentioned in *Gulliver's Travels.*

Three shillings cost the first, the last seven groats;
Sullen you turn from both, and call for oats.
    Others bring goods and treasure to their houses,   55
Something to deck their pretty babes and spouses;
My only token was a cup-like horn,
That's made of nothing but a lady's corn.
'Tis not for that I grieve; no, 'tis to see
The groom and sorrel mare preferred to me!   60
    These, for some moments when you deign to quit,
And (at due distance) sweet discourse admit,
'Tis all my pleasure thy past toil to know,
For pleased remembrance builds delight on woe.
At every danger pants thy consort's breast,   65
And gaping infants squall to hear the rest.
How did I tremble, when, by thousands bound,
I saw thee stretch'd on Lilliputian ground?
When scaling armies climb'd up every part,
Each step they trod I felt upon my heart.   70
But when thy torrent quench'd the dreadful blaze,
King, queen, and nation staring with amaze,
Full in my view how all my husband came,
And what extinguish'd theirs, increased my flame.
Those spectacles, ordain'd thine eyes to save,   75
Were once my present; love that armour gave.
How did I mourn at Bolgolam's decree!
For when he sign'd thy death, he sentenced me.
    When folks might see thee all the country round
For sixpence, I'd have given a thousand pound.   80
Lord! when the giant-babe that head of thine
Got in his mouth, my heart was up in mine!
When in the marrow-bone I see thee ramm'd,
Or on the house-top by the monkey cramm'd,
The piteous images renew my pain,   85
And all thy dangers I weep o'er again.
But on the maiden's nipple when you rid,
Pray Heaven, 'twas all a wanton maiden did!
Glumdalclitch too!—with thee I mourn her case:
Heaven guard the gentle girl from all disgrace!   90
O may the king that one neglect forgive,
And pardon her the fault by which I live!
Was there no other way to set him free?
My life, alas! I fear proved death to thee.
    O teach me, dear, new words to speak my flame!   95

Teach me to woo thee by thy best-loved name!
Whether the style of Grildrig please thee most,
So call'd on Brobdignag's stupendous coast,
When on the monarch's ample hand you sate,
And holloa'd in his ear intrigues of state;   100
Or Quinbus Flestrin more endearment brings;
When like a mountain you looked down on kings;
If ducal Nardac, Lilliputian peer,
Or Glumglum's humbler title soothe thy ear:
Nay, would kind Jove my organs so dispose,   105
To hymn harmonious Houyhnhnm through the nose,
I'd call thee Houyhnhnm, that high-sounding name;
Thy children's noses all should twang the same.
So might I find my loving spouse of course
Endued with all the virtues of a horse.   110

TO QUINBUS FLESTRIN, THE MAN-MOUNTAIN

A LILLIPUTIAN ODE

In amaze
Lost, I gaze,
Can our eyes
Reach thy size?
May my lays   5
Swell with praise,
Worthy thee!
Worthy me!
Muse, inspire
All thy fire!   10
Bards of old
Of him told,
When they said
Atlas' head
Propp'd the skies: 15
See! and believe your eyes!
See him stride
Valleys wide,
Over woods,
Over floods,   20
When he treads,
Mountain heads

Groan and shake:
Armies quake:
Let his spurn   25
Overturn
Man and steed,
Troops, take heed!
Left and right,
Speed your flight!   30
Lest an host
Beneath his foot be lost.
Turn'd aside
From his hide,
Safe from wound   35
Darts rebound.
From his nose
Clouds he blows:
When he speaks,
Thunder breaks!   40
When he eats,
Famine threats!
When he drinks,
Neptune shrinks!
Nigh thy ear,   45
In mid air,
On thy hand
Let me stand;
So shall I,
Lofty Poet! touch the sky.   50

HYMN [1]

THOU art my God, sole object of my love;
Not for the hope of endless joys above;
Not for the fear of endless pains below,
Which they who love Thee not must undergo.
For me, and such as me, Thou deign'st to bear   5
An ignominious cross, the nails, the spear:

[1] The following translation was made at the desire of the Rev. Mr. Brown, chaplain to Mr. Caryl, of Ladyholt, a Roman Catholic gentleman, on Mr. Pope, our celebrated poet, making a visit there, who, being requested by Mr. Brown to translate the following hymn or *rhythmus*, composed by St. Francis Xavier, Apostle of the Indies, on the morning after produced what follows.

A thorny crown transpierced Thy sacred brow,
While bloody sweats from every member flow.
For me in tortures Thou resign'st thy breath,
Embraced me on the cross, and saved me by Thy death.   10
And can these sufferings fail my heart to move?
What but Thyself can now deserve my love?
Such as then was, and is, Thy love to me,
Such is, and shall be still, my love to Thee—
To Thee, Redeemer! mercy's sacred spring!   15
My God, my Father, Maker, and my King!

TO THE RIGHT HON. THE EARL OF OXFORD

UPON A PIECE OF NEWS IN MIST, THAT THE REV. MR. W. REFUSED
TO WRITE AGAINST MR. POPE BECAUSE HIS BEST PATRON HAD
A FRIENDSHIP FOR THE SAID MR. P.[1]

WESLEY, if Wesley 'tis they mean,
    They say on Pope would fall,
Would his best patron let his pen
    Discharge his inward gall.

What patron this, a doubt must be,   5
    Which none but you can clear,
Or Father Francis cross the sea,
    Or else Earl Edward here.

That both were good must be confess'd;
    And much to both he owes;   10
But which to him will be the best
    The Lord of Oxford knows.

TRANSLATION OF A PRAYER OF BRUTUS

The Rev. Aaron Thompson, of Queen's College, Oxon., translated
the *Chronicle* of Geoffrey of Monmouth. He submitted the trans-
lation to Pope, 1717, who gave him the following lines, being a
translation of a prayer of Brutus:

GODDESS of woods, tremendous in the chase,
To mountain wolves and all the savage race,
Wide o'er the aerial vault extend thy sway,
And o'er the infernal regions void of day.

[1] "W.," the Rev. Samuel Wesley the younger; "Father Francis," the
Bishop of Rochester then in exile; Earl Edward, Edward Harley, second
Earl of Oxford.

On thy third reign look down; disclose our fate,   5
In what new station shall we fix our seat?
When shall we next thy hallow'd altars raise,
And choirs of virgins celebrate thy praise?

LINES IN EVELYN'S BOOK OF COINS

Tom Wood of Chiswick, deep divine,
To painter Kent presents his *coin*;
'Tis the first time I dare to say,
That Churchman e'er gave coin to Lay.

LINES ON SWIFT'S ANCESTORS

"Swift put up a plain monument to his grandfather, and also presented a cup to the church of Goodrich, or Gotheridge (Herefordshire). He sent a pencilled elevation of the monument (a simple tablet) to Mrs. Howard, who returned it with the following lines inscribed on the drawing by Pope. The paper is endorsed, in Swift's hand, 'Model of a Monument for my grandfather, with Mr. Pope's roguery.'"—SCOTT's *Life of Swift*.

JONATHAN SWIFT
Had the gift,
By fatherige, motherige,
And by brotherige,
To come from Gotherige,   5
But now is spoil'd clean
And an Irish dean:
In this church he has put
A stone of two foot,
With a cup and a can, sir,   10
In respect to his grandsire;
So, Ireland, change thy tone,
And cry, O hone! O hone!
For England hath its own.

LINES TO LORD BATHURST

"A WOOD?" quoth Lewis, and with that
He laugh'd and shook his sides of fat.
His tongue, with eye that mark'd his cunning,
Thus fell a-reasoning, not a-running:

"Woods are—not to be too prolix—   5
Collective bodies of straight sticks.
It is, my lord, a mere conundrum
To call things woods for what grows under 'em.
For shrubs, when nothing else at top is,
Can only constitute a coppice.   10
But if you will not take my word,
See anno quint. of Richard Third;
And that's a coppice call'd, when dock'd,
Witness an. prim. of Harry Oct.
If this a wood you will maintain,   15
Merely because it is no plain,
Holland, for all that I can see,
May e'en as well be term'd the sea,
Or C——by [Coningsby] be fair harangued
An honest man, because not hang'd."   20

EPIGRAMS

ON ONE WHO MADE LONG EPITAPHS

Friend! for your epitaphs I'm grieved,
    Where still so much is said,
One half will never be believed,
    The other never read.

COUPLET ON HIS GROTTO

AND life itself can nothing more supply
Than just to plan our projects, and to die.

EPIGRAM

YOU beat your pate, and fancy wit will come:
Knock as you please, there's nobody at home.

EPIGRAM FROM THE FRENCH

SIR, I admit your general rule,
That every poet is a fool:
But you yourself may serve to show it
That every fool is not a poet.

EPITAPH

WELL then, poor G—— lies underground![1]
So there's an end of honest Jack.
So little justice here he found,
    'Tis ten to one he'll ne'er come back.

EPITAPH

Joannes jacet hic Mirandula—cœtera norunt
Et Tagus et Ganges—forsan et Antipodes.
            Applied to F. C. [Francis Chartres]

HERE Francis C—— lies. Be civil;
The rest God knows—perhaps the devil!

THE BALANCE OF EUROPE

Now Europe balanced, neither side prevails;
For nothing's left in either of the scales.

TO A LADY WITH "THE TEMPLE OF FAME"[2]

WHAT's fame with men by custom of the nation
Is call'd in women only reputation:
About them both why keep we such a pother?
Part you with one, and I'll renounce the other.

---

[1] John Gay.
[2] "I send you my 'Temple of Fame,' which is just come out; but my sentiments about it you will see better by this epigram."—*Pope to Martha Blount*, 1714.

ON THE TOASTS OF THE KIT-CAT CLUB,[1] ANNO 1716

> WHENCE deathless Kit-Cat took its name,
>   Few critics can unriddle;
> Some say from pastrycook it came,
>   And some from cat and fiddle.
>
> From no trim beaux its name it boasts,　　　　　　　　5
>   Grey statesmen or green wits;
> But from this pell-mell pack of toasts
>   Of old "cats" and young "kits."

A DIALOGUE

(1717)

> POPE.—Since my old friend is grown so great
>   As to be Minister of State,
> I'm told, but 'tis not true, I hope,
>   That Craggs will be ashamed of Pope.
>
> CRAGGS.—Alas! if I am such a creature　　　　　　　5
>   To grow the worse for going greater;
> Why, faith, in spite of all my brags,
>   'Tis Pope must be ashamed of Craggs.

[1] The Kitcat Club was formed about the year 1700, and met at first in a pastrycook's in Shire Lane, near Temple Bar. This person, famous for mutton pies, was called Christopher Cat, whence the name of the club. *Toasting* ladies after dinner was a rule of the club. A lady was chosen for the year by ballot, and her name written with a diamond on a drinking-glass. Poetical *jeux d'esprit* on the beauties thus selected to reign supreme were written by Addison, Garth, the Earl of Halifax, Lord Dorset, Lord Wharton, etc. Lady Mary Wortley Montagu, when a child of only eight years of age, was nominated by her father, Lord Kingston. Jacob Tonson, the publisher, was mainly instrumental in keeping the club together, and the members presented him with their portraits, painted by Kneller, all uniform in size. These portraits, forty-eight in number, Tonson hung up in a room which he had added to his residence at Barn Elms for the meetings of the club. They are now in the National Portrait Gallery.

ON DRAWINGS OF THE STATUES OF APOLLO, VENUS, AND HERCULES, MADE FOR POPE BY SIR GODFREY KNELLER

WHAT god, what genius, did the pencil move,
    When Kneller painted these?
'Twas friendship warm as Phœbus, kind as love,
    And strong as Hercules.

EPITAPH ON LORD JOHN CARYLL [1]

A MANLY form; a bold, yet modest mind;
Sincere, though prudent; constant, yet resign'd;
Honour unchanged; a principle professed,
Fixed to one side, but moderate to the rest;
An honest courtier, and a patriot too;   5
Just to his Prince, and to his country true:
All these were joined in one, yet failed to save ⎫
The wise, the learn'd, the virtuous and the brave; ⎬
Lost, like the common plunder of the grave.
    Ye few, whom better genius does inspire   10
Exalted souls, informed with purer fire!
Go now, learn all vast science can impart;
Go fathom nature, take the heights of art!
Rise higher yet: learn ev'n yourselves to know;
Nay, to yourselves alone that knowledge owe.   15
Then, when you seem above mankind to soar,
Look on this marble, and be vain no more!

ON A PICTURE OF QUEEN CAROLINE, DRAWN BY LADY BURLINGTON [2]

PEACE, flattering Bishop! lying Dean!
This portrait only paints the Queen!

[1] Never used, nor published by Pope. He made the first six lines serve for Sir William Trumbull.
[2] The bishop was Gilbert; the dean, Dr. Alured Clarke, satirised in *Epilogue to the Satires*.

ON BENTLEY'S "MILTON"

Did Milton's prose, O Charles, thy death defend?
A furious foe unconscious proves a friend.
On Milton's verse did Bentley comment? Know
A weak officious friend becomes a foe.
While he but sought his author's fame to further,   5
The murderous critic has avenged thy murther.

ON CERTAIN LADIES

When other fair ones to the shades go down,
Still Chloe, Flavia, Delia, stay in town:
Those ghosts of beauty wandering here reside,
And haunt the places where their honour died.

UPON A GIRL OF SEVEN YEARS OLD

Wit's Queen, (if what the poets sing be true)
And Beauty's Goddess childhood never knew,
Pallas they say sprung from the head of Jove,
Full grown, and from the sea the Queen of Love;
But had they, Miss, your wit and beauty seen,   5
Venus and Pallas both had children been.
They, from the sweetness of that radiant look,
A copy of young Venus might have took:
And from those pretty things you speak have told,
How Pallas talked when she was seven years old.   10

EPIGRAM

ENGRAVED ON THE COLLAR OF A DOG WHICH I GAVE TO HIS ROYAL HIGHNESS

[Frederick, Prince of Wales, father of George III.]

I am his Highness' dog at Kew;
Pray tell me, sir, whose dog are you?

This is taken from Sir William Temple's *Heads designed for an Essay on Conversation*. "Mr. Grantam's fool's reply to a great man that asked whose fool he was—'I am Mr. Grantam's fool—pray tell me whose fool are you?'"

VERBATIM FROM BOILEAU

Un jour, dit un Auteur, etc.

ONCE, says an author—where I need not say—
Two travellers found an oyster in their way;
Both fierce, both hungry, the dispute grew strong,
While, scale in hand, Dame Justice pass'd along.
Before her each with clamour pleads the laws,   5
Explain'd the matter, and would win the cause.

Dame Justice, weighing long the doubtful right,
Takes, opens, swallows it, before their sight.
The cause of strife removed so rarely well,
"There,—take," says Justice, "take ye each a shell;   10
We thrive at Westminster on fools like you:
'Twas a fat oyster—live in peace—Adieu."

BISHOP HOUGH

A BISHOP, by his neighbours hated,
Has cause to wish himself translated;
But why should HOUGH desire translation,
Loved and esteemed by all the nation?
Yet if it be the old man's case,   5
I'll lay my life I know the place:
'Tis where God sent some that adore him,
And whither Enoch went before him.

Dr. John Hough was made Bishop of Oxford in 1690; Bishop of
Lichfield and Coventry in 1699, and Bishop of Worcester in 1717.
He died in 1743, at the great age of ninety-three.

EPIGRAM

MY Lord complains that Pope, stark mad with gardens,
Has cut three trees, the value of three farthings.
"But he's my neighbour," cries the peer polite:
"And if he visit me, I'll waive the right."
What! on compulsion, and against my will,   5
A lord's acquaintance? Let him file his bill!

Pope had cut three walnut-trees, which hindered the view from
his garden. Warton says the peer alluded to was Lord Radnor.

EPIGRAM

The Countess of Hertford sends the following to the Countess of
Pomfret, in their correspondence between the years 1738 and 1741,
observing, " The severity of the weather has occasioned greater
sums of money to be given in charity than was heard of before. Mr.
Pope has written two stanzas on the occasion."

YES! 'tis the time (I cried) impose the chain,
    Destined and due to wretches self-enslaved;
But when I saw such charity remain,
    I half could wish this people should be saved.

Faith lost, and Hope, our Charity begins;   5
    And 'tis a wise design in pitying Heaven,
If this can cover multitude of sins,
    To take the *only* way to be forgiven.

ADDITIONAL POEMS

A PARAPHRASE

ON THOMAS À KEMPIS; L.3, C.2.[1]

SPEAK, Gracious Lord, oh speak; Thy servant hears:
  For I'm Thy servant, and I'll still be so:
Speak words of comfort in my willing ears;
  And since my tongue is in Thy praises slow,
And since that Thine all rhetoric exceeds;   5
Speak Thou in words, but let me speak in deeds!

Nor speak alone, but give me grace to hear
  What Thy celestial sweetness does impart;
Let it not stop when entered at the ear
  But sink, and take deep rooting in my heart.   10
As the parched Earth drinks rain (but grace afford)
With such a gust will I receive Thy word.

Nor with the Israelites shall I desire
  Thy heav'nly word by Moses to receive,
Lest should I die: but Thou who didst inspire   15
  Moses himself, speak Thou, that I may live.
Rather with Samuel I beseech with tears
Speak, gracious Lord, oh speak; Thy servant hears

Moses indeed may say the words but Thou
  Must give the Spirit, and the Life inspire;   20
Our love to Thee his fervent breath may blow,
  But 'tis Thy self alone can give the fire:
Thou without them may'st speak and profit too;
But without Thee, what could the prophets do?

They preach the doctrine, but Thou mak'st us do't;   25
  They teach the mysteries Thou dost open lay;
The trees they water, but Thou giv'st the fruit;
  They to Salvation shew the arduous way,
But none but You can give us strength to walk;
You give the practise, they but give the talk.   30

[1] Done by the Author at twelve years old.—POPE.

Let them be silent then; and thou alone
  (My God) speak comfort to my ravished ears;
Light of my eyes, my consolation,
  Speak when thou wilt, for still thy servant hears.
What-e'er thou speak'st, let this be understood;   35
Thy greater Glory, and my greater Good!

AN EPISTLE TO HENRY CROMWELL ESQ.[1]

DEAR Mr. Cromwell, may it please ye!
Sit still a moment; pray be easy—
Faith 'tis not five; no play's begun;
No game at Ombre lost or won.
Read something of a different nature,   5
Than *Evening Post*, or *Observator*;
And pardon me a little fooling,
—Just while your coffee stands a cooling.

  Since your acquaintance with one Brocas,[2]
Who needs will back the Muses cock-horse,   10
I know you dread all those who write,
And both with mouth and hand recite;
Who slow, and leisurely rehearse,
As loath t' enrich you with their verse;
Just as a still, with simples in it,   15
Betwixt each drop stays half a minute.
(That simile is not my own,
But lawfully belongs to Donne)
(You see how well I can contrive a
Interpolatio Furtiva)   20
To Brocas's lays no more you listen
Than to the wicked works of Whiston;[3]
In vain he strains to reach your ear,
With what it wisely, will not hear:
You bless the powers who made that organ   25
Deaf to the voice of such a Gorgon,
(For so one sure may call that head,
Which does not look, but read men dead.)

---

[1] Cromwell was a friend of Pope's early years.
[2] Beau Brocas. Little is known of him.
[3] Succeeded Newton at Cambridge; was suspected of heterodoxy.

I hope, you think me none of those
Who shew their parts as Pentlow does,   30
I but lug out to one or two
Such friends, if such there are, as you,
Such, who read Heinsius and Masson,
And as you please their doom to pass on,
(Who are to me both Smith and Johnson) [1]   35
To seize them flames, or take them Tonson.

But, Sir, from Brocas, Fouler, me,
In vain you think to 'scape rhyme-free,
When was it known one bard did follow
Whig maxims, and abjure Apollo?   40
Sooner shall Major-General cease
To talk of war, and live in peace;
Yourself for goose reject crow quill,
And as for plain Spanish quit Brasil;
Sooner shall Rowe lampoon the UNION   45
Tydcombe take oaths on the Communion;
The Granvilles write their name plain Greenfield,
Nay, Mr. Wycherly see Binfield. [2]

I'm told, you think to take a step some
Ten miles from Town, t' a place called Epsom,   50
To treat those nymphs like yours of Drury,
With—I protest, and I'll assure ye;—
But though from flame to flame you wander,
Beware; your heart's no Salamander!
But burnt so long, may soon turn tinder,   ⎫   55
And so be fired by any cinder-   ⎬
(Wench, I'd have said did rhyme not hinder)   ⎭
Should it so prove, yet who'd admire?
'Tis known, a cook-maid roasted Prior,
Lardella fired a famous author,   ⎫   60
And for a butcher's well-fed daughter   ⎬
Great D——s roar'd, like ox at slaughter.   ⎭

(Now, if you're weary of my style,
Take out your box of right Brasil,
First lay this paper under, then,   65
Snuff just three times, and read again.)

34 Their Doom to pass on] *all texts, however, read* to pass their
Doom.   (Ault.)

[1] Friends of Bays (Dryden) in *The Rehearsal.*   [2] Binfield. Where Pope lived.

I had to see you some intent
But for a curst impediment,
Which spoils full many a good design,
That is to say, the want of coin.   70
For which, I had resolved almost,
To raise Tiberius Gracchus' ghost;
To get, by once more murdering Caius,
As much as did Septimuleius;
But who so dear will buy the lead,   75
That lies within a poet's head,
As that which in the hero's pate
Deserved of gold an equal weight?

Sir, you're so stiff in your opinion,
I wish you do not turn Socinian;   80
Or prove reviver of a schism,
By modern wits called Quixotism.
What moved you, pray, without compelling,
Like Trojan true, to draw for Helen:
Quarrel with Dryden for a strumpet,   85
(For so she was, as e'er showed rump yet,
Though I confess, she had much grace,
Especially about the face.)
Virgil, when called *Pasiphae Virgo*
(You say) he'd more good breeding; *Ergo*—   90
Well argued, faith! Your point you urge
As home, as ever did Panurge:
And one may say of Dryden too,
(As once you said of you know who)
He had some fancy, and could write;   95
Was very learn'd, but not polite—
However from my soul I judge
He ne'er (good man) bore Helen grudge,
But loved her full as well it may be,
As e'er he did his own dear lady.   100
You have no cause to take offence, Sir,
Z—ds, you're as sour as Cato Censor!
Ten times more like him, I profess,
Than I'm like Aristophanes.

To end with news—the best I know,   105
Is, I've been well a week, or so.
The season of green peas is fled,
And artichokes reign in their stead.

Th' allies to bomb Toulon prepare;
G—d save the pretty ladies there!   110
One of our dogs is dead and gone,
And I, unhappy! left alone.

If you have any consolation
T'administer on this occasion,
Send it, I pray, by the next post,   115
Before my sorrow be quite lost.
    The twelfth or thirteenth day of July,
    But which, I cannot tell you truly.

LINES ON DULNESS

THUS dulness, the safe opiate of the mind,
The last kind refuge weary wit can find,
Fit for all stations and in each content
Is satisfied, secure, and innocent:
No pains it takes, and no offence it gives,   5
Un-feared, un-hated, un-disturbed it lives.
—And if each writing author's best pretence,
Be but to teach the ignorant more sense;
Then dulness was the cause they wrote before,
As 'tis at last the cause they write no more;   10
So wit, which most to scorn it does pretend,
With dulness first began, in dulness last must end.

TO EUSTACE BUDGELL, ESQ.

ON HIS TRANSLATION OF THE CHARACTERS OF THEOPHRASTUS

'TIS rumoured, Budgell on a time
Writing a sonnet, could not rhyme;
Was he discouraged? no such matter;
He'd write in prose—To the *Spectator*.
There too invention failed of late: 5
What then? Gad damn him, he'd translate,
Not verse, to that he had a pique—
From French? He scorned it; no, from Greek.
He'd do't; and ne'er stand shilly-shally,
Ay, and inscribe to Charles Lord Halli——   10
Our Gallo Grecian at the last

Has kept his word, here's Teophraste.
How e'er be not too vain, Friend Budgell!
Men of ill hearts, you know, will judge ill.
Some flatly say, the book's as ill done,   15
As if by Boyer, or by Gildon; [1]
Others opine you only chose ill,
And that this piece was meant for Ozell.[2]
For me, I think (in spite of blunders)
You may, with Addison, do wonders.   20
But faith I fear, some folks beside
These *smart, new characters* supplied.
The *honest fellow out at heels*
Pray between friends, was not that Steele's?
The *rustic lout* so like a brute,   25
Was Philips's beyond Dispute.
And the *fond fop* so clean contrary,
'Tis plain, 'tis very plain, was Cary.[3]
Howe'er, the *coxcomb*'s thy own merit,
That thou has done, with life and spirit.   30

VERSES SENT TO MRS. T. B.[4]
WITH HIS WORKS

BY AN AUTHOR

THIS book, which, like its author, you
By the bare outside only knew,
(Whatever was in either good,
Not looked in, or, not understood)
Comes, as the writer did too long,   5
To be about you, right or wrong;
Neglected on your chair to lie,
Nor raise a thought, nor draw an eye;
In peevish fits to have you say,
"See there! you're always in my way!"   10
Or, if your Slave you think to bless,
"I like this colour, I profess!"
That red is charming all will hold,
I ever loved it—next to gold."

[1] Miscellaneous writers and critics. For Gildon see "Prologue to the Satires," line 151.
[2] Translated Boileau's *Le Lutrin* and Tassoni's *La Secchia Rapita*.
[3] Walter Carey. See "Three Gentle Shepherds."
[4] Teresa Blount, with the folio Works of 1717.

Can book, or man, more praise obtain?   15
What more could G—ge or S—te gain?[1]

Sillier than G–ld–n could'st thou be,
Nay, did all J–c–b[2] breathe in thee,
She keeps thee, book! I'll lay my head,
What? throw away a "fool in red":   20
No trust the Sex's sacred rule;
The gaudy dress will save the fool.

IN BEHALF OF MR. SOUTHERNE.
TO THE DUKE OF ARGYLE[3]

EPIGRAM

ARGYLE his praise, when Southerne wrote,
First struck out this, and then that thought; ⎫
Said *this* was flatt'ry, *that* a fault.   ⎬
    How shall your bard contrive?   ⎭

My Lord, consider what you do,   ⎫   5
He'll lose his pains and verses too;   ⎬
For if these praises fit not you,   ⎭
    They'll fit no man alive.

EPITAPH ON LADY KNELLER[4]

ONE day I mean to fill Sir Godfrey's tomb,
If for my body all this church has room.
Down with more monuments! More room! (she cried)
For I am very large, and very wide.

[1] Count Gage, and Southcote, the priest who had saved Pope's life.
Possibly "George or Senate."
[2] Giles Jacob. Gildon, of course, in the line above.
[3] Southerne had dedicated his last play to Argyll in fulsome terms.
[4] Lady Kneller proposed to erect a vast monument in Twickenham
Church, thus obscuring the tablet in memory of Pope's father.

EPIGRAM
IN A MAID OF HONOUR'S PRAYER-BOOK

WHEN Israel's daughters mourned their past offences,
They dealt in Sackcloth, and turned Cinder-Wenches:
But Richmond's fair-ones never spoil their locks,
They use white powder, and wear holland-smocks.
O comely Church! where females find clean linen   5
As decent to repent in, as to sin in.

EPITAPH [OF BY-WORDS [1]]

HERE lies a round woman, who thought *mighty odd*
Every word she e'er heard in this church about God.
To convince her of *God* the good Dean did endeavour,
But still in her heart she held *Nature* more *clever*.
Though he talked much of virtue, her head always run   5
Upon something or other, she found better *fun*.
For the dame, by her skill in affairs astronomical,
Imagined, to live in the clouds was but *comical*.
In this world, she despised every soul she met here,
And now she's in t'other, she thinks it but *queer*.   10

TO THE EARL OF BURLINGTON
ASKING WHO WRIT THE LIBELS AGAINST HIM

You wonder who this thing has writ,
So full of fibs, so void of wit?
Lord! never ask who thus could serve ye?
Who can it be but fibster H—y.[2]

---

[1] By-words; fashionable semi-slang of the time.
[2] Lord Hervey, who had attacked Pope in a document published 1733.

BOUNCE TO FOP

AN HEROICK EPISTLE FROM A DOG AT TWICKENHAM
TO A DOG AT COURT [1]

To chee, sweet Fop, these lines I send,
Who, though no spaniel, am a friend.
Though, once my tail in wanton play,
Now frisking this, and then that way,
Chanced, with a touch of just the tip, 5
To hurt your Lady-lap-dog-ship;
Yet thence to think I'd bite your head off!
Sure Bounce is one you never read of.

Fop! you can dance, and make a leg,
Can fetch and carry, cringe and beg, 10
And (what's the top of all your tricks)
Can stoop to pick up strings and sticks.
We country dogs love nobler sport,
And scorn the pranks of dogs at court.
Fye, naughty Fop! where'er you come 15
To f—t and p—ss about the room,
To lay your head in every lap,
And, when they think not of you—snap!
The worst that envy, or that spite
E'er said of me, is, I can bite: 20
That sturdy vagrants, rogues in rags,
Who poke at me, can make no brags;
And that to towze such things as flutter,
To honest Bounce is bread and butter.

While you, and every courtly fop, 25
Fawn on the Devil for a chop,
I've the humanity to hate
A butcher, though he brings me meat;
And let me tell you, have a nose,
(Whatever stinking fops suppose) 30
That under cloth of gold or tissue,
Can smell a plaster, or an issue.

[1] Bounce was Pope's Great Dane bitch; Fop, Lady Suffolk's lap-dog.

Your pilfering Lord, with simple pride,
May wear a pick-lock at his side;
My master wants no key of state,　　　　　　　35
For Bounce can keep his house and gate.

When all such dogs have had their days,
As knavish Pams, and fawning Trays;
When pampered Cupids, beastly Veni's,
And motly, squinting Harvequini's,　　　　　40
Shall lick no more their Lady's br—,
But die of looseness, claps, or itch;
Fair Thames from either echoing shore
Shall hear, and dread my manly roar.

See Bounce, like Berecynthia, crowned　　45
With thund'ring offspring all around,
Beneath, beside me, and a top,
A hundred sons! and not one Fop.

Before my children set your beef,
Not one true Bounce will be a thief;　　　50
Not one without permission feed,
(Though some of J—'s hungry breed)
But whatsoe'er the father's race,
From me they suck a little grace.
While your fine whelps learn all to steal,　55
Bred up by hand on chick and veal.

My eldest-born resides not far,
Where shines great Strafford's glittering Star:
My second (child of fortune!) waits
At Burlington's Palladian gates:　　　　　60
A third majestically stalks
(Happiest of Dogs!) in Cobham's walks:
One ushers friends to Bathurst's door;
One fawns, at Oxford's, on the poor.

Nobles, whom arms or arts adorn　　　　65
Wait for my infants yet unborn.
None but a peer of wit and grace,
Can hope a puppy of my race.

And O! would Fate the bliss decree
To mine (a bliss too great for me)   70
That two, my tallest sons, might grace
Attending each with stately pace,
Iülus' [1] side, as erst Evander's,
To keep off flatt'rers, spies, and panders,
To let no noble slave come near,   75
And scare Lord Fannys from his ear:
Then might a royal youth, and true,
Enjoy at least a friend—or two:
A treasure, which, of royal kind,
Few but himself deserve to find.   80

Then Bounce ('tis all that Bounce can crave)
Shall wag her tail within the grave.

And though no doctors, Whig or Tory ones,
Except the sect of Pythagoreans,
Have immortality assigned   85
To any beast, but Dryden's Hind:
Yet Master Pope, whom truth and sense
Shall call their friend some ages hence,
Though now on loftier themes he sings
Than to bestow a word on kings,   90
Has sworn by *Sticks* (the poet's oath,
And dread of dogs and poets both)
Man and his works he'll soon renounce,
And roar in numbers worthy Bounce.

LINES ON BOUNCE

AH Bounce! ah gentle beast! why wouldst thou die,
When thou had'st meat enough, and Orrery? [2]

---

[1] Iülus; that is, Frederick, Prince of Wales.
[2] Two years before Pope's death he gave Bounce into the care of Lord Orrery. The dog died a few weeks before Pope.

INDEX OF FIRST LINES